Engaging Putnam

Berlin Studies in Knowledge Research

Edited by
Günter Abel and James Conant

Volume 17

Engaging Putnam

Edited by
James Conant and Sanjit Chakraborty

DE GRUYTER

Series Editors
Prof. Dr. Günter Abel
Technische Universität Berlin
Institut für Philosophie
Straße des 17. Juni 135
10623 Berlin
Germany
e-mail: abel@tu-berlin.de

Prof. Dr. James Conant
The University of Chicago
Dept. of Philosophy
1115 E. 58th Street
Chicago IL 60637
USA
e-mail: jconant@uchicago.edu

ISBN 978-3-11-153212-7
e-ISBN (PDF) 978-3-11-076921-0
e-ISBN (EPUB) 978-3-11-076934-0
ISSN 2365-1601

Library of Congress Control Number: 2022933783

Bibliographic information published by the Deutsche Nationalbibliothek
The Deutsche Nationalbibliothek lists this publication in the Deutsche Nationalbibliografie;
detailed bibliographic data are available on the Internet at http://dnb.dnb.de.

© 2024 Walter de Gruyter GmbH, Berlin/Boston Typesetting: Integra Software Services Pvt.
Ltd. Printing and binding: CPI books GmbH, Leck
This volume is text- and page-identical with the hardback published in 2022.

www.degruyter.com

Contents

List of Abbreviations

AA	*Kant's gesammelte Schriften* (Akademieausgabe)
AE	Attitude Externalism
AI	Artificial Intelligence
APA	American Philosophical Association
BIV	Brain in a vat
CA	Capabilities Approach
CLT	Categorical Level-Theory
LT	Level-Theory
LT_{int}	Level-Theory, internalized
MIPOV	Metaphysical Independence of One's Point of View
MIT	Massachusetts Institute of Technology
MP	Methodological Principle
MT	Model Theory
MT_{int}	Model Theory, internalized
OC	Ludwig Wittgenstein, *On Certainty*
PA	Peano Arithmetic
PA_{int}	Peano Arithmetic, internalized
PI	Ludwig Wittgenstein, *Philosophical Investigations*
PS	Proof System
RHF	Hilary Putnam, *Realism with a Human Face*
SA	Spatial Autonomy
TTC	Hilary Putnam, *The Threefold Cord*
UCLA	University of California, Los Angeles
WL	Hilary Putnam, *Words and Life*
ZF	Zermelo-Fraenkel set theory

https://doi.org/10.1515/9783110769210-203

James Conant
An Introduction to Hilary Putnam

> The holes in our lives that the dead leave behind should not be ignored.
>
> Hilary Putnam[1]

The hole that the death of Hilary Putnam left behind, not only in the lives of those who knew him as a philosophical colleague and interlocutor, but also in the landscape of contemporary philosophy, is as capacious in extent as it is unique in shape. Perhaps no one of the respects in which Putnam is an unusual philosopher – his colorful life, his distinctive conception of philosophy, his extraordinary intellectual breadth, his proclivity for changing his mind, the metamorphoses in his forms of political and religious engagement – is fully peculiar to him, but what is unique is the manner in which he combines and blends them into a single lifelong way of doing philosophy and exemplifying what it means to be a philosopher.

I From Paris to Jerusalem and From Positivism to Judaism

The richness of Putnam's thought and the many-layered character of his philosophical identity may in part be traced to the unusual trajectory of stations his life traverses, geographically as well intellectually: first from Paris to Philadelphia, then from MIT and Harvard to Tel Aviv and Jerusalem, while never ceasing to think of himself as a citizen of the world – from logical positivism and computational theories of the mind, to Marxism and externalism, and, finally, to Pragmatism and Judaism, while never ceasing to think of himself as an analytic philosopher.

Hilary Whitehall Putnam was born in Chicago on July 31, 1926 to a Jewish mother and a father who, though from a Christian family, was himself the farthest thing from a practicing Christian. Samuel Putnam (1892–1950) practiced journalism as his first métier and at one time wrote for the *Daily Worker*, a publication of the American Communist Party. Shortly after Hilary's birth his family moved to France. The Putnam family lived in Paris until the 6th of February 1934

---

1 Joost Alleblas and Randy Eisinger, "An Interview with Hilary Putnam," *Cimedart* (Magazine of the Faculty of Philosophy of the University of Amsterdam), 2001.

https://doi.org/10.1515/9783110769210-001

Crisis when anti-parliamentiarist demonstrations and riots fomented by far-right leagues rocked the city. As a child, Hilary Putnam grew up hearing and speaking both French and English. Later in life, in his Harvard classes on the philosophy of language, his favorite example of co-referential names was an autobiographical one. He would contrast the name by which he was mostly known as a child with the one by which he was known as an adult. To bring the example into auditory view for the class, he would first pronounce it in the accent, tonality, aspiration, and stress on each of the four syllables characteristic of the French pronunciation of his name, following it up with the very different American pronunciation of "Hilary Putnam."

Samuel Putnam conducted both his active literary working life – as a critic, editor, and translator – and his no less lively and no less literary Parisian social life largely within the walls of the family's apartment. He wrote a best-selling autobiography, *Paris was Our Mistress*, about the community of expatriate literary and artistic figures who formed his circle of friends and contemporaries in Paris during the 1920s and early '30s and who stepped in and out their door every day.[2] The book brings vividly to life how the Putnam family domicile doubled as a Bohemian salon at which much of the anglophone literary and artistic community then resident in Paris would gather with their Francophone counterparts to debate intellectual, political, and aesthetic issues of the day. Hilary's father's Parisian autobiography thereby depicts not only the extraordinary intellectual milieu but also, indirectly, the chaotic household in which his one and only child first tried to make sense of the world around him.[3] One of those who frequented that salon, the young Ernest Hemingway, in his own posthumously published memoir of that same Parisian epoch, spoke not only for himself at the time, but also for many of those who belonged to the Putnam circle he frequented, when he observed in a remark that Hilary Putnam later

---

[2] Samuel Putnam, *Paris Was Our Mistress: Memoirs of a Lost and Found Generation* (New York: Viking, 1947; most recent reprint: Carbondale: Southern Illinois University Press, 1970).

[3] The Viking Press's press release for the original 1947 edition of the book not only nicely summarizes its aim, but therewith also the character of the milieu which formed the backdrop to Hilary's childhood: "This is much more than a Left Bank record – it is autobiography, it is a critical appraisal, and highlights the background of the new American school of writers, from the Chicago group to the start of the flow towards Paris. It is chatty, anecdotal – a collection of pen sketches, vignettes and profiles of leading figures, American, English, and French, writers largely, but artists as well. Here was that decade, 1922–1933, in Montparnasse and Montmartre – the figures who made literary history then, Gertrude Stein, Elliott Paul, Ernest Hemingway, Ezra Pound, Elliot, Joyce, Ford Madox Ford, Aldington, and Ehrenburg, Cocteau, Aragon, Derain, Picasso, Pirandello. A very distinguished sidelight on the passing literary scene, perceptive, humorous, entertaining, written by a critic and editor who was one of the group of which he writes."

liked to quote: "If you are lucky enough to have lived in Paris as a young man, then wherever you go for the rest of your life, it stays with you, for Paris is a moveable feast."[4] Samuel Putnam made his living translating classic literary works from a variety of Romance languages into English. His most lasting contribution has proved to be his monumental translation of Cervantes's *Don Quixote*.[5] It is a thousand pages in length, each of which is elegantly rendered, and supplemented with scholarly endnotes providing background into a dazzlingly wide array of historical, literary and intellectual matters – including one footnote thanking his undergraduate son, Hilary Whitehall Putnam, by that point in life now an aspiring logician, for help with a logical matter.[6] Daniel Eisenberg, comparing the available English-language translations of *Don Quixote*, singles out the Putnam translation as the most "sensitive," as well as being by far the best annotated.[7]

The Putnam family returned to the U.S. in 1934, when Hilary was nine years old, and settled in Philadelphia.[8] It was while attending Central High School there, that Hilary first met his lifelong friend Noam Chomsky, who was one year his junior. Their lives moved along parallel tracks for a stretch. They both went on to attend the University of Pennsylvania and the two of them rapidly distinguished themselves from their undergraduate classmates, not least through the prodigious number of graduate seminars in which they enrolled. The most formative of these for both of them was the one taught by Zellig Harris, called *Linguistic Analysis*. There were the only two undergraduates in the class; the course material was difficult and filled with technicalities.[9] Looking back many years later,

---

4 Ernest Hemingway, *A Moveable Feast* (New York: Vintage, 1964).
5 Miguel de Cervantes, *Don Quixote de la Mancha: The Putnam Translation* (New York: Viking, 1947).
6 In Chapter 51 (on page 842 of the Putnam translation), in a ruling handed down by a judges' tribunal adjudicating the fate of Sancho Panza, a paradox figures – one in which a reason is adduced for why the defendant should be hanged, but also why, if he is for that reason to be hanged, then he should go free. The commentary in the footnote thanks the young Hilary for assisting the author with some of the details supplied there regarding the history of such logical paradoxes (see pp. 1019–1020 of the Putnam edition of "*Don Quixote de la Mancha*").
7 "Samuel Putnam (1949) is of all the English translators the one who shows the most sensitivity, and gives us the most information about competing editions of the Spanish text." (Daniel Eisenberg, "*Don Quixote* as Seen through the Eyes of Its Modern English Translators," *Cervantes: The Bulletin of the Cervantes Society of America*, Spring-Fall (2006): 104)
8 Some of the sentences in the paragraphs to follow draw on ones originally written for the headnote on Hilary Putnam in James Conant and Jay Elliott (eds.), *The Norton Anthology of Western Philosophy*. Vol. 2: *After Kant: The Analytic Tradition* (New York: Norton, 2017), 1577–1581.
9 At the time, Harris was completing work on his *Methods in Structural Linguistics* (Chicago: University of Chicago Press, 1951).

Putnam writes: "[T]he powerful intellect and personality of Zellig Harris drew me like a lodestone, and, although I majored in Philosophy, I took every course there was to take in Linguistic Analysis from then until my graduation."[10] Though he enrolled in and audited numerous courses in physics and mathematics, in addition to ones in linguistics, his favorite undergraduate courses at Penn were in philosophy, especially those taught by C. West Churchman and Morton White.[11] Putnam received his B.A. from Penn in 1948. He then began work on a Ph.D. in philosophy at Harvard, where he studied briefly with W.V.O. Quine and C.I. Lewis. Harvard at that moment in its history, however, soon came to seem to the young Hilary Putnam not to be the most exciting place in the United States to study philosophy. He was drawn at that moment especially to the ideas of the logical empiricists. For this reason, as well as others (primarily financial in nature[12]), he decided to transfer to the University of California, Los Angeles, where he completed his Ph.D. in 1951.[13] This allowed him to write his dissertation, on the concept of probability,[14]

---

10 Hilary Putnam, "Preface" to *The Form of Information in Science*, edited by Zellig Harris et al. (Berlin: Springer, 1988), xi.

11 Putnam describes Churchman as "the first teacher who really influenced me." For the full context of his account of Churchman's influence on him, as well as that of White, see Michela Bella, Anna Boncompagni and Hilary Putnam, "Interview with Hilary Putnam," *European Journal of Pragmatism and American Philosophy* 7, no. 1 (2015), 1–2.

12 He reports in his intellectual autobiography: "In fact, my year of graduate study at Harvard was only made possible by the generosity of my uncle Peter Sampson. I obviously needed a scholarship, but when I asked about the possibility, the Harvard Department told me that I would have to pass the full set of 'prelims,' the written exams for Ph.D. candidates. Those exams were not to be given until the spring, and it seemed foolish to me to wait that long to find out if I would have any support the following year. So I applied for admission and financial assistance elsewhere. I don't know how many schools I applied to, but I do recall that I was offered teaching assistantships at Penn, where I had already spent four years, and UCLA, and I naturally chose to go to UCLA where I would meet a new set of philosophers." (Hilary Putnam, "Intellectual Autobiography," in *The Philosophy of Hilary Putnam*, edited by Randall E. Auxier, Douglas R. Anderson, and Lewis Edwin Hahn (Chicago, IL: Open Court, 2015), 15)

13 He spent a total of two years in the UCLA Ph.D. program, matriculating in fall, 1949 and successfully defending his dissertation and graduating in spring, 1951.

14 *The Meaning of the Concept of Probability in Application to Finite Sequences* (1951). It was reprinted in 1990 by Garland Press – the year in which I defended my own Ph.D. Upon completing my own defense, Putnam presented me a copy of the reprint, hot off the press. On the inside cover it bears in Hilary's handwriting the following four-line inscription, with the first, second, and fourth lines written from left to right and the third from right to left: "May 14th, 1990. From one Ph.D. to another. מזל טוב. Hilary."

under the supervision of the philosopher whose work most excited him at that particular moment, namely Hans Reichenbach.[15]

After a research year at Rockefeller University and a teaching year at Northwestern, Putnam moved to Princeton in 1953, where he was hired into a tenure-track position as a philosopher of science. The bulk of Putnam's work during his early Princeton years was in mathematics and mathematical logic.[16] Though he receives tenure on the strength of this work in mathematical logic, it is during these early years that he first begins to nourish the seeds of philosophical ideas that later bear fruit. He gets to know Carnap already during his first year at Princeton. The encounter proves to be a decisive one:

> Although I worked very hard at becoming a mathematician during my years at Princeton, I also needed to learn to be a philosopher . . . . [W]hen I arrived in Princeton in the fall of 1973 I did not yet have any original philosophical ideas, or even a program of research . . . . [I]t was the mentorship of someone who was at the Institute for Advanced Studies that got me started. The "someone," in this case, was Rudolf Carnap, who was still at the Institute in 1953–54, my first year in Princeton.[17]

It is only after receiving tenure at Princeton in 1957 that he publishes the first of his characteristically bold and original papers in philosophy, "The Analytic and the Synthetic."[18] Looking back on the paper many years later, Putnam concludes:

> A lot of my later philosophy is already in "The Analytic and the Synthetic": the idea of externalist semantics (although I did not realize it at that time), the idea that reference is preserved across theory change, contrary to Carnap's view, and therefore also preserved across changes in method of verification, the idea of law-cluster concepts – they are all in

---

15 "Reichenbach . . . fascinated me from day one. A wonderful human being and one of the greatest teachers on the planet . . . Reichenbach was a great teacher. It was not just a natural gift, although a natural gift he certainly had, it was not just his charisma: he loved pedagogy, he loved thinking about how to teach. But he also could do it and not just think about it." (Bella, Boncompagni and Putnam, "Interview with Hilary Putnam," 2–3)

16 See the section titled "Becoming a Mathematician" in Putnam, "Intellectual Autobiography," 27–30, and especially the engaging quotations from Martin Davis about his collaboration with Hilary Putnam on work that eventually, several years later, led to their important co-authored publication with Julia Robinson, which contributed decisively to the solution of Hilbert's Tenth Problem: Martin Davis, Hilary Putnam, and Julia Robinson, "The Decision Problem for Exponential Diophantine Equations," *Annals of Mathematics* 2, no. 74 (1961): 425–436. For some colorful background on the Davis-Putnam collaboration during Putnam's Princeton years, see Martin Davis's remarks in "Interview with Martin Davis," *Notices of the American Mathematical Society* 55, no. 5, 564–5.

17 Putnam, "Intellectual Autobiography," 30.

18 "The Analytic and the Synthetic" (1962), reprinted in *Mind, Language, and Reality: Philosophical Papers*, Vol. 2, 33–69 (Cambridge: Cambridge University Press, 1975).

that paper . . . . I really think that "The Analytic and the Synthetic" is the paper in which I found my philosophical voice.[19]

Many of the ideas touched upon in these remarks only start to be more fully elaborated by Putnam in the mid-1970s. In the meantime, he lays an additional layer of groundwork for those further developments by first returning to the set of interests that most captivated him in his undergraduate years when he and Noam Chomsky were studying with Zelig Harris at Penn.

This formed part of the reason for his deciding to switch departments, going on to spend four formative years at MIT from 1961 to 1965. At MIT, he had two colleagues, Jerry Fodor and Jerrod Katz, who were also close to Chomsky and equally fascinated by his project of generative linguistics. The four of them together advanced a new research program – one that was animated by the conviction that the right blend of methods and ideas drawn from generative grammar, the newly emerging science of semantics, and computational modeling of the mind would hold the key either to solving all outstanding problems in philosophy of mind and language or for allowing them to be reformulated and outsourced as strictly scientific problems. It is difficult to overstate how influential this MIT research program proved to be on the subsequent development of analytic philosophy. As it gradually moved from the periphery to the center of mainstream philosophical research, Putnam himself, however, gradually moves in the opposite direction: from being one of its foremost proponents to – starting in the late 1980s – being its foremost critic.

This fundamental shift in Putnam's overall philosophical orientation had numerous enabling causes, the first of which, no doubt, was his move from MIT to Harvard in 1965. From thenceforth the Harvard Philosophy Department would become the center of his intellectual life for the next three and a half decades. He taught there until his retirement in 2000, at the age of 74. Characteristically, he does not just allow himself to be influenced by, but also reacts against this new academic environment – above all, against the ways in which he perceives it to be a bastion of the privileged and the wealthy, as well as an intellectual product of the political status quo.

Shortly before arriving at Harvard, and for all of the next decade, he becomes immersed in a wide range of left-wing political causes and groups, including the civil rights movement, as well as several of the movements at the forefront of opposition to the war in Vietnam.[20] Already at MIT in 1963, he had helped to organize

---

19 Putnam, "Intellectual Autobiography," 35.
20 For a summary of Putnam's anti-war engagement in this period, see Lance Hickey, "Hilary Putnam," in *American Philosophers, 1950–2000*, edited by Philip B. Dematteis and Leemon

one of the first faculty cum student committees against the war. It is only after he moves to Harvard, however, that such activities move to the center of his life for a time. For a time, he sees his intellectual and political work as integrally inter-twined strands in a single endeavor: studying the writings of Marx, Lenin, and Mao on his own, teaching courses that challenge the reigning philosophical ortho-doxies of the day in the classroom, while overseeing campus protests outside the classroom in his capacity as the main faculty advisor at Harvard to the anti-Vietnam war organization Students for a Democratic Society. On campus, he co-organized frequent protests, featuring civil disobedience initiatives and the pub-lic burning of draft cards; off campus, as a member of the Progressive Labor party (promoting, in his own words, an "idiosyncratic version of Marxism-Leninism"), he would stand outside factory gates at 7am to sell copies of the magazine *Challenge* and discuss politics with the workers. Aside from the Vietnam War, his activ-ist public ventures and experiments were conducted in opposition to forms of racism and social and political inequality – especially as these manifested them-selves within the walls of the academy. On campus, he disrupted the classes of Richard Herrnstein,[21] and he lived in a commune together with students. He be-came known as a brilliant, captivating teacher, but students at his lectures during these years were often sitting on the floor with the professor in their midst, needing to contort their bodies to look at him, because he wished to eschew all forms of hierarchy, refusing to stand at the podium at the front of the room. Needless to say, the Harvard establishment was often in despair over what they viewed as his politically theatrical antics. This brought him not only into very visible forms of public conflict with the university administration, but also into sometimes painful private forms of personal conflict with a number of his colleagues at the Harvard Philosophy Department – relationships that he subsequently strove to repair over the ensuing decades.

1972 is a watershed year in Putnam's biography – one in which he turns away from his immersion in Marxist political activity and back towards full time work on topics in the philosophy of science, language, and mind. He him-self retrospectively describes the moment as follows:

B. McHenry, 226–236 (Detroit: Gale Group, 2003). For some retrospective reflections from Put-nam on this topic, see the section titled "The Vietnam War" in his "Intellectual Autobiogra-phy," 80–82.

21 Richard J. Herrnstein, a professor of psychology at Harvard, advocated social policies – al-ready not uncontroversial at the time (and which only gained in notoriety over the following decades) – based on purported connections obtaining between a person's race and their aver-age intelligence and capacity for success.

I resigned from the "Progressive Labor Party" in December 1972, after months of reflection and rethinking of my entire relation to Marxism and to communism. I decided to abandon political activism for the time being, apart from supporting Amnesty International. . . . The first fruit of that decision was "The Meaning of 'Meaning'" which I wrote that same month. I had been thinking about the issues for a long time, and evidently the text had been composing itself in my subconscious, because that paper flowed from my fingers via a new electric typewriter onto the paper as if it had been "there" waiting for a joyous release.[22]

The publication in 1975 of "The Meaning of 'Meaning'" (to which we will return below) no doubt marks a moment in which Putnam's philosophical work achieves a new degree of recognition and begins to draw the attention of philosophers working in areas not directly related to the philosophy of science, mind or language.[23] What it does not mark is a sudden shift in Putnam's views on topics in theoretical philosophy. That had already been underway for some time, starting almost a decade earlier. His break with radical political activism notwithstanding, Putnam's work in the philosophy of mind and philosophy of science in the late 1970s continues a trend already clearly discernible in his thought from the late 1960s on – one which reflects his commitment to the materialist and anti-individualist outlook he draws from his reading of Marx. He becomes an opponent of all forms of methodological solipsism – not just those that constituted the then regnant research programs in psychology, linguistics, and the philosophy of mind, but also those in economics, ethics, and political theory. Just as Marx had argued that Hegelian philosophy was upside-down and tried to stand it on its head, so Putnam in this period of his work is concerned to argue that much of mainstream analytic philosophy of mind was similarly upside-down and needed to be set on its feet. In this initial attempt to turn analytic philosophy right-side up, he strove to reveal the extent to which our capacity for thought depends upon the embeddedness of our minds in a physical, social, and linguistic environment.[24] Although Putnam publicly and vehemently came to abandon communism as a political stance in the early 1970s, he remained politically active and never lost his admiration for the anti-individualist and anti-reductionist strands of thought in Marx's

---

22 Putnam, "Intellectual Autobiography," 82.

23 Hilary Putnam, "The Meaning of 'Meaning'," in *Mind, Language and Reality: Philosophical Papers*, Vol. 2, 215–271 (Cambridge: Cambridge University Press, 1975).

24 Putnam makes the connection between his Marxism and externalism explicit in a number of his later retrospective reflections on this period of his work. One contemporaneous context in which it is made explicit – which appeared two years prior to the publication of "The Meaning of 'Meaning'" – is in the opening pages of his 1973 essay "Explanation and Reference," in *Mind, Language, and Reality: Philosophical Papers*, Vol. 2, 196–214 (Cambridge: Cambridge University Press, 1975), see 196–197.

philosophical writings. Certain aspects of his late '60s political awakening therefore never ceased to exert an influence on his later philosophical work.

Putnam's wife Ruth Anna Jacobs, was not only his companion throughout much of his life, but also became his most important intellectual interlocutor. Her own biography is relevant to an understanding of her husband's later intellectual development in a variety of ways, especially with regard to two dimensions of reorientation that Putnam's later philosophy acquires when it seeks to incorporate ideas drawn from pragmatism, on the one hand, and, Judaism, on the other.

Ruth Anna was born in Berlin on September 20, 1927. Her parents were both German citizens, again one Jewish and one Christian. Like her husband's parents, they, too, saw themselves as committed atheists and communists. An only child, in the wake of the Reichstag fire, shortly before her sixth birthday, she was sent by them for her own protection to live with her Christian grandparents, while her own parents, who had actively protested against the Nazis, went into hiding. Ruth Anna emigrated to the United States in 1948, when she was 21, and it was only then, fifteen years later, that she was finally reunited with her parents in 1947 in Los Angeles. Those fifteen years marked a defining trauma of her life, one to which she returned in her activity as a philosopher, seeking to comprehend its significance. It formed a background against which she, in her later philosophical work, she sought to gauge the strengths and limitations of the analytic tradition in philosophy – the one in which she, like her husband, was originally been trained – measuring them against those of the comparatively capacious conception of philosophy she found in the American pragmatist tradition, and especially in the writings of William James and John Dewey.

Once they settled in the United States, Ruth Anna's father, having been a well-known Communist in Germany, was rightfully fearful of deportation from the United States. He therefore changed his name to "Martin Hall" and she herself went by this surname in public life as a young adult though, as she later told her family, she chose not to legally change her birth name until she married Hilary. Her initial work as a philosopher was in fairly technical areas of philosophy of science; and she, too, received her Ph.D. in philosophy at UCLA, though over a decade after Hilary, in 1962, with a dissertation titled *The Interpretation of Theoretical Statements*, written under the supervision of Carnap. Her own philosophical interests eventually broadened out as widely as did those of her husband. She became known, above all, as an important historian of American pragmatism, teaching at MIT and at Wellesley College during the years when Hilary taught at Harvard. One seminal intellectual influence she had on her husband was to teach him to take the philosophical achievement of especially James and Dewey with a degree of seriousness with which he had initially been reluctant to

credit their writings.[25] Their conversations and collaborations on these philosophers eventually culminated in their enormous, jointly authored book, *Pragmatism As a Way of Life*, edited by David Macarthur and published in the year after
Hilary's death.[26] Another more gradual but no less profound philosophical influence she exerted on her husband's development as a thinker had to with the
ways in which she encouraged and accompanied him through the various stages
in his gradual transition from an unapologetically firebrand atheist to a practicing religious Jew. Ruth Anna and Hilary had each had been raised in a secular
home with ambivalent relations to the Jewish side of its legacy, but the crucial
difference is that hers had been one that was devastated and split asunder by the
holocaust. As she grew older, she became ever more curious about this side of
her original roots, as well as in the philosophical significance of the events that
had exerted such an enormous impact on her early life, severing her from that
side of her heritage. Her concern with these topics had been that of a secular
Jew, until 1975 – the year in which the older of their two sons announced that he
wanted to have a bar mitzvah. This first event of family participation in Jewish
religious observance proved to be a decisive catalyst, leading to further such
events, and gradually over time reshaping their lives. As Ruth Anna explored
these avenues, from 1975 on Hilary became equally curious about his own Jewish
heritage, as well as eager to seek instruction more broadly in all aspects of Jewish
thought, history, and religious observance. Hilary began to take Hebrew lessons,
to study the Torah and Talmud under the tutelage of Rabbi Ben-Zion Gold,[27] regularly to attend meetings at the Harvard Hillel Society, to observe the major Jewish
holidays, and to familiarize himself with the writings of major Jewish thinkers – all

---

25 Putnam's first probing yet sympathetic published engagements with the writings of Dewey,
James, and Peirce begin appear in the late 1980s and early 1990s; in the case of Peirce, see
especially the discussion of Peirce on chance in *The Many Faces of Realism* (La Salle, IL: Open
Court, 1987), 80–86, as well as his essay "Peirce: The Logician," in *Realism with a Human
Face*, edited by James Conant, (Cambridge, MA: Harvard University Press, 1990), 252–260; in
the case of James and Dewey, see especially "Pragmatism and Moral Objectivity" and "Pragmatism and Relativism" in *Words and Life*, edited by James Conant, (Cambridge, MA: Harvard
University Press, 1994), 151–181 and 182–197; as well as "The Permanence of William James" in
Pragmatism: An Open Question, 5–26 (Oxford: Blackwell, 1995).
26 Hilary Putnam and Ruth Anna Putnam, *Pragmatism as a Way of Life*, edited by David Macarthur (Cambridge, MA: Harvard University Press, 2017). Ruth Anna and Hilary's earliest co-
authored essays on these topics are their "William James's Ideas" (collected in *Realism with a
Human Face, 217–231*) and their "Education for Democracy" (collected in *Words and Life,
221–244*).
27 Rabbi Gold was the Rabbi of the Hillel at Harvard University. For a brief discussion of Putnam's indebtedness to him, as well as of Putnam's own self-understanding of the distinctive
kind of Jew he strove to be in his later life, see his "Intellectual Autobiography," 88–89.

of which, in turn, set the stage for his later book *Jewish Philosophy as a Guide to Life* in which he sets forth some of the ideas in the Jewish philosophical tradition he finds to be most significant.[28]

On a memorable occasion for all those who were present, at the age of 68, Putnam celebrated a much belated bar mitzvah in 1994. Four years later, Ruth Anna celebrated her bat mitzvah, in 1998, memorably remarking to those present on that occasion that part of the point of her doing so was to send the following message: "We are not going to finish Hitler's work for him. We are not going to assimilate!" Hilary retired from his regular faculty post at Harvard in 2000, and became Harvard's Cogan University Professor Emeritus. Though he had begun to teach and visit Israel, off and on, either at Tel Aviv University or at the Van Leer Institute in Jerusalem, starting in the late 1980s – taking his entire sabbatical years there and spending many a Harvard winter break during his non-sabbatical years in the country he came to regard as his second homeland – it was only after his official retirement from Harvard that the center of his teaching and intellectual activity shifted from Cambridge and Harvard to Tel Aviv and Jerusalem. Hilary Putnam died on March 13, 2016 at his home in Arlington, Massachusetts, at the age of 89.

II A Distinctive Conception of Philosophy and Its Practice

The first thing about Putnam as a philosopher, apt immediately to strike any newcomer to his work, is his astonishing combination of breadth with depth. He is well versed not only across a diverse range of areas of philosophy, but in an equally wide number of fields outside philosophy – mathematics, physics, economics, linguistics, cognitive psychology, artificial intelligence, and history of science. As he moves from one sort of debate to a very different one, he is seldom out of his depth and there appears to be hardly any area of philosophy and its allied fields about which he does not have something interesting to say. Yet he wears his prodigious learning extremely lightly and gracefully, never drawing

---

28 Hilary Putnam, *Jewish Philosophy as a Guide to Life* (Bloomington: Indiana University Press, 2002). In an interview in 2015, he says: "Judaism is my tradition, but I interpret it in my own way. When my friend, a wonderful critical philosopher, Sidney Morgenbesser, died . . . one of the speakers at his memorial, said that 'Sidney proved that one can be rooted in a tradition without being a plant.' I think that is what I want: I want to be rooted in a tradition without being a plant!" (Bella, Boncompagni and Putnam, "Interview with Hilary Putnam," 8)

upon it except where it is absolutely pertinent. This is in part due to the fact that the difference between the character of his philosophical conversation and that of his philosophical writing is remarkably slight. This is both because he was able to speak spontaneously in perfectly worded paragraphs and because his style of philosophical writing itself possesses a conversational fluidity and accessibility, punctuated with mischievous asides and friendly nods to his audience befitting a presentation to friends. His approach to philosophical problems is, in every sense of the word, *unassuming*. Each time he writes about a problem he seeks to make a fresh start on it: to motivate everything from scratch, to adduce non-canned examples, to purge his discussion of second-hand formulations of the problem, and to rethink every aspect of the issue from the ground up. The result is sometimes a philosophical style which can at first appear naïve and unlettered. But it usually requires only a short exposure to his work before it becomes evident that his philosophical naïveté is cultivated with Socratic ulterior motives.[29] When engaging with Putnam's work – at least when it comes to any philosophical topic about which he cares deeply – it is no mean feat to bring to bear a point of view on the discussion which he has not already considered and thoroughly explored. As his age measured in biological years gradually increased, he never ceased to strike his friends and acquaintances as philosophically youthful. He always brought to philosophy an exuberance and awe that usually wears off after extended exposure to the subject, while also bringing to his discussion of each problem a form of wisdom that can come only with age: never ceasing to wonder at how extraordinarily strange and deep philosophy's central problems are, while tempering his approach to them with a foresight stemming from having already traveled down the countless dialectical paths that branch off from each of them.

A second striking fact about all of Putnam's work is its philosophical *independence*. His work combines a protean capacity constantly to reexamine the grounds of his philosophical conviction with a deep passion for getting things right – a passion he hopes will infect his reader. His work is everywhere

---

29 In Putnam's writings from the mid-1980s on this involves the employment of a strategy he terms one of deliberate 'naiveté' – where the difficulty lies in showing how such a strategy is so much as possible and why it is necessary for the attainment of a philosophically uncluttered view of the nature of the human mind and the cognitive capacities it brings into exercise: "The difficulty is in seeing how . . . a move in the direction of deliberate 'naiveté' can possibly help after three centuries of modern philosophy, not to mention a century of brain science and now cognitive science. The problem now is to *show the possibility* of a return to what I called 'deliberate naiveté'. [I]t seems to me that that is the direction in which we need to go." (Hilary Putnam, "Realism without Absolutes," collected in *Words and Life*, 284)

characterized by a deep distrust of intellectual fashion and a tendency to recoil from any philosophical position – even if he himself helped to originate it – as soon as it begins to acquire the cast of a new philosophical orthodoxy. At no point in his life was he without philosophical heroes, but he made a point of always having several very different such heroes at once, both past and present. He had no compunctions about eventually outgrowing any of them and in trading them in for new philosophical exemplars. Yet he was also truly delighted and surprised by the small handful of philosophers (Aristotle, Kant, Wittgenstein) who proved to be much harder for him to outgrow than the others – those who seemed to have always already taken the next step in philosophical thinking ahead of him, somehow standing there waiting for him down the road, at the other side of the arduous recent dialectical turn he himself had just managed to complete.[30]

Not only is there a very significant sense in which Putnam never remained anyone's philosophical follower, but it was very much part of his aim in philosophy never to be one. He was eager to learn as much as he could from the great philosophers of the past and the present, but equally concerned not to allow his philosophical horizons to be defined by his admiration for any one of them. It is one thing to adopt this as one's aim in philosophy, quite another to make good on it. It requires a wonderful facility for not getting stuck in philosophy, as most of us do. Usually, as one's philosophical convictions mature, they harden: so that one's thought is able to move smoothly forward only along a single groove. If these once hardened convictions are then at a later stage undermined, usually the capacity for conviction itself sustains permanent damage in the process. (The result is a disillusioned skepticism, so familiar nowadays, and not only in departments of philosophy.) Putnam's sort of nimbleness of mind seems always only to deepen – rather than to corrode – his capacity for philosophical conviction. This requires, among other intellectual virtues, a remarkable ability to penetrate deeply into a philosophical problem along a single angle of approach without

---

30 The following is an example of a remark he makes in a wide number of contexts, sometimes just as an observation about his experience of reading some single philosopher to whose work he keeps returning – Aristotle, or Kant, or Wittgenstein – in this case as a more general remark about philosophers whom he admires: "I find that reading – Kant, or Aristotle, or Wittgenstein, or John Dewey, or William James, or Habermas, or one of my colleagues here at Harvard – always opens new possibilities. As I get smarter, Kant, Aristotle, etc., all get smarter as well" (Josh Harlan, "Hilary Putnam: On Mind, Meaning, and Reality," Interview with Josh Harlan, *Harvard Review of Philosophy*, Spring (1992): 24). An earlier and snappier version of such a remark is his quip: "As I get older, I find Aristotle gets smarter" (reported by Emrys Westacott, "Review Essay: Hilary Putnam, *Words and Life*", *Philosophy and Social Criticism*, 1998 Vol. 24, 104).

allowing one's overall perspective on the problem in any way to narrow. It is this that allows Putnam repeatedly to articulate a genuinely fresh and subtle philosophical view, without ever precluding him, only shortly thereafter, from also being able completely and mercilessly to rethink or reject that very same view in the light of some sudden new insight.

A further striking feature of Putnam's work is that it operates with an extremely robust yet nuanced conception of the *difficulty* of philosophy. He is someone who not only thinks long and hard about both how and why certain philosophical problems are difficult, but also about what ought to count as making satisfying progress with them. His tendency when exploring a received philosophical view is generally not to consider it simply on its own terms, but rather to attain an understanding of the shape of the entire dialectic of which that particular view forms a part. The underlying methodological premise is that you are not going to be able to see clearly what is wrong with a philosophical view (and therefore reject it in a way that allows you to head out of the problem in the right direction) unless you are also able to see clearly what it is that makes the view seem so attractive to others. Hence when Putnam thinks about a philosophical problem, he often first attempts to formulate the problem in the sharpest possible terms, so that it assumes the form of an intolerable aporia, and then undertakes to map the topography of the most natural responses to it, partly in order to see how each response bears the image(s) of those it wishes to reject, and partly in order to isolate and examine the presuppositions that remain invariant throughout the established field of philosophical play. Though this dimension of his philosophical method becomes ever more pronounced in his later work, it runs throughout all of his work. The common denominator in the philosophical work of the figures in the history of philosophy whom he came most to admire – such as Aristotle, Kant, and Wittgenstein – their many differences notwithstanding, was that he regarded each of them as practicing a variant of some such method for making progress in philosophy.[31]

When it came to the process of making his philosophical ideas available to a wider public, writing always came a distant third after conversation and teaching for Putnam, in the order of genesis, clarification, and expression of thought. He would write once he was ready – as he liked to put it – "to write up" a set of ideas he had recently been trying out in various conversational and pedagogical contexts. This was no less exploratory a procedure in Putnam's hands than were

---

31 For a brief overview of Putnam's Aristotelianism, see *Words and Life*, xv–xxiv; of his Kantianism, see *Realism with a Human Face*, xvi–xxxiv; of his Wittgensteinianism, see *Realism with a Human Face*, xxxiv–xlii.

his improvisatory modes of conversation and teaching themselves. Each time he would "read out" a lecture he had "written up," he would – sometimes even while he was giving it – take his pencil out and begin to alter it. After dozens of such alterations, what would emerge was often a remarkably different article – and not always one that, in retrospect, he deemed superior to some of its prede-cessors, leading him to dive back into his earlier versions to recover an idea he felt he should not have been as quick to abandon. Working with him as the editor on two of his collections of essays – *Realism with a Human Life* and *Words and Life* – required carefully going back over a raft of mutually overlapping texts, both published and unpublished, selecting out the best versions of ones that did not substantially overlap one another, eliminating common paragraphs, adding ones from other versions of the papers, and simply leaving out altogether some nicely turned essays whose inclusion would have involved introducing too much repetition into the volume.[32] It is therefore in no way an exaggeration to say that Hilary Putnam's corpus of books and easily accessible published essays repre-sents only a fraction of his overall body of work.[33]

More generally, Putnam's manner of practicing philosophy was one in which the role of philosophical conversation was preeminent. He would spend hours talking with students and colleagues, as well as attending conferences through-out the world – not only giving lectures and conducting mini-seminars, but also actively seeking out young philosophers to ask them what presently excited them in what they were reading and learning, self-consciously striving to expose himself to novel forms of philosophical provocation. Always eager to acquire fruitful new conversation partners, when he found someone with whom he wished to remain in contact, he was ingenious at devising ways to do so. Aside from conversation, the other great engine of intellectual exploration in his life was teaching. Given the choice, he would never teach his already published work – unless it was to criticize something in it – preferring to take advantage of the classroom environment to try out and refine his latest ideas.

Putnam approached almost everything in life – each new person, trip to a new country, or experience of an unfamiliar culture, religion, or way of life – as an opportunity to expand his education. One good way to get a sense of this

---

32 This is one of the reasons that there is a substantial number of published articles not col-lected in any of his volumes – because they overlap with ones that are published, even though the uncollected ones often also contain interesting philosophical insights that do not figure in any of the collected articles.
33 A further reason for this is that Putnam himself would simply lose track of things that he published in obscure venues.

side of his philosophical life – as well as of the impact he had on those whom he thus encountered – is to read some of the many reminiscences penned by those who thereby came to know him or even by those who had no more than a brief chance to meet and interact with him on a single occasion.[34] Here is Michael P. Lynch recollecting his first encounter with Putnam, when they met at Syracuse when Lynch was a graduate student there:

> I remember having dinner with Hilary Putnam when he came to Syracuse University around 1994 to give some lectures. I was a graduate student working on a dissertation on realism and truth. Putnam was my philosophical hero and he was incredibly generous with his time during the week he was there, meeting with me and offering me advice and philosophical wisdom. During this particular dinner he told me about traveling to Mexico when he was 18 and going to Diego Rivera's house and getting invited in for dinner by Frida Kahlo. He told me about his discussions with Einstein. Near the end of the dinner he turned to me and remarked on how lucky he was to have met such great minds, and how grateful he was to them for their willingness to talk to a young person. I remember thinking then, as I do now, that I was having the exact same experience talking to Hilary. How lucky I was, and am, for having met him. He was one of the greats.[35]

I have chosen this particular report because of the direct and unadorned manner in which it touches upon many of the things that recur throughout such reminiscences: the smiling openness with which Putnam would approach students, the active and warm interest he would take in them and their lives, his delight in sharing anecdotes and in adducing a perfectly fitting story (including especially ones drawn from his own life) to illustrate a point, his sense of how lucky he himself had been in life and especially in the gift of his teachers, his desire to pass this gift on to the next generation in philosophy, and – last but not least – the sense he often left on those with whom he came into contact that they had, indeed, been privileged to meet "one of the greats" and yet in the end were struck as much by his humility and generosity as by his brilliance and erudition.

III A Moving Target

Putnam is unusual among philosophers for the sheer number of times in which he alters his fundamental ideas, the openness with which he acknowledges those changes, and the vehemence with which he later turns on and seeks to

---

34 One nice collection of such reminiscences may be found in Roy T. Cook and Geoffrey Hellman, "Memories of Hilary Putnam," in *Hilary Putnam on Logic and Mathematics*, edited by Roy T. Cook and Geoffrey Hellman (Cham, Switzerland: Springer, 2018), 1–8.
35 Cook and Hellman, "Memories of Hilary Putnam," 3–4.

dismantle the very philosophical doctrines he himself originally pioneers.[36] Daniel Dennett's humorous publication, *The Philosophical Lexicon*, which compiles neologisms based on the names of famous philosophers, offers the following definition: "*hilary*, n. (from hilary term). A brief but significant period in the intellectual career of a distinguished philosopher." It includes an example of how to use the word in a sentence: "'Oh, that's what I thought three or four hilaries ago.'"[37] *The Lexicon* thereby suggests that a hilary might be roughly equivalent in length – and perhaps even etymologically related – to an Oxford Hilary Term, in effect suggesting the temporal unit in question is around six weeks. This surely involves a drastic underestimation of the average length of time for which Hilary Putnam tended to hold a philosophical view. Nonetheless, what is true in this bit of hyperbole is that Putnam arguably already begins wondering what might be wrong with the view he has just published, as soon as it appears in print and others begin developing an enthusiasm for it. He is often asked in interviews why he is so prone to change his philosophical mind and in response he suggests that his willingness to approach his own previous writings in this mercilessly critical manner proved to be essential to the very manner in which he found he himself was best able to make genuine progress in philosophy.[38]

His ready willingness to retract the philosophical doctrines for which he was most famous is not a feature of his philosophical development that Putnam ever feels the slightest need to apologize for. He tends rather to regard it as an expression of commitment to a central aspect of his own conception of the subject: "Philosophy is not a subject that eventuates in final solutions, and the discovery that the latest view – no matter if one produced it oneself – still does not clear away the mystery is characteristic of the work, when the work is well done[39] This remark of Putnam's – "philosophy is not a subject that eventuates in final solutions" – drew the ire of some of his critics. Indeed, for just this

---

36 Authors placed in the awkward position of having to provide an introduction to Putnam's thought therefore tend to begin by saying something like this: "Putnam, almost uniquely among the philosophical greats, is willing to rethink his views continuously and to reengage with the issues that have preoccupied him for six decades." Maria Baghramian, "Introduction" to *Reading Putnam* (New York: Routledge, 2012), 1.

37 Daniel Dennett (ed.), *The Philosophical Lexicon* (Newark, Delaware: American Philosophical Association, 1987), 11. Another neologism presented in that book is this: "*putname*, n. A presumed expert authorized by a society to name a natural kind and determine its members."

38 "I am always dissatisfied with something about what I have previously written, and locating that something, and trying to think why I am dissatisfied and what to do about it, often sets the agenda for my next piece of work." (Harlan, "Hilary Putnam: On Mind, Meaning, and Reality," 24)

39 Hilary Putnam, *Representation and Reality*, (Cambridge, MA: MIT Press, 1988), p. xii.

reason, some of his most frustrated critics sometimes dismissively labeled him a "moving target." Why bother to criticize a philosopher's position, if the philosopher himself tells you he that is present view is not his final view and, in effect, acknowledges that he is about to abandon it anyway?

Others, however, have seen his refusal to regard as final any solution to a philosophical problem – including those he himself proposes – as itself constituting an important part of the singular character of what he came to stand for in philosophy. John Passmore, a distinguished historian of twentieth-century Anglo-American philosophy, documents some of the dazzling number of different influential philosophical views Putnam respectively originates and then abandons over the course of his career and then concludes: "Hilary Putnam is . . . the Bertrand Russell of contemporary philosophy in this respect."[40] We will touch below upon other reasons why a comparison of Putnam with Russell might suggest itself to someone writing an intellectual profile of him, but for now let us focus only on Passmore's reason for being drawn to such a comparison. He begins by noting that "Putnam shares Russell's capacity for changing his mind as a result of learning from his contemporaries" and remarks that any attempt to characterize "Putnam's philosophy [in particular, his swings between realism and anti-realism] is like trying to capture the wind with a fishing net."[41] But he resembles Russell in a further related respect for Passmore as well. Just as Passmore found in writing his celebrated account of the prehistory, origins, and development of the history of analytic philosophy – in his famous 1957 book *A Hundred Years of Philosophy* – that he could not confine his discussion of Russell to some isolated part of that book, he made a similar discovery when he turned to the task of writing its sequel.[42] In *A Hundred Years of Philosophy*, when it came to narrating the first three decades of the history of analytic philosophy, no matter which topic is at issue, it was impossible to discuss the period without some detailed presentation of Russell's views on the topic and his criticisms of other contemporaneous figures working on it. So, too, when Passmore, twenty-three years later, turns to writing his 1980 book *Recent Philosophers*, a history of the decades of philosophical activity not yet covered in his previous history, here he finds that some discussion of Putnam's work crops up in virtually every chapter, as if it were undeniably the case that several of the most important philosophers of that then recent period all happened to be

---

40 John Passmore, *Recent Philosophers* (London: Duckworth, 1988), 104. My discussion below of Passmore on Putnam draws on my editor's introduction to *Realism with a Human Face*.

41 John Passmore, *A Hundred Years of Philosophy* (London: Duckworth, 1957; the most widely accessible reprint is the 1978 Penguin edition).

42 Passmore, *A Hundred Years of Philosophy*, 92.

named "Hilary Putnam." Passmore himself notes the oddity of this, and the effect it has on his own procedure for narrating how these debates unfold in this later period of the history of analytic philosophy, pausing to remark at one point in the book: "Putnam's Russellian capacity for changing his mind makes him very useful for our purposes. He is the history of recent philosophy in outline."[43]

As noted above, Putnam's entire philosophical career takes the form of a series of pendulum swings, in which he first internalizes and creatively develops ideas he takes from his adopted philosophical teachers and heroes, and then turns on those ideas, subjecting them to rigorous and radical critique. Focusing on nothing more than Putnam's philosophical work up till the 1970s, it already becomes possible to say something like this:

> Philosophy experiences few seismic shifts in the course of centuries. Hilary Putnam has been responsible for at least two in a single generation: functionalism about mental phenomena, and externalism about meaning.[44]

What this leaves out, as we shall briefly see below, is that Putnam, starting in the mid-1980s, becomes a vociferous critic of standard functional accounts of mental states and vehemently repudiates the received understanding of what it is to be an externalist about meaning. It is impossible within the compass of an introduction such as this to document all of the shifts in Putnam's philosophy with respect to the diverse areas and topics of which he treats. This is a more sensible task for individual essays each devoted to one aspect of Putnam's philosophical development – as are some of the ones collected in this volume. Tim Maudlin's contribution to this volume, for example, provides a wonderful critical overview of the twists in turns in the development of Putnam's thought when it comes specifically to the philosophy of quantum mechanics. Mario De Caro performs a similar task, tracing a parallel trajectory of development, when it comes to the topic of how to reconcile the truth in determinism with the possibility of free will. A volume with many more contributions than this one could contain many dozens of further such overviews of main lines of development in some one aspect of Putnam's thought – pertaining to his conception of, say, the objectivity of ethical statements, or of the value of a religious way of life (to mention just two of the many philosophy topics about which his views shifted dramatically over the course of his life), or his successive attempts at interpreting and critically assessing, say, Aristotle's hylomorphism or Wittgenstein's rule-following considerations (to mention just two of the many interpretative

---

43 Passmore, *A Hundred Years of Philosophy*, 97.
44 Maxmilian de Gaynesford, "Introduction" to *Hilary Putnam* (Chesham: McGill-Queens University Press/Acumen, 2006), 1.

topics to which he recurred, and took up anew, once every decade or so over the second half of his life).[45]

In what follows, in charting some twists and turns in his philosophical development, I will not attempt descriptions of Putnam's thought anywhere near as fine-grained as those offered in the aforementioned individual contributions to this volume. My focus below will rather be on how the whole of this thought hangs together and alters its overall shape as it develops. The aim will be selectively to trace a handful of interrelated lines of thought and criss-crossing paths in his evolution as a thinker in a manner that conveys both how wide and how variegated the philosophical terrain is he traverses over the course of the whole of his life.[46]

IV Some Pendulum Swings in Putnam's Philosophical Development

As a young man who starts his graduate career in philosophy with an unusually strong background in theoretical linguistics, physics and formal logic, as well as in the foundations of probability and number theory, Putnam is drawn to the work of philosophers who take these disciplines seriously and wish to explore the intellectual challenges they pose for philosophy. The first major pendulum swing

---

45 For Putnam on Aristotle, see especially the first three essays – originally respectively published in 1986, 1992, and 1993 – collected in *Words and Life*, the second of which is the magisterial essay co-authored with Martha Nussbaum, "Changing Aristotle's Mind" (collected in *Words and Life*, 22–61) and also see his 2000 essay "Aristotle's Mind and Contemporary Science," collected in *Philosophy in an Age of Science*, edited by Mario De Caro and David Macarthur, (Cambridge, MA.: Harvard University Press, 2012), 584–607. For Putnam on Wittgenstein on rule-following, see especially the chapters on Wittgenstein in that same book. Putnam himself believed there were deep philosophical affinities between Aristotle and Wittgenstein and tried to bring these out in the readings he sought to offer of each on these topics. This thought finds its first expression in his co-authored essay with Nussbaum: "We suggest that Aristotle's thought really is, properly understood, the fulfillment of Wittgenstein's desire to have a 'natural history of man' . . . As Aristotelians we do not discover something behind something else, a hidden reality behind the complex unity that we see and are. We find what we are in the appearances. And Aristotle tells us that if we attend properly to the appearances the dualist's questions never get going." (*Words and Life*, 55)

46 For a bibliographical essay on Putnam's oeuvre, as well as some of the most important secondary literature on it, see the appendix to Conant and Elliott (eds.), *The Norton Anthology of Western Philosophy*, Vol 2, A125–A126. For a straight bibliography of Putnam's publications, see Auxier, Anderson, and Hahn, *The Philosophy of Hilary Putnam*.

in his philosophical trajectory comes when, after sitting at Reichenbach's feet in UCLA, reading everything recent of Carnap's, and writing a Ph.D. dissertation under their mentorship, Putnam strikes out on his own in the philosophy of science and mathematics, largely by criticizing the views of these first two of his philosophical heroes. According to them and their fellow logical positivists or empiricists, mathematics should be conceived not as a substantive body of knowledge in its own right, but as a language for stating scientific truths. On this positivist view, mathematical language itself carries no ontological commitments. Its value is purely as an instrument in scientific investigation. In this way, the positivists sought to avoid the traditional controversy over the nature of mathematical entities, and especially the idea of a "Platonic" realm of mathematical objects existing outside of observable nature. The positivists were determined to avoid the idea of unobservable mathematical entities. The Hilary Putnam of the late 1950s, shortly after receiving tenure, parts company with his teachers on this point. He concludes for a time that Quine, over his series of recent publications, has managed successively to show that fundamental ontological questions – such as "Do numbers really exist?" – are well-posed: not only do they admit of an answer, but that Quine even succeeds in showing precisely how a scientifically-minded philosopher may go about answering them. This paves the way for Putnam to embrace a robust form of metaphysical realism for the next quarter of a century, only to vehemently abandon it in the mid-1970s.

In his 1960 paper "What Theories Are Not," Putnam seeks to build on Quine's criticisms of the central doctrines of logical positivism by mounting an internal critique of his own, in this case of the positivist dichotomy between observational terms and theoretical terms. Putnam seeks to show that even Carnap's most sophisticated and nuanced attempt to draw such a distinction still eventuates in problems that render the distinction itself untenable.[47] This turns out to be the first step in what becomes a lifelong philosophical project. The distinction between the merely observational and the purely theoretical becomes only the first of a series of dichotomies which Putnam identifies as central to the outlook of logical positivism and which he subjects to scathing critique. He eventually, however, also comes to think that none of these influential dichotomies constitutes a mere philosophical mistake on the part of their progenitors. Each such distinction harbors an important truth – one that it takes considerable intellectual work properly to tease out and formulate adequately – but the truth in

---

47 Hilary Putnam, "What Theories Are Not" (1960), collected in *Mathematics, Matter and Method: Philosophical Papers*, Vol. 1, 215–227 (Cambridge: Cambridge University Press, 1975).

the underlying distinction becomes philosophically crippling as soon as it is erected into an absolute dichotomy. The philosophical task becomes one of rescuing the distinction while rejecting the dichotomy.[48]

The positivists were also skeptical of the traditional idea that geometry, as well as other branches of mathematics and logic, discovers necessary truths. By construing logic and mathematics on the model of a language rather than a body of fact, the positivists hoped to explain away necessary truth, in geometry and elsewhere, as merely a kind of trivial linguistic truth. Given certain definitions, certain truths would necessarily follow. But, they argued, the definitions could always be changed, and so the "necessary truths" could be changed, without changing our view of any "real" truth or matter of fact. The positivists had been particularly impressed by the way the advent of relativity theory challenged traditional views of geometry. Before the late nineteenth century, philosophers and scientists largely took it for granted that Euclidean geometry described the real structure of physical space. Relativity theory, however, showed that there were physical applications for non-Euclidean geometry. The positivists concluded that *no* geometry should be seen as "the real" geometry of space. Instead, different geometric languages can be adopted as a matter of convenience or utility in different scientific contexts. In "It Ain't Necessarily So" (1962), Putnam argued that the positivists had drawn the wrong moral from the success of relativity theory. In his view, the presuppositions of Euclidean geometry – such as that one never comes back to the same place when traveling along a single path in the same direction – were not merely convenient but *necessary* presuppositions from the point of view of classical Newtonian physics.[49] The shift to relativistic physics does not merely involve a change in the meaning of such terms as "place" or "path." It involves a fundamentally different conception of what a "place" or a "path" is – a conception that cannot be made consistent with the old Newtonian worldview. From Putnam's point of view, examples like the shift from Newtonian to relativistic physics show that it is possible to revise our mathematical beliefs for empirical reasons. In "It Ain't Necessarily So," he contended that all truths

---

48 This distinction – between a "distinction" and a "dichotomy" – continues to play a central role in Putnam's thought until the end of his life; see, for example, *The Collapse of the Fact/ Value Dichotomy* (Cambridge, MA: Harvard University Press, 2002), 9–11, 60–61.

49 Hilary Putnam, "It Ain't Necessarily So" (1962), collected in *Mathematics, Matter, and Method: Philosophical Papers*, Vol. 1, 237–249 (Cambridge: Cambridge University Press, 1975). For a broader retrospective glance at his early disagreements with Carnap and Reichenbach on geometry, his critique of Grünbaum's account of physical geometry, as well as the development of his own positive views on the philosophy of geometry in this period, see his "Intellectual Autobiography," 38–39, 46–50.

were in principle empirically revisable – even basic logical truths such as the law of non-contradiction, which he suggested might be revised in the light of quantum mechanics.

At the same time, Putnam proposes that we might think of certain truths, such as those of logic and mathematics, as possessing a kind of *relative necessity*. The old idea that there is a body of truths, such as the truths of Euclidean geometry, which are "simply" necessary, he argued, should indeed be jettisoned. But a given statement can be necessarily true *relative to* a certain theory or body of knowledge, so that to give up that truth is at the same time to reject a whole set of fundamental theoretical commitments. Putnam argues that we need this idea of relative necessity in order to make sense of moments of radical scientific change, such as the shift from classical to relativistic physics. How exactly best to formulate the idea that certain truths are relative to a certain framework – as well as how to specify which truths these are, how to characterize the sort of necessity they possess, and how best to conceive of the framework in question (as a language?, a theory?, a certain tradition of thought?) – remains a task to which he repeatedly returns as his views within the philosophy of logic, language, and science themselves evolve.

His profound criticisms of the central doctrines of logical positivism notwithstanding, Putnam never ceased to credit the positivists with having taught him a number of important philosophical lessons. Looking back in later years, he would particularly single out the following as foremost among these: philosophy cannot be done simply independently of knowledge of the sciences – both of the history of science and of the present state of science. Putnam especially liked to remind certain sorts of readers that it had been Carnap himself who had not only hailed Thomas Kuhn's *The Structure of Scientific Revolutions* but had also played an instrumental role in seeing to it that the book was published – and that what Carnap most appreciated about it was how Kuhn so convincingly made the case for the indispensability of the history of science to philosophy.[50] Putnam's own further engagements, however, both with the sciences of his day, as well as in his own investigations into certain moments in the history of physics, biology, linguistics and computer science led him to the conclusion that the picture of science with which both Carnap and Quine operated was rife with metaphysical assumptions – assumptions that he increasingly became concerned to make visible and criticize in his later work.

---

50 See the remarks about Carnap in this connection in Hilary Putnam, "A Half Century of Philosophy, Viewed from Within," *Daedalus: Journal of the American Academy of Arts and Sciences*, Winter (1997): 176.

Putnam's conception of the relative a priori and his increasing disenchantment with especially Quine's philosophical worldview had their roots in a series of decisive philosophical encounters which took place when he spent a sabbatical semester in the fall of 1960 visiting Oxford University, where he found himself in constant philosophical conversation with Elizabeth Anscombe, Philippa Foot, and Paul Grice. Part of what impressed him about these three figures was the sheer breadth of their respective conceptions of philosophy, the way they did philosophy with one eye trained on the history of philosophy, and the robust intellectual independence with which they each followed out their own interests and developed their views. A description Putnam offers of the impression that Anscombe made on him in this period parallels remarks he would later make about other philosophers whom he came greatly to admire – not only about how Foot and Grice struck him at that time, but also in later years about what drew him to the writings of figures such as John McDowell and Bernard Williams. The description I have in mind is the following: "Anscombe was interested in just about every question of philosophy, and although she had been a student and close friend of Wittgenstein's, her own philosophical style is markedly different."[51] This came to represent a philosophical ideal for Putnam: to learn to be someone on whom nothing philosophical is lost – so that one is able to be interested in just about every question of philosophy and equally able to become fast philosophical friends with any one of the great philosophers of one's time whom one admires, while never falling under the spell of any one of them so as to become unable to develop a philosophical style of one's own, markedly different from theirs.

The decisive recent event in the history of Oxford at that time of his 1960 visit was that J.L. Austin had just passed away. The debate between Austin and Grice continued in his absence. Austin's followers maintained that the meanings of the words in a sentence do not themselves determine exactly what is being said in a given context; many different things may be said using those same words with those same meanings. Grice maintained, on the contrary, that there is such a thing as the standard meaning of a sentence and the various further non-standard things we can use a sentence to say are all to be explained by conversational implicatures. In his subsequent writings in the 1960s and 1970s, Putnam became increasingly interested in identifying and exploring examples of a sort to which he thought proponents on neither side of this debate could do full justice – examples of sentences whose truth-value do not fluctuate through a mere alteration of an Austinian context of use, yet whose significance

---

51 Putnam, "A Half Century of Philosophy," 184.

is not fixed once and for all in the manner required by a Gricean theory of language. By the mid-1980s – partly due to the influence of Charles Travis – he concluded that Austin's own views, properly understood, were far more compatible with his own earlier account of the contextual a priori and his own overall conception of language than he had originally supposed, eventually coming around to the view that he was in complete agreement with Austin – or at least with what Austin holds on Travis's reading of him.[52]

Putnam's move in 1965 from MIT to Harvard – that is, from one side of Cambridge, Massachusetts to the other side of the same town – did not mark a step towards Quine in anything other than a merely geographical direction. Though the early phases of the first pendulum swing away from positivism in Putnam's thought are mediated by Quine's criticisms of Carnap, they eventually lead, especially after Putnam's visit to Oxford, to no less vehement criticisms of Quine himself. As a former student of Reichenbach, Putnam never ceases to be engaged with questions about the philosophical presuppositions of the natural sciences and the proper place of a scientific outlook in philosophy. Early in his career, he embraced the details of Quine's criticisms of Carnap, and especially of the analytic/synthetic distinction; later Putnam, however, concludes that, in so doing, he implicitly committed himself to features of Quine's own strident brand of empiricism that were nothing short of philosophically disastrous. In his early enthusiasm for Quine's critique of Carnap, Putnam simply and unequivocally rejects the traditional empiricist distinction between the substantive content of a scientific theory and the conceptual vocabulary in which that theory is couched. Over the next three and a half decades of his life, he repeatedly revisits this issue, devoting considerable energy to trying to sift through and extract what he later thinks might still be sound in Quine's critique of Carnap, while endeavoring to hive off that sliver of philosophical insight from the larger portion of philosophical overkill he concludes characterizes most of the rest of Quine's overall conception of philosophy. This leads to the beginning of Putnam's subsequent lifelong concern not only to criticize philosophical scientism and related forms of naturalistic excess in analytic philosophy, but also to provide a philosophical account of the nature and depth of the forms of diversity within the natural sciences themselves,[53] as well as of the autonomy and irreducibility of the various forms of

---

52 For a brief discussion of his 1960 visit to Oxford, the debate between Austin and Grice, his early view of that debate, and his eventual later move towards Austin, see the section titled "Oxford in 1960" in Putnam, "A Half Century of Philosophy," 184–185.
53 See, for example, his 1987 essay "The Diversity of the Sciences," collected as Chapter 25 of *Words and Life*.

non-scientific knowledge – forms of knowledge he endeavors to show are fundamentally misconstrued when conceived on the model of the natural sciences.[54]

From this point on, a central point of continuity in Putnam's views across the decades is that our terms embody theoretical commitments and that these terms cannot be changed without overturning those commitments. This leads him also to a nuanced reconsideration of what is right and what is wrong in traditional ways of drawing the analytic/synthetic distinction, as well as in the related distinction between the a priori and the a posteriori. It fuels his later advocacy of what he calls "realism with a small 'r'" and the development of a philosophical conception of language fully consonant with such a form of realism.[55] By the mid-1980s Putnam regards the ensuing conception of language as a natural consequence of an appropriately metaphysically modest form of realist epistemology – one that is able to allow that what we say, and what we mean, reaches all the way to the things we talk about, and does not stop anywhere short of them. Rather than doing what he had originally been trained to do and continued to do throughout his Quinean and MIT periods – namely, to begin with issues in the philosophy of science and language and then work out from there to the implications of a putatively sound philosophy of science and language for other areas of philosophy – thereby essentially holding the rest of philosophy hostage to some preferred set of views about the nature of science and/or language – Putnam increasingly comes to adopt the reverse methodology. He concludes that one first think hard and long about what is distinctive about each of the diverse forms of knowledge we need to make room for in philosophy – how to do philosophical justice to the full diversity of our forms of scientific, logical, mathematical, ethical, aesthetic, and political discourse – and

---

54 In a comparatively late retrospective essay "Pragmatism and Nonscientific Knowledge" (2002), Putnam summarizes "what has been a focus for my philosophical interests for the past twenty years" as follows: "the existence of and the importance of knowledge outside of the exact sciences ('nonscientific' knowledge) and in particular the existence and importance of knowledge of values in the widest sense – what is it to know that something is better or worse than something else: a better way of life, or a better course of action, or a better theory (in science), or a better interpretation (of a text, etc.). This focus has naturally led me to point out how 'paradigmatic' science (physics) itself depends on judgments which are 'nonscientific'." (in James Conant and Urszula M. Zeglin (eds.), *Hilary Putnam: Pragmatism and Realism* (London and New York: Routledge, 2002); reprinted in *Pragmatism as a Way of Life*, 55)
55 Putnam draws a distinction between what he calls "Realism with a capital 'R'" (which he took to be the then regnant metaphysical image of the world in analytic philosophy) and "realism with a small 'r'" (which is his label for a form of philosophy that seeks to recover our common-sense image of the world from philosophical distortions of it). The distinction is perhaps drawn in its sharpest terms by him in the 1988 title essay of *Realism with a Human Face*.

then to develop an adequate philosophy of knowledge and language in the light of such an overall conception of the task of philosophy.

This larger transition in Putnam's thought is encouraged through his increasing engagement with the writings of Ludwig Wittgenstein and philosophers influenced by him – including several already mentioned above: Anscombe and Foot in the 1960s, McDowell and Travis in the 1980s. When Putnam moves his office in 1965 to the Harvard Philosophy Department in Emerson Hall, it is to a building in which there are three philosophers passionately interested in later Wittgenstein: Rogers Albritton, Stanley Cavell, and Burton Dreben.[56] The respective influences they each have on him are diverse and in each case quite distinct.[57] The figure who has the most immediate impact is Albritton, with whom he discusses questions such as: could it turn out that pencils are really organisms? Is this so much as possible? If we are to allow that it is in some sense *possible*, what does it require of an adequate philosophical account of modality that it be able to do justice to such a possibility? If it is not even possible, then why not? What sort of *necessity* could it be that pencils cannot turn out upon further discovery really to be organisms? Dreben's influence on Putnam proves in the long run to be far more consequential than Albritton's, but largely for reasons having to do with ways in which Putnam himself strongly reacts against the conception of philosophy Dreben finds in Wittgenstein. What initially bothers Putnam most in that putatively Wittgensteinian conception is the feature he takes it to share with logical positivism: namely, the idea that the central aim of philosophy, if properly conducted, should be to free us from the illusion that when we grapple with the traditional problems of philosophy we have to do with a set of important issues.[58] In his philosophical conversations in Emerson Hall, Putnam was fond of quoting a passage from Étienne Gilson – "Philosophy always buries its undertakers."[59] – but whenever he quoted it, the undertaker of philosophy he most had in mind

---

56 See the section titled "Wittgenstein at Harvard" in "A Half Century of Philosophy," 191–195.

57 For some of Putnam's own subsequent major writings on Wittgenstein, see the essays collected as Chapters 12–15 in *Realism with a Human Face*; Chapter 2 of *Pragmatism: An Open Question*; chapters 7 and 8 of *Renewing Philosophy* (Cambridge, MA: Harvard University Press, 1992); Chapter 1 of *Jewish Philosophy as a Guide to Life*; and those collected as Chapters 22–28 of *Philosophy in an Age of Science*). His attitude towards Wittgenstein takes a markedly critical turn in the last of these essays – Chapter 28 – written in 2011: "Wittgenstein: A Reappraisal."

58 I am here paraphrasing remarks of Putnam's from "A Half Century of Philosophy," 193.

59 The remark comes from the concluding sequence of Gilson's *William James Lectures*, delivered at Harvard in 1936, reprinted as Étienne Gilson, *The Unity of Philosophical Experience* (New York: Scribners, 1965), 305–306. Here is an example of a context in which Putnam quotes the remark in print: "A simple induction from the history of thought suggests that metaphysical discussion is not going to disappear as long as reflective people remain in the world. As

was Dreben. In the writings and teachings of Cavell, on the other hand, Putnam finds a reading of Wittgenstein that he takes to be the diametric opposite of Dreben's: "For Stanley Cavell's Wittgenstein, philosophical confusions are not just matters of language gone wrong, but an expression of deep human issues that also express themselves in a variety of other ways – political, theological, and literary."[60]

Among the propositions that Putnam concludes an adequate philosophy must learn to make room for – and for which many philosophies fail to provide a coherent account – are the propositions we call upon when we ourselves philosophize: those propositions we come out with, for example, when we formulate philosophical truths about the nature of non-philosophical discourse. This initiates what proves to be a recurring project – one Putnam refines partly through the evolution in his own ways of reading Kant and Wittgenstein: the project of investigating the conditions of the very possibility of philosophical discourse, along with the related task of criticizing philosophical views that are self-refuting precisely on the ground that they fail to account for the status of the sentences in which they themselves are formulated. The roots of his interest in this issue may be traced back to Putnam's earlier criticisms of verifiability theories of meaning for resting on theoretical pronouncements about what is meaningful that cannot stand up to the theory's own test for meaningfulness, his related criticism of Carnap's propositions purporting to elucidate the analytic/synthetic distinction for being neither analytic nor synthetic, and his charge against putatively Wittgensteinian criterial theories of meaning (such as the one advanced by Norman Malcolm) for themselves failing to meet their own criteria. This concern eventually broadens out, as Putnam increasingly appreciates that the gambit he originally employed to showed that certain positivist and neo-Wittgensteinian views were self-refuting "is *deep* because it refutes every attempt to argue for a criterial conception of rationality."[61] What comes to disturb him most about such theories about particular topics in philosophy (what is meaningful, analytic, etc.) is that they implicitly commit themselves to *"philosophies which leave no room for a rational activity of philosophy."*[62]

The topic of the status of the propositions of *philosophy* and that of the status of genuinely *logical* propositions are seldom treated by Putnam as completed unrelated. In his mid-career writings on logical and mathematical necessity, Putnam

---

Gilson said at the end of a famous book, 'Philosophy always buries its undertakers'." (*Realism with a Human Face*, 19)

60 Putnam, "A Half Century of Philosophy," 194.

61 Hilary Putnam, *Reason, Truth and History* (Cambridge: Cambridge University Press, 1981), 111.

62 Putnam, *Reason, Truth and History*, 113.

struggles to retain the core of what he takes to have been true in the argument of "It Ain't Necessarily So," while reining in what he came to see as its worst excesses. The topic of logical necessity – and how it relates to the sorts of truths one formulates when doing philosophy – is one that he wrestles with throughout his philosophical career, with his changes of view in this area influencing his views in many other areas of philosophy, and vice versa. A characteristic expression of his mid-career wrestling with the issue may be seen in his article "There is at Least One A Priori Truth" (1978), in which he seeks to draw some limit to the extreme revisability of logic that he had defended in his early writings.[63] At least one truth is unrevisable, Putnam declares there, in the sense that it would never be rational to give it up. His candidate for such an a priori truth, at this point in his career, is (what he calls) the minimal principle of non-contradiction: the principle that *not every statement is both true and false.* Putnam argues that there are no circumstances under which it would be rational to revise this principle, and that it therefore provides us with an example of at least one "absolutely, unconditionally, truly, actually, a priori truth."[64] Twenty-two years later, in his even more historically informed 1990 paper "Rethinking Mathematical Necessity," Putnam again returns to the question: what is the status of the laws of logic?[65] Are they analytic or synthetic, a priori or a posteriori? As is typical of him, he once again approaches the question completely afresh. At the outset of the paper, he describes contemporary philosophy as faced with two equally unsatisfying alternatives – alternatives he associates with the names of Carnap and Quine respectively. The Carnapian view is a linguistic conventionalism, according to which the laws of logic are analytic truths. The Quinean view is a naturalized epistemology, according to which the laws of logic are synthetic a posteriori and hence not dissimilar in kind from ordinary empirical truths. Putnam then goes on to sketch a third way, whose roots he finds in Kant and Frege, which turns on the crucial idea that logical truths do not have negations that we are able to understand. The point is not that these propositions express a content that we grasp and then reject as false; rather, it is that we are simply unable to make sense of these propositions in a way that allows the question of their truth value

---

63 Hilary Putnam, "There Is at Least One A Priori Truth" (1978), collected in *Realism and Reason: Philosophical Papers*, Vol. 3, 98–114 (Cambridge: Cambridge University Press, 1983).

64 Putnam, "There Is at Least One A Priori Truth," 101.

65 Hilary Putnam, "Rethinking Mathematical Necessity" (1990), collected as Chapter 12 of *Words and Life*, 245–263; for a brief discussion of the relation between the views of the 1990 article and his earlier work on the a priori, see Hilary Putnam, "Reply to James Conant" in *The Philosophy of Hilary Putnam*, edited by Christopher. S. Hill (Fayetteville: The University of Arkansas Press, 1992), 374–77.

to arise in the first place. As Putnam puts it there: "the negation of a theorem of logic violates the condition for being a thinkable thought or judgment."[66]

Putnam's work in the philosophy of mind moves along a track that parallels these shifts in his conceptions of language, logic, and philosophy. He begins from a challenge to one of the logical positivists' central themes. The positivists had been strong proponents of what they called the "Unity of Science": their ultimate ambition was to show how all of science, including psychology, sociology, and economics, could be reduced to fundamental physics. In "Reductionism and the Nature of Psychology" (1973), Putnam develops an influential criticism of this reductionist program, while at the same time showing how anti-reductionism can be consistent with a commitment to a materialist worldview and a scientific approach to the study of certain aspects of the mind.[67] Putnam's fundamental argument in this essay is that materialism – the belief that there are not any things that are immaterial – does not imply reductionism, insofar as reductionism requires that fundamental physics provides the complete *explanation* of all higher-level phenomena, such as psychological phenomena. To show that fundamental physics is limited in its explanatory scope, he points out that fundamental physics does not even include the complete explanation of biology. Even such basic biological phenomena as the existence of life on Earth do not follow merely from truths of fundamental physics, since the existence of life on Earth depends on what he famously calls "auxiliary hypotheses" that do not figure in fundamental physical theory, e.g., the presence of liquid water on the Earth's surface. Putnam's point is not that biology has to point to some mysterious *non-physical* fact, such as an *élan vital*. The auxiliary hypotheses required by biology, such as that there is liquid water on the Earth's surface, are themselves physical facts. But this fact about the Earth is not *relevant* to fundamental physical theory, and so is not included among the basic laws of physics. The presence of water on the Earth's surface is, however, essential for biology, and in this sense "higher-level" sciences such as biology do not simply follow from "lower-level" ones like physics.

This leads to a larger philosophical theme that Putnam brought to prominence in post-war analytic philosophy: the nature of emergent phenomena. His original interest in this topic stemmed from his having closely studied Marx's account of the nature of emergent economic phenomena. But Putnam saw a way of generalizing the insight and applying it across the entire panoply of

---

66 Putnam, "Rethinking Mathematical Necessity," 257.
67 Hilary Putnam, "Reductionism and the Nature of Psychology" (1973), not reprinted in its original form until it was collected much later as Chapter 23 of *Words and Life*.

natural and human sciences, arguing that psychology, economics, and sociology each study their own proprietary phenomena and that they each stand in a relation to biology that is logically akin (in the depth of difference in the forms of phenomena to be characterized) to biology's relation to physics. An economic development such as the rise of capitalism does not *follow* from a biological description of *homo sapiens*, even though it is, in principle, possible to explain how creatures with our biological constitution came to practice capitalism without introducing anything mysterious or supernatural.

Putnam had long opposed reductionism, initially favoring a functionalist view of the mind. In early essays such as "Psychological Predicates" (1967; later reprinted as "The Nature of Mental States"[68]), he argues that mental states cannot be identical with brain states or any material states because mental states are "multiply realizable" in different material substrates. Thus pain, for example, could be the same mental state in a human and a fish, even if the material composition of the nervous systems in a human and a fish were quite different. What matters for Putnam now is functional architecture, of which he initially proposes to conceive on the model of a digital computer and its computational states. On this model, the mind is to be identified with the functional structure of the computer and its program, not with their material realization in hardware and software. As Putnam pungently put it, "we could be made out of Swiss cheese and it wouldn't matter."[69] Shortly after it becomes a mainstream position in analytic philosophy of mind, however, Putnam rejects the functionalist view he himself had championed. His most famous statement of this recantation comes in his book *Representation and Reality* (1988).[70] Functionalism had initially seemed attractive to him as a way of preserving materialism without reductionism, but he subsequently broadens his reductionist target to include such methodological assumptions as the supposition that social structure can be reduced to individual psychology, and the idea that meanings can be reduced to decontextualized semantic structures. This eviscerates the foundations of his own earlier functionalism. Hence Putnam concludes – to the dismay of many of his earlier admirers – that his own earlier functionalism, its overt anti-reductionist ambitions notwithstanding, reflects just one characteristic and comparatively subtle species of a much broader misguided reductionist

---

68 Hilary Putnam, "The Nature of Mental States," collected as Chapter 21 of *Mind, Language and Reality*: *Philosophical Papers*, Vol. 2, 429–440 (Cambridge: Cambridge University Press, 1975).
69 Hilary Putnam, "Philosophy and our Mental Life" (1973), reprinted in *Mind, Language and Reality*: *Philosophical Papers*, Vol. 2, 291–303 (Cambridge: Cambridge University Press, 1975).
70 Hilary Putnam, *Representation and Reality* (Cambridge, MA: MIT Press, 1988).

impulse that typifies what is philosophically most retrograde in the mainstream of post-war analytic philosophy.

Possibly Putnam's single most celebrated essay, "The Meaning of 'Meaning'" (1975), marks his first effort to extend his critique of reductionism into the area of the philosophy of language. The centerpiece of "The Meaning of 'Meaning'" is Putnam's much-discussed "Twin Earth" thought experiment. Imagine, Putnam writes, that in the future a spaceship from Earth lands on a distant planet that resembles Earth in many surprising respects, and which we may call "Twin Earth." On Twin Earth, there are large bodies of liquid that resemble, to the naked eye, our rivers and lakes. Also, on Twin Earth, there are people who use a language that looks and sounds exactly like English. So they refer to the stuff that constitutes these rivers and lakes using a word that looks and sounds exactly like our word "water." Now, as it happens, the stuff in the Twin Earth rivers and lakes is *not* water, i.e., it is not H_2O. It is instead another substance; Putnam memorably proposes we call it XYZ. His question is this: does the Twin Earth word "water" *mean* what our word "water" means? Putnam argues that the answer is *no*, and he takes this argument to have far-reaching implications.[71] In particular, Putnam argues that the meaning of our word "water" is not to be explained in terms of any set of associated appearances and ideas that ordinary English speakers have when they use the word, since these could be exactly the same for the speakers on Twin Earth. As Putnam memorably put it, "'meanings' just ain't in the head."[72] The meanings of many of our terms, including natural-kind terms like "water" are *beholden* to the way the world is, because when we use a natural-kind term we mean to refer to a single substance or kind of stuff, and thus what we mean depends on what kind of stuff we are referring to. In the case of "water," most grown-up English speakers today know that it's H_2O. But in many other cases – for example, when it comes to knowing what distinguishes an elm from a beech or aluminum from molybdenum – the average modern English speaker is not in possession of the relevant knowledge. Still, Putnam argues, lay-speakers can succeed in referring to elms and aluminum because 1) they can exploit the presence of a sample, and 2) they belong to a linguistic community in which someone – such as a botanist or a chemist – does have the relevant knowledge. Through what Putnam calls a

---

71 What exactly these implications should be taken to be is a matter that will preoccupy him for some years. Some of the problems that stem from Putnam's initial manner of formulating the twin-earth experiment and the ways in which he later seeks to address these are illuminatingly discussed in Sanjit Chakraborty, *The Labyrinth of Mind and World: Beyond Internalism-Externalism* (London and New York: Routledge, 2020).
72 Putnam, "The Meaning of 'Meaning'," 227.

"division of linguistic labor," a whole community of speakers can come to refer successfully to elms even if only some of its members know what distinguishes an elm from a beech. Putnam argues that traditional semantics, by focusing on what is in the head of the individual speaker, has missed two essential dimensions that enter into securing the meaning of a term like "water": first, the way the world is, and second, the speaker's linguistic community.

On the basis of his account of natural-kind terms in "The Meaning of 'Meaning'," Putnam then goes on to elaborate, first, a criticism of Quine's thesis of the indeterminacy of translation, and then later of Donald Davidson's conception of radical interpretation. He argues that the world- and community-involving character of natural-kind terms imposes substantive constraints on translation and interpretation that are not recognized by Quine and Davidson. Together with similar arguments made by Saul Kripke, Putnam's "Meaning of 'Meaning'" helped to initiate one of the central controversies of late analytic philosophy: the controversy over what has come to be called "externalism" in the philosophy of mind and language. This controversy revolves around the question: to what extent are the contents of our thoughts and utterances constituted by the environment in which they occur? The way this controversy is usually understood, there are two distinct self-standingly intelligible realms: the physical realm of the environment in which a thinker and speaker of language finds herself, and "the mental realm" in which her thoughts are "located" and to be individuated. In his later writings, this picture of two distinct self-standingly intelligible realms increasingly comes under pressure. As he memorably summarizes the crux of his later view in the preface to arguably his most famous book *Reason, Truth and History*:

> I shall advance a view in which the mind does not simply 'copy' a world which admits of description by One True Theory. But my view is not a view in which the mind *makes up* the world, either. . . . If one must use metaphorical language, then let the metaphor be this: the mind and the world jointly make up the mind and the world. (Or, to make the metaphor even more Hegelian, the Universe makes up the Universe – with minds – collectively – playing a special role in the making up.)[73]

The aspiration to make fully good on this picture eventually leads Putnam first to excavate and identify, then to reconsider and jettison, a surprising number of assumptions that he originally viewed as utterly trivial but now concludes are philosophically consequential and which underlay his own particular ways of arguing in his earlier writings for functionalist and externalist theses.

To take just one example: readers of "The Meaning of 'Meaning'" tended to assume Putnam's employment of the term "environment" in that essay aimed to

---

73 Putnam, *Reason, Truth and History*, xi.

refer to a realm utterly external to the mind – a realm fully relevantly describable in merely natural-scientific terms. Putnam himself deplored this misunderstanding of his work and it arguably gave rise to a very different focus to much of his subsequent philosophical life. Looking back, at the end of his life, on the subsequent reception of his most famous essay, he made of the following attempt to repudiate (what he termed) "the supposed scientism" that many readers attributed to that essay:

> In "The Meaning of 'Meaning'," I did not claim that what is and is not water (for example) is simply decided by science. In fact, I wrote, "To be water . . . is to bear the relation "same$_L$" [same liquid] to certain things. But what is the relation "same$_L$"?? And I replied that "in one context, 'water' may mean chemically pure water, while in another it may mean the stuff in Lake Michigan." In "Meaning Holism" I went even further to distance myself from a "scientistic" reading of my externalism, when I wrote: "In physics, 'water' means chemically pure water; in ordinary language, things are more complicated. On the one hand, 'water', in the ordinary sense, may have impurities; on the other hand, tea and coffee are not 'water'. What sort of or degree of departure from ideally "pure" taste, color, or odor disqualifies H_2O-cum-impurities from being 'water' in ordinary circumstances is interest relative and context-sensitive. But this is not to say that 'water', in ordinary language, is an operationally-defined word, pure and simple."[74] And I ended the section by saying, "Ordinary language and scientific language are different but interdependent."[75]

Only one year later, in *Meaning and the Moral Sciences* (1976), the scientistic assumption highlighted here (that Putnam himself never endorsed but which informed the generally received understanding of what "externalism" is) begins to become a central target of his work, and the contrary assumption (regarding science's entanglement in and dependence upon the ordinary) begins to become a central preoccupation of his work.[76] Putnam begins to attack (what he calls) "the very idea of metaphysical realism" in all its guises (of which regards scientism to be just one species) and instead argues for a form of "internal realism" – one in which the framework which is internal to our very capacity to form beliefs encompasses not only our "factual" beliefs about our "natural" environment, but much more. This marks the beginning of Putnam's ever more concerted effort to illuminate the extent of the entanglement of fact in value in every domain of human thought and activity, of non-scientific ways of thinking in a non-scientific background body of knowledge that makes scientific thinking possible, of scientific language in ordinary language, and of our intellectual

---

74 Hilary Putnam, "Meaning Holism" (1986), collected as chapter of *Realism with a Human Face*, 282.
75 Putnam, "Intellectual Autobiography," 80.
76 Hilary Putnam, *Meaning and the Moral Sciences* (London: Routledge, 1976).

present in a historical tradition of thought. The first book largely devoted as a whole to exhibiting and elucidating these forms of entanglement is *Reason, Truth and History* (1981). In it he develops his famous "brain in a vat" thought experiment in order to show how internal realism forms the basis of a response to radical skepticism. In the series of four books that follow – *The Many Faces of Realism* (1987), *Renewing Philosophy* (1992), *Pragmatism: An Open Question* (1995), and *The Threefold Cord: Mind, Body, and World* (1999) [77] – Putnam continues to prosecute his case against the varieties of philosophical dichotomy that obscure from view these forms of entanglement, while arguing now for the relevance of ideas he finds in thinkers outside the mainstream of analytic philosophy to the illumination of these questions.

The fourth of the aforementioned books, *The Threefold Cord*, contains Putnam's 1994 *Dewey Lectures* – "Sense, Nonsense, and the Senses" – in which he attempts to identify a widespread assumption that he claims runs throughout early modern philosophy – he dubs the assumption in question "the interface conception" – and he argues that, three centuries later, it continues to be responsible for many of the difficulties that plague contemporary philosophy.

Putnam characterizes the consequences of the continuing hold of this assumption on the philosophical imagination of our time as nothing short of a "disaster." His summary statement of how contemporary philosophy managed to place itself in its present disastrous position runs as follows:

> [T]he key assumption responsible for the disaster is the idea that there has to be an interface between our cognitive powers and the external world – or, to put the same point differently, the idea that our cognitive powers cannot reach all the way to the objects themselves.[78]

If we could overcome the assumption expressed by these words, Putnam suggests, we would be in a position to embrace with a sound philosophical conscience what Putnam (following William James) calls "the natural realism of the common man." This locution – "natural realism" – as Putnam deploys it, is not meant to be a label for an alternative philosophical position; rather it is meant to denote something both more familiar and more elusive: our own prephilosophical understanding of the character of our cognitive relation to the world, prior to its corruption by certain forms of philosophizing that have now come to seem to be forms of post-scientific common sense. In issuing his call for a return to a lost state of epistemological innocence, Putnam knows he is

---

77 Hilary Putnam, *The Threefold Cord: Mind, Body, and World* (New York: Columbia University Press, 1999).

78 Putnam, *The Threefold Cord*, 10.

bound to appear to many of his colleagues to be merely the most recent incarnation of the proverbial philosophical ostrich burying his head in the sands of our everyday ways of talking and thinking. What makes it inevitable that things will so appear to many of his colleagues, according to Putnam, is the interface conception: it is what makes it look as if the recommended species of naiveté cannot be anything other than mere naiveté. Putnam credits John McDowell, in his book *Mind and World*, with having identified (what Putnam calls in the passage above) the "key assumption."[79] The *Dewey Lectures* seek to expose the various guises this assumption assumes in contemporary philosophy of perception and mind, and in the theory of linguistic reference.

From the mid-1980s on, it is not an exaggeration to say that a whole new Hilary Putnam bursts onto the philosophical scene – often to the dismay of some of his earlier colleagues, past doctoral students, and former philosophical fellow travelers – someone whose philosophical thought is still concerned with the topics that animated him from the beginning, but whose horizon of philosophical reference points and favorite authors has now vastly expanded and whose overall philosophical orientation has dramatically shifted. He undertakes a closer study of historical figures such as Aristotle, Kant, and Wittgenstein, with a renewed interest in how each of them anticipates ideas that Putnam himself arrives at by a very different route, seeking now to refine and deepen his own formulations of those ideas by drawing upon theirs. He develops an interest in the philosophical relevance of the writings of literary figures, poets and novelists, devoting whole essays to authors ranging from Alexander Pope to Henry James. In parallel, he begins a careful study of Dewey, James, and Peirce, and begins teaching a seminar on the writings of William James – one which he retaught and rethought several times from the mid-1980s on. At the same time, the constellation of philosophers among his contemporaries with whom he enters into most immediate and fervent dialogue comes to broaden out considerably, featuring as his most frequent interlocutors now, no longer

---

79 John McDowell, *Mind and World* (Cambridge, MA: Harvard University Press, 1994). Putnam later becomes quite critical of certain strains of thought in *Mind and World* which he originally celebrated; see, for example, Hilary Putnam, "McDowell's Mind and McDowell's World," in *Reading McDowell: On Mind and World*, edited by Nicholas H. Smith (London: Routledge, 2002), 174–190. This gives rise to a larger dispute between Putnam and McDowell, culminating in McDowell's "Putnam on Natural Reason," his contribution to Auxier, Anderson, and Hahn, *The Philosophy of Hilary Putnam* (3–110) and Putnam's response to McDowell in that same volume. For an overview of the terms of the initial shape of this dispute, see my "Two Varieties of Skepticism," in *Rethinking Epistemology*, Vol. 2, edited by Guenter Abel and James Conant (Berlin: De Gruyter, 2012), 1–73.

Chomsky, Fodor, and Quine, but rather figures such as Jürgen Habermas,[80] Richard Rorty,[81] and Bernard Williams[82] – philosophers whose interests are not primarily centered around topics in the philosophy of logic, mind, or science. His list of philosophical heroes from the generation preceding his own comes also to foreground more prominently than before thinkers from the post-war British tradition, beyond his early Oxford friends Elizabeth Anscombe and Philippa Foot, one now encounters frequent allusions in his classes and articles to writings of Iris Murdoch,[83] David Wiggins,[84] as well as others already mentioned above, such as John McDowell and Bernard Williams. He also, in this same period, begins to make a close study of authors in the Jewish philosophical tradition such as Buber, Levinas, and Rosenzweig. As his list of favorite authors thus expands, so, too, does the list of contemporaneous philosophical heroes whose ideas he seeks to engage, inherit and

---

80 His serious engagement with Habermas begins in the late 1980s, beginning with *The Many Faces of Realism*, and continues throughout the 1990s and beyond. Perhaps his single most sustained response to Habermas is his "Antwort auf Jürgen Habermas," in *Hilary Putnam und die Tradition des Pragmatismus*, edited by Marie-Luise Raters and Marcus Willaschek (Frankfurt am Main: Suhrkamp, 2002), 306–324.

81 "Rorty influenced me – to *combat* Rorty. We were not enemies, we loved each other, but we differed very much, and the differences were stimulating. I think I clarified my own positions in my head by seeing where I disagreed with Rorty" (Bella, Boncompagni and Putnam, "Interview with Hilary Putnam," 6). For an overview of some of their disputes, see *Words and Life*, xxiv–xxxiii; his most intensive period of debate with Rorty was in the late 1980s and early '90s; see especially the three essays collected as Chapters 14, 15, and 17 in that book. His two earliest major critical statements of Rortian ideas predate this period and are collected as Chapters 12 and 16 of *Philosophical Papers*, Vol. 3. His two final major responses to Rorty are found in his "Richard Rorty on Reality and Justification," in *Rorty and His Critics*, edited by Robert Brandom, (Oxford: Blackwell, 2000), 81–86; and in their conversation with James Conant about truth published as "What Is Pragmatism?" *Think* 8 (Autumn) (2004), 71–88.

82 For some of Putnam's most sustained engagements with Williams's philosophy, see, for example, Chapter 11 of *Realism with a Human Face*, Chapter 5 of *Renewing Philosophy*, and Chapter 2 of *Naturalism, Realism, and Normativity*, edited by Mario De Caro (Cambridge, MA: Harvard University Press, 2016).

83 Putnam's interest in Murdoch is in part stimulated by his increasing interest in this period in the philosophical – and especially ethical – significance of literary works. He credits Martha Nussbaum with helping him to appreciate the importance of this topic; see, for example, his discussion of both Murdoch and Nussbaum in "Taking Rules Seriously," collected as Chapter 13 of *Realism with a Human Face*. This essay of Putnam's is discussed in Max de Gaynesford's contribution to this volume.

84 One essay that particularly captivates Putnam's attention in this period is David Wiggins's "Truth, Invention, and the Meaning of Life" (reprinted in his book *Needs, Values, Truth* (Oxford: Blackwell, 1987), 87–138).

modify. His seminars, conversations, essays and books begin regularly to feature names which at most only rarely occur in his writings prior to the mid-
1980s – with perhaps the most prominent four such newcomers in the period
between 1985 and 2000 being the following: Stanley Cavell,[85] Cora Diamond,[86]
John McDowell, and Charles Travis.[87]

As he takes the turn into the twenty-first century, the themes Putnam is led
to explore acquire a more public-facing aspect and acquire a renewed note of
ethical and political urgency – one that becomes especially pronounced in
books such as *The Collapse of the Fact/Value Dichotomy and Other Essays*
(2004) and *Ethics Without Ontology* (2005). In the former of these, he builds on
and radicalizes ideas he finds in philosophically insightful economists, such as
Amartya Sen and Vivian Walsh.[88] Putnam argues with a new passion now, not
only that the central questions of contemporary meta-ethics are informed by
dubious and dispensable metaphysical presuppositions, but that this has social
and not just intellectual costs: it is itself an expression of a cultural and political, rather than (whatever this might mean) a merely philosophical, disorder of
our age. The critiques that Putnam proposes in these two books aim not merely
to transform how we think about our lives, but also at transforming our ways of
living themselves – where the elicitation of the latter sort of change (in how we
live) and the elucidation of the former (having to do with how we think) are conceived as two sides of a single form of philosophical activity. After having in the
early 1970s gradually stepped back from the politically most activist period in his
life, now thirty some years later, in the final decade and a half of his life, we
again find Putnam expressing a conception of philosophy that has great affinities

---

85 For an overview of some of what Putnam takes from Cavell, see *Realism with a Human
Face*, lvii–lxxiv. For his own homage to Cavell, see Hilary Putnam, "Philosophy as the Education of Grownups: Stanley Cavell and Skepticism" (collected in *Philosophy in an Age of Science*), 552–566.
86 For a discussion of some of what Putnam takes from Diamond, see *Words and Life*,
xxxiii–lviii.
87 Putnam becomes fascinated already in the late 1980s in Travis's account of occasion-
sensitivity and begins to draw on it throughout the 1990s and beyond in connection with the
treatment of a range of philosophical problems. See, for example, the following two essays:
"Skepticism and Occasion-Sensitive Semantics" (1998) "Skepticism, Stroud, and the Contextuality of Knowledge" (2001) respectively collected as Chapters 30 and 29 of *Philosophy in an Age of
Science*.
88 Putnam, *The Collapse of the Fact/Value Dichotomy*, is dedicated to Vivian Walsh. See also
the essays (some of which are co-authored with Walsh) by Putnam in the jointly authored
book: Hilary Putnam and Vivian Walsh, *The End of Value-Free Economics* (New York: Routledge, 2012).

with the one he embraced at the height of his overtly Marxist period – only now the philosophical blades he employs to sharpen the political cutting edge of his politico-philosophical thought are furnished by Kant, Dewey and Wittgenstein and the very distinctive readings of each of those three thinkers that Putnam himself had previously elaborated over the course of the 1980s and '90s.

In an interview Putnam gives in Amsterdam in 2001, we find him criticizing his Parisian Continental philosophical contemporaries, such as Jacques Derrida, in terms strikingly reminiscent of those he deployed at the heyday of his Marxist phase to criticize his Harvard analytic colleagues in 1968:

> The project of enlightenment is a double project of, on the one hand, *reflective transcendence*, which means standing back from the way we live both individually and socially, and seeing what needs to be criticized and criticizing it. And this means, as Dewey said, criticizing even our ways of criticism: the criticism of criticism. This means, on the other hand, making sure those criticisms issue in change, which requires the willingness to propose radical reform. To me it seems that for philosophers such as Derrida his political moment and his philosophical moment have become disjoined. There is a disjunction between the way he will talk when he sees himself as doing philosophy and the way he will talk when he sees himself as doing politics. But that is a pathological idea of philosophy – one which Kant rightly attacked, the idea that some things are 'valid in practice but not in philosophy': 'Das gilt in der Praxis, aber in der Philosophie nicht'. Pragmatists and Wittgenstein join Kant in rejecting that disjunction. It should be a constraint on philosophy that it be congruent with and can guide our practice.[89]

The swings in Putnam's philosophical development from 1951 to 2016 are not confined merely to particular varieties of philosophical doctrine he espouses over those six and a half decades; they exhibit equally dramatic zigzags in his conception of how best to conceive the relation between the higher reaches of abstract contemplative philosophical theory and the concrete ground of engaged everyday human practice. In the closing decade and a half of his life, in characteristic fashion, he once again strives try to rethink his whole conception of philosophy anew and from the ground up – seeking a new fulcrum for its reorientation in a new conception of how to strike the proper balance in philosophy between reflective detachment and activist engagement.

---

89 Alleblas and Eisinger, "An Interview with Hilary Putnam."

V Putnam's Later Conception in Which Philosophy, Like Virtue, Is Entire

When I first took courses from Hilary Putnam as an undergraduate, at Harvard in the late 1970s, I was a physics major, and the courses I took from him were courses in the philosophy of physics, mathematics, and/or logic. As I became both more serious about studying philosophy and as I came to know Putnam himself better, he chastised me for taking courses only in these areas. First, he urged me to take his own course on *Forms of Non-Scientific Knowledge*; thinking it would help to broaden my philosophical horizons. Then he enjoined me to enroll for credit in courses on ethics, aesthetics, political philosophy, and especially in the history of philosophy, taught by his colleagues in the Philosophy Department. I will never forget what he said to me then on that occasion: "You have to learn about all of philosophy and to understand why each part is *part of philosophy* in order to understand what philosophy is."

Once I entered the Ph.D. program and began to study more seriously with Putnam as a graduate student, I came to appreciate that this was only the tip of the iceberg with respect to what was heterodox in his conception of what a serious study of the subject of philosophy ought to require of a serious student. Putnam encouraged his students to resist the forms of institutionalization and professionalization that were then – and are certainly still – shaping the character of philosophical graduate training and credentialization. He deplored how these tendencies led to an ever further speciation of philosophy into putatively distinct subdisciplines that went out of communication with one another. He would reminisce about how even back as recently as in the 1960s and '70s there was always a canon of recent books or articles that you could count on all analytic philosophers to all have read and whose central terms and concepts would comprise a lingua franca among them, facilitating intellectual communication and debate. He deplored how by the later 1980s and early '90s, it was already the case that most admirers of John McDowell's writings would never have read anything by Jerry Fodor and vice versa.

Partially in reaction to this tendency within the academic profession of philosophy, Putnam in his own work, starting with *Reason, Truth and History*, becomes ever more concerned to push back against such developments, seeking to exemplify how the very possibility of doing path-breaking work in philosophy requires (what the Germans call) the attainment of an *Übersicht* – a synoptic overview – of the intellectual landscape of the subject as a whole. The aim was not merely to attain a wider view, one that encompassed a vaster intellectual terrain, but rather to see how each of the regions of that territory formed aspects of an interconnected whole. Putnam became fond of the following passage from Paul Grice:

> [I]t is my firm conviction that despite its real or apparent division into departments, philosophy is one subject, a single discipline. By this I do not merely mean that between different areas of philosophy there are cross-references, as when, for example, one encounters in ethics the problem whether such and such principles fall within the epistemological classification of *a priori* knowledge. I mean (or hope I mean) something a good deal stronger than this, something more like the thesis that it is not possible to reach full understanding of, or high level proficiency in, any one department without a corresponding understanding and proficiency in the others; to the extent that when I visit an unfamiliar university and (as occasionally happens) I am introduced to, 'Mr Puddle, our man in Political Philosophy' (or in 'Nineteenth-century Continental Philosophy' or 'Aesthetics', as the case may be), I am immediately confident that either Mr Puddle is being under-described and in consequence maligned, or else Mr Puddle is not really good at his stuff. Philosophy, like virtue, is *entire*. Or, one might even dare to say, there is only one problem in philosophy, namely all of them.[90]

Putnam regarded this passage as articulating a touchstone which one could employ to distinguish two different types of philosophers. He was well aware that an increasingly small fraction of his philosophical contemporaries belonged to the type he hoped his students would become: philosophers who would resonate to Grice's remarks, regarding them as voicing something essential to the very nature of the philosophical enterprise – something that not only was in danger of being lost through its forms of institutionalization and professionalization, but also, once it was completely lost, would mark the death knell of philosophy itself. He knew that most of his colleagues belonged to the other type of philosopher: those who regard pronouncements such as Grice's as vestigial traces of a vanishing philosophical era – one we can leave behind without great intellectual cost to anything in philosophy about which we should care. He viewed this disagreement about how philosophy should be institutionalized – and hence how it should be pursued as a course of study – as itself constituting a significant crossroads within the heart of analytic philosophy. It was a disagreement in which he saw the very soul of philosophy – what it is, what it aspires to be, and what it shall become – at stake. That philosophy for him, like virtue, is entire – so that *au fond* there is only one problem in philosophy: namely all of them – is one of the reasons he was so fond of saying "any philosophy that can be put in a nutshell belongs in one."[91]

---

90 Paul Grice, "Reply to Richards," in *Philosophical Grounds of Rationality*, edited by Richard Grandy and Richard Warner (Oxford: Clarendon Press, 1986), 64.
91 Putnam, *Words and Life*, xi.

VI The View from 2004: A Figure of Russellian Intellectual Stature

In 2004, Putnam received an honorary degree from the University of Chicago. As it happens, I was asked to head up the honorary degree committee that solicited outside testimonials from distinguished academics around the world, in order to make the case that the nominee was fully deserving of the honor. Such testimonials were solicited not only from philosophers, but also from economists, political scientists, theorists of literature, physicists, and historians of science. It was in the context of looking over these letters to our committee that I first came fully to appreciate the degree to which Putnam was regarded as a towering figure not only by those who worked within the narrower world of academic philosophy, but also by writers, thinkers, and scientists of all sorts and types throughout the wider intellectual world.

At that time, Richard Rorty and Noam Chomsky were two of the other most prominent living examples of individuals whose career had started within anglophone philosophy of language and mind, but who in later life achieved widespread international recognition as public intellectuals. So it was natural for the University of Chicago honorary degree committee to solicit a letter from each of them regarding Putnam's candidacy. Rorty's letter – in sharp contrast to Chomksy's – somewhat surprised the committee by showing absolutely no interest in the wider intellectual significance of Putnam's achievements, instead focusing entirely on (what Rorty at least took to be) the uniqueness of Putnam's place within the discipline of philosophy itself:

> Putnam is unquestionably the most distinguished and influential of living American philosophers. Throughout a long career, he has always been at the leading edge of analytic philosophy – constantly coming up with original and provocative ideas. His range has been vast: from contributions to symbolic logic to restatements of Dewey's account of the relation between philosophy and democracy. All of us who teach philosophy have felt obliged to think about each of his books as they have appeared – to keep track of his changing views and to grasp the course of his thought.

In his testimonial, Amartya Sen, one of the world's leading economists, concentrated instead on the breadth of Putnam's achievements:

> Putnam is one of the leading philosophers of our age, whose contributions have transformed our understanding of a great many philosophical issues. The range of his contributions has varied from epistemology to metaphysics to ethics and the philosophy of mathematics, and from the understanding of communication to the assessment of natural and social sciences. Hilary Putnam's contributions in each of the particular areas in

which he has worked could, taken separately, more than justify the award of an honorary doctorate by a leading university in the world. Taken together, they make a case that must be hard to question.

Peter Galison, one of the finest living historians of science, echoed this note, but also highlighted the fact that, unlike those of most contemporary analytic philosophers, it was reasonable to anticipate that Putnam's writings would continue to be read and studied well into the future:

> Hilary Putnam is, without any doubt, one of the leading philosophers in the English-speaking world. He has made major contributions in a staggering range of fields – from important articles in the history of physics, to classic articles on scientific realism, and philosophy of language . . . My own view is that in 50 years, Putnam will still be read, avidly, by philosophers but not only philosophers.

What all of the authors of the testimonials submitted to that committee emphasize, each in their own manner, is how there simply is no one among his own contemporaries with whom Putnam can easily be compared.

If one seeks a comparison, then it is hard to identify a comparable figure unless one goes all the way back to that towering figure of a previous generation, namely Bertrand Russell – to whom we already saw John Passmore comparing Putnam above. If one looks over the testimonials supplied to the Chicago honorary degree committee, the comparison recurs in this context for three reasons. First, Putnam, to a degree equaled by no one in the recent history of philosophy other than Russell, managed to do outstanding technical work in logic, mathematics, and the philosophy of science, while publishing a great many highly accessible and readable general works in philosophy that enjoyed – and still enjoy – a wide following. Second – as we already saw Passmore note – Putnam abandoned more original and influential ideas than anyone else in the recent history of philosophy other than Russell. Third, Putnam managed to remain extraordinarily productive for over three quarters of a century, showing no visible signs of a flagging in productivity in his later years.

If one looks at the comparison between Russell and Putnam in more detail, it becomes clear just how extraordinary Putnam's achievement really is. For a detailed comparison will show that Putnam enjoys the advantage over Russell on each of the three aforementioned points. Putnam's technical work is on a par with Russell's, including important contributions to logic (his first short book, titled *Philosophy of Logic*,[92] is still considered by some to be the best overview of the subject), to mathematics (he contributed toward the solution of

---

92 Hilary Putnam, *Philosophy of Logic* (New York: Harper and Row, 1971).

Hilbert's tenth problem), to philosophy of science (his famous early defense of quantum logic still enjoys many adherents), to cognitive science and the philosophy of mind (in particular, as the originator of the functionalist program for the explanation of the nature of mental states). Putnam's more general work in philosophy, beyond comparatively technical areas of specialization, however, is of a far higher quality than Russell's. Most of Russell's writings on ethics, political philosophy, and the history of philosophy are no longer taken seriously by those who work in those subjects, and even at the time of their appearance were largely regarded as merely popular publications – ones that many of his philosophical colleagues sometimes found to be embarrassingly casual in their treatment of serious topics. By contrast, Putnam's work outside of the core areas of theoretical philosophy – outside of logic, philosophy of science, epistemology and metaphysics – has been singled out as path-breaking by leading philosophers who work in history of philosophy, practical philosophy, philosophy of social science, and the theory of value. He has, in particular, done important and influential work in ethics (especially his critique of the fact/value distinction, his vindication of thick ethical concepts, and his refutations of various forms of proceduralism in ethics), in political philosophy (his defense of Dewey's conception of democracy, his critique of Habermas's account of norms of validity, and his criticisms of traditional welfare economics), and in history of philosophy (his proto-functionalist reading of Aristotle's *De Anima*, his defense of aspects of Kantian epistemology, his interpretation of William James as a common-sense realist, and, more broadly, his recovery and vindication of the pragmatist tradition in American philosophy). His contributions to these areas continue to enjoy a lively reception on the part of specialists working on the topics and figures on whom Putnam has published an article or book. Finally, whereas there is a widespread consensus that the quality of Russell's work gradually declined with each passing decade throughout the second half of his life, there is no such consensus about Putnam's work.

On the contrary, contemporary philosophers tend to be evenly split in their view of Putnam. About half of them hold that the high point of Putnam's career was his seminal papers in defense of functionalism, scientific realism, and cognitivism in the philosophy of mind, language, and science in the 1960s and '70s; while the other half hold that Putnam's deepest and most lasting contribution lies in his criticism of just those views, developed in his papers in 1980s and beyond, issuing in the anti-scientistic, anti-reductionist philosophy of mind and language that he continues to elaborate over the later phase of his career in opposition to his own influential earlier positions. Immediately prior to his nomination for the Chicago honorary degree, his book *The Collapse of the Fact/Value Dichotomy* appeared in print. Though it was certainly not without its critics, a number of leading philosophers and social scientists heralded it in contemporaneous reviews as ranking among his most important books. Amartya Sen made it a centerpiece of the case in his testimonial for why Putnam should be awarded the honorary degree: "*The Collapse of the Fact/Value Dichotomy*, for the methodology of the social sciences, is a work of very powerful relevance and impact." In the letter he provided to the honorary degree committee, Richard Rorty argued the same point in more general terms: "In his seventies, Putnam is still responding to critics with force and precision."

In 2004, the other notable figure who was both a professional anglophone philosopher and yet someone of an international intellectual stature comparable to that of a Rorty or a Putnam was my Chicago colleague Martha Nussbaum. It was therefore also natural for the degree committee to seek her view of the case. This is part of what she had to say in her testimonial submitted to the committee:

> Although Putnam is in his middle seventies, he is currently doing some of his most exciting work. *The Collapse of the Fact/Value Dichotomy*, published last year and soon to appear in paperback, is one of his best books, and probably the most important for our public culture. Written from the vantage point of Putnam's immense expertise in philosophy of science and in technical notions of rationality, it attacks the facile use of a distinction between fact and value that pervades economic discourse and, through economics, much of our public life. Putnam argues effectively that an inclusive humanistic notion of objectivity is the best one we have available in both science and ethics, and that the attempt to build social choice upon a theory that treats preferences as utterly distinct from judgments about the world is scientifically naive as well as humanly impoverished. Similar conclusions have been defended by moral philosophers, but Putnam's technical mastery gives his argument a singular importance, making it impossible for economists to dismiss it. The book shows a great philosopher at the height of his powers making a crucial intervention in public debates.

Nussbaum here makes a crucial point. It is not just that Putnam happened to be someone with a laudable if peculiarly schizophrenic combination of forms of competence – so that he somehow managed to be someone with immense technical expertise (making path-breaking contributions to logic, philosophy of physics, and related technical branches of analytic philosophy) *and* someone who had an interest in contributing to philosophical topics with a wider bearing on human life (such as ethics, the philosophy of economics, social thought, and the theory of democratic institutions). Rather the way he was the one sort of philosopher cannot be understood apart from the way he was the other. It is precisely because he was the former sort of philosopher that he was uniquely able to intervene in debates about the latter variety of topics in the singularly influential manner that he did. Moreover, he sought to do this precisely in a way that would help to heal the very rift in our contemporary intellectual culture that makes it appear as if someone must suffer from an academically debilitating multiple-personality syndrome if she seeks to be a leading logician and philosopher of physics and, at one and the same time, a significant ethicist and critic of our democratic institutions. Now that Hilary Putnam is no longer amongst us, is there a philosopher alive today who even aspires to heal this rift?

Sanjit Chakraborty
Introduction to this Volume

Hilary Putnam was one of the truly great philosophers of the twentieth century. In a memorial essay I published elsewhere, I wrote:

> Leading philosophy towards constant dynamic expeditions and holding on to an incredible style of self-critique, Hilary Putnam (1926–2016), over five decades, has been in the process of making laudable contributions in philosophy and philosophy of science by being a beacon to a series of philosophical generations. He was a profound scholar full of wisdom, morality, and love of humanity, in a word a "Philosopher's Philosopher."[1]

Hilary Putnam, whom I called "Gurudev" (mentor), was a *renaissance man of philosophy* for his laudable and novel contribution in the fields of philosophy and philosophy of science. The impetus for bringing out this honorary volume on his fundamental contributions to philosophy and philosophy of science began after his peaceful death on March 13, 2016 in Arlington, Massachusetts. In its aftermath, I, along with my co-editor James Conant, decided to pursue the task of editing a volume dedicated to the memory of our beloved mentor, teacher, and friend Hilary Putnam. By 2019 we had assembled an excellent set of essays for this celebratory volume. Despite the new and often frightening situation worldwide, our contributors swiftly sent us their marvelous essays on time. We profusely apologize to our distinguished authors for the delay on the part of the editors in this atmosphere of mayhem.

The notices published shortly after Putnam's death, such as Martha Nussbaum's obituary in *Huffington Post* (March 14, 2016),[2] my own reflection on Putnam,[3] David Macarthur's introduction,[4] and Geoffrey Hellman and Roy Cook's preface,[5] all explicitly underlined two extraordinary parts of Putnam's life and work: first, Putnam's profound wisdom and influential contributions in every

---

1 Sanjit Chakraborty, "Hilary Putnam: An Era of Philosophy Has Ended," *Philosophia* 45, no. 1 (2017): 1–6.
2 See Martha C. Nussbaum, "Hilary Putnam (1926–2016)," Obituary published in the *Huffington Post*, March 14, 2016, https://www.huffpost.com/entry/hilary-putnam-1926-2016_b_9457774 (last accessed March 13, 2021).
3 Chakraborty, "Hilary Putnam."
4 David Macarthur, "Introduction," in Hilary Putnam and Ruth Anna Putnam, *Pragmatism as a Way of Life: The Lasting Legacy of William James and John Dewey*, 1–9 (Cambridge, MA and London: Belknap Press of Harvard University Press, 2017).
5 In Geoffrey Hellman and Roy T. Cook (eds.), *Hilary Putnam on Logic and Mathematics*, 1–7 (Cham, Switzerland: Springer, 2018).

https://doi.org/10.1515/9783110769210-002

field of philosophy could only be measured up to Aristotle; second, how, as he persistently changed and re-engaged his philosophical perspectives, deploying his iconic style of self-criticism in order to know the truth behind an argument, Putnam displayed an unwaveringly beautiful mind (*schöne Seele*), a grand combination of intellect and humanity. As Cornel West beautifully says:

> Ironically, in the end, Putnam is most like Socrates – the founding father of Western philosophy and the First Enlightenment. Putnam is *atopos* – no label can subsume him, no "ism" can define him, and no school of thought can contain him. Like a jazzman in the life of the mind, Putnam is forever on the move in search of persuasive pictures of the position of human beings in the world mindful of the wise words of Rabbi Tarphon, "The task is not yours to finish, but neither are you free to desist from it."[6]

It was truly impressive when Maria Baghramian and the University College Dublin celebrated Hilary Putnam's 80th birthday with an exciting and enormous conference, titled "Putnam at 80," where a wide range of renowned philosophers, former students, and friends of Putnam presented their papers on his seminal philosophical contributions. Later, a dozen of the papers presented at that event were collected and published together as a volume titled *Reading Putnam*[7]. Personally, I myself felt it to be an immense honor to organize an international conference on *The Philosophy of Hilary Putnam* at the Indian Institute of Technology, Bombay, in October 2015, where he delivered (on October 3, 2015) his last talk over Skype on "Thought and Language."

Many collections of essays on his works were published during his lifetime. The following half dozen stand out: Christopher Hill's *The Philosophy of Hilary Putnam* (1992), Peter Clark and Bob Hale's *Reading Putnam* (1995), Yemima Ben-Menahem's *Hilary Putnam* (2005), Maximilian de Gaynesford's *Hilary Putnam* (2006), Maria Baghramian's *Reading Putnam* (2012) and Randall Auxier, Douglas Anderson, and Lewis Hahn's *The Philosophy of Hilary Putnam*[8] (2015). These are admirable honorary volumes, all of which appeared during his lifetime and reflect on the many-faced twists and turns in Putnam's philosophical explorations. He

---

6 Cornel West, "The Third Enlightenment," in *The Philosophy of Hilary Putnam*, edited by Randall Auxier, Douglas Anderson, and Lewis Hahn, 757–767 (Chicago, IL: Open Court, 2015).
7 Maria Baghramian (ed.), *Reading Putnam* (New York: Routledge, 2012).
8 Christopher. S. Hill (ed.), *The Philosophy of Hilary Putnam* (Fayetteville, AR: The University of Arkansas Press, 1992); Peter Clark and Bob Hale (eds.), *Reading Putnam* (Cambridge and Oxford: Blackwell, 1995); Yemima Ben-Menahem (ed.), *Hilary Putnam. Contemporary Philosophy in Focus* (Cambridge: Cambridge University Press, 2005); Maximilian de Gaynesford, *Hilary Putnam* (Montreal: McGill-Queens University Press/Acumen, 2006); Baghramian, *Reading Putnam*; Randall E. Auxier, Douglas R. Anderson, and Lewis Edwin Hahn (eds.), *The Philosophy of Hilary Putnam* (Chicago, IL: Open Court, 2015).

deeply cherished interpretative criticism and offered his own trenchant replies to the contributors in most of the aforementioned volumes.

Yet *Engaging Putnam*, our ambitious memorial volume, aims to make a new contribution. It is the first volume to appear after his death that seeks to take stock of his lifetime achievement as a whole. It comprises twelve outstanding essays exploring the innovative contributions of Hilary Putnam in the emerging fields of philosophy and philosophy of science. Putnam's emblematic theories are searchingly explored in these essays, and his older views are shown to lead to cumulative progress. The approach of the volume is distinctive in outlining Putnam's philosophical contributions within a single volume, with an emphasis on avoiding distortion while providing critical analysis that will prove helpful for readers. A summary suffices: all the essays collected here are self-explanatory and fine-grained in their Putnam-inspired thoughts.

* * *

Turning to Putnam's philosophical contributions, an immensely complicated topic involving vast areas, Joshua Thorpe and Crispin Wright, in their magnificent paper "Putnam's Proof Revisited," look again at Putnam's *Brain in a Vat* thought experiment. The argument challenges the familiar idea of an embodied mind that interacts causally with the external world, imagining a Brain in a vat [henceforth BIV] not causally hooked up to a real world and stimulated by engineered electro-chemical signals. Looking back at Putnam's thought experiment, Thorpe and Wright debunk the VAT scenario that purports to expose "the skeptical conclusion that you lack the vastly greater part of the empirical knowledge you ordinarily take yourself to have." More specifically, they think that Putnam rules out the VAT scenario by defending semantic externalism, a view evolved from the interconnected and equally celebrated Twin Earth case.[9] This opening essay also shows us how the VAT argument expresses Putnam's thinking not only about reference but also about concepts. Significantly, the authors reject any epistemic distinction between the reasoning of Putnam's BIV argument and that of the McKinsey paradox (1991), and make a foray into Putnam's account of warrant transmission as a question-begging proof! Using Putnam's interpretation to harness the possibility of metaphysical realism and the VAT argument, Thorpe and Wright highlight two vital elements – *Mind-Independence* and *Robust Correspondence* respectively – to check whether Putnam's VAT scenario could serve as a parable for an Ideal Error situation or not.

---

9 Hilary Putnam, "The Meaning of 'Meaning'," in *Language, Mind, and Reality: Philosophical Papers*, Vol. 2, 215–271 (Cambridge: Cambridge University Press, 1975).

In his essay, "Language, Meaning, and Context Sensitivity: Confronting a 'Moving-Target,'" Sanjit Chakraborty picks up three major interrelated aspects of Putnam's philosophy of language and epistemology: language, meaning, and the context-sensitivity of "truth-evaluable content." In the first part of the essay, he briefly describes how Putnam's semantic externalism challenges both internalist theories based on the idea of a "language of thought" (often called "mentalese") and theories that prelude meanings as abstract entities. Putnam construes meanings, or more accurately, ascriptions of meaning, as descriptions of the world involving competencies that speakers possess. For instance, as an externalist, Putnam argues against the natural language proposed by Chomsky and especially the early Fodor, who postulate an innate language realized by computer programs in the brain. Chakraborty explores the relationship between Putnam's hypothesis that "language precedes thought" and theses of his such as that "language is a social art" or that linguistic acquisition is an ability that presupposes human intelligence operating in a physical and cultural environment, or to use Putnam's words, involves the acquisition of a "socio-linguistic hypothesis."[10] The second section of his essay focuses on Putnam's celebrated causal theory of reference that refutes the view that the semantic features of a term are determined by its epistemic descriptive features (e.g., Russellian "descriptions") by considering how meaning can be determined by referential functions that are publicly sharable (i.e., be subject to a constraint of publicity). Putnam's "normal forms" is a regimentation of a way talking about the meanings of words not indeterminate in a Quinean sense, and which supports a claim of the non-ambiguity of "the meaning" of words in a linguistic sense, namely what is represented in dictionaries and by linguists. Interestingly, for Putnam, the reference of terms is also context-sensitive. In fact, this is the main reason why the truth-conditions of sentences are themselves context-sensitive. Chakraborty later examines the trajectory of a "moving-target" philosopher like Putnam, especially showing a magnificent expedition from the meaning and language towards "truth-evaluable content," paving the way to "context sensitivity."

Sanford C. Goldberg's brilliant paper "Externalism and the First-Person Perspective" consists of two parallel inquiries: first, an epistemic investigation into externalism's compatibility with first-person perspective, and second, some metaphysical qualms about mind and brain, language and thought, and especially meaning and mental content. The linked series of logical argumentation throughout the essay produces a collection of these implications and they are then brought together in a single package. The implications Goldberg presents

---

10 Putnam, "The Meaning of 'Meaning'," 227.

should by now be familiar; the outcome of packaging them together Goldberg anticipates may not initially seem feasible. To make explicit how the arguments work: he shows externalism to require a revision of the standard account of the *first-person perspective*. And if externalism is true, we will need to reconsider clear-cut conventional views about what it is to occupy an epistemic standpoint on the world. Goldberg puts his interesting conclusion as follows: "The result would be a view on which one's point of view yields one's epistemic perspective on the world – all of which is *causally* dependent on, but *metaphysically* independent of the world itself."

Garry Ebbs, in his stimulating essay entitled "Putnam on Trans-Theoretical Terms and Contextual Apriority," vindicates the nuances of the philosophical approach he finds in Putnam's paradigm-changing explanations of the methods of scientific inquiry concerning the world. The key problem of the paper is the dilemma of how to reconcile the methodological role of statements accessible in synchronic, practical ways with Putnam's view of diachronic, theoretical reasoning, whose contours conceive whole new theoretical structures. Ebbs brings out Putnam's point here by considering a range of examples. For example, if one holds with Putnam that if the only way a statement can be overthrown is by a new theory, then it should count as contextually a priori, one thereby commits oneself to a very different conception than Quine's for what counts as a theory-laden observation. Looking back on a scientist in the eighteenth century, Putnam holds that it would not have been epistemically reasonable for an agent to accept that physical space is Euclidean. Hence the statement was not contextually a priori for them, even if a century later it will come into focus for us as one that is contextually a priori. An important *methodological* principle that Putnam derived from this consideration is, in Ebbs's words, that, if a person cannot specify any way in which a statement S may be false, it is reasonable for her to accept S and hold it immune from disconfirmation. As we know, in defense of the analytic-synthetic distinction, Putnam notably introduced the idea of a "law-cluster" concept that requires multifaceted criteria such as laws and specifiable predictions. Whereas Quine denied any rules that create a sharp line between evidence and theory, for Putnam the notion of being immune to revision for an analytic sentence rests on an epistemic basis. This permits Putnam to use *trans-theoretical* terms to refer (for example, to kinetic energy) across either side of an episode of radical change in our theory of kinetic energy. In the concluding part of the paper, Ebbs criticizes Putnam's proposed elucidation of what counts as contextually a priori in terms of conceptual schemes. Ebbs concedes that Putnam's deployment of the latter notion is helpful in showing how there are important methodological differences in the character of, for example, Einstein's discovery that the geometry of physical space is non-Euclidean and Russell's discovery that Frege's Basic Law V is inconsistent. Ebbs concludes, however, that Putnam's conceptual schemes explanation of the contextual a priori does not deliver what it promises. For the methodological differences upon which Putnam focuses in elucidating the differences between such cases fails to explain the difference between having and not having a contextually a priori entitlement to accept a statement.

Keeping in mind Ebbs legitimate points, let us now turn to Quine who challenges Carnap and his followers who maintained the logical positivist commitment to the analytic-synthetic distinction. Quine's naturalistic perspective frames observational sentences in terms of holophrastic ones in which the notion of conjunction is delimited. Quine says that, "The observation sentence is the means of verbalizing the prediction that checks a theory. The requirement that it commands a verdict outright is what makes it a final checkpoint. The requirement of inter-subjectivity is what makes science objective."[11] Putnam objects that for Quine, there is no fact of the matter as to whether an observation sentence is "theory laden" or "not theory laden," because there is no fact of the matter as to what it means. Of course, once we accept a translation manual, we may say that a word is a "theoretical term" and that an observation sentence "contains theoretical terms." Even if consider any translation manual that fails to preserve the stimulus meaning of observation sentences unacceptable, there still remains no fact of the matter as to whether a translation manual is right.

In his insightful essay "Mathematical Internal Realism," Tim Button carefully assesses Putnam's internal realism in terms of his philosophy of mathematics. Button investigates internalism about arithmetic, set theory, and model theory separately, revisiting Putnam's mathematical internal realism by means of a speculative connection between the Skolem-Gödel Antinomy and conceptual relativism. For Putnam, an ontological assumption seems internal to a conceptual scheme, and he later rebuffs any scheme-independent facts underneath the panorama of internal realism. The sophisticated turn that Button sketches on internal categoricity results in mathematical internal realism. He thinks that these results speak in favor of a non-metaphysical view that lends support to Putnam's dictum that models "have names from birth." This analysis forms one horn of Putnam's impasse since internal categoricity conflicts with Putnam's internal realism, which disdains the claims of mathematical objectivity as hinging on mathematical objects by promoting a formal link between quantification "over mathematical entities" and quantification over natural kind terms.

---

11 W.V.O. Quine, *Pursuits of Truth* (Cambridge, MA and London: Harvard University Press, 1992), 4–5.

In investigating the topic of mathematical entities that might be taken up as true on some crucial realist interpretation, one should consider the sphere of quantum mechanics. Putnam's notable writings in this area, bearing titles such as "The Logic of Quantum Mechanics" (1979)[12]. "Quantum Mechanics and the Observer" (1981),[13] "A Philosopher Looks at Quantum Mechanics (Again)" (2005),[14] and "The Curious Story of Quantum Logic" (2011),[15] reveal his strong disagreement with prevalent interpretations of quantum mechanics. In the first of these, his paper "A Philosopher Looks at Quantum Mechanics" (1965)[16], Putnam talks about "quantum potential," i.e., some unknown force for which there is scant evidence, but could encompass the disturbance by the measurement. Putnam infers that, "'measurement' can never be an undefined term in a satisfactory physical theory . . ."[17] But David Bohm, who postulated an electron (quantum particle) along with a hidden "guiding wave" that controls its motion, subsequently nourished the idea that the *Principle of Non-Disturbance* is a valid means to measure the position of the electron. Originally Putnam considered this as a failed interpretation of quantum mechanics and resisted the validity of the *Principle of Non-Disturbance* for any quantum measurement. Later (in "A Philosopher Looks at Quantum Mechanics (Again)") he changed his mind, admitting that his early argument doesn't ultimately succeed, since the notion of live functioning does not require a rigid interpretation. Such interpretations of quantum mechanics, in my own view, supplement empirically testable predictions about the probabilities of experimental results with forms of description of quantum phenomena that exaggerate the reality of hidden variables.

Tim Maudlin, in his seminal paper, entitled "The Labyrinth of Quantum Logic" argues that the two-slit interference of electrons embedded in quantum mechanics predicts many surprising phenomena. Maudlin lucidly explains the span of quantum mechanics and its central conceptual difficulty, known as the

---

12 Hilary Putnam "The Logic of Quantum Mechanics," in *Mathematics, Matter and Method: Philosophical Papers*, Vol. 1. 174–198 (Cambridge: Cambridge University Press, 1979).

13 Hilary Putnam, "Quantum Mechanics and the Observer," *Erkenntnis* 16, no. 2 (1981): 193–219.

14 Hilary Putnam, "A Philosopher Looks at Quantum Mechanics (Again)," *British Journal for the Philosophy of Science* 56 (2005): 615–634.

15 Hilary Putnam, "The Curious Story of Quantum Logic," in *Philosophy in an Age of Science: Physics, Mathematics and Skepticism*, edited by Mario De Caro and David Macarthur, 162–177 (Cambridge, MA: Harvard University Press, 2012).

16 Hilary Putnam, "A Philosopher Looks at Quantum Mechanics." in *Beyond the Edge of Certainty: Essays in Contemporary Science and Philosophy*, edited by. Robert G. Colodny, 75–101 (Englewood Cliffs, N.J.: Prentice-Hall, 1965).

17 Putnam, "A Philosopher Looks at Quantum Mechanics," 132.

measurement problem in physics. Maudlin observes a development in Putnam's response to the problem. In his early career, Putnam stressed modifications to classical logic that could resolve the measurement problem and account for the two-slit phenomena. Maudlin shows how this foray of Putnam's into his own version of quantum logic ended in self-contradiction and failure, but also how he himself came to recognize this. Culminating in his final contributions to the topic, forty years later, in which Putnam became a trenchant critic of the entire approach to quantum mechanics that he himself had pioneered. He came to appreciate that one can't just stipulate how so-called "measurement interactions" work and then trim logic to fit. That is, he came to appreciate that the form of the difficulty that quantum theory here faces – in seeking to bring "measurement interactions" and "measurements" under the same physical laws and principles of physical analysis – is one that plagues natural scientific inquiry elsewhere as well. Maudlin concludes his piece as follows: "Putnam wandered for three decades in the labyrinth of quantum logic, but he finally found his way out again." The essay's detailed account of how he did so not only interestingly delineates the trajectory from Putnam's earlier views to his later views but also thereby illustrates the intricacies involved in any attempt to unravel physical problems through modifications of mathematics and logic.

Roy Cook's fantastic paper, "Fulfillability, Instability, and Incompleteness," carries out the deductive account of Gödel's first incompleteness theorem pertaining to the sentence G constructed via diagonalizing on the negation of the provability predicate. In addition, Cook does not introduce meta-level deductivism, according to which sentence G nor the negation of G could be proven from modulo familiar assumptions or axioms of arithmetic. Putnam recapitulates the whole debate by bringing in the concept of "semantic," which seems to enter in the course of the object-language level as it entails a predicate that blends a minimal "correctness" criterion for sentences of arithmetic, as well as semantic at the meta-level to get the truth-value of a sentence in a model-centric theorem. Cook raises a question: Can we mix-and-match these methods to obtain proofs of the incompleteness theorem that are deductive at one level and semantic at the other? A moderate stance comes from Cook's thought that it looks inevitable to diagonalize on the negation of the semantic "correctness" predicate in order to obtain a sentence that is neither provable nor refutable in arithmetic. Putnam and Kripke's model-theoretic argument holds that the most intelligible way to prove the incompleteness theorem in accord to a sentence expressing a syntactic/deductive claim. The theory is not beyond doubt. Cook's alternative argument is motivated by the reasons he lays out for the collapse of Putnam-Kripke's model-theoretic argument. Subsequently, it opens up a scope for the non-standard model of arithmetic.

Martha C. Nussbaum's outstanding essay "Putnam's Aristotle" addresses Putnam's special affinity for Aristotelian philosophy. His reverence for Aristotle is embodied in his remark: "As I get smarter, Aristotle gets smarter." She explores Putnam's receptive stance toward Aristotle, as expressed in his co-authored paper "Changing Aristotle's Mind" with Nussbaum[18] and a solo-authored paper "Aristotle after Wittgenstein."[19] Nussbaum argues that this reverence is not anchored in mere argumentation, but in a more general affinity of philosophical methods and thoughts, such as his adoption of Aristotle-inspired ideas (the *Capabilities Approach, Hylomorphism, Functionalism, Realism*), his procedure of organizing a metaphysical inquiry into natural kind terms and properties and, especially his refusal to split animal minds from bodies. Cornel West appreciates that "Putnam and Nussbaum are claiming that Aristotelian realism undermines Platonic distinctions between deep reality and surface appearances, and modern dichotomies between mind and body."[20] In the final section of her essay, Nussbaum discusses tragic conflicts in ethics and literature, taking issue with Putnam in arguing that a deeper appreciation of such conflicts is an integral part of an Aristotelian approach to human flourishing.

In his critical essay, "Davidson and Putnam on the Antinomy of Free Will," Mario De Caro takes up Putnam and Davidson's respective accounts of free will and seeks to explore how and why those views are governed by the twofold motive of finding a way to conjoin adequate accounts of mind-body relation and causal reference with our ordinary and scientific explanatory practices. Both their accounts represent a quest for liberal forms of naturalism, in which normative notions are pertinent to scientifically explicable phenomena without being reducible to them. By thus employing Davidson as a foil, De Caro is able to bring out what is distinctive in Putnam's own variety of such a liberalized from of naturalism. This enables De Caro to illuminate both the strengths and weaknesses of Putnam's own accounts of determinism and free will. He argues that Putnam's attempt to strengthen a libertarian account of free will through an appeal to consideration drawn from the indeterminism of quantum mechanics fails. But he also shows that Putnam, by the end of his life, came to realize this and therefore accepted compatibilism as the correct account of free will. Putnam thus came to agree with Davidson that an action is free as long as it is

---

18 Martha C. Nussbaum and Hilary Putnam, "Changing Aristotle's Mind," in *Essays on Aristotle's De Anima*, edited by Martha C. Nussbaum and Amelie Rorty, 27–56 (Oxford: Clarendon Press, 1992).
19 Hilary Putnam, "Aristotle after Wittgenstein," in *Modern Thinkers and Ancient Thinkers*, edited by Robert W. Sharples, 117–137 (London: UCL Press, 1993).
20 West, "The Third Enlightenment," 761.

adequately caused by some relevant intentional state. However, he never wavered in his disagreement with Davidson on one crucial point: his rejection of Davidsonian *monism*. Putnam denied that all causal relations instantiate a universal (physical) law. De Caro details Putnam's reasons for thinking it is not the case that causal powers must only belong to physical events. It is this consideration that renders the mental epiphenomenal in Davidson's framework and in no way epiphenomenal in Putnam's thought. It is this dimension of Putnam's thought – his resolute *pluralism* in ontology and in epistemology – that De Caro singles out as his lasting contribution to this area of philosophy. De Caro's concerns find an important resonance in Putnam's thought of patronage libertarianism with the indeterminism of quantum mechanics that goes wrong, and due to this failure in the last part of his life, Putnam admits compatibilism as an acceptable explanation of free will.

Wittgenstein, in conversation with G.E. Moore, argues against the notion of contents, calling them "shadows." The problem is that on this conception, "contents" are themselves unambiguous, and to disambiguate a sentence is to say which of a number of contents it has. Still, those contents themselves are not held to have different interpretations. Putnam taught me to take this problem seriously and said, "Philosophers before Quine spoke of sentences as 'expressing propositions'; those propositions were like the shadows that Wittgenstein attacked. Quine made 'proposition' talk unfashionable, but now it seems to have crept in under the new terminology of 'contents.'" Following Travis in his *Unshadowed Thought*[21] and elsewhere, I think that "meanings," as in the things dictionaries and grammars seek to describe, do not determine what Travis calls "truth-evaluable content." The latter depends on the meaning plus the context of use. But now you will ask, "how can you yourself use the word 'content,' if you object to the notion?" The answer is that the notion of content I object to is one on which (i) contents are supposed to be the meanings of sentences and (ii) they determine the truth-conditions of sentences in all possible worlds. My "truth-evaluable contents" are not the meanings of sentences, and they only serve to disambiguate sentences to the extent that is appropriate to employ them on a particular occasion of use. If I can decide whether a sentence is true, false, or not clearly either on a particular occasion given enough relevant information, then I know its truth-evaluable content on that occasion. What its truth-evaluable content would be if some other logically possible world were actual, I may not be able to determine in my present situation – nor do I need to be able to do so.

---

21 Charles Travis, *Unshadowed Thought: Representation in Thought and Language* (Cambridge, MA: Harvard University Press, 2000).

Thus knowing the truth-evaluable content is a species of knowing how, not knowing that. (I critically discuss this in my essay "Language, Meaning, and Context Sensitivity: Confronting a 'Moving-Target'" – earlier presented at the *International Conference on The Philosophy of Hilary Putnam* that took place at the Indian Institute of Technology Bombay in 2015.)[22]

With regard to the notion of unformalizability, Putnam refused to endorse any account of the ability of a hearer to understand the truth-evaluable content of an utterance on a particular occasion of use that rested upon an axiomatic algorithmic analysis of that ability. Fodor's compositionality account vindicates at most the claim that that some words, particularly logical words, contain formal properties, but it hardly suffices to show that nouns such as *gold*, or *diamond*, or *tree* have context-insensitive meanings, or that there is such a thing as *the property of being gold*, to which an agent is causally connected such that the extension of "gold" in (almost) every sentence containing that words may be analyzed in terms of "the" collection of things having that purportedly unique property.

It is against the background of Putnam's rejection of such mainstream analyses of the meanings of natural kind terms and his own later endorsement of occasion-sensitive semantics that Duncan Pritchard explores the implications of this dimension of Putnam's philosophy for central debates in contemporary epistemology. In his startling contribution to this volume, titled "Putnam on Radical Scepticism: Wittgenstein, Cavell, and Occasion-Sensitive Semantics," Pritchard considers how Putnam's ingenious style of reasoning enables him to bring the panorama of considerations he originally adduced in his writings on content externalism to bear on the epistemological dilemma posed by radical skepticism. This paper reconstructs the arc of Putnam's journey towards such an anti-skeptical line in epistemology – one that draws its inspiration from Putnam's own distinctive and penetrating understanding of the lessons to be learned from Wittgenstein, Cavell, and, most recently, Travis's respective ways of articulating the insights underlying *occasion-sensitive semantics*.

Pritchard's essay helps to bring out crucial aspects of Putnam's conception of language. For Putnam, a language is like an art form that each user modifies and adds to. There is a constant interaction between the subjective and the intersubjective. Thinking of utterances as vehicles for "propositions" obscures this, since "propositions" are not supposed to be human creations. The mental event that is someone's thought on a particular occasion is part of the mental life of a subject, and admittedly is subjective in that sense but this does not

---

22 See in detail, https://www.hss.iitb.ac.in/en/international-conference-philosophy-hilary-putnam (last accessed March 13, 2021).

preclude its content (unless it contains the indexical "I") from being shareable. The question of whether anyone else can think exactly what I think when I think "my name is Sanjit Chakraborty," or "I have an antique pen in my hand" is an intricate one, which Putnam leaves to philosophers like David Kaplan. One should resist sweeping generalizations here. Putnam's outlook is perhaps closer to Kant's than to that of the post-Kantian idealists, but none of them thought about the phenomenon of context sensitivity nor arrived at Wittgenstein's insight that we land ourselves in paradox if we hold both that all understanding of signs requires interpretation and that every interpretation of a sign can itself be further interpreted. In Putnam, we encounter the unique case of a philosopher who combines the internal diversity of a systematic approach to philosophy of the sort we find in Kant, with one who is exquisitely attuned to the sorts of considerations that Wittgenstein brought to light – ones that make it so difficult to achieve the forms of systematic insight to which philosophy aspires.

In her interesting essay "Natural Laws and Human Language," Yemima Ben-Menahem, decisively examines the issue in Putnam's philosophy regarding realism, understood as an objective understanding of natural laws, and how it might appear to conflict with the vista of human language in which sensitivity to context and what is ineluctably personal in experience may play a role in shaping the contours of our beliefs and methods of justification. Ben-Menahem puts forth an alternative conception of realism, one that commits her neither to the naïve view (a meticulous description of the world that is simply correct) nor to the view that all correct descriptions are requisite parts of the language of fundamental physics. In addition, the authenticity and efficacy of a range of descriptions do not fully look up physical concepts and physical categories that fend off reductionism. Ben-Menahem's account draws on Putnam's nuanced discussion in his later writings of what is required of an adequate philosophy of objectivity and language – one which faces up to the depth of the entanglement of these issues in questions about the limits of reductionism. She follows Putnam in trying to offer an account that does equal justice to scientific knowledge and to the irreducible character of our various forms of non-scientific knowledge.

This raises the question of what the place of conceptual necessity is in the alternative conception of realism that Ben-Menahem sets forth and attributes to Putnam. The supervenience principles advocated by contemporary naturalists are certainly not conceptual truths; for Putnam they are substantive metaphysical assumptions in their own right. For instance, contemporary naturalists hold that all the properties of material objects (except for *existing in this particular universe – if that counts as a property at all*) are supervenient on the total *physical* states of the world; but no naturalist ever claims that this is a *conceptual* truth any more than they would claim that "All brown things are colored" is true in virtue of the truth of some supervenience principle. Putnam himself came to reject any form of naturalism that conceives of what happens "in the mind" as happening in an isolable region of physical reality. Such a conception, he concludes, rests on a solipsistic conception of what a mind is that is not simply false, but incoherent. As Putnam later puts it:

> To have concepts it is necessary to have appropriate causal connection with an environment. Semantic externalism implies externalism about the mind; if to have a mind is to have thoughts, then to have a mind it isn't sufficient to have the right goings-on in the brain and the rest of the body; to have a mind you have to be hooked up to an environment in the proper way, or at least to have a mind that can think about an external world, you have to have causal interactions that extend into the environment. One might call this an anti-solipsist conclusion: If externalism is right, pace Descartes, an isolated disembodied mind would have no thoughts about the world at all, not even false thoughts. In Kantian language, the pseudo-thoughts of Descartes' isolated mind are an empty play of representations and not thoughts at all.[23]

The question, however, is how exactly this conception of "appropriate causal connection with an environment" is to be spelled out. Putnam's answer to this question undergoes considerable fluctuation over the course of his philosophical development, reflecting tensions in his thought on this matter. In my own effort to get clearer about what he himself was committed to here, I once addressed the following question to him:

> Even you regarded truth as a non-relative property. You also claimed that the truth of a belief must be 'warranted assertible.' Here do you think that, in the linguistic representation of our belief, norms are assertible with the concept of causal constraint in our external world?

Putnam responded as follows:

> I claimed (and now think that was a *mistake*) that to be true a belief must be warrantedly assertible (or in other words confirmed by the evidence), not necessarily at the present time, but in the future, *provided the epistemic situation is good enough.* [This is the point at which I helped myself to a notion that the internal realist is not really entitled to.] As to the second part of your question, concerning causal constraints: I accepted the idea that we must have causal connection of the right sort to things in our environment BEFORE, DURING, AND AFTER my "internal relativist" period (1976–1990). BUT – and this is a big "BUT" – during my internal realist period whether we have such causal connection was just a part of our "theory," and thus also mind-dependent, whereas now, as a realistically minded naturalist, I say that whether we have such causal connection or not isn't a matter of whether our beliefs are or could be confirmed.

---

23 Hilary Putnam, "Sixty-Five Years of Philosophy," in *Naturalism, Realism, and Normativity*, edited by Mario De Caro (Cambridge, MA: Harvard University Press, 2016), 223.

For the internal realist, the so-called external world – the world outside the brain and body – is itself *mind-dependent*; for a real realist of the sort Putnam later became when he abandoned this feature of his earlier internal realism, it isn't. Qua internal realist, Putnam held that truth has everything to do with assertibility; qua the real realist he became, he holds that truth and assertibility are logically independent. From his later vantage, therefore, his own earlier internal realism was insufficiently realist. In finding his way back to this fully realistic view, Putnam reported to me that he had been inspired by ideas that he found in the Indian realistic school of thought of Nyāya and Vaiśeṣika.[24]

Maximilian de Gaynesford's "Balance in *The Golden Bowl:* Attuning Philosophy and Literary Criticism," is a worthy attempt to further explore Putnam's favorite novel. One aim of his contribution is to highlight a dimension of Putnam's thought that he feels has gone underappreciated, namely his view that philosophy and thoughtful appreciation of literature have much to contribute to each other. The essay seeks to bring out why this ought not to be regarded as a topic peripheral to Putnam's central concerns in philosophy, noting ways in which the influence of figures such as Stanley Cavell, John McDowell, and Iris Murdoch helped Putnam to arrive at an unusually capacious conception of rationality – and especially of moral reasoning. At the outset of the essay, de Gaynesford quotes Putnam's remark that moral thinking requires "reasoning in the full sense of the word," something that "involves not just the logical faculties, in the narrow sense, but our full capacity to imagine and feel, in short, our full sensibility." The aim of the essay is, on the hand, to explore Putnam's own reasons for thinking such reasoning "in the full sense of the word" requires that we cultivate a capacity to describe the sorts of situations that call for nuanced ethical evaluation in the language of a sensitive novelist; while, on the other hand, it does so by supplementing and challenging certain details of Putnam's own conception of what this involves. It prosecutes this dual aim by developing an alternative reading of *The Golden Bowl* – one that offers a different account of wherein the philosophical significance of the novel lies, when approached anew with Putnam's interest in seeing what philosophy might be able to learn by attending to the perspective on human life and action that such a novel affords.

This strikes me as a fitting note on which to conclude this volume, underscoring how literature can serve as a guide for living ethically through a gradual expansion of self-realization toward a universal realization of humanity

---

24 In a personal communication, Putnam wrote to me: "I did have a course in Indian philosophy in graduate school, and I remember being impressed with Nyāya and Vaiśeṣika."

and its values. In the context of what it means to do analytic philosophy, Putnam once wrote to me:

> As I mentioned in a recent message, your gurudev is an analytic philosopher, though not
> a scientistic one, and the first principle of analytical philosophy is to be sure that ques-
> tions have a clear sense before you try to answer them. If they don't, you don't always
> need to dismiss them, but you had better find at least one way to make them clear. An-
> other principle is that questions (especially philosophical questions), have presupposi-
> tions that need to be subjected to critical examination.

An extended introduction is often freighted by its context, and this possibility
grows when someone writes about the person whom he admires most and loves
very much. So I feel I should not extend it more. My sincere thanks go to my co-
editor, James Conant for his conceptual inputs and his team Garrett Allen, Ryan
Simonelli, Elena Comay del Junco for her careful editing. Besides, I would like
to thank Cornelia Meinig and Sreetama Misra for keeping everything updated
and their commitments to get the volume published in a timely fashion. We are
grateful further to our publisher De Gruyter and Christoph Schirmer for his appreciation and various editorial help. We pay our heartfelt homage and gratitude to Noam Chomsky, Martha Nussbaum, and John Perry, all of whom read
the volume in manuscript form and shared their precious endorsements in a
timely fashion. Without the encouragement and incessant moral support of
Martha Nussbaum, Maximilian de Gaynesford, Mario De Caro, Duncan Pritchard, and Sanford Goldberg, I personally could not prevail over the difficult hur-
dles faced during the completion of such daunting editorial tasks.

This honorary volume is dedicated to all Hilary Putnam's students and
followers!

Joshua R. Thorpe and Crispin Wright

Putnam's Proof Revisited

Abstract: The enigmatic few paragraphs around pages 14–15 of *Reason, Truth and History* that offer the "proof" of our title have probably generated more interpretative reaction than any other short argument in recent philosophy. Their achievement and significance, however, have remained stubbornly controversial. We reckon that, through the settling dust of the debates over the last 35 years, it is now possible to make out the contours of a reasonably clear set of lessons. Stable answers are in prospect to each of the three main issues: Does the proof work? If so, what exactly does it show? And of what, if any, significance, metaphysical or epistemological, is the result? We outline these answers in this paper.

Towards the end of the Preface to the *Philosophical Investigations*, Wittgenstein remarked that he "should not like [his] writing to spare other people the trouble of thinking." In this, as in many other respects, Hilary Putnam seems to have taken Wittgenstein's example to heart. As the extent of bibliographical section of Sanford Goldberg's recent edited anthology makes vivid,[1] the enigmatic few paragraphs around pages 14–15 of *Reason, Truth and History* that offer the "proof" of our title have probably generated more interpretative reaction than any other short argument in recent philosophy. Their achievement and significance, however, have remained stubbornly controversial. We reckon that, through the settling dust of the debates over the last 35 years, it is now possible to make out the contours of a reasonably clear set of lessons. Stable answers are in prospect to each of the three main issues: Does the proof work? If so, what exactly does it show? And of what, if any, significance, metaphysical or epistemological, is the result? We outline these answers in what follows.

---

1 Sanford Goldberg (ed.), *The Brain in a Vat* (Cambridge: Cambridge University Press, 2016).

Acknowledgments: It is an honor and a great pleasure to contribute to this volume in celebration of the magisterial philosophical achievements of the late Hilary Putnam, and we are very grateful to Jim Conant and Sanjit Chakraborty for giving us the opportunity to do so. Thorpe gratefully acknowledges a research grant from the São Paulo Research Foundation (grant ID no. 2016/03277-1), which allowed him to work on this paper.

https://doi.org/10.1515/9783110769210-003

I The VAT Argument Developed in Terms of Reference

Suppose the following skeptical scenario occurs to you.

> *The Classical VAT Scenario*: You always have been and always will be a brain in a vat of nutrients, fed sensory experiences by a supercomputer. The computer ensures that the experiences you have are consistently and exceptionlessly of a character that is fully coherent with your normal, more congenial though false assumptions about the kind of creature you are and the world you inhabit. In fact, the world contains nothing, and never has contained anything except your brain in its vat, and the supercomputer.

It seems that, challenged to do so, it would be impossible to rule out the claim that you are actually in this scenario – that you are actually, as we shall follow custom in saying, a "BIV" – if only appeal to the course assumed by your actual sensory experiences is allowed as evidence. For the rub is that those experiences are exactly as they ought to be on the hypothesis that you are indeed in the scenario described. The question therefore arises, how – if you can – *can* you rule it out?

This question is pressing. For if it transpires that you cannot rule out the classical VAT scenario, it is difficult to resist the skeptical conclusion that you lack the vastly greater part of the empirical knowledge you ordinarily take yourself to haves. One very familiar skeptical argument to secure this conclusion exploits the following plausible principle:

> *Closure*: for any subject S, and propositions p, q: if S knows that p, and S knows that p entails q, then S is in a position to know that q.

Since you know, naturally, that the proposition that you are right now reading a philosophy paper entails that you are not a BIV, it follows, by Closure, that if you know that you are reading a philosophy paper, you are in a position to know that you are not a BIV. So if you are indeed not in a position to know that you are not a BIV, then you don't know that you're reading a philosophy paper. The same reasoning applies to any other proposition that you know to be incompatible with being a BIV, that is, to most of the propositions that you usually take yourself to know empirically. Thus you lack most of the empirical knowledge that you usually take yourself to have. Or so runs one skeptical thought.[2]

---

2 The classical VAT scenario clashes with the *truth* of almost all your empirical beliefs. But it is also inconsistent with your perceptual good functioning, and hence with your being in position to acquire perceptual knowledge. A skeptical argument building specifically on the latter point will need to be a tad more complicated that the simple Closure-based reasoning just outlined. Save at one point, though, this distinction will not be important on the sequel. For

Putnam's ingenious suggestion[3] was that you *can* rule out the VAT scenario. You can do so by employing the following *VAT argument.*

(1) If you were in the VAT scenario, you could not refer to BIVs.

However:

(2) You can refer to BIVs (since, of course, your word "BIV" refers to BIVs)

Therefore:

(3) You are not in the VAT scenario.

That seems easy! But what is the support for the premises?

Famously, Putnam supported premise (1) by an appeal to a generic form of semantic externalism. One motivation for such semantic externalism is the pattern assumed by what seem to many to be intuitively correct verdicts about certain imaginary cases, paramount among which is Putnam's own "Twin Earth" case.[4] Putnam imagined a planet, Twin Earth, which is indistinguishable from Earth at the macro level. In fact, however, wherever there is water on Earth there is something with a different chemical structure, XYZ, on Twin Earth. Let us call the stuff on Twin Earth "twater." What does your Twin Earth doppelgänger refer to when s/he utters the word "water"? Most are inclined to say that s/he refers to twater, which is XYZ, and not to water, which is H_2O. A natural explanation of why your doppelgänger refers to XYZ and not to water is that in order to be able to refer to certain kinds of things, including especially natural kinds, a thinker must have been in some form of appropriate causal contact with such things.[5] But this is just to accept a form of semantic externalism. The idea, then, is that if you were in the VAT scenario as described, you would not

---

further discussion, see Crispin Wright, "Facts and Certainty," *Proceedings of the British Academy 71 (1986):* 429–472.

3 For this is what we take the crucial paragraphs of Chapter 2 of *Reason, Truth and History* to boil down to.

4 The case is used in support of semantic externalism in Hilary Putnam, "Meaning and Reference," *The Journal of Philosophy* 70, no. 13 (1973): 699–711 and "The Meaning of 'Meaning," in *Language, Mind, and Knowledge*, Vol. 2, edited by Keith Gunderson, 131–193 (Minnesota: University of Minnesota Press, 1975).

5 It is usually allowed that relevant such contact can be causally remote, mediated by the activities of one's linguistic ancestors, and also that reference can be accomplished by means of concepts which, even if one has had no contact with their instances, are definable in terms of concepts that meet the causal contact condition.

have been in appropriate causal contact with brains or vats,[6] and so could not refer to BIVs for the same reason that your doppelgänger on Twin Earth cannot refer to water. This argument for premise (1) requires only that we acknowledge an analogy between your relationship to brains and vats, were you in the VAT scenario, and your doppelgänger's relationship to water in the Twin Earth scenario. It does not, as has sometimes been supposed, require that we endorse any particular causal *theory* of reference, but only a causal necessary condition on reference.[7]

Premise (2), for its part, might ordinarily be thought to require no support. Of course you can refer to BIVs. Are you not doing so right now as you intelligently read this paper?

However, at this point some philosophers have tended to suffer a misgiving. Once one accepts premise (1) is it not then question-begging to suppose that you know that you can refer to BIVs? If it is agreed that you couldn't refer to BIVs if you were in the VAT scenario, don't you have to know that you are *not* in the VAT scenario before you can know that you can refer to BIVs – and thus know exactly the thing that the VAT argument is supposed to prove?[8] This misgiving will be the topic of section III.

II The VAT Argument at the Level of Concepts

Putnam's argument is formulated above in terms of reference.[9] However, the argument has sometimes also been formulated in terms of concepts, as follows.

---

6 Nor with any kinds of thing suitable concepts of which would provide for a definition of the concept of a BIV.

7 Jesper Kallestrup, "Brains in Vats, Causal Constraints on Reference and Semantic Externalism," in *The Brain in a Vat*, edited by Sanford Goldberg, 37–53 (Cambridge: Cambridge University Press, 2016) argues that premise (1) can be supported even on semantic views that are not traditionally thought of as externalist, thus broadening the dialectical appeal of the vat argument. However, we shall assume that the argument relies on some form of semantic externalism throughout this paper.

8 Jane MacIntyre, "Putnam's Brains," *Analysis*, 44, no. 2 (1984): 56–61, makes this objection. Marian David, "Neither Mentioning 'Brains in a Vat' nor Mentioning Brains in a Vat Will Prove that We Are Not Brains in a Vat," *Philosophy and Phenomenological Research* 51, no. 4 (1991): 891–896, and Bredo C. Johnsen, "Of Brains in Vats, Whatever Brains in Vats May Be," *Philosophical Studies* 112, no. 3 (2003): 225–249, make objections in a similar vein, although the details differ since they use a formulation of the VAT argument different from ours.

9 See Anthony Brueckner, "Brains in a Vat," *The Journal of Philosophy* 83, no. 3 (1986): 148–167, Thomas Tymoczko, "In Defense of Putnam's Brains," Philosophical Studies 57, no. 3

(1*) If you were in the VAT scenario you could not have any concept of a BIV.

But:
(2*) You do have a concept of a BIV.

Therefore:
(3*) You are not in the VAT scenario.[10]

The support for the premises runs parallel to that for the premises of the argument as formulated in terms of reference. Thus premise (1*) is defended by appeal to a mild form of externalism about thought content, according to which in order to have certain concepts one must be in particular kinds of favorable environment. Again, this idea gains support from our intuitive verdicts about scenarios like Putnam's Twin Earth case. On reflection, most philosophers are inclined to say that it is not merely that your doppelgänger on Twin Earth cannot refer to water; s/he cannot even have the *concept* of water. Correspondingly, the idea is that if the VAT scenario were true you would not be in an environment in which you could so much as understand what it would be to be a BIV. And of course premise (2*) is true; after all, have you not perfectly understood the discussion so far?

We doubt whether the argument formulated in terms of concepts differs in any important respect from the argument formulated in terms of reference. Note that the former, at least as we have presented it, is formulated in terms of what we have concepts *of*. But to have a concept of a kind of thing is just to have a concept whose linguistic expression would refer to that kind of thing. On the plausible assumption that we can only refer to what we have concepts of, and that we can only have concepts of what we can refer to, the version of the VAT argument formulated in terms of concepts and the version of the VAT argument formulated in terms of reference raise no separate issues. We shall proceed on that assumption.[11]

(1989): 281–297, and Tim Button, *The Limits of Realism* (Oxford: Oxford University Press, 2013) for three quite different versions of the VAT argument formulated at the level of reference.

10 Crispin Wright, "On Putnam's Proof that We Are Not Brains-in-a-Vat," *Proceedings of the Aristotlian Society* 92, no. 1 (1992): 67–94 and "On Putnam's Proof that We Are Not Brains in a Vat," in *Reading Putnam*, edited by Peter Clark and Bob Hale, 216–242 (Cambridge, MA: Blackwell, 1994) and Kevin Falvey and Joseph Owens, "Externalism, Self Knowledge, and Skepticism," *The Philosophical Review* 103, no. 1 (1994): 107–137 give versions of the VAT argument formulated in terms of concepts.

11 It should be noted that in the relevant use, having a concept of something and having a device of reference to it are *intentional*: when one says that, in one's language, "BIV" refers to BIVs, one is not, of course, presupposing that there actually are any BIVs to be the objects of reference, extensionally understood.

III Misgivings about the Significance of the Argument – Question-Begging

Let's return to the misgiving we flagged above. The concern was that in the context of an acceptance of premise (1), or (1*), the ground is cut from under any easy confidence that you do indeed have the ability to refer to (or have a concept of) BIVs – for premise (1) entails, after all, that a BIV does not have that ability, and you are supposed to be taking seriously the possibility that you might be in that predicament. So, the objection is, to accept (1) is to abrogate your grounds for premise (2).

As a first pass at a reply, it may be observed that this way of questioning Putnam's argument is obviously problematic for any actual or hypothetical adversarial skeptic who is encouraging you to worry that, for all you can know, you could be in the classical VAT scenario. For you cannot so much as entertain the scenario unless you are able to refer to (have a concept of) BIVs. The adversarial skeptic thus faces a dilemma: either she allows that you can refer to BIVs, and so allows premise (2), thereby making it available for use in Putnam's argument against her; or she denies that you can take it that you can refer to BIVs – but then you may retort that in that case you are in no position to take the skeptical worry seriously since you have no right to assume you understand it.

That's a point about dialectics. But it has a counterpart in the setting of a "solitary skeptical worrier." Simply: if premise (1) is acceptable, then one must accept that an understanding of the skeptical scenario is possible only in circumstances when it fails to obtain. So do you understand it or not? If you do, premise (2) is secure and – granted premise (1) – the specter of envatment dispelled. If you don't, there is nothing that *you* can worry about in the first place.

These points do have some traction. They show that, whatever its detail, a skeptical argument based on the VAT scenario is nothing that can engage the attention of a fully reflectively coherent thinker who accepts premise (1)/(1*). To credit oneself with an understanding of the argument is, in the presence of premise (1)/(1*), a commitment to believing that the scenario does not obtain. But that is not the same as saying that the VAT argument itself *develops a reason* for discounting the scenario. It is not the same as saying that Putnam gives a *proof* that the scenario does not obtain. A proof, in the intuitive sense relevant here, is a valid argument such that someone who is so far justifiably open-minded about its conclusion can rationally agree that there is sufficient evidence to accept its premises and, by running through the argument, thereby justifiably come to the view that the conclusion is true. In short, a proof, in the intuitive sense relevant here, is a valid argument that *transmits* the epistemic warrant for its premises to its conclusion. Does the VAT argument do that?

When Putnam published *Reason, Truth and History*, there had not been the attention to issues concerning warrant transmission, closure of knowledge and justification over (known) entailment, and their relations that has burgeoned in the literature since. We are accordingly unsure whether he would have wished to claim that his argument is indeed a proof in the sense just glossed. There is, however, a prima facie forceful reason for denying that it is: namely, its close resemblance to the so-called McKinsey paradox[12] that purports to disclose a tension between semantic externalism and the way we ordinarily think of the authority that subjects have for their contentful states of mind. Here is a version of McKinsey's paradox, albeit tweaked in such a way as to align as closely as possible with Putnam's argument:[13]

(1^{m}) If neither you nor anyone in your historical speech community had ever had any contact with water, you would not be able to refer to (would not have a concept of) water.

(2^{m}) You are able to refer to (do have a concept of) water.

Hence:

(3^{m}) someone in your historical speech community has had contact with water.

Premise (1^{m}) is assumed to be established a priori on the basis of reflection on the externalist character of the concept *water* – viz. that it is a natural kind concept whose intension is fixed by the kind of thing, if any, that it actually denotes. This is something we are assumed to be able to know by pure philosophical reflection. Premise (2^{m}) is assumed to be established as an item of ordinary self-

---

12 McKinsey first gave the argument in his "Anti-Individualism and Privileged Access," *Analysis* 51, no. 1 (1991): 9–16, reiterating and defending it in his "Externalism and Priviliged Access Are Inconsistent," in *Contemporary Debates in the Philosophy of Mind*, edited by Brian P. McLaughlin and Jonathan D. Cohen, 37–53 (Oxford: Blackwell, 2007). Paul Boghossian, "What the Externalist Can Know A Priori," *Proceedings of the Aristotelian Society* 97, no. 2 (1997): 161–175 also gives a version of this argument. James Pryor, "What's Wrong with McKinsey-Style Reasoning?" in *Internalism and Externalism in Semantics and Epistemolgy*, edited by Sanford Goldberg, 177–200 (Oxford: Oxford University Press, 2007) and André Gallois and John O'Leary-Hawthorne, "Externalism and Scepticism," *Philosophical Studies* 81, no. 1 (1997): 1–26 take it that the VAT argument is just a particular instance of McKinsey-style reasoning.

13 McKinsey writes that, ". . . if you could know a priori that you are in a given mental state, and your being in that state conceptually or logically implies the existence of external objects, then you could know a priori that the external world exists." ("Anti-Individualism and Privileged Access," 16)

knowledge – you know that you are capable of water thoughts: thoughts that configure the concept of water in their content. So both premises can be known without rising from the armchair. But then it appears that, if the McKinsey argument is indeed a proof in the sense we are concerned with, you can come to know a substantial and contingent piece of socio-linguistic history from the comfort of the armchair as well.

Some philosophers have, on reflection, been inclined to accept this conclusion.[14] Probably the majority, though, would disagree. There is then the option of treating the argument as a *reductio* of the armchair-knowability of its premises, and much of the literature has followed one of the two directions that then open.[15] What is relevant to the appraisal of Putnam's argument, however, is the possibility of a different response. On this diagnosis, the McKinsey argument is a valid argument with justified premises – at least, it is so if one accepts the conception of the semantics of natural kind terms that underwrites its first premise, and allows that "water" in ordinary English may be known to be such a term by an ordinary reflective English speaker – which nevertheless *fails to transmit* their justification to its conclusion. It fails to do so because, to resort to metaphor, justification for its conclusion is, in the context of the assumptions of the argument, *epistemically upstream* from the warrants described for accepting its premises.

Dispensing with the fluminal metaphor in favor of a precise theoretical description has proved a complex and controversial endeavor.[16] But we can illustrate

---

14 For example Sarah Sawyer, "Privileged Access to the World," *Australasian Journal of Philosophy* 76, no. 4 (1998): 523–533.

15 For example Pryor, "What's Wrong with McKinsey-Style Reasoning?," attempts to avoid the paradox by qualifying the idea that we have armchair knowledge of the content of our own thoughts. His suggestion is that although (1^m) and (2^m) can individually be warranted a priori, no subject can be a priori warranted in believing both at the same time. McKinsey's own response, in "Externalism and Privileged Access," is to give up on externalism about thought content.

16 Early discussions are Crispin Wright, "Cogency and Question-Begging: Some Reflections on McKinsey's Paradox and Putnam's Proof," *Philosophical Issues* 10, no. 1 (2000): 140–163 and "Some Reflections on the Acquisition of Warrant by Inference," in *New Essays On Semantic Externalism And Self-Knowledge*, edited by Susana Nuccetelli, 57–77 (Cambridge, MA: MIT, 2003). Probabilistic accounts of transmission failure are explored in Martin Smith, "Transmission Failure Explained," *Philosophy and Phenomenological Research* 79, no. 1 (2009): 164–189, Geoff Pynn, "The Bayesian Explanation of Transmission Failure," *Synthese* 190, no. 9 (2013): 1519–1531 and Matthew Kotzen, "Dragging and Confirming," *The Philosophical Review* 121, no. 1 (2012): 55–93. A useful informal conspectus of the issues and a purportedly deflationary treatment of the phenomenon is given in James Pryor, "When Warrant Transmits," in *Mind, Meaning and Knowledge: Themes from the Philosophy of Crispin Wright*, edited by Annalisa Coliva, 269–303 (Oxford: Oxford University Press, 2012). Crispin Wright, "Replies Part IV," in

the essential point with a couple of examples. Consider first an argument of the kind that features in Stewart Cohen's work[17] on "easy knowledge":

(1^c) It looks to you right now as if the rain has stopped.

So (2^c) The rain has stopped.

So (3^c) On this occasion appearance and reality coincide.

Here (1^c) provides good though defeasible justification for (2^c); and (1^c) and (2^c) together entail (3^c). You are, we may suppose, fully introspectively justified in reporting (1^c) – your experience is as of bright sunshine and steam rising off the pavements – and the truth of (1^c), absent any other relevant information, is naturally excellent evidence for (2^c). So you are fully justified in simultaneously accepting both (1^c) and (2^c). But your justification for doing so is ultimately just the experience reported by (1^c) – and surely *that* isn't evidence for its own accuracy, as (3^c) avers.

The argument is valid, and its premises are justified. But it doesn't provide a justification for its conclusion. Why not? One answer would be this. In order for the argument to work as a proof in the sense we are concerned with, it must be rationally possible to start from a position of agnosticism about its conclusion while simultaneously appreciating the warrant for its premises. But if you start from a position of agnosticism about (3^c), then you are not in position to take the experience reported by (1^c) as the excellent evidence it is for (2^c), and thus you lose your warrant for (2^c). So the argument is grounded.

Here's a second example. Suppose you are a field zoologist on an expedition in the Amazon basin. You have heard that an especially large and impressive male jaguar has been sighted on a number of occasions a few miles higher up the Rio Purus and, notwithstanding a bout of malaria, set off upstream in your canoe in the hope of filming the big cat. Sure enough, rounding a bend in the river, you see – or so it seems to you – a huge spotted feline lazing in the sun on a sand bar mid-stream. You think to yourself: Gosh, that cat really is a magnificent specimen! Then, feeling pretty shaky and remembering your malaria, you wonder whether you can trust your senses. Can you reassure yourself by the following argument?

Mind, Meaning and Knowledge: Themes from the Philosophy of Crispin Wright, edited by Annalisa Coliva, 451–472. (Oxford: Oxford University Press, 2012) responds to Pryor.
17 Stewart Cohen, "Basic Knowledge and the Problem of Easy Knowledge," *Philosophy and Phenomenological Research* 65, no. 2 (2002): 309–329.

(1^j) A singular indexical token thought features an object as part of its *de re* truth-condition and thus has determinate content only if a suitable such object exists in the context of the thought. (Premise delivered by so-called Strong Singular Thought theory.[18])

(2^j) My thought: <that cat really is a magnificent specimen>, is a singular-indexical thought.

So (3^j) My thought: <that cat really is a magnificent specimen>, has a referent

So (4^j) I am not hallucinating the cat.

Well, clearly not. And the reason, plausibly, is as before. In a context in which you are open-minded about the possibility of feverish hallucination – that is, open minded about the conclusion, (4^j) – but accept (1^j), the introspective phenomenology of attending to the apparent jaguar and thinking to yourself, "That cat really is a magnificent specimen," is insufficient to justify premise (2^j). Rather, it is only in a context where (4^j) is not in question that you have the justification for its premises that the argument assumes.

One diagnosis of the McKinsey paradox is very close to this.[19] The relevant question is: what would be the status of those of your thoughts that apparently feature reference to, or exercise of a concept of water in the event that (3^m) is false – so that neither you nor anyone in your historical speech community has had any contact with water? Specifically, what if you now entertain it as an open possibility that you inhabit Boghossian's Dry Earth, where there simply is no watery substance of any kind and all experiences to the contrary are illusion?[20] In that case premise (2^m), that you do have the ability to refer, or have a concept of water, can no longer be grounded in ordinary self-knowledge and the phenomenology of your thought – at least, not when you accept (1^m), the semantic externalist premise, at the same time. So you cannot rationally be open-minded about the conclusion of the McKinsey reasoning yet simultaneously avail yourself of the "armchair" grounds for its premises that the appearance of paradox exploits.

---

18 The *locus classicus* for such a conception of the truth-conditions of genuinely singular thoughts as a class is Gareth Evans, *The Varieties of Reference* (Oxford: Oxford University Press, 1982). A useful recent discussion is Imogen Dickie, "We Are Acquainted with Ordinary Things," in *New Essays on Singular Thought*, edited by Robin Jeshion, 213–245 (Oxford: Oxford University Press, 2010).

19 One way of developing the diagnosis in detail, superseding Wright, "Cogency and Question-Begging" is offered in Crispin Wright, "McKinsey One More Time," in *Self-Knowledge*, edited by Anthony Hatzimoysis, 80–104 (Oxford: Oxford University Press, 2008).

20 Boghossian, "What the Externalist Can Know."

A general model of warrant-transmission failure suggested by these examples may be framed if we now draw on the standard epistemologist's notion of *undermining*, whereby the basis of a belief is, wholly or partially, undermined by any information that – whether or not bearing directly on the truth-value of the belief – is suggestive that it was not reliably formed. The model is this. If one specific kind of epistemic basis for the premises of a valid argument is such that it would be *undermined* by doubt about its conclusion, then one cannot rationally be open-minded about the status of that conclusion yet simultaneously avail oneself of that basis to accept the premises. In that epistemic situation then, there is no possibility of availing oneself of that particular basis to advance, by the argument, to justified confidence in its conclusion.[21]

Suppose we sustain this diagnosis of the McKinsey paradox. All the same, it's notable that the argument still has the kind of dialectical effectiveness that at the start of this section we credited to Putnam's argument. For imagine a water skeptic who attempts to disconcert you with Boghossian's imagined scenario:

> *The Dry Earth scenario*: Neither you nor anyone in your speech community have ever had any encounter with any water. All your and everyone else's apparent experiences with water have been bizarre hallucinations, somehow merging seamlessly with otherwise mostly veridical experience of the external material world. All your thoughts about water, as well as all other thoughts you or others have had whose truth would require, directly or indirectly, the existence of water, are consequently false.

Clearly, and exactly as before, you may simply dismiss this skeptic. For if you understand the scenario, then, in the presence of premise (1^m) backed by a relevant semantic externalism, it cannot be true. And if you do not understand it – if your uses of "water" token no genuine concept – then nothing is presented with which *you* can be rationally concerned.

There need be then, in parallel, no tension between granting that Putnam's argument has the kind of dialectical effectiveness noted earlier while denying that it is, properly speaking, a transmissive argument that establishes a warrant for its conclusion. But should we deny that?

We – the present authors – do not think so. But the question interacts with what one should suppose the intellectual capacities of a BIV would be. Putnam himself tends to write as though an inhabitant of the vat may be credited with thoughts about aspects of the machine program, or electronic impulses, or whatever it is that it does causally interact with in appropriate reference-fixing ways.

---

21 Note that, on this diagnosis, one and the same argument may be transmissive with respect to one kind of basis for its premises but not with respect to another.

But it is not clear whether any of the modes of causal interaction that a BIV could have with its environment would be of the kind necessary to establish semantic reference. Putnam himself said vanishingly little by way of a positive externalist account of content-fixation, and later work has hardly filled the lacuna. Suppose accordingly we take seriously the idea that a subject of the VAT scenario would actually not be able to think thoughts with any specific truth-conditional content *at all*. In that case, we suggest, there really would be no relevant epistemic difference between the reasoning of Putnam's argument and that of the McKinsey paradox.

That, however, is not the situation to which the skeptical train of thought challenges us to respond. In order to convict Putnam's argument of warrant-transmission failure on the model we have proposed of that phenomenon, we need to ask whether someone who is antecedently open-minded about the conclusion of the argument can rationally avail themselves of the presumed warrant for its externalist premise while maintaining an unchallenged assurance that they can refer to/have a concept in good standing of BIVs. And now, provided the VAT scenario is not supposed to entrain any threat to one's capacity for any contentful thought whatsoever, but only to impact – via semantic externalism – on *which* thoughts one is capable of having, then we may continue to take it, absent reasons for doubt in specific cases, that we do have just the concepts of and capacities of reference to things that we take ourselves to have, that they are in good standing and that we may specify them homophonically.

The concern of this section has been with the charge that Putnam's argument is somehow question-begging. So what should we conclude? We have proposed one model, viz. warrant transmission failure, for what one relevant kind of question-begging might consist in and argued that, on an assumption that the skeptical argument based on the VAT scenario is not intended to question – namely that, absent reason for doubt in specific cases, we may take it that we have the referential and conceptual capacities that we think we have – Putnam's argument deserves the cautious Scottish acquittal: "Charge Not Proven." The reason for caution is that the case required by the proposed model for a full "Not Guilty" would demand that a thinker who is agnostic about the conclusion of Putnam's argument could nevertheless perfectly rationally move to accept its premises on the given grounds. And it may be doubted that we have really canvassed any *specific* ground for the second premise, beyond the point that the skeptical argument is not challenging our capacity to think contentful thoughts and to specify our concepts and referential intentions homophonically. That's a point about our dialectical situation as we attempt to frame a response to the skeptical argument, not a point of evidence.

At this point, though, one misgiving about question-begging rapidly morphs into another. For even if the VAT scenario is not supposed to undercut the capacity of its subject for any contentful thought at all, still as lately remarked the kind of semantic externalism that Putnam was appealing to must be allowed to impact on the *identity* of their thoughts. Even allowing, then, that Putnam's argument is indeed a proof of *something*, can you know – without presupposing that you know that you are not in the VAT scenario – what it is that the argument proves?

This is the specter of another kind of question-begging: that the argument may indeed be warrant-transmissive but that you are in no position to be sure that its conclusion is what was intended. We'll turn to this the next section.

IV Misgivings about the Significance of the Argument (Continued): Can we be sure what it is that we have proved?

Some philosophers have suggested that although you can successfully work through the VAT argument to establish its conclusion, there is a sense in which you do not know what it is that you have proved.[22] After all – on the assumption that such a creature could have contentful thoughts and referential intentions at all – could not a BIV run through exactly the VAT argument and thereby be rightly convinced of *something*? And whatever that was, it would not be the conclusion that it was not a BIV! So how are you better placed? Mightn't you actually be a BIV running this very argument but proving thereby not that you are not a BIV but who knows what?

Our experience suggests that this is a common first-pass reaction to Putnam's argument but it is, needless to say, almost embarrassingly confused. A BIV could – or so let's suppose – comprehendingly run through an argument whose linguistic formulation was word-for-word identical with either of the formulations of the VAT argument that we gave above in English. But it would not be an argument in English and it would not be an argument whose execution involved employment of the concept of a BIV. Putnam's argument, by contrast, does involve essential employment of that concept and it is that concept – one a BIV cannot possess – which it shows you do not fall under. So no: you (epistemically) *could not* be a BIV reading this very paper and running through Putnam's argument. *Punkt.*

---

22 For example Johnsen, "Of Brains in Vats," Brueckner, "Brains in a Vat."

Still, this may seem too quick. Some sort of worry that a kind of opacity of content, consequent on externalism, may compromise the significance of Putnam's argument may be apt to linger. It is a familiar point that the ability to identify something – to recognize it, or to specify which object it is – need not involve an ability to discriminate it from other things in any possible presentation. You may get a good look at the assailant in a street robbery, sufficient to be able to recognize him if you see him again in a normal context, but insufficient to pick him out with confidence from a range of similar looking candidates in an identity parade. Externalism may be taken to entrain analogous discriminative limitations where content is concerned, so that knowledge of *what* you are thinking is compatible with significant kinds of inability to identify and distinguish your thought among a range of alternatives. To illustrate, consider an imaginary eighteenth-century chemist, who is working at a time when the basic categories of Daltonian chemistry are understood but before Avogadro's finding that water is H_2O. The scientist is confident that water molecules involve some kind of binding of atoms of hydrogen and oxygen, though the exact structures involved remain conjectural. He thinks that H_2O is one possibility but that so is H_2O_2, and – correctly – that both combinations would be chemically stable. He gives the name "acqua" to the former substance and "hydra" to the latter. Suppose he now thinks that water flows in the Thames. He can perfectly well identify what he is thinking, namely, that water flows in the Thames. However, he does not know, and is in no position to know from the armchair, that when he thinks that water flows in the Thames, he is thinking a thought that – assuming externalism – is identical to his thought that acqua flows in the Thames, and distinct from his thought that hydra flows in the Thames. Once intension (sense) is regarded as fixed, for suitable concepts, by extension (reference), the ability to identify what you think can stop short of the ability to discriminate that thought from others.

Does this reflection do damage to the significance of Putnam's argument? Suppose a BIV thoughtfully tokens a series of sentences indistinguishable from those you token when you run through a version of the VAT argument. Externalism about thought content ensures that the BIV does not thereby express the VAT argument, and does not prove that it is not in the classical VAT scenario. What exactly – if anything[23] – it does prove when it reaches the end of the argument and tokens "I am not in the VAT scenario"[24] will depend on the BIV's conceptual repertoire and, as already remarked, in the absence of a developed

---

[23] We have of course, no reason to suppose that the relevant sequence of thoughts in the language of the BIV amounts to a proof of anything at all.

[24] We adopt the convention of representing sentences tokened in the thought of the BIV by underlining.

externalist theory of reference, the extent and nature of that repertoire is imponderable.[25] Let us allow, nevertheless, that the BIV has indeed worked through a proof and that when it tokens its conclusion, "I am not in the VAT scenario," it expresses a thought whose truth-conditions *we* can capture by a particular English sentence, *E*, leaving it open whether this is a thought about the BIVs sensory experiences, the electrical signals that cause them, the features of the computer program that are responsible for the electrical signals, or whatever else.

Now there is indeed something unimpressive about the BIV's performance, despite the fact that – or so we are supposing – it has successfully worked through an argument and proved its conclusion. But what is unimpressive about it is not that the BIV does not know what it has proved. There is no reason to think that the BIV does not know *what* it has proved, knowledge it might express by thinking "I am not in the classical VAT scenario." The point is rather that, like our imaginary scientist, the BIV cannot discriminate that thought from among certain relevant others: in particular, it cannot identify the thought that it expresses when it says "I am not in the classical VAT scenario" with the thought that *E*, and cannot distinguish it from the thought that it is not in the classical VAT scenario. And because of these limitations, it has accomplished little of significance. In particular, its conclusion is compatible with the (realized) possibility that it is a (mere) BIV.

Can you coherently bring an analogue of this concern "home," and apply it to your own case? It would have to be something like this: that unless you suppose that you are not in the VAT scenario from the outset, you cannot guarantee that when you run the VAT argument you have not merely done something in no important way different to what the BIV has done. That is, you cannot guarantee that although you have successfully established a thought, and you know what thought this is in the sense that you can identify it in your language, you lack the *discriminatory* knowledge required in order to vouchsafe that it is incompatible with the skeptical possibility which should have been your real concern.

But this is still a muddle. The conclusion that the BIV expresses by saying "I am not in the VAT scenario" is indeed compatible with the possibility that it is in the VAT scenario, but this – lest we forget – is a possibility that the BIV itself *cannot think*. It is not as if, like our imagined scientist, it can *formulate* a

---

25 Candidates for the relevant concepts suggested by Putnam himself include concepts of the BIVs sensory experiences, concepts of the electrical signals that cause these experiences, and concepts the features of the computer program that are responsible for the electrical signals. Hilary Putnam, *Reason, Truth and History* (Cambridge: Cambridge University Press, 1981), 14–15.

pair of truth-conditionally distinct thoughts and realize that it is in no position to determine which of them its conclusion is. It cannot think: well, I have proved that I am not in the VAT scenario but I do not know whether that is to have proved that I am not in the classical VAT scenario or merely that *E*. The thoughts among which the BIV cannot discriminate its conclusion are thoughts which can only be distinguished in a language which, such is its predicament, it necessarily cannot understand. Bringing the worry home to your own case will thus enforce a retreat from any expression of it that involves your *grasping* the putative possibility, of putatively real concern, that you have failed to rule out. Once such a retreat has been made, however, it is unclear whether anything worth calling a *skeptical* worry can be preserved.[26] You might try saying that, for all you know, there is some possibility that you cannot think, and that you have failed to rule out by running the VAT argument. But of course there are *innumerable* possibilities that you have not ruled out by running the argument! And some of them may, plausibly, be beyond your powers of understanding. Nothing too untoward there.[27]

V Misgivings about the Significance of the Argument (Continued): Surely there are other skeptical scenarios, suitable to underwrite very similar skeptical arguments, that may not be discounted on externalist grounds?

A number of commentators have remarked that the features of the classical VAT scenario as characterized by Putnam on which his externalist antidote depends are not essential to the genre of skeptical argument concerned. A simple skeptical argument that is structurally similar to, and in no way less challenging than that we outlined at the start can, for instance, simply make use of a scenario such as the following:

---

26 That is, a worry that questions the truth, or good standing, of whole swathes of your ordinary beliefs. It may be felt that a different kind of worry does still linger. We'll return to this in the concluding section.

27 For further discussion of the issues of this section, see Joshua Rowan Thorpe, "Semantic Self-Knowledge and the Vat Argument," *Philosophical Studies*, forthcoming.

The Recent Envatment scenario: Up until yesterday your brain was functioning normally within your body, and you moved around in a world that was more-or-less as you took it to be. As you slept last night, however, evil scientists drugged you and removed your brain from its body, placing it in a vat and hooking it up to a supercomputer ensuring that you have sensory experiences that smoothly dovetail with those you had before, and that are congenial to your usual assumptions about the kind of creature you are and the world you inhabit. Now, however, insofar as these assumptions are about the current state of the world, they are false, since after envatting you, the scientists accidentally destroyed most of what exists, except for your brain in its vat.[28]

No plausible semantic externalism will prevent you from referring to BIVs if you have spent most of your life living in normal, English-speaking Western society, so there is no possibility of a VAT argument-style proof that you are not in the Recent Envatment scenario. But the Recent Envatment scenario is incompatible with your having perceptual knowledge that you are right now reading a philosophy paper. So, cannot a skeptic just argue that your inability to rule out the Recent Envatment scenario combined with Closure entails that you don't know that you are reading a philosophy paper, or anything else that you take yourself to know about your current environment on the basis of current perception? And if that's so, isn't Putnam's argument largely a distraction, at least so far as the project of responding to skepticism is concerned?[29]

Arguably, this popular objection proceeds too quickly. To see why, first consider that a skeptical argument based on the Recent Envatment scenario will at least do *less extensive* damage to your empirical knowledge than one based on the classical VAT scenario. This is because many of your empirical beliefs are compatible with the Recent Envatment scenario, and so Closure does not require that you must be able to rule out the Recent Envatment scenario if those beliefs are to be regarded as knowledgeable. For example, your beliefs about where you were born, where you grew up, where you were educated and indeed where you were and what you were doing last week, are all compatible with the Recent

---

28 A skeptical argument based on this scenario does not actually need the flourish at the end. It is enough that, whatever is now taking place in the external world, you no longer have, according to the scenario described, the appropriate cognitive connections to acquire knowledge about it. (Cf. n. 3 above.) But we include the flourish for the sake of symmetry with the skeptical argument based on the classical VAT scenario.
29 This objection to the VAT argument can be found in, among other places, David Christensen, "Skeptical Problems, Semantical Solutions," *Philosophy and Phenomenological Research* 53, no. 2 (1993): 301–321, Graeme Forbes, "Realism and Skepticism: Brains in a Vat Revisited," *The Journal of Philosophy* 92, no. 4 (1995): 205–222, Wright, "On Putnam's Proof" and Anthony Brueckner, "Transcendental Arguments from Content Externalism," in *Transcendental Arguments: Problems and Prospects*, edited by Robert Stern, 229–250 (Oxford: Clarendon Press, 1999).

Envatment scenario. An appeal to Closure thus imposes no requirement that you be in position to know that the Recent Envatment scenario is false before you can continue justifiably to regard these beliefs as knowledgeable.

This reflection points up a strategic weakness in the attempt to run a skeptical argument based on any modified scenario of this kind. Not that it is in any important sense a weakness merely that the damaging effects of such an argument will be more limited than one based on the classical VAT scenario, however. They are still extensive enough and thoroughly unwelcome. The strategic weakness is rather that because any closure-based argument that utilizes the Recent Envatment scenario or similar is in the way noted more limited in scope, there is nothing to prevent you from appealing to presumable empirical knowledge that lies *outside its scope* in order to justifiably rule the relevant scenario out. Take, for example, your belief that as recently as last week envatting technology did not exist, and that we were nowhere near developing it. Or your belief that up until last week doctors were nowhere near being able to remove a brain from someone's body without causing massive permanent damage to the brain. A skeptical argument based on the Recent Envatment scenario does not threaten the status of either of these beliefs as knowledge. But both provide perfectly good reasons to think that you are not in any scenario of that kind.

It may be worthwhile pausing to note why no similar problem arises for the skeptical argument based on the classical VAT scenario. You cannot rule out that scenario by appealing to your belief that as recently as last week envatting technology did not exist, and that as recently as last week doctors were nowhere near being able to remove a brain from someone's body without damaging it beyond repair. The classical VAT scenario does not, to be sure, rule out those beliefs by virtue of being strictly *incompatible with their being true* – at least not if each is construed as featuring a wide-scope negation. But what it is incompatible with is the assumption that, when whatever caused you to form those beliefs occurred, you were functioning as a competent knowing subject, appropriately connected to relevant matters in an external world. Thus a skeptical argument that employs the classical VAT scenario *does* undercut the status of these beliefs as presumable knowledge. To appeal to them and thereby to assume that they are knowledgeable as part of an attempt to refute the original skeptical argument would be question-begging.

So, the attempt to monger a skeptical paradox along the now familiar lines faces a dilemma: if the mooted skeptical paradox employs the classical VAT scenario, you can use the VAT argument to rule that scenario out; but if the Recent Envatment scenario is invoked, you can appeal to aspects of your still presumable empirical knowledge that are unthreatened by that scenario to justifiably discount it.

Can a skeptic finesse this dilemma by coming up with a different kind of skeptical scenario – one which cannot be ruled out by either the VAT argument or by appeal to certain of your empirical beliefs whose knowledgeability it fails to challenge? Such a scenario would have to allow you to have or retain the concepts necessary to describe it even if you were in it, whilst being incompatible with the knowledgeability of any empirical belief you hold to which you could appeal to rule it out.

One possible ploy for a skeptical argument that squeezes between the horns is to resort to a high degree of abstraction, thus aiming to avoid the use of any concepts in the description of the skeptical scenario that externalism about thought content might prevent one from having if the scenario were actual. To this end, someone might propose something like the following

> *Abstract scenario*: the experiences you have are consistently and exceptionlessly of a character that is fully coherent with your empirical beliefs. However, these beliefs are all false.

The Abstract scenario falsifies all of your empirical beliefs, and so there is no possibility of ruling it out by appeal to your empirical knowledge. But grasp of this scenario arguably involves only concepts such that that externalism about thought content would not prevent you from having them if you were in it. It is not clear whether the concepts of *empirical belief* and *experience* are concepts your grasp of which requires that you stand in causal relations to their referents. But even if they are, there is no evident reason to think that you could not enter into the relevant relations were the Abstract scenario to be true. For you do have experiences and empirical beliefs, after all, even in the Abstract scenario.[30]

If the Abstract scenario does indeed subserve a skeptical paradox that is no less challenging than the classical VAT scenario paradox, we should conclude that the details of the classical VAT scenario were mere ornamental flourishes which a skeptic can dispense with once it is noticed that they set up Putnam's counter-argument. But is any prospective Abstract scenario paradox truly no less challenging? The skeptical claim that your experiences provide no sufficient reason to discount the VAT scenario turns on the idea that, as we expressed it at the beginning, "those experiences are exactly as they ought to be

30 Thomas Nagel, *The View from Nowhere* (Oxford: Oxford University Press, 1986), Janet Folina, "Realism, Scepticism, and the Brain in a Vat," in *The Brain in a Vat*, edited by Sanford Goldberg, 155–173 (Cambridge: Cambridge University Press, 2016) and Duncan Pritchard and Chris Ranilli, "Putnam on BIVs and Radical Scepticism," in *The Brain in a Vat*, edited by Sanford Goldberg, 75–89 (Cambridge: Cambridge University Press, 2016) object to the VAT argument essentially on the grounds that it does not rule out the Abstract scenario.

on the hypothesis that you are indeed in the VAT scenario as described." The VAT scenario, that is to say, provides an *explanation* of your experiences – and one, the skeptic must claim, that you have no sufficient epistemic reason to think is worse than the explanation provided by your usual beliefs about how things are. However, it is doubtful that the Abstract scenario can match this. The Abstract scenario cannot be said to provide an explanation of your sensory experiences that competes with the explanation provided by your usual beliefs about your worldly situation, because the Abstract scenario says nothing about the causation of your experiences at all. It simply says that you have your sensory experiences, and that while they are broadly consonant with your usual empirical beliefs, they are not to be explained in terms of the truth of those beliefs. This simply conjoins a statement of what needs explaining with the denial of one possible explanation. Unlike the VAT scenario, the Abstract scenario offers no competition to your usual beliefs as an explanation of your experiences.

If needed, a simple analogy will serve to drive home the significance of this point. Suppose you are a senior detective leading a murder investigation. So far as you can see, all of a considerable body of evidence suggests that Jon did it: the murder weapon is Jon's knife, Jon's fingerprints and no-one else's are on the handle, a man of Jon's description was seen leaving the scene of the crime shortly after the murder, Jon has no alibi for the time of the slaying, Jon stood to benefit considerably from the death of the victim, and he is a man with a previous conviction for stabbing. So, you naturally form the belief that Jon is the murderer, on the basis that it is an excellent explanation of the evidence. Your two subordinates are not convinced, however. One simply suggests that perhaps, despite all the evidence, Jon didn't do it. It doesn't seem that, if you are rational, this suggestion should move you at all. The reason is that it introduces no new hypothesis to challenge your own in the competition of explaining the evidence. The other subordinate, by contrast, points out that Jon has an identical twin who had access to Jon's knife, and that some of the prints on the handle are smudged in a way consistent with its being wielded by a hand in a rubber glove, that the twin stood to benefit from the death of the victim just as much as Jon, that he too has no relevant alibi, and like his brother has a history of violence. Moreover, he has a strong motive to incriminate his brother. Perhaps, your subordinate suggests, Jon's twin is the murderer. It seems that this should be regarded as a serious contender as an explanation of the evidence, and that until further evidence emerges to give an edge to the hypothesis that Jon is the murderer, you should conclude that the investigation should remain open – that you do not after all at this point know that who the murderer is.

The point, then, is that, like the first subordinate's suggestion, the Abstract scenario simply fails to provide any competing explanation of the relevant evidence, and therefore stands no chance of occasioning reasonable doubt about an apparently adequate explanation that is already on the table.

Three constraints have now emerged which a skeptical scenario must meet if it is to perform as the original skeptical argument advertises. They are, as noted,

(i) that the scenario deploy only concepts that will be available to you if you are in it;

(ii) that it undermine the knowledgeable status of any of your empirical beliefs that might be adduced against it; and

(iii) that the scenario offer at least some explanation of your on-going experiences to rival that provided by those of our normal beliefs that skepticism challenges.

The classical VAT scenario fails the first constraint, the Recent Envatment scenario the second, and the Abstract scenario the third. Can there be an envatment-style scenario that meets all three constraints?

We can see what shape it must take. Unlike the VAT scenario, it must, assuming content externalism, allow you a sufficiently extended period of normal education and experience to ground the concepts needed to characterize it, but unlike the Recent Envatment scenario, it must also undermine the epistemic pedigree of those of your ordinary beliefs that you could reasonably marshal against it. And unlike the Abstract scenario, it must offer an explanation of your experience to rival, at least prima facie, the explanation provided by your normal beliefs about the world you live in and the routine causes of your experiences.

We have not shown that there is no possible such scenario, and we shall not here take a definite stand on the matter. Certainly, one should not be discomforted merely by the epistemic possibility that an ingenious skeptic will yet come up with an effective skeptical scenario meeting all three constraints. One should, after all, be moved only by paradoxes with which one is actually confronted, not by the bare idea that there *might* be arguments to the same effect. That said, it may interest the reader to ponder the

> *Relatively Recent Envatment* scenario: You were successfully envatted a few years ago after a normal upbringing and education, but not so long ago that the radical dislocation of your sensory experience from the physical world around you has had time, for externalist reasons, to materially impact on the referential/conceptual repertoire that you acquired during your pre-envatted days. So your understanding of this depiction of your predicament is just as it would have been before your envatment. The course your experience now assumes in general is to be explained in terms of your brain's neural connections to impulses emanating from your controlling computer and the details of its program, exactly as in the classical VAT scenario. Finally, while you have a range of seemingly-well attested beliefs that suggest that such a mishap is technologically impossible and has been throughout your life,

these beliefs have all been acquired – either by direct programming or suitable illusory experiences of learning – since you were envatted.[31]

VI The VAT Argument vs. Metaphysical Realism

Our discussion hitherto has focused on the potential force of the VAT argument in addressing traditional skeptical paradoxes in epistemology. We should not conclude, therefore, without acknowledging that fashioning a response to skepticism was not, or not primarily, Putnam's purpose. Rather, he believed that his argument strikes a powerful blow against the broad view about the relationship between our thought and the external world that he entitled *metaphysical realism*. What did he understand by that, and is the VAT argument successful when harnessed to that project?

Putnam's characterizations of metaphysical realism are many and various.[32] For our purposes here it will suffice to say that there are essentially two core components in the metaphysical realist outlook. The first concerns the nature of the world treated of by the natural sciences: it is a world that is "mind-independent" – a world whose characteristics have no form of metaphysically interesting dependence on activities and properties of minds. The second concerns the nature of truth and meaning: metaphysical realism involves a robust correspondence conception of truth, according to which the truth of a thought (concerning the relevant type of subject matter) is subject to no form of epistemic constraint but consists simply in a relationship of pure depiction of an objective state of affairs. Call these two elements *Mind-Independence* and *Robust Correspondence* respectively.

In Putnam's handling, these ideas are taken to enforce a conception of our cognitive endeavors as aspiring to *mirror*, in Rorty's famous image, a natural world from which we are, in something like an Hegelian sense, *alienated*: a "brutely other" realm of fact and law whose correspondence to any purported account of it that satisfies our most refined standards of enquiry and evidence is

---

31 The issues raised in this section are discussed at greater length in Joshua Rowan Thorpe, "Closure Scepticism and the Vat Argument," *Mind* 127, no. 507 (2018): 667–690.

32 The discussion to follow will rely on the perspective articulated in *Reason, Truth and History*, where Putnam offers the following characterization of metaphysical realism (there called "external realism"): "On [the metaphysical realist perspective] the world consists of some fixed totality of mind-independent objects. There is exactly one true and complete description of 'the way the world is.' Truth involves some sort of correspondence relation between words or thought-signs and external things and sets of things." (*Reason, Truth and History*, 49) See also Putnam, *Realism with a Human Face* (Cambridge, MA: Harvard University Press, 1990), 30–33.

a matter of deep contingency. Metaphysical realism, Putnam proposed, is thus committed to the view that a total empirical theory that was *unimprovable* by our methodological standards, and adequate to all data that this actual world might in principle offer up, might nevertheless just be extensively false. Call a scenario in which that alleged possibility obtains one of *Ideal Error*. Putnam's idea seems to have been that the VAT scenario, as he characterizes it, may be taken as a parable, or epitome, for any situation of Ideal Error, and hence that its refutation would dispose not only of the possibility of Ideal Error but also of the theses that provide its metaphysical springs – Mind-Independence and Robust Correspondence.

It is striking that Putnam himself contributed very little to the extensive debates in the literature that Chapter 2 of *Reason, Truth and History* has generated. An exception is his 1994 Reply[33] in the Clark and Hale anthology to Wright's article in the same volume.[34] Wright there argued that, granted its semantic externalist assumptions, the VAT argument is successful but that its potency against metaphysical realism is seriously qualified by its failure to engage a certain more abstract worry.[35] The argument turns on the thought that it is a side-effect of the externalism that an envatted brain in the VAT scenario is barred from any adequate conception of its specific predicament. But that is to be barred from recognition, indeed from any understanding, of fundamental aspects of its own nature and of the world it lives in. *We* can understand its predicament in such general terms. Can we not understand accordingly how we might be in some such broadly structurally analogous predicament ourselves, even if the specifics of it would elude our grasp for the same reasons that the specifics of the VAT scenario elude the grasp of the envatted brains? If that remains an intelligible possibility, then acknowledging it still brings in train the metaphysical realist conception of a brutely other world, set over against and transcending our powers of understanding and discovery.

Putnam dismisses this worry. But the way he framed his response to it reads as if he took it to be an attempt to reinstate a skeptical argument. So we should stress that skepticism – understood as the claim that we cannot rationally rule out massive error – is beside the point. The predicament bruited is one not of massive error but rather of fundamental and ineluctable ignorance – *Cosmic Ignorance*. And the point is not, or not really, whether such a scenario is "worrying" – for why, it may be asked, should the heart grieve over what the mind cannot comprehend? – but rather that to grant its possible reality is exactly

---

33 Hilary Putnam, "Comments and Replies," in *Reading Putnam*, edited by Peter Clark and Bob Hale, 242–296 (Cambridge, MA: Blackwell, 1994).
34 Wright, "On Putnam's Proof" (1994 version).
35 We here pick up on the worry prefigured in n. 27.

to conceive of the world as the metaphysical realist conceives it, as brutely alien with a population, at least in significant part, of things we cannot refer to in thought and states of affairs we cannot conceptualize.

Still, with the dialectical situation so clarified, it is clear how Putnam's reply should run. He must charge that any attempt to describe even such a general and non-specific scenario must still have recourse to concepts which would not be available to us were we in it – in general, that *any* hypothesis that postulates circumstances either of extensive undetectable error *or* extensive ineluctable ignorance must be "semantically auto-disruptive."[36] This must hold no matter at what level of abstractness and generality the description proceeds. And in Putnam's reply this is exactly what he tries to do.[37] His strategy is to press for some further specification of how we should conceive of the "broadly structurally analogous predicament" to that of the envatted brains that we allegedly might be in and to make a case that natural ways of trying to provide that – involving notions such as cause, fundamental law, and space – will require a conceptual repertoire which would not be available to the envatted brains and whose availability to us is, by semantic externalism, contingent on the falsehood of the specification in question.

The extreme generality of this new kind of scenario claim, and the lack of specification of exactly what semantic externalism requires of the good standing of concepts for which a straightforwardly causal account of reference looks implausible in any case, makes it difficult to predict whether this response can succeed. Since we will shortly canvass independent reasons to doubt that the VAT argument can exert any real pressure against metaphysical realism, we here, for reasons of space, will leave it to the reader to ponder the issue. In doing so, however, (s)he may want to reflect that at least one, bare bones, characterization of the predicament needs only *logical* concepts, concepts of *ourselves as thinking, epistemic agents*, concepts of *metasemantics* and certain kinds of *evaluative* concepts: it is the predicament in which *there are* states of affairs to which *we* are so related that we cannot *refer to* their constituent *objects* and *properties*, nor therefore represent them in *true thoughts*, and whose obtaining would be of *enormous significance* to us could we but *know* of it. If that is admitted as a possibility whose intelligibility is unthreatened by any generalization of the

---

36 Wright, "On Putnam's Proof," 85 (1992 version): "Say that a hypothesis H is *semantically auto-disruptive with respect to language L* if and only if, were H true, some elements in the L-expression, S, of H would differ in meaning in such a way that S would no longer express H. And now define H as *absolutely* semantically auto-disruptive . . . if and only if for *any* expression, S, of H, in whatever language, if H were true some elements in S would so differ in meaning that S would no longer express H."
37 Putnam, "Comments on Replies."

VAT argument, then the argument presents no obstacle to ways of thinking about the world and our cognitive situation within it characteristic of metaphysical realism.[38]

However that may be, there are three other, as it seems to us, cogent reasons for doubting that the VAT argument can carry the metaphysical significance that Putnam wanted. First, assume that the VAT scenario can indeed function as an epitome for any of the forms of cognitive dislocation whose possibility is supposedly distinctively implicit in metaphysical realism. There is a worry nevertheless about the *modality* of the conclusion of the VAT argument. Insofar as metaphysical realism may be taken to involve commitment to possibilities of Ideal Error, or Cosmic Ignorance, it is *metaphysical* possibility that is at stake. The idea is that the determinants of truth and falsity are metaphysically unconstrained – across all possible worlds – by the thoughts and standards of ideal investigators. Putnam's argument, by contrast, establishes only that we are not *actually* brains-in-a vat. We are not so because we actually have the conceptual repertoire necessary to characterize the predicament of the envatted brains. But that is a contingency. Had we been brains-in-a vat, we would have lacked that repertoire. The conclusion of the VAT argument, while of potential comfort in the context of addressing (one kind of) skepticism, thus has no bearing on the conception of the relationship between thought and reality that metaphysical realism is invested in, since it carries no implication that we could not, in different circumstances, have been brains-in-a vat.

Second, the VAT scenario is in any case arguably not well suited to serve as an epitome of Ideal Error. Interpreted as the basis for a skeptical argument, it offers a situation in which the subjects' beliefs are supposedly massively false because almost all the things they putatively concern fail to exist. It is – before any semantic externalist ideas are brought to bear – a scenario of massive reference failure. But there are other kinds of possibilities for Ideal Error. One such, for example, attends the kind of strong version of the thesis of underdetermination of empirical theory by data that Quine invoked to argue for the indeterminacy of

---

38 As we remarked at the beginning, it is a dialectical strength of the original VAT argument that it needs only relatively modest assumptions about reference – essentially just that a necessary condition for being in position to refer to brains and vats is that one have had – or that the speech community in which one acquires one's language have had – some appropriate kind of causal interaction with brains, and vats, or items in terms of which "brain" and "vat" can be defined. But this is a place where a more exact understanding of the requirements of a plausible causal semantic externalism becomes important since the acausality of many quotidian subject matters, as intuitively conceived, entails that far too much of our everyday conceptual repertoire in presumable good-standing will be incapable of satisfying any simple "causal interaction" condition on reference.

translation. On one understanding of that thesis, it is possible for two theories to agree in their respective ontologies and ideologies but to propose incompatible yet empirically adequate theoretical accounts of the same range of observable phenomena and to score similarly for other theoretical virtues. If that is a possibility, then an ideal theory can be false for reasons quite unlike anything epitomized by the classical VAT scenario.

Finally, it is doubtful whether Mind-Independence and Robust Correspondence really do entail possibilities of Ideal Error in the first place. At any rate, there are a variety of proposals that philosophers have defended that, while consistent with Mind-Independence and Robust Correspondence, precisely exclude the possibility of massive error. One dramatic kind of view with that intended effect is Donald Davidson's interpretationism.[39] According to Davidson, a subject's beliefs are to be identified with whatever best interpretation of their sayings and doings would take them to be. Since, in Davidson's view, best interpretation must be charitable – must maximize the range of true beliefs ascribed – and since, while there are no limits on how knowledgeable interpreters may in principle be taken to be, interpretation is generally better the more knowledgeable its agent, it follows that any rational subject must for the most part be best interpreted as having true beliefs, even when truth is conceived as robust correspondence to a mind-independent world.

According to this train of thought, Ideal Error is excluded, quite consistently with metaphysical realism, by a thesis about the metaphysical nature of belief. However, we appeal to Davidson's famous proposal here not to endorse it but merely to highlight the gap it illustrates between metaphysical realism, understood as throughout this discussion, and Ideal Error. In general, whether the latter is a possibility, even when Mind-Independence and Robust Correspondence are assumed, will depend on one's theory of the metaphysics of concepts and reference – on what view one takes of the scope and nature of the concepts and beliefs that a subject can form in a world conceived as by metaphysical realism. One would have supposed that the potential lacuna here would be especially evident to anyone of semantic externalist leanings. That it seems not to have been more salient to Hilary Putnam is one more puzzle about the thought of this brilliant yet enigmatic philosopher.

---

39 Donald Davidson, "A Coherence Theory of Truth and Knowledge," in *Truth and Interpretations*, edited by Ernest Lepore, 307–319 (Oxford: Blackwell, 1986).

Sanjit Chakraborty

Language, Meaning, and Context Sensitivity: Confronting a "Moving-Target"

Abstract: This paper explores three important interrelated themes in Putnam's philosophy: language, meaning, and the context-sensitivity of "truth-evaluable content." It shows how Putnam's own version of semantic externalism is able to steer a middle course between an internalism about meaning that requires a "language of thought" (or "mentalese") and a mind-independent realism about meaning that requires Platonic objects (or other such "abstract entities"), while doing justice to how ascriptions of meaning are causally related to the objective world. The following account is able to allow for the primacy of language over thought while ensuring that the content of thought is partially fixed by the external world. The emphasis in Putnam's later writings on the "context sensitivity" of meaning are often construed as marking a major departure from his earlier thought. It is here argued that such an interpretation involves a misunderstanding both of the commitments of Putnam's original form of semantic externalism and of the implications of the version of context sensitivity he embraces.

In his book *Renewing Philosophy*, Putnam claims, "A central part of human intelligence is the ability to make inductive inferences, that is, to learn from experiences."[1] Chomsky and his followers believe in the conceptual aspect of thought and Chomsky refutes the idea that the content of a thought can be the same as the meaning of the sentence by arguing in favor of a cognitive account of linguistic competence.[2] He articulates the method of language use in terms of the rule-governed processes that seem innate, while Fodor, at an intense level, safeguards the innate "language of thought." For Fodor, all expressions and concepts of human being that are used in our natural language are in liaison with the primitive thought, which precedes language by leading towards the doctrine of innateness. Chomsky does not support as extreme a view as Fodor does.[3] Instead, Chomsky believes in an ample number of concepts and conceptual abilities that we can express through innate language. He is reluctant to make any distinction

---

1 Hilary Putnam, *Renewing Philosophy* (Cambridge, MA: Harvard University Press, 1992), 8.

2 Noam Chomsky, "Problems of Projection," *Lingua* 130 (2013): 33–49.

3 Jerry Fodor, *Language of Thought* (Cambridge, MA: Harvard University Press, 1979). See Sanjit Chakraborty, *The Labyrinth of Mind and World: Beyond Internalism-Externalism* (London and New York: Routledge, 2020), 195–196.

https://doi.org/10.1515/9783110769210-004

between innate abilities and innate concepts. However, Putnam rejects Chomsky's thesis and says,

> The view that language learning is not really learning, but rather the maturation of an innate ability in a particular environment (somewhat like the acquisition of a bird call by a species of bird that has to hear the call from an adult bird of the species to acquire it, but which also has an innate propensity to acquire that sort of call) leads, in its extreme form, to pessimism about the likelihood that human use to natural language can be successfully stimulated on a computer – which is why Chomsky is pessimistic about projects for natural language computer processing, although he shares the computer model of the brain, or at least of the "language organ," with AI researchers.[4]

Chomsky, who believes in the computer model of brain in some particular areas, does not believe that artificial intelligence can attain the level of biological adaptation. For Chomsky, "language use" is not a separate ability of human beings like throwing a cricket ball. In the case of "language use," an agent needs to undergo the process of total human intelligence capacity, whereas, in order to throw a cricket ball, one does not require to stimulate total human intelligence capacities. This is a very controversial topic where, I think, Putnam misunderstood Chomsky, as Chomsky has repeatedly argued that the computational model works only for the generative grammar in I-language in the context of parsing a program that determines the structure of presented expressions, and is not related to the system of language use. Chomsky also believes in the "creative aspect of language use" that is different from the way a computer processes language. The believers, in the theory of the innateness of language, like Chomsky or some other internalists (Devitt, Fodor, and Jackson) think that thought precedes language in three different senses:

(1) Conceptual competence is ontologically prior to linguistic competence. We cannot take on conceptual competence without developing the capacity to acquire linguistic competence.

(2) Linguistic competence is an amalgam of conceptual competence and processing competence. Hence, we should distinguish between conceptual capacities and processing capacities. The merit of the processing capacity can, thus, be considered as a tool of thought. Besides, there are some philosophers like Pinker, who takes "processing capacity" as an adaptation (something that was selected for), but this view is rejected by both Chomsky and Putnam who claim that if we consider linguistic competence as an

---

4 Putnam, *Renewing Philosophy*, 15.

adaptation, it will follow that conceptual capacity can be prior to it because of this adaptation.[5]

(3) Unless we admit linguistic capacity as an adaptation, an analysis of exploring processing capacity in relation to linguistic competence would not execute anything until it is coped with conceptual capacity.

Conceptual competences are interrelated to certain thoughts that cannot adapt to suitable reasoning. An ontological priority defines conceptual competence as prior to linguistic competence. The best explanation of this theory is found in the behavioral attributes of animals, as animals do not possess language by which they can express their thoughts. Even in psychology, it is well proven that babies who do not speak any spoken natural language, have a very rich mental life like that of the higher-level animals, which may remind us that our ancestors (apes) had thoughts, but no language per se. Thought, no doubt, precedes language, as thought cannot pervade language.

However, Putnam would not like to put "psychological states" in the brain in retrospect of language by treating the environment as the primary cause of psychological states. Rather, through language, agents can make a sense of the world that affects us. Putnam accepts language use to be competent to identify "concepts," by putting forth his hypothesis that underscores the primacy of language over thought. Concepts are in no sense Platonic objects. Having concepts means an ability to use words in our linguistic communication. Putnam seems to agree with Fodor in the fact that only syntax is formed in the brain, but semantics locate in the world, as language is an art that the world creates, and this is entirely different from an individual's brain.

Language speaking is a human ability that one cannot theoretically explicate by piecemeal procedures. It is rather allied to complete "human functional organization." The "constitutive fact" about the natural kind terms like "human being" or "hydrogen atoms" is not the same, since they stipulate different explanatory models. The inquiry about "hydrogen atoms" depends on an intelligible explanatory theory that bestows importance on natural science. However, language speaking and other human abilities that are linked to the system of language fall outside the realm of naturalistic inquiries. Neither neuroscience nor the mental approach helps us to learn anything about meanings. "Human being" as a concept can be a part of our human understanding mainly based on common sense and particular human actions and attitudes. And the same process is followed in the case of language speaking.

---

5 Chakraborty, *The Labyrinth of Mind and World*, 67.

Of significance here is that when a person believes something, the meaning of their belief cannot be an isolated thing that can only exist in their mind. If I believe that I have a mole under my eye, I tend to believe, at the same time, that there are people with moles under their eyes, just like me. The conception of others' claims for the concepts and beliefs from a non-intrinsic sense; these are external and publicly shareable in our language. It could hardly be possible that people can think and write the meaning of a sentence without intending this relation to the certain beliefs of the others. Putnam upholds language as a social phenomenon, so the intentions, beliefs and conventional meaning rely on the socio-linguistic framework and the public shareability of meaning.[6]

Putnam seems right in that there may be a possible way in which language precedes thought. In order to make a distinction between justified and unjustified thoughts we have to take language as an implement. In the case of a prelinguistic organism, we do not make such a distinction. I think that, even when thought is in the form of a proposition (even in an interrogative sense), it can have a justification derived from language and previous experience. The perception and visual processes have some tendencies to be reformulated in verbal propositions and these verbal propositions, in the way of thought, need language to give it a structural milieu. Chomsky himself believes that one's thought about how one could avoid a traffic jam does not hinge on any linguistic competence but rather on the visual imagery. This is a farfetched justification, unless and until we reformulate it verbally. Even the plan that an agent envisages acquire its meaning through other related cognitive capabilities of the agent's *I-language*. But, the conceptions of driving a car or how to avoid a traffic jam are not bound by mere visual imagery or innate rules. Rather the processes are related to rules that are applied by people and also by their instant common senses which can be achieved through practices and experiences from one's community.[7]

In *Reality and Representation*,[8] Putnam, who always tends toward realism, tries to endorse externalism from a scientific background by claiming that people's beliefs or knowledge can change but the referent of the words or terms remain unchanged.[9] Putnam tries to make a link between the word and the world

---

6 See, in particular, Sanjit Chakraborty, "Pursuits of Belief: Reflecting on the Cessation of Belief," *Sophia* 60, no. 3 (2021): 639–654.

7 I am personally indebted to Noam Chomsky for these thought-provoking notes.

8 Hilary Putnam, *Representation and Reality* (Cambridge, MA: MIT Press, 1988).

9 I wrote elsewhere, "Putnam raises a severe objection against Popper by defending the account of primary practices in science as any scientific ideas conduit its practical application in science, technology, and human life. Even in our practice, we could find out the correctness or the failures of an idea to see its successful long run practice or its unsuccessful and

to rebuff any kind of mentalism and *Platonic entities*.[10] The logical positivists, especially Carnap, strive to reconstruct the understanding of language in terms of scientific methods (physics plus mathematics) and the synthetic formulation of logical consequences.[11] In contrast, terms like virus, quark, or gene, which are not perceivable, are labeled as theoretical terms. The dualism of observational terms and theoretical terms puts forward a kind of intricacy in philosophy of mind and language. Logical positivists sketch an overpass between statements of the status of verification with the theoretical one by arguing that an observational statement can be directly verified, whereas a theoretical statement is indirectly verifiable. They talk about a hierarchy between the two statements. The observational statements are fully meaningful and intelligible, even as the theoretical statements turn out to be partially meaningful with the help of the observational statements.[12] In his early years (1950s), Putnam shows that Carnap makes the wrong effort to integrate the false assumptions regarding the dependence relation between theoretical statements and observational statements. We know that, first, a strict challenge came from Quine in 1951, where he analyzed the marginal boundary between theoretical statements and observational statements of our language using the notion of meaning and the dependence of truth-values.[13] In his article "What Theories Are Not,"[14] Putnam concludes that it would not be a justified to think that the meaning of theoretical terms depends

---

insignificant application in our daily life. The whole process of knowing the significant or insignificant practices of the theories or ideas in the private life of the human could be understood only based on experience." (Sanjit Chakraborty, "Scientific Conjectures and the Growth of Knowledge," *Journal of Indian Council of Philosophical Research* 38, no. 1 (2021): 97)

10 Hilary Putnam, "The Meaning of 'Meaning',", in *Mind, Language and Reality: Philosophical Papers*, Vol. 2 (Cambridge: Cambridge University Press, 1975), 222.

11 Rudolf Carnap, *The Logical Syntax of Language* (New York: Humanities, 1937).

12 Rudolf Carnap, *The Philosophical Foundation of Physics*, edited by Martin Gardner (New York: Basic Books, 1966).

13 Travis writes, "Quine supposes that there is a class of privileged facts. Quine is prepared to tell us what these facts are. Roughly, they are what is 'really' observable as to how things are. There may then be, he allows, other nonprivileged or not obviously privileged facts only so far as these are analyzable in terms of privileged facts . . . (Quine supposes a notion of proof such that the obtaining of what proves a nonprivileged fact leaves no logical possibility of that fact's nonobtaining. So in effect, what is demanded is that, for any nonprivileged fact, there be some set of privileged ones that are logically equivalent to it.) Ultimately, for Quine, the privileged facts are facts about our own sensations." (Charles Travis, "Engaging," in *The Philosophy of Hilary Putnam*, edited by Randall E. Auxier, Douglas R. Anderson, and Lewis Edwin Hahn (Chicago, IL: Open Court, 2015), 284–285)

14 Hilary Putnam, "What Theories Are Not" (1960), reprinted in *Mathematics, Matter and Method: Philosophical Papers*, Vol. 1, 215–227 (Cambridge: Cambridge University Press, 1975).

on observational terms. Now, one can question: how could we derive the meaning of the unperceivable terms like "quark," "gene" etc.? In this case, Putnam accepts a function-based approach that talks about the linguistic practices that specify the way of learning the terms in our society. The meaningfulness of a term, for Putnam, can be determined through the common language. A term means how it is used and expressed in our ordinary language. This approach of finding out meaningfulness of the terms through causal links underpins theoretical terms in the periphery of common language. We can say that Quine tries to see the agreement or disagreement of linguistic practices in relation to logical incompatibility. For Quine, two sentences would exhibit disagreement only if there is a logical incompatibility between them. Moreover, these sentences would be in agreement only if there is a conjunction of the sentences, which allows for the assertion of the negation of the particular sentence that talks about an inconsistency between the assertions expressed by the two original sentences. All these deflationary accounts avert us from the notion of an agreement and disagreement between the speakers regarding practical identification. Here, two speakers in the same natural language believe each other's words as true and justified without any special query. The practices that teach us to treat others' words as significant make an integration of our understanding of truth with the understanding of sameness of denotation and satisfaction. Language, for Putnam, is an art that we can share through practices and uses. With this point in mind, Putnam urges that the competent speaker does not have any semantic marker (an intrinsic natural system to exhibit meaning) in their brain as Katz argued.[15] Meaning becomes public because of similar paradigms, not because of shared knowledge. According to Putnam, an individualistic conception of knowledge cannot be possible at all. Every speaker needs a standard minimum account of information about the used words through which they can able to participate in any kind of collective discussion in linguistic community.

I Putnam on Meaning

The concept of language, and the way Putnam tries to see language, is clearly related to his "theory of meaning," an externalist appraisal. Putnam's doctrine

---

15 Hilary Putnam, "Explanation and Reference" (1973), reprinted in *Mind, Language, and Reality: Philosophical Papers*, Vol. 2 (Cambridge: Cambridge University Press, 1975), 204.

of "causal theory of reference"[16] gets a full-fledged form of externalism in his brilliant paper "The Meaning of 'Meaning'" (1975) which is a challenge to the popular idea of science. In this paper, he argues that, by claiming change in the beliefs in favor of scientific progress, one cannot change the meaning and the referent of terms. Putnam's semantic externalism, a seminal contribution to the history of analytic philosophy, specially puts forward the argument that the meaning cannot be ambiguous, and that psychological states (intentional form) cannot determine the physical states (extension), as the knowledge of meaning is in no way an individual property (in a *Platonic sense*), which locates in the agent's brain or mind. If we positively describe Putnam's semantic externalism, we arrive at three interconnecting arguments that underlie his claims to externalism. The first claim brings up the notion of meaning just by avoiding mental entities. It is in fact the world oriented that mainly signifies by its reference. The second claim talks about a grasp of meaning that cannot be intrinsic; it exists in the public or social sphere. Finally, the third claim holds that concepts and beliefs, including meaning, can be determined by manifold ways connected with "socio-linguistic" background, "division of linguistic labor," and "stereotypes." Putnam blends these three elements (division of linguistic labor, stereotypes, and socio-linguistic background together) by calling them *meaning-vectors*.[17] In a deep foundational sense, Putnam minimally defends a sentence component that he calls *meaning vector*, which he sensitively designates as "myth-eaten," a picture of meaning that contrasts with the internalist claims about knowing the meaning of a term, which is just a matter of being in a certain psychological state. Mental states and mind as a manipulation of meaning cannot be intrinsic or located in the head or in the speaker's skin. In his *John Locke* lectures (1975–76), Putnam discusses a richer version of the causal theory of reference that he calls "social co-operation plus contribution of the environment of the theory of specification of reference."[18]

More generally, Putnam has charged Frege with some explicit allegations. However, he agrees with Fregean thought on certain points. Putnam first argues against Frege's speculation on intentions as abstract entities and "mock proper names." Secondly, though Putnam appreciates Frege's stance on "anti-

16 Hilary Putnam, "The Psychological Predicates," in *Art, Mind and Religion*, edited by W.H. Capitan and D.D. Merrill, 37–48 (Pittsburgh: University of Pittsburgh, 1967). Reprinted as "The Nature of Mental States," in *Mind, Language and Reality: Philosophical Papers*, Vol. 2, 429–440 (Cambridge: Cambridge University Press, 1975).

17 Putnam, "The Meaning of 'Meaning'," 269.

18 Noam Chomsky, *The New Horizons in the Study of Language and Mind* (Cambridge: Cambridge University Press, 2000), 41.

psychologism" – an inspiration for his thought that meanings cannot be mental entities that can be publicly sharable – he argues that Fregean analysis of "anti-psychologism" seems quite weak. Frege's argument against psychologism is actually an argument against mental concepts in particular instead of abstract entities in general.[19]

The dilemma that verificationists cherished (except Quine) is that if we admit the desirable theory of "linguistic meaning," it goes towards the adherence theory, which sounds close to "the network theory of meaning." One could emphasize that any considerable amendment of the total theory also entails a consequent change of the constituent words and statement that are associated with the theory. However, a realist does not face such a dilemma. They consider that the change of meaning does not entail a subsequent change of reference. Putnam accepts this, but worries about the claim of realism regarding references that are determined by "Platonic entities" or intensions (the mentalese approach). Rather he claims that, in science, there are some cases in which belief about the referents can change instead of the knowledge of the terms. In this case, Putnam thinks that an amendment of the implicit meaning of a term like "chlorophyll" would be unable to bring about a consequent change to the explicit belief associated with it, that being of the referent "tree." From 1960 onwards, Putnam tried to advocate a way out of the worry, for example, of how the meaning and reference of a term could assist in the development of scientific theories. Another problem is that the conception of an unchanging definition of a term that could allow its reference to be fixed cannot be error free. We find a causal and referential link between what terms refer to and its unchanging definition. In this case, the reference is fixed by the physical world and not by any mental process. This leads to Putnam's celebrated externalist plea, "Cut the pie any way you like, 'meaning' just ain't in the head."[20]

In the first case, in order to know the inner construction of a natural kind term, we do not know the paradigmatic instances of the entities through an ostensive definition or mere description of properties. Here the "stereotype" of the term can be easily perceptible, which helps to inform the speaker about the common and distinctive features of the terms that they perceive. The functionally based externalist approach that Putnam once espoused (1960–75)[21] mainly eliminates the thesis that knowing a term occurs through its mere description. For him the process of 'knowing' may be possible because of its referent and ability

---

19 Sanjit Chakraborty, *Understanding Meaning and World: A Relook on Semantic Externalism* (New Castle and London: Cambridge Scholars Publishing, 2016), 16.

20 Putnam, "The Meaning of 'Meaning'," 227.

21 Putnam, "The Psychological Predicates" and *Mind, Language and Reality: Philosophical Papers*, Vol. 2 (Cambridge: Cambridge University Press, 1975), xiii–xiv.

to use these in our linguistic systems. There is even mutual understanding and co-operation between non-professionals and the experts regarding the terms in our language use. Putnam considers the background of this co-operation as the "socio-linguistic background," which leads to a hypothesis of universality, later popularly known as the "division of linguistic labor" and which discards "knowledge as persona." Putnam adds that natural kind terms decipher to fix reference, which he says, the "shared paradigm," i.e., a kind of agreement amongst the community members. This stereotype or "shared paradigm" can partly fix the meaning of a term, while the other parts of the same paradigm may be fixed by the scientific research to find out the decisive aspect, which categorizes the reference of the natural kind term, as in the case of the term "water" which means H_2O (two hydrogen atoms bonded with one oxygen atom).

Putnam's talk about the "division of linguistic labor" in his theory of meaning considers that a speaker is fully competent in the use of language concerning the relevance of words and sentences. It illustrates that the meaning should be implicitly known, and the whole process is called the *constraint of publicity*. My understanding of Putnam makes it incumbent upon a fully competent speaker, one who has the ability to use their own words pertinently, to understand the expressions of the other members' words properly of their linguistic community. This process may depend on the subject's interaction with others in the same community who vary in interests, capacities and expertise. The practical ability of a speaker to engage in linguistic behavior may have relevance here. There will be a problem of requirement of meaning in the case of beliefs. Moreover, if any of my beliefs change, the meanings of my words will also change simultaneously. Therefore, the question would be whether the understanding of the meaning of a sentence depends on the process of understanding the general belief of the community or not. Putnam emphasizes the linguistic sense of meaning. An agent can understand the meaning of a sentence in terms of the beliefs that constitute the stereotypes being associated with the words. Here, an agent does not have to believe the stereotypes, but they should be able to recognize them *as* stereotypes. The crucial point is that for Putnam, most of the beliefs of an agent can change without any change in the meaning of an agent's word, as in the case of photosynthesis and stereotypes of trees. Another important concern is that the meaning of an agent's word does not rely on the agent themselves, but on the community they belong to. Putnam believes that if a person forgets the stereotype of a natural kind term or non-natural kind term, it does not show that the word changed its meaning. Rather, the speaker or the agent has forgotten or made a mistake about what the meaning of the word is. Now, what would be the position of words in communication? The shareability method of beliefs that remains context sensitive since it deals with the matter of common sense or the general intelligence. The idea of "grasping of meaning" in our communication is powerful but also sounds like *Platonic entities*. If we talk about the complete or partial understanding of the meaning of a term, it falls into the realm of the *Platonic idea* of understanding. Putnam considers, "Meanings are not a function of what we believe, but at most of what is stereotypical" as meaning is world involving component that the speaker possesses. That is a key point of "The Meaning of 'Meaning'."[22]

I think that ordinary people have a partial grasp of the meaning of a natural kind term like "water" or "tree," but the comprehensive grasp of the meaning of the natural kind term can only be well identified by the experts. My point is that there is a gradation of the criteria of experts or of the knowledge of experts that can be verified as it gradually increases over the course of time and social change.[23] For me, the picture of communication is relied on the meaning and I agree with Putnam that the meaning is not any entity in the *Platonic sense*. However, the communication system and the linguistic sense of using words are causally liked to the contexts and common sense of individuals. Speakers are not bound by any semantic rules. The meaning of a sentence and the content of our thoughts rely on a particular occasion of use that looks contextually sensitive with our understandings. In this sense, the idea of comprehensive grasp of meaning and the partial grasp of meaning are significant. Ordinary people, through observational properties can give an "operational definition" of a word that may go towards "context sensitivity." In this context, their understanding has various syntactic structures that are associated with the description of the sentences. Even for me, the "knowing how" process of linguistic practice is very close to context sensitivity. If we claim that the meaning is context sensitive rather than truth conditions itself (Putnam will disagree), then it would be reasonable to argue that comprehensive and partial grasp of meaning could both be possible and this thesis also leads to one of indeterminacy of meaning since we do not have any concrete idea of meaning except its reference. I am well aware that the reference fixation of a term as "water" does not hinge on the comprehensive meaning of the term "water" for a layman. In fact, the common belief and the succession of the belief procedures that we named as "reference borrowing" have taken a significant role as a prerequisite. The interesting point that Putnam raised is that "what the speakers had to be causally linked to 'is the correct extension' not the correct description of the extension. Moreover, extensions, as opposed to descriptions of extensions, are not things we grasp with our minds; they

---

22 I am indebted to Hilary Putnam for this personal correspondence.
23 Chakraborty, *The Labyrinth of Mind and World*, 122.

are out there in the world."[24] I strongly agree with his point in favor of semantic externalism, which is coping with "meaning vectors" cum "knowing how" processes in which "division of linguistic labor" along with the meaning on the constraint of publicity also take a relatable part.

A note to remember is that, here, the meaning for Putnam is "speaker's meaning" not the meaning that linguists apprehended in their own sphere. Putnam does not admit that the knowledge of one's belief and the meaning of the term are context sensitive. Let me discuss these issues in the last section of my paper, in which I focus on Putnam's position on context sensitivity.

II Putnam on Content and Context Sensitivity

A significant recent development in Putnam's philosophy has been the towards "occasion sensitive" semantics, in which content, truth and meaning play in significant roles. In this period, Putnam declined to treat content as related to the meaning of a sentence, since content is unable to determine the truth condition of the sentence. Putnam favors "truth-evaluable content,"[25] which cannot be regarded as a meaning of the sentence. The truth-evaluable content essentially assists to disambiguate the sentences on particular occasions. Putnam writes, "The thesis of contextualism is that in general the truth-evaluable content of sentences depends both on what they mean (what a competent speaker knows prior to encountering a particular context) and on the particular context, and not on meaning alone."[26] For Putnam, "truth-evaluable content" relies on context sensitivity plus speakers' meaning rather than on dictionaries' meanings, which are actually "forms of descriptions," prioritized by linguists. Meanings provided by dictionaries are incapable of resolving what exactly the "truth-evaluable content" of a sentence is in a given context. One thing is very clear here, namely that Putnam does not consider that meanings are individuated or determined by the

---

24 We have a very fascinating dialogue in detail on this issue that is available on Hilary Putnam's own blog: http://putnamphil.blogspot.com.

25 Putnam writes, "I call these understandings 'truth-evaluable contents' (this is my terminology, not Travis') because in the contexts we (very roughly) described they are typically sufficiently precise to be evaluated as true or false. (Note that even a vague sentence – 'He stood roughly there' – can often be evaluated as true or false *given an appropriate context*. But it is also the case that these 'contents' themselves admit of further specification, admit of different understandings in different contexts." Hilary Putnam, *Philosophy in an Age of Science*, edited by Mario De Caro and David Macarthur (Cambridge, MA: Harvard University Press, 2012), 497.

26 Putnam, *Philosophy in an Age of Science*, 496.

truth conditions. Putnam fixes the meaning in the sense of externalism and he thinks that the (possible) truth conditions of the sentence have changed depending on the context of the issues.

Once in a discussion, I asked Putnam, "If a person accepts the notion of content as '*shadow*,' it could not be the meaning of a sentence. Now the question is, how could it be compatible with the context?" (Since the meaning and context of use can assign a "truth-evaluable content" of a sentence as Putnam himself claimed.)

Putnam answered me that, for him, the question of meaning and context assigned to "a truth condition of a sentence" seemed extremely convoluted. Putnam said,

> To explain why, let me use an analogy. In a context (or, as Travis prefers to say, on a particular occasion of use), a noun, say, an automobile, refers to, say, particular objects that we drive, ride in, etc. But, to say that it does that because the meaning plus the context "assign a reference condition to the noun," would be to adopt a particular metaphysical picture, on which mental entities such as the empiricists' "ideas," or entities such as Husserl's "noemata" (that pertains to a supposed transcendental ego), or perhaps Platonic entities such as Frege's *Sinne* (translated as "intensions" sometimes) determine a "reference condition" whose satisfaction, in turn, determines what "automobile" refers to. This inserts a "shadow" (the "reference condition") between the noun and the automobiles. This is a pseudo-explanation. That is why Wittgenstein regarded all of these mental, or transcendental-mental, or Platonic and mental, entities as mere "shadows." We do refer to objects, including automobiles, and we have evolved so as to be able to do that.[27]

One may ask, "what is the externalist picture here?" Externalists can refer to things, but I do not think that reference conditions depend on any kind of descriptive theory. The concept of "reference" is a primitive unnaturalized function that refers to the external world. The "state of affairs" that make the sentence true can be determined by a "truth condition" that is also "assigned" by speakers' meanings and context of uses but is not grasped by mere description.[28]

For Putnam, the "state of affairs" (which Wittgenstein mentions as an external affair) are not "mental entities" or "linguistic entities" that can be understood as a sentence. Moreover, the "truth-evaluable content" cannot be considered as meanings, propositions or shadows in any sense. And, for Putnam, the phrase

---

27 I am extremely grateful to Hilary Putnam for this valuable note that he once shared with me in a personal correspondence.

28 To refute the traditional theory of meaning like Putnam I strongly believe that the truth condition of a sentence rest on the reference of the terms that is used in the sentence in a particular context or occasion through the abilities (biological and linguistic capabilities together) of the competent speakers. For further discussion of the issues, see Chakraborty, *The Labyrinth of Mind and World*.

"state of affairs" generates complexity, as he does not take "state of affairs" to stand for mental entities or meanings. Putnam refutes any description as a "state of affairs." We can take an example here; the noun "bird" can be described in different linguistic ways, but that does not show that the noun itself is bird. The point is that it can have different interpretations based on context sensitivity. Putnam suggests that we describe "truth-evaluable content" as describing the "state of affairs" that would make the speaker's utterance true on the relevant occasion.

However, one can also consider the "meaning" as an object. This means that the conception of ambiguity cannot be sited here. It looks true that some words may be ambiguous. The "truth-evaluable contents" of a sentence depend on a range of distinctive conditions of the sentence. Putnam convinced me that "truth-evaluable contents" are determined by "meaning plus context of use." In fact, the notion of "truth-evaluable content" that I label as "truth conditions" depends on the process of "knowing how," an ability that is correlated with speakers' competence and linguistic words. Meaning can be regarded as the usual linguistic sense, which is determined in terms of linguistic uses (akin to occasion sensitivity) and comprehension (sometimes it may be the conventional grasp of understanding). The difference between Putnam and me is that according to Putnam, context sensitivity is assigned with the "truth-evaluable content" and not with the meaning, but I think context sensitivity partly also depends on the meaning. I shall discuss the reason why I think that the meaning is partly context sensitive later.

Let us see what we generally think about terms. Putnam does not believe that every term is occasion sensitive. Logical words cannot be occasion sensitive, such as the essential indexical terms, as these fail to designate anything in the external world. This is undoubtedly an externalist appeal. The example that Putnam frequently offers to clarify "context sensitivity" is, "There is milk in the refrigerator."

Following Putnam's argument, the "first context" would be as follows:

> There may be no container of milk in the refrigerator now, but there may be a spill of a little milk in the refrigerator that needs to be wiped. In this sense, the sentence comes true.

The "second context" is that in which one of my family members asks me whether we have any milk to drink in the refrigerator or not. Somehow, I have forgotten that we are out of milk and reply: "There is milk in the refrigerator." Now, I am mistaken and the sentence that I said in response, is false. Even if there is a little spilled milk in the refrigerator, this does not count as milk in this context. Putnam says that the meaning cannot be regarded as context sensitive but that truth conditions are context sensitive and are determined by the meaning plus context.

You might try saying that, context sensitive truth conditions are endorsed in terms of the "reference" of the constituent terms of a sentence. Therefore, changeability of the reference in relation to context sensitivity makes "truth-evaluable contents" more context sensitive. Let us take a sentence: "there is cheese on the table." Here, "cheese" may refer only to "some edible cheese" or "some moldy cheese" or "a few grams of dehydrated cheese" etc. that has a different reference in a different sentence. Here, "common sense and the general intelligence" of a speaker can determine or understand the exact reference of the word like "cheese" in a particular context sensitive sentence. Our understanding does not have any propositionally rigid structures, but they have syntactic structures that are verified by different occasions. Therefore, the content of our thought not only depends on reference, but is also involved with reference imposed by context sensitivity. Putnam considers that the synthetic structure of a sentence like "There is milk in the refrigerator" cannot be context sensitive, as it remains the same in both the contexts. Even the two uses of milk do not illustrate a differentiation of "meaning" or in short, the different senses in any lexicon. Here, the charge of "ambiguity" is a misleading effort to put context sensitivity in the artificial box of "ambiguity." We can consider a term like "bank" as an ambiguous term as it is quite unclear if it means the bank of a river or a bank where people deposit their money. "Bank" has two different conventional linguistic senses that milk does not have. Putnam writes, "Note that the contextual variability of truth value is explained by the context sensitivity of the reference of individual words and phrases. That – reference of words in contexts – is what isn't fixed by rigid rules. The connection with externalism is that both context sensitivity and externalism attack the descriptivist picture."[29]

However, I am not satisfied with Putnam's argument. This account underlines a strategic weakness. My point can be put as follows: "How far would it be justifiable to claim that truth is 'context sensitive' in a sentence?" It seems to me that if truth takes a pertinent position in the context of meaning and their uses, then the changing of truth value can consequently result in a change in meaning. Here, the question will be "how could the 'sameness of meaning' be possible within our communication process?"

Putnam maintains a promising ploy in his previous example, "There is milk in the refrigerator," and the sentence is broadly consistent with his proclamation as it does not have diverse meanings in the mentioned two contexts. So, there is

---

29 I am thankful to Hilary Putnam for his thought-provoking analysis.

no question about its two meanings or, in my words, the changing of truth value is not the product of a change of meaning. Putnam espouses that here we will not find any change in the meaning of the term ("milk") that is directed by the "stereotypes" and the semantic markers in the mentioned two contexts. The changeability of reference in terms of context sensitivity makes "truth-evaluable contents" more occasion sensitive. Sameness of meaning could be possible due to the fixation of the speaker's meaning that copes with the "normal form of description" of the sentences that helps a speaker use the term meaningfully in linguistic communication.

The point, I think, is that Putnam introduced the idea of "truth-evaluable content" first, but the distinction as depicted by Charles Travis in relation to *the meaning of a sentence in language* and *what a speaker says by uttering the sentence on a particular occasion* is the source of Putnam's attention to "truth-evaluable content."[30] Travis and Putnam are in accord regarding the ingenious aspect of "truth-evaluable content" that does not rely on the linguistic meaning. Both of them believe in "truth-evaluable content" of speaker's meaning only, which seems beyond the meaning of the referred terms. Travis's point is that the meaning has no role to play in the case where a word comes out true. The meaning of a word imposes a condition (definite) on its truth. Travis, unwilling to accept understanding as an extract content that remains outside of circumstances as circumstances do not have any relevance to determining the required conditions of truth. The description that one has given compared to understanding words are fixed by the "circumstances." Travis inclines to give importance to a conception of 'understanding' that is bound by sensitivity, and writes, "Understanding requires sensitivity. Understanding word consists, in part, sensitivity to how they fit with the circumstances of their speaking. Part of that is sensitivity to how they need to fit in order to be true. So adequate sensitivity requires grasping what truth is, and how that notion applies in particular cases."[31] These arguments consist of some interesting traction. We can point up that the notion of understanding does not have any propositionally rigid structure, but only syntactic structure that is verified by different occasions. Therefore, the content of thought is not only relying on the reference but on the sense that is tangled to the reference enacted by context sensitivity. The description of word that sounds occasion sensitivity also correlates with the truth that depends on the truth and

---

30 Charles Travis, *The Uses of Sense: Wittgenstein's Philosophy of Language* (Oxford: Clarendon Press, 1989) and *Unshadowed Thought: Representation in Thought and Language* (Cambridge, MA: Harvard University Press, 2000).
31 Charles Travis, "Meaning's Role in Truth" (1996), reprinted in *Occasion-Sensitivity: Selected Essays* (New York: Oxford University Press, 2008), 102.

the use of words together. In short, what determines truth conditions is nothing but word meaning as understood by a speaker in a context.

III Postscript

The semantic postulates are of no avail in cases indeterminacy. Our linguistic communication has a meaning and, here, the concept of meaningfulness might play a relevant role. Otherwise, there will be a communication gap, which actually should not come up in our discourse. I may be wrong, but still I think that to explain the meaning of a sentence we should hear the speaker's verbal behavior (utterances) and consider the surrounding circumstances (context of uses). Moreover, the knowledge of the meaning of a sentence is gradually increased in epistemic situation and speakers do not know the meaning of the whole sentence or web of beliefs at a time. In support of my point Putnam once urged,

> Quine is, of course, right that there is no scientifically precise criterion for "same meaning", but he is wrong in believing that only what is scientifically precise has cognitive value, Historical hypothesis, e.g., the hypothesis that European imperialism, and particularly the struggle to acquire and retain colonies, was a primary cause of World War I, are meaningful, true or false (I believe that one is true), and justified by evidence. Quine's extreme scientism was wrong.[32]

We can follow the same approach in the context of "truth-evaluable content." The reason is that through a description of the "state of affairs," we can identify the "truth-evaluable content" of an utterance that does not lie within any sort of systematic description in a language. The science of linguistics can stress meanings as objects. However, the problem is that if we would like to describe all the possible "truth-evaluable contents," we should have to describe all human nature, which no science can reasonably do.

I do not think that the speakers are bound by any *a priori* semantic rules. The productivity of language and the causal history of content are jointly involved in a shared language. However, I am afraid to seeing that for Putnam "meanings are neither individuated by truth conditions, nor enough, on their own to determine truth conditions." How could it be possible that the endless number of possible truth conditions for the sentence "there is milk on the table" simply rely on context sensitivity rather than on the changeability of meaning of

---

32 My thanks go to Hilary Putnam for this note and analysis.

the sentence in our understanding? I think that there is a certain "change of meaning" that in the sentence according to the context and the users' capability of understanding the meaning, which may be conventional. This change can inform various possible truth conditions of the sentence, but all these are reliant on a trivial sense. Here, I think Putnam needs to clarify the idea of "sentence meaning" in his philosophy from the perspective of "word meaning." We saw that for Putnam, "truth-evaluable contents" are not meanings, propositions or shadows. For Putnam, "truth-evaluable contents" are "states of affairs" that make the speaker's utterance true on some relevant occasions by maintaining a relation to the objective world. Putnam rebuffs the notion of content on the basis of two different assumptions that I already discussed. Putnam refutes the first assumption, according to which contents are supposed to be the meaning of a sentence. Moreover, he also rejected the second assumption according to which content can determine the truth condition of sentences in all possible worlds. I appreciate his notable attempt to erase "state of affairs" from the bondage of "mental entities." However, I wonder about the relation between the "content" that he rejected and the idea of "states of affairs" that he accepted to describe the "truth-evaluable content." This looks like a puzzle leading to a contradiction. I fully believe that truth conditions of meaning can alter in terms of the context in which sentences are uttered, as truth is relative to the meaning of such sentences. Putnam thinks that truth is context sensitive. There is no question concerning further relativity, as the meaning and context are fixed. However, Putnam does not agree with my understanding, as he instead believes that "utterances have truth conditions." The change in the truth condition of the sentence, "the milk is in the refrigerator" from one content to another is not a change in the meaning but a change in the "truth-evaluable content" in the mode of asserting the sentence. It is clear that, for Putnam, "truth-evaluable content" cannot be regarded as "meaning." Putnam argues that we give meanings (in my sense) by giving what I called 'core facts' in "Is Semantics Possible?" and these can be systematized and presented in a textbook; we give the 'truth-evaluable content' of an utterance by describing the 'state of affairs' that the speaker alleges to obtain in other words. There is no systematic description of 'truth-evaluable contents' of possible utterances in a language. Meanings are objects that can be studied by the science of linguistics. To describe all the possible 'truth-evaluable contents' one would have to be able to describe all of human nature, which no science can reasonably hope to do. An internalist trend (represented chiefly by Frank Jackson) claims that the context sensitivity of meaning depends on the ambiguity of words. In his paper, "Narrow Content and Representation or Twin Earth Revisited," Jackson discusses the concept of centered world content, where the differences in the referents of our beliefs are mainly caused by the differences in the

centered as these are consistent with the sameness of the particular context.[33] Keeping Jackson's point in mind, this idea is taken to endorse a reflection on the notion of context sensitivity.

Besides, another question that I intend to mention here is the following: how could Putnam assign the truth value of a sentence, where the meaning and the context of use are covered by "shadow," understood as the "states of affairs" at an occasion sensitive condition? Putnam's speculation looks weak here. One possibility that Putnam hinted to me is that meanings do not have truth conditions. Rather, utterances have truth conditions. The change that we find in the truth conditions of a sentence like "the milk is in the refrigerator" is, nonetheless, a change from one context to another that does not entail a consequent change in meaning. Putnam argues that truth is not relative to the meaning of the uttered sentence, but rather depends on the truth-evaluable content of the utterance.

This is an intriguing point. However, I find a contradiction here that once I brought to my mentor Hilary Putnam's notice, which he highly appreciated. The argument is: If Putnam believes that 'truth-evaluable content' can be identified in terms of 'state of affairs,' we should accept, from a logical stance that 'states of affairs' are objects related to our real world. The contradiction arises because, for Putnam, contents are not objects; they are rather mental or Platonic entities that can perceive somehow be perceived by reason. In what follows, then, it would be difficult to identify "truth-evaluable content" in terms of "states of affairs." During the last few months of his life, a moving target philosopher like Putnam was working to find out a solution to this problem. Unfortunately, however on March 13, 2016 time stopped the genius's thought.

33 Frank Jackson, "Narrow Content and Representation – or Twin Earth Revisited," *Proceedings of the American Philosophical Association* 77, no. 2 (2003): 55–71.

Sanford C. Goldberg

Externalism and the First-Person Perspective

Abstract: In "The Meaning of 'Meaning'," Putnam presented an argument on behalf of an externalist approach to linguistic meaning. In due course, this argument was extended to support externalism in the philosophy of mind as well. In this paper I argue that this extension has significant implications for how we are to understand the notion of a subject's point of view.

I

Putnam's "The Meaning of 'Meaning'" presented a bold thesis about linguistic meaning. We might formulate this as the thesis of *Linguistic Externalism* (LE), according to which the meanings of expressions of a speaker's language depend on factors 'external to' the speaker herself. Somewhat more explicitly, LE claims that

LE For all languages L and speakers S of L, there are some expressions e of L for which the standing meaning of e as used by S does not supervene on S's bodily states.

Putnam himself did not explicitly state that this was true for all languages and speakers. But several considerations suggest that this captures his intention. For one thing, he presented the Twin Earth thought experiment as involving a subject, Oscar, who could be any human person – thereby allowing for an implicit generality in what is claimed about Oscar. For another, he theorized about a kind of terms – *natural kind terms* – that we might think are present in any human language. In addition, in the latter part of the paper Putnam advanced the hypothesis of the Division of Linguistic Labor, which is a hypothesis about human language itself – all human language. Consequently, it seems that he had in mind an implicit generality for the claim he made about language, precisely as LE has it.

Two important clarifications and comments were needed in order to appreciate the full significance of LE itself.

First, while Putnam's argument was pointed to a dependence of linguistic meaning on context, this dependence is not like the sort of dependence one finds in connection with such straightforwardly context-sensitive expressions as indexicals and demonstratives – Putnam's own original thinking to the

https://doi.org/10.1515/9783110769210-005

contrary notwithstanding. Putnam himself was tempted by the thought that we can disaggregate the meaning of the relevant sorts of expressions (those of which LE is true) into a component that could be specified independently of context and a component that had to be specified in context, much in the way that we might think to specify the meaning of "I" as involving a context-independent element (the semantic rule to the effect that a use of "I" refers to the person who produced the token) and a context-specific element (i.e., a specification of the particular person who produced the relevant token of "I"). Subsequent authors – most prominently, Gareth Evans, John McDowell, and Tyler Burge – argued that this was not the way to understand the meaning of an expression like "water."[1] Using a distinction introduced by Saul Kripke, we might put the point as follows: the features that subjects use to *fix the reference* of an expression is not (or at least not necessarily) part of *the meaning* of the expression, as the latter is given simply in terms of the contribution of the use of an expression to the truth conditions of sentences in which the expression figures (or the statements made by the use of such sentences).

Second, while Putnam himself had restricted his claims in "The Meaning of 'Meaning'" to linguistic meaning and natural language, many philosophers came to hold that his reflections bore on mental content and thought as well – once again, his comments to the contrary in that article notwithstanding. In that paper, Putnam wrote as if the two doppelgängers meant different things with their respective uses of "water" *despite being in the same (type of) psychological state*. Subsequent authors went on to argue that we do best to see Putnam's point about the individuation of linguistic meaning carrying over to bear on the individuation of (the mental content of) the propositional attitudes. Consequently, they endorsed what we might call an Attitude Externalism (AE), according to which the contents of a subject's attitudes – and hence the attitudes themselves – depend on factors 'external to' the subject herself. More specifically, AE is the thesis that

AE For all subjects of the propositional attitudes S, there are some attitudes A of S's which are such that the fact that S instantiates A does not supervene on the facts constituting S's bodily states.

AE captures what has come to be known as "Externalism" in the philosophy of mind.

---

1 Although it is worth noting that versions of so-called two-dimensionalist semantics have tried to recover this idea of a two-component analysis of the meaning of the relevant terms.

In what follows I will be embracing these clarifications as constituting the core of an externalist position in the philosophy of mind and language. Consequently, I will be assuming that both LE and AE are true, and that they are understood as just described. My interest will be in drawing out an implication of these views. Since my implication will concern the nature of a point of view, I want to begin by developing some (I hope, familiar) thoughts regarding what it is to have a point of view.

II

As subjects, each of us occupies a distinctive point of view on the world. Without doing violence to this idea, we might identify one's point of view with one's cognitive or epistemic perspective on the world.

I submit that there are two familiar ways of conceiving of what it is to have a point of view – what it is to have an epistemic perspective on the world.

The first conception is *spatial* to have a point of view – an epistemic perspective on the world – is to occupy a particular spatial location at every moment at which one exists. As a corollary, we can trace one's point of view by following that spatial location across time.

The second conception is *informational*: to have a point of view – an epistemic perspective on the world – is to be such that one's cognitive life can be represented as an ever-evolving stock of information resident "in" one's information-processing system. Here, one's information-processing system is taken to be a system that
(1) starts off with some information (though it could be empty at the outset as well),
(2) acquires new information,
(3) stores, retrieves, and manipulates the information it has acquired,
(4) updates its informational state when new information comes in, and
(5) draws inferences from that information.

If we wish, we can add that all of this is at least partly in the service of action. As a corollary, we can capture the evolution of one's epistemic perspective over time by keeping track of changes in the overall informational state of the system over time.

While these two conceptions are distinct, it is natural to suppose that they fit nicely together. One's position in space determines the novel empirical information one acquires, and so, assuming that one's position in space is the position of a cognitive subject (with its own cognitive capacities for acquiring, storing, retrieving, and manipulating information), we can regard the spatial conception as spelling out how the information-processing system itself acquires new (empirical) information. This, of course, is the task of a theory of sensation and perception.

There is no particular reason to doubt that these two conceptions can be combined to form a seamless whole. At the same time, these conceptions encourage a fuller picture which itself will be the target of my reflections. We reach this fuller picture by adding two further assumptions into the mix. The first is the identification of the informational system itself with the occupant of a particular position in space (or space-time): the informational system just is a physical system that traces a spatial position through time. The second is the reduction of novel empirical information to what has causal impact on that physical system. According to this second assumption, empirical information can be exhaustively characterized in terms of changes pertaining to the physical system in question. If we put these two additional assumptions together, we reach the idea that *one's point of view can be exhaustively captured in terms of the spatial position one occupies, the initial state of one's cognitive system, together with all of the physical goings-on within that system that reflect the (history of the) causal impacts of the surrounding world.*

I suspect that this is a familiar conception of what it is to have a point of view over time. It suggests the metaphysical independence of one's point of view from the world around one, including the social world around one. Although such a view can allow for the *causal* relevance of items in one's environment (including other people) to one's epistemic perspective, in principle this exhausts their relevance. We might summarize this familiar conception by characterizing the status of everything beyond the physical occupant of the spatial position itself. Where S is the subject in question, anything beyond the physical boundaries of S is (on this picture) of *merely causal relevance* to S's mind and language.

It is by now familiar that AE poses a central challenge to this conception. If AE is true, then we should reject this thesis of merely causal relevance: the objects and properties in one's environment, and/or the other subjects in one's language community, are *metaphysically* relevant to a characterization of one's mental life. This is a point long recognized.

But what I think we have failed to appreciate is the bearing of this on our understanding of a point of view as our epistemic perspective on the world. In particular, once we appreciate the challenge AE poses to the traditional conception of a point of view, we must also recognize that it challenges the standard conception of the *autonomous epistemic subject*. As I say, it is a familiar lesson of AE that the materials that go into one's cognitive/epistemic perspective – the concepts that compose to form the mental content of our attitudes – cannot be specified in a way that is independent of all features of the subject's environment. Even for those who grant this, however, it can be tempting to suppose that there remains a sphere of our mental life that, though it involves information and content, nevertheless remains beyond the reach of the sorts of considerations that motivate AE. The temptation might be put in terms of the distinction between concepts and conceptions: whereas our concepts (or many of them, at any rate) are "externalist" in nature, our *conceptions* remain our own, unaffected by the sorts of "externalist" considerations relevant to one's concepts. What I want to claim is that this alleged sphere of individual autonomy – this last "refuge" of individualism in the philosophy of mind – is itself a target of Putnam's reflections, properly understood. In particular, I want to argue that if AE is true, then insofar as we think of a subject's conceptions – how she conceives of things – as the materials out of which we construct her epistemic perspective on the world, then we should not think that *how she conceives of things* can be specified independent of the world in which she lives and of the linguistic community of which she is a part.[2] On the contrary, AE suggests that the facts that individuate how one conceives of things, like the facts that individuate the concepts through which one thinks, do not supervene on individualistic facts. In this way, the idea of the autonomous epistemic subject is in even bigger trouble than many have realized.

III

As I say, it is tempting to think of one's point of view – one's epistemic perspective on the world – as a domain whose layout is metaphysically (though not causally) independent of the world itself. I will call this tempting view *Metaphysical Independence of One's Point of View*, or MIPOV for short. Why would one

---

2 I have presented several arguments for conclusions in this vicinity; see Sanford Goldberg, "Do Anti-Individualistic Construals of the Attitudes Capture the Agent's Conceptions?" *Noûs* 36, no. 4 (2002): 597–621; *Anti-Individualism: Mind and Language, Knowledge and Justification* (Cambridge: Cambridge University Press, 2007); "Anti-Individualism, Content Preservation, and Discursive Justification," *Noûs* 41 (2007): 178–203; "Experts, Semantic and Epistemic," *Noûs* 43, no. 4 (2009): 581–598; "Anti-Individualism, Comprehension, and Self-Knowledge," in *Externalism, Self-Knowledge, and Skepticism*, edited by Sanford Goldberg, 184–194 (Cambridge: Cambridge University Press, 2015).

endorse MIPOV? I believe that MIPOV derives its apparent support from two separate, but ultimately related, types of consideration. The first type reflects an "inward"-looking orientation. On this score, MIPOV might be thought to be motivated by focusing on how a subject is epistemically related to her own point of view. Here we find characteristic arguments for something in the neighborhood of MIPOV from the nature of one's self-knowledge of – or first-person authority regarding – the materials that constitute one's point of view, namely, one's attitudes (doxastic and otherwise). The second type of consideration that can be used to support MIPOV appeals to the very notion of a *conception*. Here we find characteristic motivations for something in the neighborhood of MIPOV from how one takes the world to be. It is thought that unless we capture how a subject is "conceiving of" the various objects and properties in her world, we will fail to capture how she takes the world to be; and it is thought that we cannot capture an agent's conceptions if these are held to vary with variations in the properties and objects in the world itself (including properties of others' mental states and linguistic acts). I say that these are two "separable" sources of would-be support for MIPOV; but after presenting each, I will argue that they derive from a common source. This is the common assumption that the materials that constitute a subject's point of view cannot do what is expected of them – cannot constitute part of her epistemic perspective on the world – unless these materials are such that, by their very nature, all of their attitudinal- and content-relevant features are discernible by the subject from her armchair.

Let us begin with the "inward"-focused motivation (or alleged motivation) for MIPOV. This one should be familiar to anyone who followed the literature on Attitude Externalism (AE) in the 80s, 90s, and early 2000s, since it is intimately related to the debates regarding the compatibility of AE and first-person authority. To be sure, that debate rarely made an explicit connection between first-person authority or self-knowledge and the subject's point of view,[3] but it appears to have been premised on the idea that accounting for the former is an essential task for any adequate understanding of the latter. In a nutshell, the basic line of argument (which I will call The *Argument from Inwardness*) is this:

---

3 Katalin Farkas, *The Subject's Point of View* (Oxford: Oxford University Press, 2008) stands as an exception to the rule.

Premise 1_{Inw} Having a point of view involves having an epistemic perspective on the world.

Premise 2_{Inw} One's epistemic perspective on the world is constituted (at least in part) by how one mentally represents the world, how one takes it (in thought) to be.

Premise 3_{Inw} One's mental representations form the background against which one assesses new information and from which one reasons to further conclusions.

Premise 4_{Inw} One's mental representations can't play this role unless one can discern from the armchair what one is committed to when one represents the world in this way.

Premise 5_{Inw} If Attitude Externalism is true, then there are cases in which one mentally represents the world in a certain way, yet one cannot discern from the armchair what one is committed to when one represents the world in this way.

Conclusion$_{Inw}$ Attitude Externalism fails to capture the subject's point of view.

The familiar debate over the compatibility of AE and first-person authority/self-knowledge was focused, of course, on Premise 5_{Inw}: so-called incompatibilists endorsed this premise and tried to provide arguments for it,[4] while so-called compatibilists denied it and tried to show that appearances to the contrary could be explained away. But it was not merely an interest in the truth-value of Premise 5_{Inw} that brought the compatibilist debate to the attention of the philosophical community in the two decades after Putnam's "Meaning of 'Meaning'";[5] it was the (perhaps implicit) worry that if that premise is true, then Attitude Externalism is in trouble *for failing to be able to capture the subject's point of view*. The aim of the Argument from Inwardness is to bring out this charge.

---

4 A particularly explicit set of arguments to this effect can be found in Åsa Wikforss, "Social Externalism and Conceptual Errors," *The Philosophical Quarterly* 51, no. 203 (2001): 217–231; "Externalism and Incomplete Understanding," *The Philosophical Quarterly* 54, no. 215 (2004): 287–294; "Self-Knowledge and Knowledge of Content," *Canadian Journal of Philosophy* 38, no. 3 (2008): 399–424; "Semantic Externalism and Psychological Externalism," *Philosophy Compass* 3, no. 1 (2008): 158–181.
5 Hilary Putnam, "The Meaning of 'Meaning'," in *Mind, Language and Reality: Philosophical Papers*, Vol. 2, 215–271 (Cambridge: Cambridge University Press, 1975).

Each of the premises in the argument can seem very plausible. Premise 1_{Inw} simply spells out what we have in mind when we speak of a subject's "point of view"; it should be common ground to all parties. Premise 2_{Inw} seems unexceptional: whatever else is involved in having a point of view, it involves how one takes the world to be; and it is natural to think that this is captured in how one represents the world in thought. This premise could do without talk of mental representation altogether; talk of thought would suffice (so long as we made corresponding adjustments to the subsequent premises). Premise 3_{Inw} seems to be a truth of human psychology, or perhaps of all of cognitive psychology more generally (whether of human subjects or other cognitive non-human subjects): our mental representations constitute the stock of information we have about our world, and it is this information that guides us as we assess new incoming information (for plausibility or coherence with our background beliefs), update our beliefs and credences to reflect new evidence, and reason from the information we currently have to draw new conclusions about our world. To be sure, this premise appears to be rather intellectualist in orientation: a good deal of our information-processing is done subcognitively. But it would seem that even here our cognitive systems are sensitive to our background information: we don't accept the perceptual appearances, and we refrain from making certain judgments or drawing certain inferences, if something doesn't seem right – even when we can't articulate what it is that isn't proper.[6] Premise 4_{Inw} might initially seem controversial, but it does capture a highly intuitive point: if a subject S fails to appreciate what she is committed to when she mentally represents the world as she does, it would seem that she is not in a position to know what inferences to draw, nor is she in a position to determine how this information bears on new information coming in to the system. To be sure, this point may be moot for the information-processing done at the subcognitive level: arguably, *she* need not be in a position to discern precisely what she is committed to in mentally representing the world as she does, in order for *her cognitive system* to "draw" the relevant inferences or update in the relevant ways. But even if this is so, still, at the level of conscious thought and inference, the premise would stand. And insofar as we are thinking of her "point of view," we must include her conscious thought and inferences. So the premise seems defensible

---

6 The psychology and epistemology of this is described in Kent Bach, "A Rationale for Reliabilism," *The Monist* 68, no. 2 (1985): 246–263 and Cristina Bicchieri, *The Grammar of Society: The Nature and Dynamics of Social Norms* (Cambridge: Cambridge University Press, 2006), Chapter 1. Sanford Goldberg ("The Psychology and Epistemology of Self-Knowledge," *Synthese* 118, no. 2 (1999): 165–199) uses these considerations to raise worries for leading theories of self-knowledge.

after all. And as I said, Premise 5_{Inw} was the issue in the compabilist debate in the 1980s–2000s; the very persistence of that debate suggests that this premise is thought plausible by a good many philosophers. (Precisely why is something I will get to below, when I consider the second, "outward"-focused source of would-be support for MIPOV.)

The thrust of the argument above is that one's point of view must have as its constitutive components mental representations, where the content features of these must be discernible from the armchair – on pain of not being able to play the cognitive roles they are tasked with playing. As I say, the orientation of this argument is "inward"-looking: it is asking what relation must we have to our own thoughts if these are to play to roles we regard them as playing in our epistemic lives. And I suspect that something like the argument above motivates many to conclude, with MIPOV, that one's point of view – one's epistemic perspective on the world – is a domain whose layout is metaphysically independent of the world itself. Such a view can and should allow that this domain is *causally* affected by the world; but its proponents will insist that the dependence of our point of view on the world is merely causal.

This is not the only route to MIPOV; there is also the route that runs through the notion of a subject's *conceptions*. The basic idea behind this route is as follows. A subject's point of view – her epistemic perspective on the world – is captured by how she takes things to be, where this is to be understood in the broadest sense (as including the entirety of her doxastic system). We might then understand "how a subject takes things to be" as consisting of the totality of her "takings," where these are doxastic attitudes whose contents are composed of concepts as constituents – roughly, her beliefs about the world.[7] We might then introduce "conceptions" as designating the way that the subject comprehends these constituents in turn – that is, how she "grasps" or "understands" the concepts that figure in her first-order beliefs or takings. The distinction between concepts and conceptions would then hold out the possibility for a distinction between how the subject represents the world in thought – that is, how she takes it to be – and how she comprehends her own representations, that is, what she takes her own first-order takings to amount to. Insofar as we theorists want to understand how a subject understands her world, it is not unreasonable on such a picture to think that it is at the level of the subject's conceptions – how she conceives of the world, where this is determined by (i) how she takes things to be

---

7 I suspect that a version of this picture could be developed where we treat credences or degrees of belief as basic. My points here are semantic, not epistemic, so this difference between beliefs and credences need not detain us here.

and (ii) how she understands *those very takings* – at which we most fundamentally characterize the subject's point of view, her epistemic perspective on things. To reach the conclusion of MIPOV, the strategy would then be to argue that the level of conceptions is a level of description of the subject's mind that is metaphysically independent of how things are.

To articulate the relevant sense of "metaphysically independent," as well as to capture why one might think this, consider the following argument for a qualified "autonomous" account of how a subject conceives of things. The argument (which I will designate as the *Argument from the Nature of Conceiving*) would go something like this:

Premise 1_{Cn} A subject's point of view must include how she is conceiving of the various objects and properties in her world.

Premise 2_{Cn} How a subject conceives of things depends on how she takes them to be.

Premise 3_{Cn} At least on those occasions on which she accepts or presupposes that how things seem to her is indicative of how they are, how a subject takes things to be is determined by how things seem to her, how they appear to her to be.

Premise 4_{Cn} Even in the restricted set of cases in which a subject accepts or presupposes that how things seem to her is indicative of how they are, how things seem to her how they appear to her to be – can be held fixed, even as we radically vary the nature of the world around her.

Conclusion$_{Cn}$ At least in the relevant restricted set of cases, how a subject conceives of things can be held fixed, even as we radically vary the nature of the world around her.

In a nutshell: how a subject conceives of the world is a matter of how she grasps or understands her own mental representations of the world; in a broad set of cases these representations are determined by the world's appearances; but we can hold the appearances fixed while varying the underlying reality; so at least in this set of cases, how a subject conceives of the world is metaphysically independent of the nature of that world.

Now I suspect that many philosophers will endorse some version of this sort of argument. Stronger still, I suspect that there are some who endorse a stronger (non-qualified) version of this argument.[8] In any case each of the premises can appear to be plausible. Premise 1_{Cn} seems truistic: insofar as we think of *conceivings* as capturing how a subject is thinking about the objects and properties she represents in thought, it seems uncontestable that these will be relevant to her point of view. It is hard to see how one could deny this. Premise 2_{Cn}, the claim that how a subject conceives of things depends on how she takes them to be, can be taken to reflect what, by definition, conceptions are: they are the things we theorists postulate to represent how a subject understands or comprehends her own "takings." Here we can think of "takings" as (doxastically endorsed) mental representations whose constituents are concepts. If we put these points together, it follows trivially that how a subject conceives of things depends on how she takes them to be, since conceivings just are the way that the subject understands the concepts constituting her takings. It seems, then, that Premise 2_{Cn} should be granted by anyone who goes in for the traditional distinction between concepts and conceptions in the first place.

Premise 3_{Cn} would also appear to be a truism. It holds that, in a restricted set of cases, how a subject takes things to be is determined by how things seem to her, how they appear to her to be. The restriction is to those cases in which the subject accepts or presupposes that how things seem to her is indicative of how they are. Given this restriction, the premise appears to be truistic: when one regards the appearances as veridical, the appearances themselves determine how one takes things to be (in that respect).

Premise 4_{Cn} is the most controversial of the premises. It contends that, in the restricted set of cases just described, how things seem to a subject – how they appear to her to be – can be held fixed, even as we radically vary the nature of

---

8 See e.g. Farkas, *The Subject's Point of View*; Katelin Farkas, "Phenomenal Intentionality without Compromise," *The Monist* 91, no. 2 (2008): 273–293; Katelin Farkas, "Constructing a World for the Senses," in *Phenomenal Intentionality*, edited by Uriah Kriegel, 99–115 (Oxford: Oxford University Press, 2013); Terence Horgan and John Tienson, "The Intentionality of Phenomenology and the Phenomenology of Intentionality," in *Philosophy of Mind: Classical and Contemporary Readings*, edited by David Chalmers, 520–533 (Oxford: Oxford University Press, 2002); Terence Horgan, John Tienson and George Graham, "Phenomenal Intentionality and the Brain in a Vat," in *The Externalist Challenge*, edited by Richard Schantz, 297–317 (Berlin: De Gruyter, 2004); Terence Horgan, "Original Intentionality Is Phenomenal Intentionality," *The Monist* 96, no. 2 (2013): 232–251; Uriah Kriegel, "Is Intentionality Dependent upon Consciousness?" *Philosophical Studies* 116 (2003): 271–230; Uriah Kriegel, "Intentional Inexistence and Phenomenal Intentionality," *Philosophical Perspectives* 21, no. 1 (2007): 307–340; Uriah Kriegel, *The Sources of Intentionality* (Oxford: Oxford University Press, 2014); Uriah Kriegel, "The Phenomenal Intentionality Research Program," in *Phenomenal Intentionality*, edited by Uriah Kriegel, 1–26 (Oxford: Oxford University Press, 2013).

the world around her. That such a claim is controversial is unsurprising especially in the present context; below I will argue that proponents of Attitude Externalism (AE) should reject it. But before arguing for this, it is worth noting what Premise 4_{Cn} has going for it, as I suspect that it continues to exert a power over many philosophers' intuitions on these matters. Indeed, it appears to have exerted its power over Putnam in 1976, since (as noted above) he himself sharply distinguished the contents of a person's psychological states from the linguistic meanings of her words, and he appeared to use something like the subject's conceptions to do so. In what follows, then, I want to suggest the various things that can be said on behalf of Premise 4_{Cn}.

Perhaps the most obvious thing that can be said on behalf of this premise is that it appears to capture something about the nature of the appearances themselves. Everyone will agree that how things appear can come apart from how they (really) are. For this reason it can seem plausible to suppose that, while how things appear is *causally* related to how things are, this causal relation is itself a contingent fact; and accordingly it can seem plausible to suppose as well that, for this very reason, *things could have been otherwise* (i.e., with the appearances floating free of reality). That is, it can seem plausible, given the rift between appearance and reality, that the former can be held fixed, varying the latter radically. This is a familiar idea whose most vivid portrayal is the Cartesian Evil Demon.

Indeed, this first point appears to suggest a second consideration that can be offered in defense of Premise 4_{Cn}. When it comes to the appearances, *there is no appearance/reality gap*: what you "see" is what you get. Reality itself, of course, is not like this: the visual appearances can be misleading as to how things really are. But then it seems just obvious that we can vary things along the reality parameter in ways that are not reflected in the appearances. And this is but a short distance to Premise 4_{Cn} itself: in those cases in which the subject takes the appearances to be veridical, how things seem to a subject – how they appear to her to be – can be held fixed, even as we radically vary the nature of the world around her.

Given what has been said on behalf of Premise 4_{Cn}, the critic of externalist approaches to mentality makes a strategically good move when she pursues her case by focusing on the appearances. To see this, consider the argumentative burden on externalism's critic if she chooses to argue for a conclusion, not about the appearances, but about belief. In that case, Putnam's critic would need to argue that externalist construals do not capture the subject S's point of view because such construals do not capture *what S believes*. This appears to play right into the hands of those who would defend the externalist conclusion of Putnam's "The Meaning of 'Meaning'." After all, from S's point of view she has come to believe things regarding the natural (liquid) kind she observes; so, assuming that S aims in her belief to represent the natural liquid kind she observes *as* the natural (liquid) kind that it is – something we can build into the thought experiment itself – it appears that externalist construals of S's belief contents are *precisely* what we need if we aim to capture her point of view. On the other hand, if Putnam's opponent presents a counterargument focusing, not on belief, but on the appearances, then she would appear to be in a much stronger dialectical position. For she can then appeal to the appearances – to how things strike S – to argue as follows. S's point of view is determined by these appearances (when S herself takes them to be veridical); but these appearances can be held fixed even as we vary how things are in the world; so S's point of view can be invariant over how things are in the world; so any construal of her point of view that fails to appreciate this is deficient. It is noteworthy that if Putnam's opponent *does* make this sort of argument, she can *concede* that S aims to represent the natural (liquid) kind as the natural (liquid) kind that it is, and so she can go on to allow that S's belief involves the concept WATER; her point would then be that S's WATER-involving beliefs fail to capture S's point of view, for failing to capture *how she conceives* of the liquid S herself represents with the concept WATER. (Of course, Putnam's proponent may prefer not to be so concessive; she may opt instead to deny that S has any WATER-involving beliefs in the first place.)

As I say, I have little doubt but that something like the argument above continues to exert tremendous power on the thought of many philosophers of mind.[9] It is not hard to appreciate why. Doing so allows Putnam's opponent to make the case against AE without having to deny what many people have found plausible about externalism – namely, the idea that we *do* seek to mentally represent natural kinds as the (objective) kinds they are. What the concessive position just described makes clear is that one can retain such a view while still holding on to the idea that, even so, such construals fail to capture the subject's point of view, as they fail to capture *how she conceives of those kinds*. On such a view, it is the agent's conceptions, rather than her concepts, that constitute the building-blocks of her point of view – of her epistemic perspective on the world.

---

9 Arguably, something like it lies behind the recent development of so-call two-dimensionalist (2D) semantics. Such views aim to do justice to Putnam's verdicts while simultaneously capturing something close to what I am calling the subject's conceptions, where these reflect the appearances. Their proposal is to model all of this in two dimensions, one reflecting the context of interpretation, the other the context of evaluation.

Or so it might be tempting to think. I now want to suggest that, if successful, Putnam's 1976 argument undermines this possibility.

IV

Putnam's "The Meaning of 'Meaning' presents a challenge to both the "inward"-oriented motivation, and the "conception"-involving motivation, for MIPOV (the thesis asserting the Metaphysical Independence of One's Point of View). In this section I develop and defend this contention.

IV.1

Let us begin with the "inward"-oriented argument for MIPOV. Metaphysical Independence of One's Point of View (MIPOV). Here it is tempting to make short shrift of the task of rebutting the argument. To do so we might note that Premise 5_{Inw}, according to which

> If Attitude Externalism is true, then there are cases in which one mentally represents the world in a certain way, yet one cannot discern from the armchair what one is committed to when one represents the world in this way.

has been rebutted by those defending the compatibility of SE and first-person authority/self-knowledge. Still, for reasons that should emerge shortly, it is worthwhile pointing out the general lessons that emerged from the compatibilism dispute.

Burge aimed to defend the compatibility of AE and first-person authority.[10] He argued that one manifests authoritative, groundless self-knowledge of one's occurrent thoughts in the very act of self-ascribing those thoughts. The judgments one makes in such an act are self-verifying, as one thinks the thought in the very act of self-ascribing it, and so the very external conditions that go into determining one's first-order thought also go into determining one's self-ascription of that thought. However, doubts regarding Burge's argumentative strategy emerged. Some argued

---

10 Tyler Burge, "Individualism and Self-Knowledge," *Journal of Philosophy* 85, no.1 (1988): 649–663.

that it could not be generalized to cases beyond occurrent thoughts;[11] others were concerned that if successful this strategy proved too much, as it appeared to pave the way for an armchair proof of the existence of empirical properties.[12] On this score the critics of Burge's strategy[13] endorsed common diagnosis: they held that any account on which the individuation of thought involves *relational* properties will be incompatible with the doctrine of first-person authority.

However, it appears that these worries failed to appreciate the power of Burge's model,[14] or else they misconstrued the substance of the knowledge one was manifesting in the self-verifying judgment Burge had described.[15] Once we appreciate this, we see that the defender of AE is in a position from which to deny Premise 5_{Inw} of the Argument from Inwardness. In particular, AE does nothing to jeopardize the idea that whenever a subject S mentally represents the world in a certain way, S can discern from the armchair what she is committed to in mentally representing the world in this way. To be sure, what S discerns from the armchair is the very thing she self-ascribes in the self-verifying judgments Burge had characterized; this is not sufficient to enable her to distinguish the thought she has from the thought she would have had if the world had been different. Still, S's discernment does amount to "minimal" self-knowledge[16] of an item that partially constitutes her point of view – her epistemic perspective on the world. This is to say that such a model captures the sense in which S's mental representations provide the background against which S assesses new information and from which S reasons to further conclusions.

---

11 See e.g. Paul Boghossian, "Content and Self-Knowledge," *Philosophical Topics* 17, no. 1 (1989): 5–26.

12 This was owed to Michael McKinsey, "Anti-Individualism and Privileged Access," *Analysis* 51, no. 1 (1991): 9–16. For discussions and responses, see Sarah Sawyer, "The Epistemic Divide," *Southern Journal of Philosophy* 39, no. 3 (2001): 385–401 and Jessica Brown, *Anti-Individualism and Knowledge* (Cambridge: MIT Press, 2004); and see Lisa Miracchi, "Perspectival Externalism is the Antidote for Radical Skepticism," *Episteme* 14, no. 3 (2017): 363–379 for a recent defense of the use of externalism as a response to radical skepticism.

13 These critics include not only Boghossian, "Content and Self-Knowledge," and "Externalism and Inference," *Philosophical Issues* 2 (1992): 11–28, but also Laurence Bonjour, "Is Thought a Symbolic Process?" *Synthese* 89, no. 3 (1991): 331–352.

14 This is a theme explored in Sarah Sawyer, "In Defense of Burge's Thesis," *Philosophical Studies* 107, no. 2 (2002): 109–128 and in Sanford Goldberg, "The Dialectical Context of Boghossian's Memory Argument," *Canadian Journal of Philosophy* 35, no. 1 (2005): 135–148.

15 See Sanford Goldberg, "What Do You Know When You Know Your Own Thoughts?" in *New Essays on Semantic Externalism and Self-Knowledge*, edited by Susana Nuccetelli, 241–256 (Cambridge, MA: MIT Press, 2003) and "Anti-Individualism, Conceptual Omniscience, and Skepticism," *Philosophical Studies* 116, no. 1 (2003): 53–78.

16 See Goldberg, "Anti-Individualism, Comprehension, and Self-Knowledge."

And while some have doubted that this enables us to understand the role one's mental representations play in inference,[17] others pointed out that this fails to appreciate the resources available to proponents of SE with which to explain undetected vacillation in one's reasoning.[18]

Reflecting on the history of this debate, I submit that we can easily overstate what is involved in characterizing a subject's point of view. In particular, it is tempting to dismiss Burge's model of self-knowledge of content, as not providing for the grasp one has of the elements of one's own epistemic perspective. To be sure, those who give in to this temptation will acknowledge that what more is needed requires further clarification; but they will regard this as further work to be done in the metaphysics of mind. Insofar as we bring the tempting point itself to bear on issues of mental content, the further work involves articulating the reflectively accessible materials out of which the metaphysician reconstructs the mental world of the subject. This, of course, is a familiar project, from the proponents of phenomenal intentionality[19] to the proponents of 2D semantics.[20] But I believe that this project is misguided, in that it is based on a false presupposition concerning the nature of one's grasp of one's own concepts. Interestingly, we can illuminate the falsity of this presupposition by considering the second of the two motivations for MIPOV, which appeals to how a subject is conceiving of the objects and properties in her world.

---

17 See Boghossian "Externalism and Inference," 11–28.

18 See e.g. Goldberg, "Individualism, Content Preservation, and Discursive Justification."

19 See e.g. Farkas, *The Subject's Point of View*, "Phenomenal Intentionality without Compromise," "Constructing a World for the Sense"; Horgan and Tienson, "The Intentionality of Phenomenology and the Phenomenology of Intentionality"; Horgan, Tiensen, and Graham, "Phenomenal Intentionality and the Brain in a Vat"; Horgan, "Original Intentionality Is Phenomenal Intentionality"; Brian Loar, "Phenomenal Intentionality as the Basis of Mental Content," *Reflections and Replies: Essays on the Philosophy of Tyler Burge*, edited by Martin Hahn and B. Ramberg, 229–258 (Cambridge: MIT Press); Kriegel, "Intentional Inexistence and Phenomenal Intentionality," "The Phenomenal Intentionality Research Program," *The Sources of Intentionality*.

20 See e.g. Frank Jackson, *From Metaphysics to Ethics: A Defence of Conceptual Analysis* (Oxford: Oxford University Press, 1998); David Chalmers and Frank Jackson, "Conceptual Analysis and Reductive Explanation," *The Philosophical Review* 110, no. 3 (2001): 315–360; David Chalmers, "Epistemic Two-Dimensional Semantics," *Philosophical Studies* 118, no. 1 (2004): 153–226 and "The Foundations of Two-Dimensional Semantics," in *Two-Dimensional Semantics: Foundations and Applications*, edited by Manuel Garcia-Carpintero and Josep Macia, 55–140 (Oxford: Oxford University Press, 2006).

IV.2

Moving on to that motivation, I want to begin by granting Premises 1_{Cn}, 2_{Cn}, and 3_{Cn} of the argument. My target will be Premise 4_{Cn}, which I repeat here:

> Even in the restricted set of cases in which a subject accepts or presupposes that how things seem to her is indicative of how they are, how things seem to her – how they appear to her to be – can be held fixed, even as we radically vary the nature of the world around her.

My case against Premise 4_{Cn} will proceed as follows. First, I appeal to a claim that Putnam's opponent might otherwise want to be able to grant – namely, that in thought we sometimes aim to mentally represent objective kinds as the objective kinds that they are. After showing how this claim can be used in an argument against Premise 4_{Cn}, I will go on to argue that if Putnam's opponent responds by denying this claim, she plays into the hands of Putnam's defender. Finally, I will go on to suggest why Premise 4_{Cn} was thought plausible in the first place, and show how what is correct in Premise 4_{Cn} can be captured within a thoroughgoing externalist approach to the mind.

Consider the claim that we sometimes aim in thought to mentally represent objective kinds as the objective kinds that they are. As I noted above, this is a claim that even Putnam's opponent might want to grant. Doing so appears to put her in a position from which she can concede the thrust of Putnam's argument for AE without having to grant that externalist construals capture a subject's point of view. That is, she might grant that such thoughts have an "externalist" content, yet deny that this "externalist" content captures how the subject herself is conceiving of things. On the further (plausible) assumption that how the subject is conceiving of things is the level at which we characterize her point of view, Putnam's critic would then be in a position from which to deny that externalist construals capture the subject's point of view.

However, appearances are deceptive here. For once Putnam's opponent grants that we sometimes aim in thought to mentally represent objective kinds as the objective kinds that they are, she is susceptible to the following argument:

Premise 1* Subjects sometimes aim in thought to mentally represent objective kinds as the objective kinds that they are.

Premise 2* Mental representations are composed of concepts.

Premise 3* If a subject S employs concept C, aiming thereby to represent a kind as an objective kind, S will understand C (if only implicitly) as purporting to represent an objective kind.

Premise 4*   If a subject (perhaps implicitly) understands a concept as purporting to represent an objective kind, she will understand that concept as purporting to pick out an objective property (or a property
which is a construction out of some objective properties).

Conclusion₁*   If subjects aim in thought to mentally represent objective kinds
as the objective kinds that they are, then they will understand
the concept(s) involved (if only implicitly) as purporting to pick
out an objective property, or a property which is a construction
out of some objective properties.

Conclusion₂*   Subjects sometimes understand their own concepts (if only implicitly) as purporting to pick out an objective property, or a property
which is a construction out of some objective properties.

Conclusion₁* tells us that if we are externalist in our characterization of a concept
C, then we should continue to be externalist in our characterization of the subject's understanding of C. To fail to do this is to fail to appreciate that our subject
aims in thought to mentally represent objective kinds as the objective kinds that
they are. Conclusion₂* then asserts that this is a truth regarding the subjects
about whom Putnam himself was theorizing: ordinary human subjects. As a
whole, then, this argument constitutes a defense not only of SE, but also of the
idea that externalist construals capture the subject's conceptions – and so capture the subject's point of view. For in effect this argument is a defense of the
generalization that, for any concept whose individuation is "externalist," the
subject's conception of that concept must be construed externalistically as well.

To make clear how the argument is supposed to support these conclusions, I
need to clarify what is intended with Premise 1*. Here, I need to make three points.

First, the premise uses the intentionalist vocabulary of "aiming" in thought
to represent a kind as objective. All that it meant by this is that it is sometimes
proper to regard a subject as thinking of a kind as objective, and employing a
concept that captures this objectivity.[21] This need not be the result of explicit
deliberation, nor need the subject be able to make all of this explicit herself.
Still, there must be some basis on which to construe her thought in this manner. This might come out in her behavior: for example, if she were to find out
that the kind in question is not objective after all, she would no longer apply

---

21 Perhaps I should say: "*purports* to capture" this objectivity. After all, the subject's presupposition itself, to the effect that the relevant kind is objective, might be false. However, speaking of failures of this sort here would take us too far afield.

the relevant concept to it. I assume that there can be such a basis for ascribing to a subject a thought involving a concept for an objective kind.

Second, the premise speaks of representing (aiming to represent) a kind "as *objective*." The point is that the concept employed in the representation applies correctly to all and only those instances of the objective kind itself. In speaking of a kind "as objective," I mean for a contrast with kinds that are not objective. For my purposes here, the difference concerns the canonical characterization of the kind itself. To a very rough first approximation, a kind K is *absolutely objective* iff there is a canonical characterization of K which does not involve any reference to (or denotation of) any subject, or state of any subject. Thus, "water2" expresses a concept for a kind that is absolutely objective in this sense; "funny" does not. If we like, we can then frame a notion of *relative objectivity* that differs from the absolute notion in that, while we allow for references to subjects, we deny reference to any particular subject. Thus, to a very rough first approximation, a kind K is *relatively objective* iff that there is a canonical characterization that does not involve any reference to (or denotation of) any *particular* subject, or state of any *particular* subject; K might then be said to be objective *relative to group G*, where G is the most inclusive group whose members are mentioned in the canonical characterization of K. Kinds that are response-dependent, but where the response in question is elicited in most or all normal subjects (when they are in the right circumstances), would count as relatively objective.

Third, and relatedly, the objective kinds in question are represented *as* objective kinds – as the objective kinds that they are. This is crucial: the concept that represents the kind does so in a way that represents it as objective, which is to say, in a way whose canonical characterization does not depend on any reference to (or denotation of) any subject or her states.[22] Thus, if "water" expresses a concept that represents a kind as objective, then it will not do to construe the concept expressed as equivalent to the concept expressed by "the actual liquid kind responsible for this watery experience." Borrowing an expression from Kripke, we might say that such a phrase helps to fix the extension of the concept, but it does not capture its content. That is, not if the concept expressed by "water" is a concept that represents the relevant liquid kind as objective.

Clearly, Premise 1* is a substantial claim. Given its role (along with Premises 2*–4*) in defending Putnam's conclusion of AE, I suspect that it will have

---

22 Or, if the kind is merely relatively objective, then there is no reference to or denotation of any *particular* subject.

to be targeted by Putnam's opponent. I say that it will "have to be" targeted, as the other premises (2*, 3*, and 4*) seem independently plausible in their own right. Premise 2* is a shared assumption, and so is not one that will be called into question. Premise 3* merely registers the point that if one thinks of a property or kind as an objective one, then one will use a concept which one recognizes (if only implicitly) as purporting to pick out an objective property or kind. Arguably, this is part of what it is to think of a property or kind as objective; it is hard to see how Premise 3* could be false, consistent with the hypothesis that the subject in question employs concept C thinking of the relevant property or kind as objective. Finally, Premise 4* ascribes to our subject the minimal understanding involved in thinking of a kind *as* an objective kind: one who does so will understand (if only implicitly) that she is – aims to be – representing something which itself is an objective kind (or which is composed of one or more such kinds). This is plausibly construed as a minimal understanding of a kind's being objective, so that anyone who fails to have this sort of understanding is hard to interpret as aiming to represent an objective kind as objective.

Suppose, then, that an opponent of Putnam wants to deny Premise 1*. In effect, this amounts to the idea that Putnam's opponent should not concede that we sometimes aim in thought to represent kinds as the objective kinds they are. Perhaps all of our mental representations involve concepts whose canonical characterizations involve some reference to (or denotation of) states of oneself. But whatever positive views one holds on the nature of our concepts, what are the prospects for making good on the resulting position? The challenge is that this returns us to the question of the contents of belief. That is to say, the allegedly available option of *granting* to the externalist what she wants to say about the contents of belief while *denying* that externalist construals capture the subject's point of view has evaporated. Still, we might ask: why not have Putnam's critic deny Premise 1* as part of a package that also denies that externalist construals of *belief* are correct?

There are two main reasons for avoiding such a position; these correspond to the two main ways (both of which were anticipated in Putnam's "The Meaning of 'Meaning'") to argue for AE itself.

One reason why it will not do to reject externalist construals of belief as incorrect has already been anticipated. A subject's beliefs capture how she takes the world to be. But surely as subjects we can take the world to exemplify objective properties and relations – that is, properties and relations whose natures are independent of our conceptual scheme, in the sense that no change in our conceptual scheme affects the natures of those properties and relations. And if this is so, it seems that as subjects we can take a particular perceived property or relation to be objective, and aim to represent it as such in thought. So if one's point of view just is one's epistemic perspective on things, and if this is captured by how one takes the world to be – that is, by one's beliefs – then it seems that it will not do to deny that externalist construals of belief are correct. These construals are needed, on pain of failing to be able to accommodate that we take some of the properties and relations in our world to be objective.

A second reason why it is not a good idea for Putnam's critic to deny that externalist construals of belief are correct is one I have offered elsewhere,[23] so here I will be brief. Start again with the claim that one's beliefs capture how one takes the world to be. Now many beliefs are acquired through accepting the say-so of our co-linguals, when we regard them as adequately positioned to have discerned the truth. But in accepting what another says, we aim to believe the very thing to which they attest. After all, this is the content regarding whose truth the speaker is assuring us (and for which she is invoking her epistemic authority); and it is the content regarding which we can "pass the epistemic buck" if challenged to defend our testimonially-acquired belief. But if this much is true, then what we believe, when we believe through accepting another's say-so, cannot be determined by anything purely subjective, and so cannot be determined through one's own conceptions if these are taken to be subjective and potentially idiosyncratic. Rather, there must be public standards guiding the interpretation of speech in a public language: it is by aiming to conform to these standards that the speaker has a reasonable expectation of being properly understood by her audience; and it is by interpreting the speaker's utterance by appeal to these standards that the audience has a reasonable expectation of understanding the speaker, and so of having access to the very content attested to. In short, if what we want is to capture how a subject takes the world to be, we have little hope of achieving this on the assumption that the starting point is something subjective (and hence potentially idiosyncratic).

V

I just described two sources of motivations for the doctrine asserting the Metaphysical Independence of One's Point of View, MIPOV the Argument from Inwardness, and the Argument from the Nature of Conceiving. I want to conclude by suggesting that both of these arguments derive from a common assumption.

---

23 See Goldberg, *Anti-Individualism* and "Anti-Individualism, Comprehension, and Self-Knowledge."

I will call this assumption *Spatial Autonomy*, or SA for short. The assumption in question is that

SA   A subject S's point of view is fixed by what is going on at the point in space at which S herself is located.

While few defenders of MIPOV have formulated a claim as explicitly as SA, I want to argue that this assumption, or something like it, lies at the heart of MIPOV. I submit that one of the most far-reaching of the implications of Putnam's "The Meaning of 'Meaning'"is that SA is false.

It is not hard to appreciate why something like SA might be thought plausible – or, at any rate, why it might have been thought plausible prior to "The Meaning of 'Meaning'." Indeed, I hinted at this when I introduced the familiar conception of what it is to have a point of view, above. There I noted that the expression "point of view" is spatial; insofar as we take the spatial idea literally, we are thinking of a point in space from which one perceptually apprehends the world around one, and at which one assembles one's "picture" or "view" of the world. This "picture" or "view" includes not only the information acquired through perception but also the sum total of the information previously stored in one's cognitive system – one's "background beliefs." We might then think that we can capture the content of this "view" by exhaustively characterizing (i) whatever information was in the system at the outset, and (ii) whatever information is acquired over the course of the subject's life (perceptually or otherwise). If we then think of the perceptual information in (ii) in terms of how the world affects the various sensory and perceptual systems themselves, we reach the idea of a kind of autonomy: one's point of view is determined by the effects on one's current cognitive system by all of the new information arriving into the system, and when it comes to perceptual information we might think of the process as being initiated with e.g. the irradiation of the retina (the sensations on the skin; the vibrations of the inner ear drum; etc.), and proceeding from there to the downstream cognitive effects on information-processing itself. To be sure, the world is *causally* implicated in this process, as it is the source of the patterns of irradiation (the sensations on the skin; the vibrations of the inner ear drum). But this is the only respect in which the world figures; metaphysically (as opposed to causally) speaking, the world is a fifth wheel.

For those who endorse it, the model of autonomy inherent in SA can be used to characterize the nature of a subject's epistemic perspective on the world. To see the connections, we need only note that a subject's epistemic perspective on the world is how she takes the world to be – how she represents it in thought. But we might imagine that when it comes to the visual parts of the world, how she represents it to be is partly a function of how it seems to her, visually speaking; and we might think that how it seems to her, visually speaking, is captured in the process that is initiated with the irradiation of the retina and which comes to full fruition in the downstream cognitive effects of the patterns of irradiation. Of course, we might then hope to treat visual apprehension as one mode of apprehending the world; and we might hope that there are corresponding ways to capture the contributions of the other sensory modalities to one's epistemic perspective on the world. The result would be a view on which one's point of view yields one's epistemic perspective on the world – all of which is *causally* dependent on, but *metaphysically* independent of, the world itself.

One of the far-reaching implications of "The Meaning of 'Meaning'" is the falsity of SA, and with it the unacceptability of the model just described. If we like, we can continue speaking of subjects as having a point of view; but insofar as we think this is, or determines, the subject's epistemic perspective on the world, we cannot think of this in terms that are both *spatial* and *reductive*. To be sure, as physical beings whose trajectories span space and time, we do occupy spatial positions; but we cannot reduce the subject's epistemic perspective on the world to materials from the history of the physical system at those positions, as the subject moves through space-time. On the contrary, if we think of the subject's point of view as constituting her epistemic perspective on the world, and if we want to continue to think in spatial terms, we must see the subject's point of view as more like a point-of-view-in-a-world, where materials that go into making up that viewpoint include facts about the worldly individuals and properties to which the subject is related. In this sense, the rhetoric of a *point* of view is somewhat misleading as to the nature of our epistemic perspective on the world.

Gary Ebbs
Putnam on Trans-Theoretical Terms and Contextual Apriority

Abstract: A central goal of Putnam's philosophy is to investigate and clarify the methodological roles of statements that are so central to an inquirer's current theory of the topics they concern that she cannot specify any way in which the statements may actually be false. My goals in this paper are (first) to explain how the problem of clarifying the methodological roles of such statements arises in Putnam's work, (second) to explain in synchronic practical terms why it is reasonable for an inquirer to accept such statements, and (third) to contrast this synchronic practical explanation with Putnam's diachronic theoretical explanation, according to which such statements can be revised "only by conceiving of whole new theoretical structures."

Putnam concludes his classic paper, "It Ain't Necessarily So," with the following suggestive yet enigmatic remark:

> The difference between statements that can be overthrown by merely conceiving of suitable experiments and statements that can be overthrown only by conceiving of whole new theoretical structures – sometimes structures, like Relativity and Quantum Mechanics, that change our whole way of reasoning about nature – is of logical and methodological significance, and not just of psychological interest.[1]

This remark launches Putnam's career-long effort to investigate and clarify the methodological roles of statements that are so central to an inquirer's current theory of the topics they concern that she cannot specify any way in which the statements may actually be false. My main goals here are to explain how the problem of clarifying the methodological roles of such statements arises in Putnam's work (§I); to explain in synchronic, practical terms why it is reasonable for an inquirer to accept such statements (§§II–VI); and to contrast this explanation with Putnam's diachronic, theoretical explanation, according to which such statements can be revised "only by conceiving of whole new theoretical structures" (§VII).

---

1 Hilary Putnam, "It Ain't Necessarily So" (1962), reprinted in *Mathematics, Matter, and Method: Philosophical Papers*, Vol. 1 (Cambridge: Cambridge University Press, 1975), 249.

https://doi.org/10.1515/9783110769210-006

I How the Problem Arises for Putnam

Like his mentors Hans Reichenbach, Rudolf Carnap, and W.V.O. Quine, Putnam takes for granted that our everyday and scientific judgments are for the most part reasonable and not in need of philosophical justification. The task of philosophy for Putnam is not to justify our everyday and scientific judgments but to describe and clarify them.

When Putnam began his career in the early 1950s, the dominant model for clarifying our everyday and scientific judgments was that of the logical empiricists, especially Carnap. Carnap proposed that we clarify the sense in which scientific judgments are reasonable by reconstructing the methods of science in terms of explicitly formulated rules for using sentences. Given such a set of rules, he observed, some sentences, which he called analytic, are settled solely by the rules without any need for empirical observation; other sentences, which he called synthetic, are only evaluable on the basis of empirical observations. For Carnap the key methodological significance of laying down explicitly formulated rules for inquiry is that if a sentence is a logical consequence of a given system of rules, then (first) anyone who has chosen to use the system, understands its rules, and has derived the sentence from the rules is thereby committed to accepting the sentence; and (second) there is no legitimate 'higher' or 'firmer' criterion for judging whether the sentence is true.[2]

In "Two Dogmas of Empiricism,"[3] Quine argues that Carnap's method of clarifying inquiry is unscientific. He agrees with Carnap and the other scientific philosophers of the day that our pre-theoretical grasp of the supposed analytic-synthetic distinction is too vague to be of use in a properly scientific philosophy. Quine's central criticism is that the logical and mathematical methods that Carnap and others use to try to clarify the supposed distinction between analytic and synthetic sentences do not, in fact, clarify it, but simply presuppose that it is already clear. Quine concludes that philosophers who take science seriously should not rely on Carnap's analytic-synthetic distinction to clarify our everyday and scientific judgments. In the last section of "Two Dogmas," Quine sketches a new project of clarifying these judgments without relying on the logical empiricists' analytic-synthetic distinction.

---

2 Rudolf Carnap, "The Task of the Logic of Science" (1934), reprinted in *Unified Science: The Vienna Circle Monographs Series Originally Edited by Otto Neurath*, edited by Brian McGuinness, translated by Hans Kaal (Dordrecht: D. Reidel, 1987), 46.
3 W.V.O. Quine, "Two Dogmas of Empiricism," *Philosophical Review* 60, no. 1 (1951): 20–43; reprinted with revisions in *From a Logical Point of View*, 20–46. (Cambridge, MA: Harvard University Press, 1953).

Putnam was one of the earliest and most important converts to this Quinean project.[4] In his first major contribution to it, "The Analytic and the Synthetic,"[5] Putnam observes that there are some statements in natural language, such as "Bachelors are unmarried," for which (first) there is only one criterion, such as being an unmarried adult male, for applying the subject term, such as "Bachelor," to someone; and (second) by this criterion, the statement is true. This observation superficially conflicts with Quine's claim in §2 of "Two Dogmas" that the only clear synonymy relations are those established by explicit acts of definitional abbreviation. As Putnam knows, however, this is not a deep challenge to Quine's arguments in "Two Dogmas," for two main reasons. First, the relationship between a word we introduce by an explicit act of definitional abbreviation, and the expression we introduce the word to abbreviate, is similar to the relationship between our uses of a one-criterion word of an unregimented natural language and the longer phrase of that language that states the generally accepted criterion for applying the word. It is therefore not a big step for Quine to acknowledge the existence in natural language of one-criterion words, such as "Bachelor," and the corresponding sentences, such as "Bachelors are unmarried," to which everyone assents. Quine takes this step, acknowledging Putnam, in Chapter 2 of *Word and Object*.[6]

Second, like Quine, Putnam saw that for any two words at least one of which is not a one-criterion word, the question whether the words are synonymous is at best unclear. In "The Analytic and the Synthetic," Putnam develops and extends this part of Quine's criticism of the logical empiricists' analytic-synthetic distinction by highlighting a range of examples of theoretical statements that are not fruitfully classified as either analytic or synthetic. For instance, before the development of relativity theory, Putnam explains, physicists were unable to see any way in which "$e = \frac{1}{2} mv^2$," an equation for kinetic energy, could be false. They held it immune from disconfirmation by new empirical evidence, and it was reasonable for them to do so. By Carnap's logical empiricist principles, Putnam notes, the methodological role of the equation is best explained by describing it as true by definition of kinetic energy. After Einstein developed relativity theory, however, scientists revised "$e = \frac{1}{2} mv^2$," replacing it with a more complicated

---

4 Hilary Putnam, "Intellectual Autobiography," in *The Philosophy of Hilary Putnam*, edited by Randall E. Auxier, Douglas R. Anderson, and Lewis Edwin Hahn (Chicago, IL: Open Court, 2015), 16–17.
5 Hilary Putnam, "The Analytic and the Synthetic" (1962), reprinted in *Mind, Language, and Reality: Philosophical Papers*, Vol. 2, 33–69 (Cambridge: Cambridge University Press, 1975). Putnam first drafted this paper in 1957–58.
6 W.V.O. Quine, *Word and Object* (Cambridge, MA: MIT Press, 1960), 56–57.

equation that fits the new theory, and concluded that "e = ½ mv², " while approximately true, was strictly speaking false, hence not true by definition. To make sense of such cases, Putnam introduces the idea of a "law-cluster" term, which figures in many different laws of a theory. He observes that we can give up one of the laws in which such a term figures without concluding that the reference of the term has changed. For instance, we can continue to use a given term to refer to kinetic energy while radically changing our theory of kinetic energy. Putnam calls such terms *trans-theoretical*.

He deepens and extends these criticisms of logical empiricism in "It Ain't Necessarily So," where he observes that our theories of the geometry of physical space have changed since the eighteenth century, when the principles of Euclidean geometry were so central to our way of thinking about physical space that we could not then specify any way in which those principles may actually be false. He argues that while our theory of physical space has changed radically since the eighteenth century, it is nevertheless correct to regard the terms that scientists in the eighteenth century used to refer to paths through physical space as trans-theoretical and to conclude that many of the sentences about physical space that scientists accepted in the eighteenth century, such as "The sum of the interior angles of any triangle formed by joining three points in physical space by the shortest paths between them is 180°," are false. Putnam concludes that some statements are so central to our way of thinking at a given time that it would not be reasonable to give them up at that time, even if our failure to be able to specify any way in which they may actually be false is no guarantee that they are true.

Even logical and mathematical statements that we now regard as obvious and beyond any doubt should not be described as analytic, Putnam argues, since there is no methodological guarantee that we will not later judge the statements false without changing the references of the terms we use to express the statements. He therefore rejects Carnap's proposal that we clarify the sense in which scientific judgments, including scientists' acceptance of logical and mathematical truths, are reasonable and not in need of any philosophical justification, by adopting systems of rules that imply logical and mathematical truths. The problem for Carnap's proposal, according to Putnam, is that, in contrast with sentences that contain only one-criterion terms, the sentences of logic, mathematics, and much of natural science, including physical geometry, contain trans-theoretical (i.e. law-cluster) terms, and therefore have "systematic import."[7] Hence even if we are currently unable to specify any way in which a statement we express by using a sentence with systematic import may actually

---

7 Putnam, "The Analytic and the Synthetic," 39.

be false, there is no methodological guarantee that we (or future inquirers) will not revise the statement, translate the terms we use to express it homophonically into our (or their) new theory, and thereby judge it to be false.

Putnam concludes that "there is no sensible distinction between *a priori* and *a posteriori* truths."[8] The statements that traditional philosophers label *a priori* – statements of logic and mathematics, as well as, for instance, the eighteenth-century scientists' statement "The sum of the interior angles of any triangle formed by joining three points in physical space by the shortest paths between them is 180°" – should be regarded, instead, as *contextually a priori*.[9] To a first approximation, a statement is *contextually apriori* for an inquirer at a time if and only if she accepts it, it has systematic import for her overall theory, and she cannot specify any way in which it may actually be false. Although we treat such statements as immune to empirical disconfirmation, they are not immune to revision without a change in subject, for the reasons explained above, and are therefore not analytic. Putnam nevertheless remains firmly committed to his guiding methodological principle that our everyday and scientific judgments, including our acceptance of contextually a priori statements, are for the most part reasonable and not in need of philosophical justification. Instead of abandoning this principle, he seeks an alternative explanation of why it is reasonable for inquirers to accept contextually a priori statements.[10] He therefore takes his arguments in "The Analytic and the Synthetic" and "It Ain't Necessarily So" to pose an internal problem for his account of the methodology of inquiry – the problem of explaining why it is reasonable for scientists to accept statements that are contextually a priori for them even though there is no methodological guarantee that the statements are true.

II A Reconstruction of Putnam's Problem

It will help to have a sharper formulation of Putnam's problem. I see him as starting with the following

> *Methodological Principle* (MP): In our pursuit of truth, we can do no better than to start in the middle, relying on already accepted beliefs and inferences, and applying our best methods for reevaluating particular statements, beliefs and inferences and arriving at new ones.

---

8 Hilary Putnam, "'Two Dogmas' Revisited," in *Realism and Reason: Philosophical Papers*, Vol. 3 (Cambridge: Cambridge University Press, 1983), 88.
9 Hilary Putnam, "'Two Dogmas' Revisited," 95.
10 Hilary Putnam, "'Two Dogmas' Revisited," 95.

I take (MP) to imply, as both Quine and Putnam argue, that no belief, inference, or method is immune to revision, and that there are no epistemological standards higher or firmer than the ones we express in our actual endorsements of particular statements, beliefs, inferences, and methods for arriving at beliefs. We may find fault with our grounds for accepting any of our statements, beliefs, inferences, or methods, and revise them accordingly, but only if such findings or revisions are rooted in our latest, best sense of which ones to accept.

Let us consider, to begin with, an unproblematic application of (MP). Suppose, for example, that we wish to know whether or not there is an occurrence of the word "octopus" on a given page of text that we have not seen before. To make things as simple as possible, assume that prior to looking carefully at the page, we have no reason to believe there is an occurrence of the word "octopus" on it and no reason to believe there isn't. In such circumstances, to determine whether or not to believe that there is an occurrence of "octopus" on the page, we rely on a vast background of beliefs about such things as what pages are, what occurrences are, what counts as an occurrence of "octopus" on a page, and so on, and we focus on the question whether or not there is an occurrence of "octopus" on the page. To answer this question, of course, we examine the page. If we find an occurrence of "octopus" on it, we will for that reason come to accept the statement that there is an occurrence of "octopus" on the page.

In this and many other cases, both in everyday life and in science, the statements S into which we inquire satisfy two conditions:

(a) before our inquiry into whether or not S, it is both epistemically possible for us that S and epistemically possible for us that not S, and
(b) we can see how we may come to have a reason for accepting S or for accepting not S.

In the above case, for instance, condition (a) is by hypothesis satisfied, and so is (b), since I suppose that I can tell by looking whether or not there is an occurrence of "octopus" on the page. In other similar perceptual cases, I might satisfy (b) if I realize that I can tell by listening, touching, smelling, or tasting, whether or not S, for some statement S.

There are of course many statements that satisfy (a) but that we cannot evaluate by perceiving alone. In practice, for any such statement S, we rely on additional ways of answering the question whether or not S, such as deducing S from perceptual evidence and a high-level explanatory law that we infer by induction, or, more generally, by reasoning to the best explanation. I shall assume that our resources are varied and comprehensive enough that if (a) holds, so, typically, does (b).

To make sense of such cases I shall rely on a partly regimented sense of the English word "reason," i.e., a sense of "reason" that satisfies the following condition:

(R1)   A person has a reason for believing that S only if she can say why she believes that S without presupposing that S.

Just as in the "octopus" example, in general, when conditions (a) and (b) hold for a given person *x* and statement S, *x* may come to have a *reason* for accepting that S, in the sense of "reason" regimented by (R1).

We have no difficulty explaining how it can be epistemically reasonable for us to accept a statement S for which conditions (a) and (b) hold, since we understand how we may come to have a reason for accepting S, in the sense of "reason" regimented by (R1). By contrast, it is not so easy to see explain how it can be epistemically reasonable to accept a contextually a priori statement. For a statement that is contextually a priori for us is one we cannot coherently suppose to be false, where the "cannot" is practical, a matter of what cannot now do: when we try to specify a way in which a belief that S of this sort may actually be false, we find we are unable to do so. Hence condition (a) does not hold for S. Moreover, a statement that is contextually a priori for us has systematic import for our theory. For reasons I shall explain a few paragraphs below, this implies that if S is contextually a priori for us, then we cannot say why we believe that S without relying on S. We therefore cannot give a reason for accepting S, in the sense of "reason" regimented by (R1).

Putnam's problem is to explain how it may be epistemically reasonable to accept contextually a priori statements given that they are not analytic, so there is no methodological guarantee that they are true, and we cannot say why we accept them without presupposing them.

To solve this problem we need a clearer characterization of the methodological roles of contextually a priori statements. Let us examine a particular example: the statement that no statement of the form "S and not S" is true. Both my expression of this statement and my belief that no statement of the form "S and not S" is true presuppose a background of beliefs about how to define truth, about the semantics of negation and conjunction, about what follows from what, and so on. These are not beliefs that I can now suspend or reject without losing my grip on what I say when I use my sentence, "No statement of the form 'S and not S' is true." Although I have tried to make sense of challenges to my belief that no statement of the form "S and not S" is true, including challenges from Graham Priest and other dialethiests, I find I am (so far) unable to describe coherently any situation in which the belief is false.[11] Moreover, all my attempts to argue for the conclusion that no statement of the form "S and not S" is true rely at some point or other on a premise or inference rule that is either stronger than the conclusion, or equivalent to it. Consider, for instance, the following argument:

> Start with two semantic premises: (1) ⌐Not S⌐ is true if and only if S is not true, and (2) ⌐S and S′⌐ is true if and only if S is true and S′ is true. Now suppose (toward contradiction) that for some S, ⌐S and not S⌐ is true. Then, by (2), S is true and ⌐Not S⌐ is true. Hence, by (1), S is true and S is not true. *This is a contradiction, hence not true*, and so it is not the case that for some S, ⌐S and not S⌐ is true.

This argument begs the question by assuming that there can be no true contradictions.[12] More generally, my failure to find a non-circular argument for the conclusion that no statement of the form "S and not S" is true convinces me that I have no reason for accepting this, in the sense of "reason" regimented by (R1). The statement that no statement of the form "S and not S" is true is part of my best current theory and it has systematic import for my overall theory. I accordingly take my acceptance of the statement to be epistemically reasonable. By (MP), moreover, I can do no better than this – there is no higher or firmer perspective from which to judge whether the acceptance (or belief) is epistemically reasonable.

We need a word to describe the epistemological standing of such beliefs. I propose that we use the English word "entitled" (or "entitlement"), regimented as follows:

(R2)   A person is entitled (or has an entitlement) to accept S if and only if she has no reason (in the sense of "reason" regimented by (R1)) for accepting S – she cannot say why she accepts S without relying on S – but it is epistemically reasonable for her to accept S.

To make use of this regimentation, we must be guided by our own best judgments about whether a person's acceptance of the statement is epistemically

---

11 Why am I not convinced by the dialethiest's arguments? This is not the place for a full explanation, but here is a characteristic detail. Priest takes the existence of certain mathematical structures – e.g. an assignment of "t-r-u-e" and "f-a-l-s-e" to the same quadrant of a Euclidean plane – to show that a statement may be both true and false. (Graham Priest, "What Is So Bad about Contradictions?" *The Journal of Philosophy* 95, no. 8 (1998): 414) I do not see, however, how the fact that one can assign "t-r-u-e" and "f-a-l-s-e" to the same quadrant of a Euclidean plane specifies a way in which a statement can be both true and false.

12 Priest, "What Is So Bad about Contradictions?," 418.

reasonable. For instance, as noted above, if my acceptance of the statement that no sentence of the form "S and not S" is true is epistemically reasonable, then given (R2), I am entitled to accept it. In this case, of course, I am unable to specify a way in which the statement is false. And that may seem to suggest that if a person cannot specify a way in which a statement S may be false, then by (R2) she is epistemically entitled to believe that S. But this latter claim is problematic, for three main reasons. First, a person might not understand a given statement S at all, and hence might not be in a position even to consider the statement, let alone to accept, or reject it. How much understanding is required is a subtle, context-sensitive matter, but some level of understanding is required for her even to accept S, and hence also for her to have entitlement. Second, a person who understands a given statement S might not have tried to say why she accepts S without presupposing S. She may wrongly suppose she cannot say why she accepts S without presupposing S, simply due to lack of trying. In such a case, (R2) does not apply to S. Third, a person who understands a given statement might not have tried to specify a way in which it may be false. The point is that a special kind of *due diligence* is required – it is only once an inquirer has done the right kind of due diligence that her inability to say why she accepts S without presupposing S and her inability to specify a way in which a statement S may actually be false may together amount to an entitlement to accept S of the kind regimented by (R2). I investigate and try to clarify the relevant kind of due diligence in §IV–VI below.

As noted above, a statement is contextually a priori for an inquirer only if it has systematic import for her theory. As I shall understand "systematic import" in what follows, a statement S has systematic import for an inquirer's theory if and only if

(a) his explanations of a significant range of phenomena depend on S,
(b) despite doing his due diligence he has no reason for accepting S in the sense of "reason" regimented by (R1) – i.e., he cannot say why he accepts S without presupposing S, and
(c) he knows that (a) and (b) are true.

In the direct, practical way in which inquirers know what they are doing when they explicitly formulate and affirm an explanation and when they search for a reason for accepting a statement yet fail to find one, an inquirer can and typically does know whether conditions (a) and (b) obtain for a statement that he accepts. Thus all three conditions are synchronic and practical. There is therefore no special difficulty in determining whether or not conditions (a)–(c) hold for a given person and a given statement that he accepts. My statement that no statement of the form "S and not S" is true, for example, clearly satisfies all three of the conditions (a)–(c).

With these definitions in place, I propose that we explicate "statement S is contextually a priori for person x" as follows:

(R3) A statement S is contextually a priori for person x if and only if x understands S well enough to raise the question of whether or not to accept S, x accepts S, S has systematic import for x's total theory, x tries to specify a way in which S may actually be false, x exercises due diligence in this effort, but x is nevertheless unable to specify a way in which S may actually be false.

With "statement S is contextually a priori for person x" explicated in this way, let us now try to evaluate the following conditional:

(R4) If statement S is contextually a priori for person x, then it is epistemically reasonable for x to accept S.

Consider the following outline of an argument for (R4). Suppose statement S is contextually a priori for a person. Then, by (R3), S has systematic import for her, so (by the explication of "systematic import" in the previous paragraph) she is unable to say why she accepts S without presupposing S, despite doing her due diligence, and hence she has no reason (in the sense of "reason" regimented by (R1)) for accepting S. By (R2), then, we may infer that she is entitled to accept S if and only if it is epistemically reasonable for her to accept S. Also by (R3), however, she is unable to specify a way in which S may actually be false, despite doing her due diligence. She is therefore unable to see any good reason to revise S, and so, by (MP), she can do no better than to accept S – i.e., it is epistemically reasonable for her to accept S. This reasoning supports (R4). Finally, (R1)–(R4) together imply that she is entitled to accept S, in the sense of "entitled" regimented by (R2).

Putnam's problem, as I reconstruct it, is to explain in a more compelling and possibly more substantive way why (R4) is true, given (MP) and (R1)–(R3).

III Rejecting a Traditional Epistemological Assumption

Many epistemologists assume that one can be epistemically entitled to accept a statement only if there is something about the statement, or its place in one's overall theory, that makes it likely that the statement is true.[13] I shall call this the *traditional epistemological assumption*. It implies that there is no solution to Putnam's problem, as I have presented it.

The reasoning is as follows. By (MP), there is no methodological guarantee that a contextually a priori statement is true. And none of the methodological characteristics of contextually a priori statements imply that there is something about the statement, or its place in one's overall theory, that makes it likely that the statement is true. Granting the traditional epistemological assumption, then, none of the methodological characteristics of contextually a priori statements imply that one is epistemically entitled to accept a contextually a priori statement. As we have seen, however, the conjunction of (R1)–(R3) with (MP) implies (R4): if a statement is contextually a priori for a given inquirer, then she is epistemically entitled to accept it. The traditional epistemological assumption is therefore logically incompatible with the conjunction of (R1)–(R3) and (MP).

If one refuses to give up the traditional assumption, one must reject the conjunction of (R1)–(R3) and (MP). But my goal in this paper is to investigate the consequences of accepting (R1)–(R3) and (MP), which I take to frame Putnam's problem. I will therefore set aside the traditional epistemological assumption. I shall assume, provisionally at least, for the reasons explained above, (R1)–(R3) and (MP) imply (R4). The problem – Putnam's problem, as I understand it – is to explain in a more detailed and compelling way why this is so.

---

13 See for example Paul Boghossian, "Knowledge of Logic," in *New Essays on the A Priori*, edited by Paul Boghossian and Christopher Peacocke, 229–255 (Oxford: Oxford University Press, 2000) and "How Are Objective Reasons Possible?" *Philosophical Studies* 106, no. 1/2 (2001): 1–40; Laurence Bonjour, *In Defense of Pure Reason* (Cambridge: Cambridge University Press, 1998); Jerrold Katz, *Realistic Rationalism* (Cambridge, MA.: MIT Press, 1998); Christopher Peacocke, "Explaining the A Priori: The Programme of Moderate Rationalism," in *New Essays on the A Priori*, edited by Paul Boghossian and Christopher Peacocke, 255–286 (Oxford: Oxford University Press, 2000); and Georges Rey, "A Naturalistic A Priori," *Philosophical Studies* 92, no. 1/2 (1998): 25–43.

IV Tests, Riddles, and Due Diligence

The key to solving Putnam's problem, as I shall now try to show, is to describe the methodological roles of contextually a priori statements from an engaged, practical point of view. My starting point is the observation that whether or not a statement is contextually a priori for a given person at a given time depends on what she can do at that time.[14] As expressed in (R3), the point is that a statement S is contextually a priori for a person if and only if she understands a statement S well enough to raise the question of whether or not S is to be believed, she accepts S, S has systematic import in her total theory, she tries to specify a way in which S may actually be false and exercises due diligence in this effort, but she is unable to specify a way in which S may actually be false. In this context, I propose that we clarify the open sentence "person x is unable to specify a way in which S may actually be false" in terms of an oral or written test with some (perhaps vague) time limit, as follows: at the start of the test x is prompted to utter or write down a way in which S may actually be false, and x tries to do so. If, by the end of the allotted time, x has failed to utter or write down any such way, the open sentence is true; otherwise it is false.

To highlight the importance of such practical failures to the methodology of inquiry, Putnam once compared them to our failure to see the solution to a riddle, such as the following one, which he takes from Wittgenstein: A person arrived at a ball neither naked nor dressed. What was he wearing? Solution: a fishnet. Putnam wrote:

> Concerning such riddles, Wittgenstein says that we are able to give the words a sense only after we know the solution; the solution bestows a sense on the riddle-question. This seems right. . . . If someone asked me, "In what sense, exactly, was [the person] neither naked nor dressed?" I could not answer if I did not know the solution.[15]

Putnam's point here is partly obscured by the fact there are several different possible solutions to the riddle – i.e., several different ways in which a person might qualify as neither naked nor dressed. By contrast, consider the following riddle described by Reichenbach:

---

14 I am guided here by Wittgenstein's remark that "When I say 'I don't know my way about in the calculus' I do not mean a mental state, but an inability to do something." (*Remarks on the Foundations of Mathematics* III §81; quoted in Juliet Floyd, "Wittgenstein, Mathematics, and Philosophy," in *The New Wittgenstein*, edited by Alice Crary and Rupert Read (London: Routledge, 2000), 249)

15 Hilary Putnam, "Rethinking Mathematical Necessity" (1990), reprinted in *Words and Life*, edited by James Conant (Cambridge, MA: Harvard University Press, 1994), 254.

Three matches are laid on the table in the shape of a triangle; the problem is to form four triangles by adding three more matches.[16]

It is natural to try first to form the required four triangles by placing the three additional matches on the table. But there is no way to form the required four triangles in this way. If one does not revise one's understanding of the problem, one will fail to find a solution to it. Reichenbach writes:

Rarely somebody conceives the idea of arranging the three matches spatially on top of the triangle lying on the table so that a tetrahedron results.[17]

Like Putnam's riddle, Reichenbach's riddle entertains us by making us aware of "conditions we impose upon our imagination."[18] The riddles are fun and instructive because they do not stump us for long. We either solve them by ourselves or are told how to solve them, and thereby become aware of conditions we imposed upon our imagination before we knew how to solve them. By contrast, if a statement is a contextually a priori for us in the sense defined by (R3), we are unable to specify any way in which it may actually be false even after doing our due diligence.

But what is due diligence? We may assume, to begin with, that it includes searching on our own for a way in which the statement may be false and asking others if they know of a way in which it may be false. Just as in other areas of inquiry, neither our own or other's verdicts on such questions are final. As I noted above, for example, I am unconvinced by Graham Priest's arguments for his conclusion that the statement that no statement of the form "S and not S" is true is false. Despite his efforts, I am unable to specify a way in which the statement that no statement of the form "S and not S" may actually be false. A proper search for ways in which a given statement may actually be false – a search that demonstrates due diligence – must weigh a host of factors and is always provisional, subject to revision, yet no less central to our methods of inquiry for that. To clarify the relevant notion of due diligence, in the next two sections I briefly review some of the methods of inquiry in which the statements that are contextually a priori for us are embedded.

---

16 Hans Reichenbach, *The Philosophy of Space and Time*, translated by Maria Reichenbach and John Freund (New York: Dover, 1958), 41.
17 Reichenbach, *The Philosophy of Space and Time*, 41.
18 Reichenbach, *The Philosophy of Space and Time*, 41.

V Due Diligence in Logic and Mathematics

Consider first the role of due diligence in our evaluations of logicians' and mathematicians' efforts to solve three different types of problems: exercises in logic and mathematics texts; open problems in mathematics for which we conjecture that there are proofs that have not yet been discovered; and problems in mathematics that are now known to be unsolvable, but that mathematicians previously did not have the methods to prove unsolvable.

Exercises in logic and mathematics texts. Some of the exercises in logic and mathematics texts are very difficult to solve. Most of them, however, have already been solved – the solutions are known to the textbook writer, at least, and perhaps many others. A person who tries to solve a logic or mathematics exercise, sees no way to do so, yet also cannot produce a counter-example to it, should not conclude that the problem cannot be solved. In such a context, the person's failure to see any way to prove the statement has no special methodological significance. He has good reason to believe that others can prove the statement or provide a counter-example to it, and that his failure to see how to proceed is mainly of personal, psychological interest. If he announces that a statement cannot be proved simply because he has not been able to see how it to prove it, he has not done his due diligence, and his announcement is of no methodological significance.

Open problems in mathematics. A mathematician who can produce no counter-example to a plausible conjecture about a well-understood topic, yet is stumped about how to prove it, does not and should not conclude that there is no proof of it. Due diligence requires more of him than that. He cannot even be sure that if there is a proof of the conjecture, it makes use solely of proof methods that are traditionally associated with the topic of the conjecture. Logic, mathematics, and the sciences more generally sometimes advance by radical transformations of the methods for establishing statements. One spectacular recent example is Andrew Wiles's proof of Fermat's last theorem.

Problems in mathematics that are now known to be unsolvable, but that mathematicians previously did not have the methods to prove unsolvable. Here are three examples:

1. *Trisecting the Angle.* A classic problem from ancient Greek mathematics is to find a procedure for trisecting any given angle by means of compass a straightedge alone. Mathematicians searched for centuries without success for such a procedure, and gradually began suspecting that there isn't one. They therefore started to investigate the question: How is it possible to prove that certain

problems cannot be solved?[19] It was not until the nineteenth century that mathematicians discovered a method for finding, for any given angle, an algebraic equivalent to the question whether there is a procedure for trisecting the angle by using only a compass a straightedge. They discovered, for instance, that there exists such a procedure for trisecting a 60° angle if and only if the equation $8z^3 - 6z = 1$ has rational roots. They then proved algebraically that $8z^3 - 6z = 1$ has no rational roots, and concluded that one cannot trisect a 60° angle using a compass a straight edge alone.[20] Prior to the discovery of a method for finding algebraic equivalents for questions about geometrical constructions, mathematicians had no way to prove that there is no procedure for trisecting any given angle using only a compass and straightedge. The discovery of such algebraic equivalents transformed the methods of geometry: after the discovery it was no longer compatible with having done one's due diligence as a mathematician to search for a procedure for trisecting any given angle using only a compass and straightedge.

2. *Hilbert's Tenth Problem.* In 1900 David Hilbert listed 23 of the most important mathematical problems left open by work in nineteenth-century mathematics. He stated the tenth of these problems as follows:

> Given a Diophantine equation with any number of unknown quantities and with rational integral numerical coefficients: *To devise a process according to which it can be determined by a finite number of operations whether the equation is solvable in rational integers.*[21]

(A Diophantine equation is a polynomial equation in one or more unknowns with integer coefficients, such as the equation noted above, $8z^3 - 6z = 1$, and $(y - xu)^2 = 0$.) As Yuri Matiyasevich, the person whose work finally solved this problem, explains, "Hilbert asks for a universal method for deciding the solvability of all Diophantine equations."[22] The proof that Hilbert's problem is unsolvable – i.e., that there is no decision procedure for determining whether or not any given Diophantine equation has solutions in rational integers – depends on a foundational result of the theory of computability: that there exist

---

19 Richard Courant and Herbert Robbins, *What Is Mathematics? An Elementary Approach to Ideas and Methods* (New York: Oxford University Press, 1958), 118.

20 Courant and Robbins, *What Is Mathematics?*, 137–138.

21 David Hilbert, "Mathematische Probleme" (1900). Vortrag, gehalten auf dem internationalen Mathematiker Kongress zu Paris 1900. *Nachrichten von der Königliche Gesellschaft der Wissenschaften zu Göttingen, Math.-Phys. Kl.* 253–297. English translation from Yuri Matiyasevich, "Martin Davis and Hilbert's Tenth Problem," in *Martin Davis on Computability, Computational Logic, and Mathematical Foundations*, edited by Eugenio G. Omodeo and Alberto Policriti (Cham, Switzerland: Springer International, 2016), 35.

22 Matiyasevich, "Martin Davis and Hilbert's Tenth Problem," 36.

listable sets of natural numbers for which there is no algorithm for recognizing, given a natural number n, whether it belongs to the set or not.[23] The strategy for relating this result to Hilbert's tenth problem is due to Martin Davis, who conjectured in the 1950s that *every listable set of numbers is Diophantine*, where a set S of numbers is Diophantine if and only if for some Diophantine equation $P(x_1, \ldots, x_n, y_1, \ldots, y_m) = 0$,

$$(x_1, \ldots, x_n) \in S \leftrightarrow (\exists y_1, \ldots, y_m)[P(x_1, \ldots, x_n, y_1, \ldots, y_m) = 0].^{24}$$

Many mathematicians, including Alfred Tarski and George Kreisel, regarded Davis's conjecture as implausible. However, in a series of steps established by Davis, Hilary Putnam, Julia Robinson, and Matiyasevich, Davis's conjecture was finally proved in 1970. The truth of Davis's conjecture and the foundational result summarized above together immediately imply that Hilbert's tenth problem is unsolvable. In 1900, when Hilbert announced his tenth problem, it was compatible with having done one's due diligence as a mathematician to conjecture that tenth problem could be solved. Now, given the foundational result and the Davis-Putnam-Robinson-Matiyasevich proof of Davis's conjecture, it is no longer compatible with due diligence to conjecture that Hilbert's tenth problem can be solved.

3. *Gödel's Incompleteness Theorems.* In 1931 Gödel showed how to assign numbers to symbols and thereby to encode logical syntax, including all the deductive proofs that can be constructed in a given system, in elementary arithmetic. By exploiting this method, he proved his *first incompleteness theorem*: given any consistent proof system PS for a language L that is rich enough to express all the arithmetical truths, there exists a true arithmetical sentence S of L such that neither S nor the negation of S can be proved in PS.[25] Gödel's *second incompleteness theorem*, closely related to the first, is that the consistency of a consistent proof system PS for a language L rich enough to express arithmetic cannot be proved in PS.[26] Gödel's theorems radically transformed the way logicians and mathematicians think about proof systems for arithmetic – it is no longer compatible with having done one's due diligence as a mathematician to assume that there are complete and consistent proof systems for arithmetic and to conjecture that in any such system PS, one can prove that PS is consistent.

---

23 Matiyasevich, "Martin Davis and Hilbert's Tenth Problem," 39.
24 Martin Davis, *Computability and Unsolvability* (New York: Dover, 1982), 200–201.
25 S.C. Kleene, *Introduction to Meta-Mathematics* (Amsterdam: North-Holland, 1952), Theorem 29 (Rosser's Form).
26 S.C. Kleene, *Introduction to Meta-Mathematics*, Theorem 30.

VI Contextual A Priority Explained

Each in its own way, the examples in §V show how new developments in logic and mathematics transform the methodology of these disciplines, so that what seemed like reasonable questions or assumptions prior to the developments (e.g. "How can one trisect any given angle using only compass and straight-edge?," "By what universal method can one determine whether any given Diophantine equation has solutions in rational integers?," "There exist complete deductive systematizations of elementary arithmetic," and "The consistency of consistent proof system PS for a language L rich enough to express arithmetic can be proved in PS") are later seen to be without solutions or false for reasons we did not previously even conceive. I want now to suggest that the examples of §V, by extension, also help us to explain contextual a priority, by helping us to see how it may happen that at one time we may reasonably accept a given statement S, regard S as of systematic import for our current theory, and, despite doing our due diligence, be unable to specify any way in which S may actually be false, yet later come to realize, after viewing S in a new way that no one in our scientific community noticed or even formulated before, that S is false.

There are statements of this kind in logic and mathematics. Consider, for instance, Gottlob Frege's acceptance of his Basic Law V, according to which "we can convert the generality of an equality into a value-range equality and vice versa."[27] Frege emphasized that Basic Law V is indispensable to previous work in logic – "The entire calculating logic of Leibniz and Boole rests upon it."[28] – and that "one thinks in accordance with it if, e.g., one speaks of extensions of concepts."[29] He recognized that it is more doubtful than his other basic laws, but he still took it to be purely logical, and at least as obvious as any proof one might propose for it. He nevertheless immediately understood the letter he received from Bertrand Russell in 1902 – the famous letter in which Russell derives a contradiction from Frege's Basic Law V.[30] This does not imply that Frege and other logicians had been negligent, failing to do their due diligence. Frege's commitments to rigor and to establishing firm foundations in

---

27 Gottlob Frege, *Basic Laws of Arithmetic*, edited and translated by Philip A. Ebert and Marcus Rossberg (Oxford: Oxford University Press, 2013), I §9, 14.

28 Frege, *Basic Laws of Arithmetic*, I §9, 14.

29 Frege, *Basic Laws of Arithmetic*, vii.

30 Bertrand Russell, "Letter to Frege" (1902), reprinted in *From Frege to Gödel: A Source Book in Mathematical Logic, 1897–1931*, edited by Jean van Heijenoort, 124–125 (Cambridge, MA: Harvard University Press, 1967).

logic are unsurpassed. Moreover, commenting on Russell's discovery of the contradiction, Frege noted, "Every one who has made use of extensions of concepts, classes, sets in their proofs is in the same position [of having regarded law V as a logical law]."[31] For my purposes here, the key methodological point is that Russell's derivation of a contradiction from Basic Law V, though it now appears obvious and inevitable, went unnoticed by all previous logicians, despite their diligence in seeking solid foundations for logic. Russell's derivation therefore transformed how logicians and mathematicians think about the relationship between concepts and extensions of concepts. As a result of Russell's discovery, what was previously contextually a priori for Frege and other logicians immediately lost that status and was shown to be false.[32]

As we saw above, there are also cases in which we accept a statement S, regard it as fundamental to our best current science, and are unable to specify any way in which it may actually be false, yet we later discover not that S is inconsistent, like Frege's Basic Law V, but that S, though consistent, is false. Recall that according to Putnam the terms that the scientists in the eighteenth century used to refer to paths through physical space are trans-theoretical. The statements that scientists in the eighteenth century made by using such terms – statements such as *The sum of the interior angles of any triangle formed by joining three points in physical space by the shortest paths between them is 180°* – were so central to

---

31 Frege, *Basic Laws of Arithmetic*, 253.
32 There are some fine points that need to be sorted out for a final judgment about Frege's due diligence to be made. As van Heijenoort explains, in 1879 Burali-Forti observed that "On naïve set-theoretic assumptions, the set of ordinals is well-ordered, hence has an ordinal; this ordinal is at once an element of the set of ordinals and greater than any ordinal in the set." (Jean van Heijenoort (ed.), *From Frege to Gödel: A Source Book in Mathematical Logic, 1897–1931* (Cambridge, MA: Harvard University Press, 1967), 104) This paradox was much discussed at the time but there was little agreement about what it showed. Burali-Forti's paper also contained errors. In a letter to Dedekind in 1899, Cantor corrected the errors, and clarified Burali-Forti's observation in Cantor's own terms, concluding that we must distinguish between consistent and inconsistent "multiplicities." (Georg Cantor, "Letter to Dedekind" (1899), in *From Frege to Gödel*, 113–117) Cantor called the former, but not the latter, sets. In retrospect, it may appear that Cantor was already drawing something like our contemporary distinction between sets and classes. But Cantor neither formulates it sharply nor explores its relationship to logical laws about extensions of concepts. W.V.O Quine, citing Fraenkel's claim that Cantor sensed paradox in his conception of sets, calls the appearance that Cantor distinguished between sets and classes "myopic" and "hindsightful." (W.V.O. Quine, *The Roots of Reference* (La Salle, IL: Open Court, 1974), 102) In any case, however, since Cantor distinguishes between consistent and inconsistent "multiplicities" in a personal letter to Dedekind in 1899, it is unlikely Frege would have known of Cantor's reasoning about such "multiplicities" before 1902, when Frege received Russell's letter.

their theory of physical space that even after due diligence, they could not specify any way in which they may actually be false. As Putnam emphasizes, their failure to be able to specify any way in which these statements may actually be false was no guarantee that they were true. Today, after a great deal of sophisticated new theorizing in logic, mathematics, and physics, we know that the eighteenth-century scientists' statements about physical space are false.

These reflections about the role of due diligence in Frege's acceptance of Basic Law V and the eighteenth-century scientists' acceptance of statements about physical space help us to solve Putnam's problem. To see why, recall first that if a statement S is contextually a priori for a person, then by (R3) S has systematic import for her, so (by the definition of "systematic import" in §II) she is unable to say why she accepts S without presupposing S, despite doing her due diligence, and hence she has no reason (in the sense of "reason" regimented by (R1)) for accepting S. By (R2), then, we may infer that she is entitled to accept S if and only if it is epistemically reasonable for her to accept S. Also by (R3), however, she is unable to specify a way in which S may actually be false, despite doing her due diligence. She is therefore unable to see any good reason to revise S, and so, by (MP), she can do no better than to accept S – i.e., it is epistemically reasonable for her to accept S. This reasoning supports (R4) – i.e. if statement S is contextually a priori for person *x*, then it is epistemically reasonable for *x* to accept S. Finally, (R1)–(R4) together imply that she epistemically entitled to accept S. The two cases described in this section both satisfy all of these conditions. We may therefore infer that Frege's Basic Law V and the eighteenth-century scientists' statements about physical space were contextually a priori for Frege and the eighteenth-century scientists, respectively, and that by (MP) and (R1)–(R4), both Frege and the eighteenth-century scientists were entitled to accept those respective statements. Together with the observations in this and previous two sections about how the notion of due diligence in (R3) is to be understood, I submit, the examples in this section make clear why, given (MP) and the regimentations and explications of §II, it is epistemically reasonable to accept a contextually a priori statement.

VII Putnam's Conceptual Schemes Explanation

Putnam offers a different explanation of contextual a priority. His proposed explanation depends on his idea, first articulated in "It Ain't Necessarily So," that a statement may be necessary relative to a "body of knowledge" or "conceptual scheme":

when we say that a statement is necessary relative to a body of knowledge, we imply that it is included in that body of knowledge and that it enjoys a special role in that body of knowledge. For example, one is not expected to give much of a reason for that kind of statement. But we do not imply that the statement is necessarily *true*, although, of course, it is thought to be true by someone whose knowledge that body of knowledge is.[33]

Putnam later noted that this talk of necessity relative to a body of knowledge is not accurate, since to say that a statement is necessary or that a belief is knowledge implies that they are true, and the truth if the relevant statements and beliefs is never guaranteed. He recommended, instead, that we speak of "*quasi*-necessity" relative to a "conceptual scheme."[34]

It is in terms of these notions that Putnam understands the notion of a contextually a priori statement. He presupposes, in effect, the following explication of "contextually a priori":

(1) A statement or belief is contextually a priori for a given speaker at a given time if and only if it is quasi-necessity relative to her conceptual scheme at that time.

Given (1), the key additional idea is that contextually a priori statements "can be overthrown only by conceiving of whole new theoretical structures." The result is what I call Putnam's

Conceptual scheme explanation. What explains why it is epistemically reasonable for an inquirer to accept a statement or belief that is *quasi*-necessary relative to her conceptual scheme, despite the fact that the quasi-necessity for her of the statement or belief is not a guarantee that it is true, is that such a statement "can only be overthrown by a new theory – sometimes by a revolutionary new theory – and not by observation alone. . ..."[35]

The problem with this explanation is that it does not fit with the practical methodological considerations that I highlighted in §§IV–VI. For the explanation presupposes that

(2) A statement is *quasi*-necessity relative to an inquirer's conceptual scheme if and only if the statement can only be overthrown by a new theory.

And (1) and (2) together imply

33 Putnam, "It Ain't Necessarily So," 240.
34 Putnam, "Rethinking Mathematical Necessity," 251.
35 Putnam, "'Two Dogmas' Revisited," 95.

(3) A statement is contextually a priori for a given speaker at a given time if and only if the statement can only be overthrown by a new theory.

If one accepts (R3), my proposed explication in §II of the notion of contextual apriority, however, the practical methodological considerations that I highlighted in §§IV–VI show that both the left-to-right and the right-to-left directions of the conditionals in (3) are false. Consider first the left-to-right direction – namely, if a statement can only be overthrown by a new theory, then it is contextually a priori. For a scientist in the eighteenth century who did not do her due diligence, it was not epistemically reasonable to accept that physical space is Euclidean, hence that statement was not contextually a priori for her, despite the fact that it would take over a century of work to see an alternative to Euclidean geometry. Hence the truth of the antecedent of the left-to-right conditional is not sufficient for the truth of its consequent. The right-to-left direction of (3) – namely, if a statement is contextually a priori for a given speaker at a time, then it can be overthrown only by conceiving of whole new theoretical structures – is also false. As Russell's discovery that Frege's Basic Law V is inconsistent shows, sometimes all it takes to undermine a contextually a priori statement is to ask a question about it that no one even considered before. Thus a person (e.g. Frege) may have a contextually a priori entitlement to accept a given statement (Basic Law V) even if little, if any, new theorizing is needed to specify a way in which the statement is, or may actually be, false.

There are, I grant, important methodological differences between Einstein's discovery that the geometry of physical space is non-Euclidean and Russell's discovery that Frege's Basic Law V is inconsistent. The problem with Putnam's conceptual schemes explanation is that these methodological differences do not explain the difference between having and not having a contextually a priori entitlement to accept a statement. A statement S is contextually a priori for a person at a given time only if she is unable to specify a way in which S may actually be false, in the practical sense of "unable" that I explained in §§IV–VI. Putnam's conceptual schemes explanation of contextual a priority leaves out these practical methodological considerations, and substitutes for them the very different methodological consideration of whether it would take a great deal of new theorizing to overthrow the statement. One key difference between these considerations is that the former are *synchronic* – they concern what an inquirer can do at a given time (i.e., whether at that time she can specify a way in which a given statement may actually be false) – whereas the methodological considerations that Putnam highlights, by contrast, are *diachronic* – they concern whether an inquirer could later come to reject or revise a given statement without developing a whole new theory.

One might think that these two types of considerations have a closer relationship to each other than my explanation of contextual apriority implies. Let us say that a statement is *deep* for a person if and only if she would have to develop a fundamentally new way of thinking even to conceive of how that statement may actually be false. One might suppose that in order for an inquirer to have a contextually a priori entitlement to accept a given statement S, he must both satisfy the synchronic criteria I describe and in addition believe that S is deep for him. But this cannot be quite right. For if he believes that S is deep for him, he will likely also believe that with enough time and hard work the statement would cease to become deep for him. And if he believes that with enough time and hard work the statement would cease to become deep for him, he should conclude that has not yet completed his due diligence – he should continue searching for a way in which the statement may actually be false until he is confident that more work will not uncover some hitherto overlooked way in which the statement may be false. We may infer that if he has done his due diligence, hence satisfies the synchronic criteria I described above, and he believes that S is deep for him, then he does not also believe that with enough time and hard work the statement would cease to become deep for him.[36] But when an inquirer satisfies these conditions, the truth of his belief that the statement is deep for him is not relevant to whether he has a contextually a priori entitlement to accept the statement. For example, as I argued above, Frege had a contextually a priori entitlement to accept Basic Law V, but that law was, in fact, not deep for him.

One might nevertheless think that an inquirer could not take himself to have done his due diligence in accepting a statement that is contextually a priori for him unless he believes that the statement is deep for him. As we have seen, however, what matters for contextual apriority is what an inquirer can do at a given time – whether or not he can specify a way in which a given statement may

---

36 One of my central arguments in "Putnam and the Contextually A Priori" (in *The Philosophy of Hilary Putnam*, edited by Randall E. Auxier, Douglas R. Anderson, and Lewis Edwin Hahn, 389–411 (Chicago, IL: Open Court, 2015)) against the conceptual schemes explanation in effect presupposes that an inquirer believes that a statement is deep for him only if he also believes that with enough time and hard work the statement would cease to become deep for him. Putnam, "Reply to Gary Ebbs," in *The Philosophy of Hilary Putnam*, 417, rightly objects that there is no incompatibility between an inquirer's believing a statement is deep for him and his having a contextually a priori entitlement to accept it. This is so, I now see, if the inquirer does not also believe that with enough time and hard work the statement would cease to become deep for him. As I explain in the text following this footnote, however, in such situations the assumption that a person's belief that a given statement is deep for him is not what explains why it is contextually a priori for him.

actually be false – and this consideration is independent of whether or not the statement is deep for him. Moreover, it is unclear how S's being deep for him could be viewed as an additional requirement for it being epistemically reasonable to him to accept S. Inquirers cannot survey their own conceptual scheme from a standpoint outside of it.[37] They may form beliefs about whether various statements they accept are deep for them. However, unless they also believe that with enough time and hard work the statements would cease to become deep for them – an attitude that, as we saw in the previous paragraph, is incompatible with the supposition that they have done their due diligence – their beliefs that the statements are deep for them simply reflect, and do not provide any additional support for, their own best practical and synchronic judgments about whether the statements have systematic import for them and whether they can specify any ways in which the statements may actually be false.[38]

It might appear that this objection to Putnam's conceptual scheme explanation rests on a classical skeptical worry – the worry that if an inquirer judges that a given statement is deep for her at a given time, she may have overlooked something which, if she later considers it, will show her immediately that the statement was not deep for her.[39] But my central objection to Putnam's conceptual scheme explanation is not based on skepticism about what is deep for us. The objection is not that we can never know that a statement is deep for us (although that may be true), but that the methodological criteria for being contextually a priori are practical and synchronic, not theoretical and diachronic, as are the criteria for a statement's being deep.

In reply to my observation that Frege's acceptance of his Basic Law V was contextually a priori for him before he received Russell's letter – an observation I first made in "Putnam and the Contextually A Priori" – Putnam writes:

> There is a sense in which any significant group of beliefs could be overthrown by showing them to be *logically* inconsistent. The task would then the rise of finding a way of repairing the breach in our scientific system. If you like, instead of saying, as I did, that a framework principle can be refuted "only by conceiving of whole new theoretical structures," I could have written (had I worried about the problem of hidden logical inconsistencies): "only by conceiving a whole new theoretical structures, or by showing it to be inconsistent, in which

---

37 Here I agree with Putnam: "The illusion that there is in all cases a fact of the matter as to whether a statement is "necessary or only quasi-necessary" is the illusion that there is a God's-Eye View from which all possible epistemic situations case be surveyed and judged; and that is indeed an illusion." (Putnam, "Rethinking Mathematical Necessity," 258)

38 That these latter judgments are practical and synchronic follows from my proposed explications of "systematic import" (in §II) and of "person x is unable to specify a way in which S may actually be false" (in §§IV–VI).

39 Putnam raises this objection in "Reply to Gary Ebbs" on page 415.

case the scientific community will be forced to conceive of a whole new theoretical structure." And "conceive of a whole new theoretical structure" is precisely what Russell did
with his theory of types. A logical contradiction can, indeed, sometimes be overlooked; but
the possibility of non-Euclidean geometry (or, in the case of the principle of determinism,
the possibility of indeterministic quantum mechanics) is not something one simply
"overlooks."[40]

I agree with all of these methodological observations. The problem, however, is
that they do not address Putnam's problem as I formulate it in §II. Among the
statements that are contextually a priori for us at a given time are some logical
and mathematical statements that we accept without proof at that time. As Putnam of course knows, Gödel's second incompleteness theorem implies that we
cannot prove the consistency of any logical or mathematical proof system PS that
we use unless we presuppose a stronger logical or mathematical proof system PS'.
But PS' must then also be part of our total theory, and, by Gödel's second incompleteness theorem, again, the consistency of PS' cannot be proved within PS'.
There is no way to avoid taking a stand on whether one's logic and mathematics
are consistent, and no such stand has the logical or mathematical resources to
prove its own consistency. Our acceptance without proof of the consistency of logical and mathematical truths is of a piece with the synchronic, practical point of
view on the methods of inquiry that is key to understanding why it is epistemically reasonable for us to accept statements that are contextually a priori for us.
The case of Frege's Basic Law V and the methodological investigations in §§IV–VI
therefore show that the question whether a statement is deep for us – i.e., the diachronic question whether we would have to develop a fundamentally new way of
thinking even to conceive of how that statement may actually be false – is different from the question whether it is epistemically reasonable for us to accept it.
Finally, while it is true, as Putnam observes, that when a statement we once relied
on is found to be inconsistent, we are "forced to conceive of a whole new theoretical structure," this observation does not help to explain the sense in which, before
we discovered that the statement is inconsistent, it was epistemically reasonable
for us to accept it.

I conclude that Putnam's conceptual schemes explanation is unsuccessful.
If we adopt the methodological principle summarized by (MP), as I recommend,
then it is only by investigating the methods of inquiry and related requirements
of due diligence in which our contextually a priori statements are embedded
that we can make clear why it is epistemically reasonable for us to accept them.

---

40 Putnam, "Reply to Gary Ebbs," 416.

Acknowledgments: This paper is a development of ideas I first articulated in my paper "Putnam and the Contextually A Priori," which was completed in 2003. In July 2009, Putnam showed me a draft of his generous and brilliant "Reply to Gary Ebbs" (see note 36 above). Despite Putnam's reply, I remain convinced, for essentially the same reasons I presented in "Putnam and the Contextually A Priori," that his conceptual schemes explanation is unsuccessful. In the present paper I offer what I take to be a clearer, more direct explanation of why the conceptual schemes explanation fails. Several paragraphs of §I are lightly revised versions of paragraphs in my papers "Putnam on Methods of Inquiry" (*Harvard Review of Philosophy* 24 (2017): 121–125) and "Analyticity: the Carnap-Quine Debate and its Aftermath" (in *The Cambridge History of Philosophy: 1945–2015*, edited by Kelly Becker and Iain Thompson (Cambridge: Cambridge University Press, 2019), 32–48). Much of §II and parts of §§VI and VII draw on material from unpublished papers that I presented at a Harvard University Philosophy Department Colloquium and at a meeting of the Kentucky Philosophical Association in 2011, and at a University of Illinois-Urbana Philosophy Department Colloquium, a Midwest Epistemology Workshop, and a conference at the University of Sydney, Australia, in 2012. For helpful comments on these and other occasions I thank Kate Abramson, Selim Berker, Albert Casullo, Matt Carlson, Sandy Goldberg, Mark Kaplan, Maria Lasonen-Aarnio, Adam Leite, Kirk Ludwig, David Macarthur, Richard Moran, Tim O'Connor, Jim Pryor, Mark Richard, Tim Scanlon, Brian Weatherson, Steve Wagner, and Joan Weiner. I also thank Joan Weiner for pointing out to me passages by Frege in which he explains his methodological attitude toward his Basic Law V, and Matt Carlson for very helpful written comments on the penultimate draft.

Tim Button
Mathematical Internal Realism

Abstract: In "Models and Reality" (1980), Putnam sketched a version of his internal realism as it might arise in the philosophy of mathematics. Here, I will develop that sketch. By combining Putnam's model-theoretic arguments with Dummett's reflections on Gödelian incompleteness, we arrive at (what I call) the Skolem-Gödel Antinomy. In brief: our mathematical concepts are perfectly precise; however, these perfectly precise mathematical concepts are manifested and acquired via a formal theory, which is understood in terms of a computable system of proof, and hence is incomplete. Whilst this might initially seem strange, I show how internal categoricity results for arithmetic and set theory allow us to face up to this Antinomy. This also allows us to understand why "Models are not lost noumenal waifs looking for someone to name them," but "constructions within our theory itself," with "names from birth."

In "Models and Reality," Putnam sketched a version of his internal realism as it might arise in the philosophy of mathematics. The sketch was tantalising, but it was only a sketch. Mathematics was not the focus of any of his later writings on internal realism, and Putnam ultimately abandoned internal realism itself. As such, I have often wondered: *What might a developed mathematical internal realism have looked like?*

I will try to answer that question here, by reflecting on a discussion between Putnam, Dummett, Parsons and McGee which spanned nearly five decades. This paper also builds on work I have co-authored with Walsh. For readability, I have abandoned many of the historical contours in favour of "rational reconstruction," and I have relegated most of my commentary on the origins of various ideas to footnotes. But I should like to make it perfectly clear that, without the work of the people just mentioned, this paper could not even have begun.

Acknowledgements: I wrote much of this paper during a period of research leave which was funded by a Philip Leverhulme Prize (awarded by the Leverhulme Trust, PLP–2014–140). For comments and discussions on drafts of this paper, and earlier versions of these thoughts, I would like to thank Neil Barton, Sharon Berry, Cian Dorr, Hartry Field, Luca Incurvati, Mary Leng, Guy Longworth, Vann McGee, Charles Parsons, Michael Potter, Robert Trueman, Sean Walsh, Crispin Wright, and Wesley Wrigley. But I would like to thank Sean Walsh most of all: we wrote *Philosophy and Model Theory* together, and this paper owes *so* much to our collaboration.

https://doi.org/10.1515/9783110769210-007

I Acquisition and Manifestation

I want to start by considering our *natural number* concept. For clarity: I am not interested in specific number concepts, like *four* or *twenty*. I am interested in the general *natural number* concept, as used within serious mathematics.

We have to acquire our mathematical concepts. Even if we are born with the capacity to acquire mathematical concepts, we are not born with the concepts themselves. No baby has the general *number* concept.

Equally, we must be able to manifest our mathematical concepts. Whilst mathematicians sometimes work alone, mathematical practice is fundamentally communal. Mathematicians present each other with proofs and projects.[1]

In our early steps towards acquiring the *number* concept, we learn how to recite sequences like "1, 2, 3, 4, 5," and learn how to use such sequences to count out small collections of objects (fish, fingers, beads, or cows). Later, we master algorithms for adding and multiplying numbers in decimal notation. And so it goes. But my interest here is not in numerical cognition, infant or adult. It is in the *number* concept itself, as used in serious mathematics. And, whatever developmental and pedagogical steps we might take towards acquiring that concept, we qualify as having acquired it fully, only when we have grasped some full-blown arithmetical theory, such as Peano arithmetic.[2] Equally, we fully manifest our grasp of the concept, only by articulating and using some such theory.

In what follows, then, I will assume that serious mathematical concepts can be (and only can be) fully acquired and manifested by mastering and articulating some theory. Much more could be said in defence of this assumption. But I think the assumption is correct, and this paper is an attempt to work through its consequences. In §§II–IV, I will explain how this assumption threatens to constrain the precision of our mathematical concepts; then, in §§V–X, I will explain how we can overcome that threat by developing Putnam's internal realism.

---

1 Here I intend to connect with Dummett's long-held insistence on the importance of manifestation and acquisition (see e.g., Michael Dummett, "The Philosophical Significance of Gödel's Theorem" (1963), reprinted in *Truth and Other Enigmas* (London: Duckworth, 1978), 188–190).
2 For interesting discussion concerning the stage at which we (implicitly) grasp Peano arithmetic (or something like it), see Lance J. Rips, Amber Bloomfield and Jennifer Asmuth, "From Numerical Concepts to the Concept of Number," *Behavioral and Brain Science* 31, no. 6 (2008): 623–687 and the subsequent "Open Peer Commentary."

II Modelism

Consider this question: *How precise is our natural number concept?*[3] A specific philosophical character, the *modelist*, answers this question with a slogan. She says:

> The *natural number* concept is precise up to isomorphism.

But, of course, the modelist will need to flesh out this slogan. To this end, she makes the following speech:

> To consider the *natural number* concept, we can simply consider the class of all natural-number sequences. After all, that class encodes everything we could ever want to know about the *natural number* concept. So, when you ask, "How precise is our *natural number* concept?," I attack this by instead asking, "How refined is the class of arithmetical models?"
>
> Well, on the one hand: suppose we had two sequences that were not isomorphic. In that case, we would not allow that both were natural-number sequences, since they would differ in some arithmetically important respect. So: every model in the class must be isomorphic to every other.
>
> On the other hand: arithmetic does not really seem to care about the differences between isomorphic sequences. So: the class should be closed under isomorphism.
>
> Combining these two points: every model in the class must be isomorphic to every other, and the class must be closed under isomorphism. In short, the class of arithmetical models is an *isomorphism type*.[4] And that is what I mean, when I say that the *number* concept is precise up to isomorphism. I mean that we can (and should) use an isomorphism type as a surrogate for the *number* concept.
>
> Note that many mathematical concepts are not so precise. As an example: the *linear order* concept is a perfectly decent concept, but plenty of linear orders are not isomorphic, so that the *linear order* concept is not precise up to isomorphism. My view is roughly that our foundational mathematical concepts are (or, aim to be) precise up to isomorphism. Admittedly, the idea of a "foundational" concept is a little imprecise, but I hope you get a sense of my ambition.

---

3 Dummett and Charles Parsons ask roughly this question (see Dummett's "The Philosophical Significance of Gödel's Theorem," and Parsons' "The Uniqueness of the Natural Numbers," *Iyyun* 39, no. 1 (1990): 13–44). Hilary Putnam raises very similar issues, but via questions which focus more on *objects* than on *concepts* ("Models and Reality," *The Journal of Philosophical Logic* 45, no. 3 (1980): 464–482). However, objectual and conceptual versions of the question are very similar (see Tim Button and Sean Walsh, *Philosophy and Model Theory* (Oxford: Oxford University Press, 2018), Chs. 6–8). So, for simplicity, I will focus solely on the conceptual version.

4 Our modelist might do better to focus on definitional equivalence instead of isomorphism (see Button and Walsh, *Philosophy and Model Theory*, §§5.1–5.2); but this would not change the dialectic, so I will ignore this complication.

That is modelism, in a nutshell. Modelism is obviously structuralist, but it is just one version of structuralism. And its special reliance on model theory gives rise to its name, *modelism*.[5]

Modelism is appealing. Unfortunately, as Putnam taught us, it is dead wrong. It succumbs to the *model-theoretic argument*.[6]

In §I, I insisted that mathematical concepts must be tied to theories, via manifestation and acquisition. So, if the modelist is right that the *number* concept is precise up to isomorphism, then our arithmetical theory must pick out an isomorphism type. But formal theories are offered in formal languages, and formal languages have certain provable limitations. For example, we have:

The Löwenheim-Skolem Theorem. If a (countable, first-order) arithmetical theory has any infinite models, then it has models of every infinite cardinality.

A Corollary of Compactness. If a (first-order) arithmetical theory has any infinite models, then it has models containing non-standard elements.

So – assuming we are limited to (countable) first-order theories – our theory cannot pick out a unique isomorphism type. In which case, given that the *number* concept was supposed to be precise up to isomorphism, no theory will allow us (fully) to manifest or acquire our *number* concept. And that contradicts what I insisted upon in §I.

This is the kernel of the model-theoretic argument against modelism. To make it stick, though, we must defend the assumption that the modelist *is* limited to considering formal, (essentially) first-order, theories.

First, then, consider *formality*. As a practice, arithmetic is not just a list of axioms, but rather a "MOTLEY of techniques and proofs," to use Wittgenstein's

---

5 Button and Walsh coined the term "modelism"; see *Philosophy and Model Theory*, Ch. 6 for more.

6 The remainder of this section presents the central problem I extract from Putnam's invocation of the Löwenheim-Skolem Theorem in "Models and Reality." (Admittedly, Putnam raised the issue in a more "objectual" than "conceptual" key; but see footnote 3, above.) Dummett raised a similar problem, focussing on Gödelian incompleteness (see "The Philosophical Significance of Gödel's Theorem," 192). For more, see Button and Walsh, *Philosophy and Model Theory*, Ch. 7.

imagery.[7] A modelist might want to suggest that this informal motley plays some role in picking out an isomorphism type.[8]

Now, insofar as model theory (as a branch of pure mathematics) considers theories, it considers only formal theories. So, if a modelist appeals to informal mathematics, we cannot just deploy results from model theory to raise problems for her. And this might seem like a strike in favour of an "informalist" modelism.

However, this point cuts both ways. The very notion of an *isomorphism type* is something we define within model theory. So it is hard to see how anyone could even hope to explain how an informal theory could pin down a unique isomorphism type. Moreover, leaving this issue unexplained is not a viable option. After all, to treat the matter as inexplicable would be to say that it is just a brute feature of the world – a "surd metaphysical fact"[9] – that our informal mathematical practice pins down one particular isomorphism type. And this would be tantamount to the patently ridiculous claim:

> Everyone who wears this *particular* motley just happens to pick out this very *specific* thing; which is really rather fortunate, since (a priori) any of us might have picked out different things, or indeed have failed to pick out anything at all!

On pain of embarrassment, then, I take it that modelists *are* restricted to using formal theories, and will seek to explain how such theories can pin down isomorphism types.[10]

As I presented the model-theoretic argument, though, I did not just assume that the modelist's favourite theory must be formal; I also assumed that the theory must be first-order (and countable). To explain why this is a significant assumption, allow me to mention some simple technicalities. When we use the *full* semantics for second-order logic, we treat second-order quantifiers as ranging over the full powerset of the first-order domain. (This allows us to gloss "$\forall X$"

---

7 Ludwig Wittgenstein, *Remarks on the Foundations of Mathematics*, translated by G.E.M. Anscombe (Oxford: Blackwell, 1956), §46.

8 This seems to be Benacerraf's response to Putnam's "Models and Reality." See Paul Benacerraf and Crispin Wright, "Skolem and the Skeptic," *Proceedings of the Aristotelian Society 59* (1985): 108–111.

9 To use Putnam's phrase from Hilary Putnam, *Reason, Truth and History* (Cambridge: Cambridge University Press, 1981), 48. (The context of the quote is the permutation argument against metaphysical realism in general; but the same thought applies here.)

10 Admittedly, mathematicians were discussing "the natural numbers" long before they had any formal theories (in the modern sense). So, to tell the historical story of how we (collectively) acquired the *number* concept, we would certainly need to consider informal practice. But this does not affect the general point that, in terms of §1, the concept is manifested with its full precision by (and only by) use of a formal theory.

roughly as "for any subset of the first-order domain.") Neither the Löwenheim-Skolem nor the Compactness theorems hold, given this semantics. On the contrary, we have this:[11]

Dedekind's Categoricity Theorem. Given the full semantics for second-order logic, second-order Peano arithmetic is categorical (i.e., all models of the theory are isomorphic).

So, the modelist might reply to the model-theoretic argument by invoking Dedekind's result, and saying:

> The theory of second-order Peano arithmetic allows us to acquire and manifest a *number* concept that is precise up to isomorphism.

This reply is tempting, but it is fatally flawed.[12] The flaw does not concern the use of *second-order* Peano arithmetic; there is nothing intrinsically wrong with allowing quantification into predicate-position. The flaw concerns the appeal to the *full semantics* for second-order logic.

Our modelist wants to say that some (formal) theory allows us to acquire and manifest our *number* concept. Indeed, she has specified a particular theory: second-order Peano arithmetic. However, if we approach second-order Peano arithmetic using the *Henkin* semantics for second-order logic, then both the Löwenheim-Skolem and Compactness results return. So, the modelist must insist that we approach second-order Peano arithmetic using her favourite semantics: the *full* semantics.

At this point, we must ask her to explain how we acquire and manifest the concepts involved in that semantics. I expect her to reply as follows:[13]

> The key concept, i.e. *powerset*, is just the concept of *all combinatorially possible sub-collections of a collection.*

---

11 For a modern proof, and references to plenty of other proofs, see e.g. Button and Walsh, *Philosophy and Model Theory*, §7.4.
12 What follows is, in effect, one version of Putnam's famous just-more-theory manoeuvre. See Hilary Putnam, "Realism and Reason," *Proceedings of the American Philosophical Society* 50, no. 6 (1977): 486–487 and "Models and Reality," 477, 481, as well as references and discussion in Tim Button, *The Limits of Realism* (Oxford: Oxford University Press, 2013), Chs. 4–7 and Button and Walsh, *Philosophy and Model Theory*, §§2.3, 7.7–8.
13 Thanks to Mary Leng for suggesting this way of putting it.

This is true. But we are no more born with that general mathematical concept, than we are born with the general *number* concept; we must acquire it. Equally, we must be able to manifest it. The rules of §I apply.[14]

In §I, I noted that counting out small collections of objects is probably an important step on the road towards acquiring the *number* concept. In the end, though, I insisted that we grasp the general concept only when we grasp some full-blown mathematical theory. Similarly: manipulating small collections of objects may be an important step on the road towards acquiring the notion of *set*, but we grasp the general concept of *powerset* only when we grasp some full-blown mathematical theory.

As before: allowing this theory to be informal will leave everything unexplained. So the modelist must accept that the theory which gives us the *powerset* concept is formal.

Now, though, the modelist has begun on an infinite regress. To make it explicit:

(1a) To explain how we come to grasp the *number* concept, the modelist presents us with a formal theory, T_1.

(1b) However, if T_1 is to pin down the *number* concept up to isomorphism, T_1 must be understood via some "intended" semantics.

(1c) So, if T_1 is to achieve what the modelist wants, we must understand the concepts involved in T_1's "intended" semantics before being introduced to T_1.

(2a) To explain how we come to grasp those semantic concepts, the modelist presents us with a formal theory, T_2.

(2b) However, if T_2 is to pin down those semantic concepts sufficiently precisely, T_2 must be understood via some "intended" semantics.

(2c) So, if T_2 is to achieve what the modelist wants, we must understand the concepts involved in T_2's "intended" semantics before being introduced to T_2.

. . .

So it goes. This is clearly a regress.[15] Equally clearly, it is vicious. It simply cannot be a constraint, on acquiring or manifesting the concepts involved in one

---

14 It is sometimes suggested that our grasp of plural logic will deliver the required combinatorial concept. But the same question arises: what allows us to grasp *full* plural logic, rather than *Henkin* plural logic? Salvatore Florio and Øystein Linnebo, "On the Innocence and Determinacy of Plural Quantification," *Noûs* 50, no. 3 (2016): 565–583 develop this criticism elegantly.

15 Note that it is useless to suggest that $T_n = T_{n+k}$, for some n and all k, since there are guaranteed to be "unintended" Henkin-style interpretations of each T_n, and these will yield unintended interpretations of T_1.

theory, that we must first acquire or manifest the concepts involved in the theory at the next level; if it were, then we would never be able to acquire or manifest our concepts *at all*.

One final point. Earlier, our modelist moved straight from first-order logic to second-order logic with its full semantics. In fact, she might have attempted to rebut the model-theoretic argument by invoking any of several alternative logics. But there is a hard limit on this strategy. As noted above, the Compactness Theorem is sufficient to yield a model-theoretic argument. But Compactness holds for any logic with a finitary (sound and complete) proof system.[16] So: if the modelist wants to use a logic which is strong enough to pin down an isomorphism type, then the logic cannot be fully articulated proof-theoretically, but must instead be articulated semantically. And that suffices to set the modelist off on her vicious regress.

III A Dummettian Approach

Modelism has failed. We need an alternative. The obvious thought is simply to try approaching matters proof-theoretically, rather than model-theoretically. Indeed, this was Dummett's approach. His central idea can be stated as follows:

(a) Mathematical concepts are fully determined by their uses in proofs.

This idea promises to handle the requirements of acquisition and manifestation better than modelism did. After all, when it comes to teaching and learning mathematics, rules of proof are rather more tractable than isomorphism types.

Unfortunately, there is an immediate barrier to this proposal. Let P be any algorithmically-checkable proof-system, by which I mean that there is an algorithm which decides whether any putative P-proof is a genuine P-proof. Now, suppose for reductio that P-provability exhausts the arithmetical facts, i.e., that, for every arithmetical sentence φ:

$$\varphi \text{ iff there is a } P\text{-proof that } \varphi$$

Since our proof-system is algorithmically-checkable, some computable function captures the idea that n is (the code of) a P-proof of (the code of) φ. This means that there will be an arithmetical predicate, Tr, such that, for any arithmetical sentence φ:

---

16 See Button and Walsh, *Philosophy and Model Theory*, §7.9.

there is a *P*-proof that φ iff *Tr*('φ')

Combining the biconditionals, for any arithmetical sentence φ:

φ iff *Tr*('φ')

But this contradicts Tarski's Indefinability Theorem.[17] So *P*-provability does not exhaust the arithmetical facts after all. Generalising on *P*, we obtain:

(b)　No algorithmically-checkable proof-system exhausts the arithmetical facts.

Dummett is aware of this sort of reasoning,[18] but he does not take it to undermine (a). Instead, he *ponenses* where others might *tollens*. Since Dummett insists that the *number* concept *is* fully determined by its use in proofs, he takes (b) to show that "no *formal* system can ever succeed in embodying all the principles of proof that we should intuitively accept."[19] That is, combining (a) with (b), he concludes that that the *number* concept itself "cannot be fully expressed by means of any formal system."[20]

　　Unfortunately, this leads to a rather unhappy conclusion. Following Dummett, I have insisted that our *number* concept must be both acquirable and manifestable. But machines, I take it, can only manifest and acquire concepts which *can* be fully expressed by means of some formal system.[21] Given Dummett's claim that the *number* concept "cannot be fully expressed by means of any formal system," he must accept that machines cannot acquire the *number* concept itself, but can only acquire some imprecise approximation to it. In short, Dummett is committed to a startling disjunction:

(c)　Either we are not machines, or we do not possess the *number* concept.[22]

17　I have put the problem this way, rather than simply invoking the fact that the class of arithmetical truths is not computably enumerable, to emphasise that the problem does not depend a notion of arithmetical truth that is (somehow) "prior" to a notion of proof.

18　Though Dummett, "The Philosophical Significance of Gödel's Theorem," focusses on Gödelian reasoning, rather than on Tarskian undefinability.

19　Dummett, "The Philosophical Significance of Gödel's Theorem," 200.

20　Dummett, "The Philosophical Significance of Gödel's Theorem," 186.

21　Setting aside machines with access to oracles.

22　This is obviously similar to Gödel's Disjunction (Kurt Gödel, "Some Basic Theorems on the Foundations of Mathematics and Their Implications" (1951), reprinted in Kurt Gödel, *Collected Works*, Vol. 3, edited by Solomon Feferman et al. (Oxford: Oxford University Press, 1995), 310). However, the right disjunct here ("we do not possess the *number* concept") should be contrasted with Gödel's ("there exist absolutely unsolvable diophantine problems").

I cannot take seriously the possibility that we do not possess the *number* concept. Equally, though, I cannot allow that our philosophy of mathematics might require that we are not machines. I therefore have no option but to part ways with Dummett.

IV The Skolem-Gödel Antinomy

The previous three sections can be summarised as follows. We (fully) acquire and manifest our mathematical concepts via formal theories. Modelism treats such theories model-theoretically. In so doing, it succumbs to Putnam's model-theoretic argument. The obvious alternative is to treat formal theories proof-theoretically. But, to allow for the possibility that we are machines, the relevant proof-system must be algorithmically-checkable; and the *number* concept is sufficiently precise that no algorithmically-checkable proof-system exhausts the arithmetical facts. All told, then, we find ourselves in the following predicament:

The Skolem-Gödel Antinomy. Our mathematical concepts are perfectly precise. However, these perfectly precise mathematical concepts are (fully) acquired and manifested via a formal theory, which is understood in terms of an algorithmically-checkable proof-system, and hence is incomplete.

Confronted with this antinomy, one might well worry that *something must have gone wrong*: *surely* any concept which is (fully) articulated in an *incomplete* theory must be *imprecise*? I certainly feel the tension; indeed, that is why I call this predicament an "antinomy."[23] Still, I do not think that anything has gone wrong. This really is our predicament, and we must face up to it.

With that in mind, the rest of this paper outlines a position, *internalism*, which aims to resolve the Skolem-Gödel Antinomy. Moreover, as I will show, internalism amounts to a detailed development of the mathematical internal realism which Putnam sketched at the end of his "Models and Reality."[24]

---

23 Cf. Putnam's ("Models and Reality," 464) use of "antinomy."
24 The material in the second half of this paper develops joint work with Sean Walsh (Button and Walsh, *Philosophy and Model Theory*, Chs. 10–12). In that work, Sean and I did not endorse internalism; we simply wanted to articulate the best possible version of internalism. In this paper, I want to stick my neck out slightly further. Here is how.

I am confident that the Skolem-Gödel Antinomy accurately describes our predicament. Moreover, internalism strikes me as the most promising line of response to that Antinomy. Indeed, at the moment, I see no other way to face up to the Antinomy. Still, there is much more work to be

V Internalism about Arithmetic

I will start by outlining a formal theory of arithmetic which articulates the *natural number* concept *incompletely*, but still shows that concept to be perfectly *precise*.

I do not want to assume that everything is a number. So I need a primitive predicate, "$N(x)$" which is to be read as "x is a natural number." I also need a primitive function symbol, "$s(x)$" to be read as "the successor of x." To save some space in my formalisms, I will also introduce two obvious abbreviations:

$(\forall x: \Phi)\Psi$ abbreviates $\forall x(\Phi(x) \rightarrow \Psi)$
$(\exists x: \Phi)\Psi$ abbreviates $\exists x(\Phi(x) \wedge \Psi)$

Using these symbols and abbreviations, I can lay down four axioms:

(1) $(\forall n: N)\, N(s(n))$
   i.e. the successor of any number is a number
(2) $(\exists z: N)(\forall n: N)\, s(n) \neq z$
   i.e. there is a zero-element
(3) $(\forall m: N)(\forall n: N)(s(m) = s(n) \rightarrow m = n)$
   i.e. successor is injective on the numbers
(4) $\forall F([(\forall z: N)((\forall n: N)\, s(n) \neq z \rightarrow F(z)) \wedge (\forall n: N)(F(n) \rightarrow F(s(n)))] \rightarrow (\forall n: N)\, F(n))$
   i.e. induction holds for the numbers: for any property F, if every zero-element has F and F is closed under successor, then every number has F.

Let PA$_{int}$ be the conjunction of these four axioms. The name abbreviates *Peano Arithmetic*, *int*ernalised, since PA$_{int}$ is just second-order Peano arithmetic, with all the axioms relativised to "N". This is the theory which I will wield in the face of the Skolem-Gödel Antinomy.

To appreciate the virtues of PA$_{int}$, imagine that Solange and Tristan have both learned PA$_{int}$.[25] They are now happily babbling away to each other, exploring the

---

done to clarify internalism. And, although I hope otherwise, such further work may end up exposing deep flaws in internalism. So, the situation is this. If you forced me to declare for some position in the philosophy of mathematics, then I would declare myself an internalist, and hope that everything works out for the best. But, absent that compulsion, I hesitate to call myself an avowed internalist. For readability, though, I will keep these reservations buried in this footnote. In the main text of this paper, I will write as a straightforward advocate of internalism.

25 The idea here is inspired by Parsons's discussions of Kurt and Michael in "The Uniqueness of the Natural Numbers." For more on the similarities and differences between this approach and Parsons's, see Button and Walsh, *Philosophy and Model Theory*, §10.B.

theory's consequences. They shared a teacher, and so they use the same word-types as each other. Still, to keep things clear, I will use "N_1" for Solange's number-predicate and "s_1" for her successor-function, so that Solange advances PA_{int} in this subscripted vocabulary, and I will call her subscripted theory $PA(N_1, s_1)$. Similarly, I will have Tristan advancing $PA(N_2, s_2)$.

In advancing $PA(N_1, s_1)$ and $PA(N_2, s_2)$, there is of course no guarantee that Solange and Tristan are talking about the same objects (if they even think of themselves as talking about objects at all). To take a trivial example: maybe "Solange's zero-element" is Solange herself, and "Tristan's zero-element" is Tristan, so that Solange (her tummy rumbling) can rightly say "zero is hungry," whilst Tristan (satiated) rightly says "zero is not hungry." But this *is* trivial, and for an obvious reason: mathematicians basically only care about arithmetical features of the natural numbers, and not about whether the numbers are hungry. We philosophers should probably do the same.

It is, then, unreasonable to ask for a guarantee that Solange and Tristan are talking about the same objects. It is much more reasonable to ask for a guarantee that Solange's numbers and Tristan's numbers share the same arithmetical structure. And the following result provides just such a guarantee:[26]

Internal Categoricity of PA

$$\vdash \forall N_1 \forall s_1 \forall N_2 \forall s_2([PA(N_1, s_1) \land PA(N_2, s_2)] \rightarrow$$
$$\exists R \, [\forall v \forall y(R(v, y) \rightarrow [N_1(v) \land N_2(y)]) \land$$
$$(\forall v: N_1)\exists! y R(v, y) \land$$
$$(\forall y: N_2)\exists! v R(v, y) \land$$
$$\forall v \forall y(R(v, y) \leftrightarrow R(s_1(v), s_2(y))))])$$

Roughly, this says the following: given that Solange's number-property and successor-function behave PA_{int}-ishly, and so do Tristan's number-property and successor-function, there is some relation, R, which takes us from Solange's numbers to Tristan's, and is bijective, and preserves successor (and hence also preserves zero-hood). Or, more briefly:

Provably, all of Solange's arithmetical structure is mirrored in Tristan's numbers, and vice versa.

---

26 See Button and Walsh, *Philosophy and Model Theory*, §10.B, and Juoko Väänänen and Tong Wang, "Internal Categoricity in Arithmetic and Set Theory," *Notre Dame Journal of Formal Logic* 56, no. 1 (2015), Theorem 1. For the sake of exposition, I have moved freely between treating e.g. "N_1" as a predicate and treating it as a relation-variable, leaving it to context to individuate what treatment is appropriate. For a rigorous treatment, see Button and Walsh, *Philosophy and Model Theory*, Chs. 10–12.

This *internal* categoricity result evidently resembles Dedekind's categoricity result, that all models of second-order Peano arithmetic are isomorphic (see §II). But it is worth spelling out the deep differences between these results.

Dedekind's result is model-theoretic. It is stated and proved in a semantic metalanguage. The internal categoricity result, by contrast, amounts to *metamathematics without semantic ascent*. It involves no semantic considerations at all. It is proved within the ordinary deductive system for (impredicative) second-order logic (as indicated by the use of '⊢' in the statement of the Internal Categoricity Theorem). The proved sentence is in the same language as PA_{int} itself (indeed, it is a sentence of the "purely logical" fragment of PA_{int}). So it is an internal categoricity theorem, in precisely the following sense: it neither takes us beyond the object language, nor outside that language's proof-system.

Sticking with deduction has a benefit. In §II, our modelist attempted to invoke Dedekind's categoricity result. This forced her to insist that some particular semantic theory was privileged, and this set her off on a vicious regress. Since the Internal Categoricity Theorem invokes no semantic notions, no similar regress can arise.

However, sticking with deduction also has a cost. Inevitably, PA_{int} cannot prove its own Gödel-sentence. Since we are viewing PA_{int} deductively, we must therefore see it as *incomplete*.

Such incompleteness was, of course, promised to us by the Skolem-Gödel Antinomy. Nonetheless – and to address that Antinomy – I now want to explain why PA_{int} succeeds in introducing a perfectly precise *number* concept.

Let us revisit Solange and Tristan, respectively affirming $PA(N_1, s_1)$ and $PA(N_2, s_2)$. Suppose that Solange affirms (an appropriate formalisation of) "every even number is the sum of two primes," at which Tristan shakes his head and replies "some even number is not the sum of two primes." Now, we already noted that Solange and Tristan need not agree about what the numbers are. Still, we might hope that Solange and Tristan are genuinely disagreeing here, rather than merely talking past each other in their different languages. After all, Goldbach's Conjecture is purely arithmetical, and all of Solange's arithmetical structure is mirrored in Tristan's numbers, and vice versa, so, *surely* they are genuinely engaged with each other?

Indeed they are. This follows from a neat corollary of PA_{int}'s internal categoricity:[27]

---

27 For a full statement and proof, see Button and Walsh, *Philosophy and Model Theory*, §§10.5, 10.B. Note the *schematic* character of this result. This might lead us to ask the internalist questions about the *syntactic theory* (as we asked the modelist questions about the *semantic* theory), but I think these can be addressed (see Button and Walsh, *Philosophy and Model Theory*, §10.8).

Intolerance of PA. For each second-order formula φ, whose only free variables are N and s, and whose quantifiers are all restricted to N:

$$\vdash \forall N \forall s(\mathrm{PA}(N, s) \to \varphi) \lor \forall N \forall s(\mathrm{PA}(N, s) \to \neg\varphi)$$

So, when Solange affirms Goldbach's Conjecture whilst Tristan denies it (in their respective languages), Solange cannot just shrug and say: "that might hold in your numbers, but it doesn't hold in mine!" If they share a logical language, then they must hold that one of them is *wrong*; for Goldbach's Conjecture must hold of all $\mathrm{PA}_{\mathrm{int}}$-ish *number* concepts (the left disjunct of the Intolerance Theorem) or fail of all of them (the right disjunct).

More generally, we can gloss the Intolerance Theorem as follows:

> *On pain of provable inconsistency, no two PA_{int}-ish number concepts can diverge over any arithmetical claim.*

This explains why I call the result an *intolerance* theorem; it shows that $\mathrm{PA}_{\mathrm{int}}$ does not tolerate different ways of pursuing arithmetic.

The Intolerance Theorem underpins my claim that $\mathrm{PA}_{\mathrm{int}}$ articulates the *number* concept precisely. To spell out the last steps towards this conclusion, I propose that we should think about *precision* in roughly the way that supervaluationists think about *determinacy*, i.e. via this heuristic:

> If we can equally well render a claim right or wrong, just by sharpening up the concepts involved in the claim in different ways, then that claim is *indeterminate* (prior to any sharpening of concepts). Otherwise, it is *determinate*.

Now let φ be any arithmetical claim. If φ holds for *every* $\mathrm{PA}_{\mathrm{int}}$-ish *number* concept, then we cannot render φ wrong, just by considering Tristan's *number* concept rather than Solange's, or whatever. So, by the above heuristic, it is determinate that φ. More generally, this suggests that we should gloss $\forall N \forall s(\mathrm{PA}(N, s) \to \varphi)$ as "it is determinate that φ." And this allows us to restate the Intolerance Theorem as follows:

Glossed Intolerance. For each second-order formula φ, whose only free variables are N and s, and whose quantifiers are all restricted to N:

$$\vdash \forall N \forall s(\mathrm{PA}(N, s) \to \varphi) \lor \forall N \forall s(\mathrm{PA}(N, s) \to \neg\varphi)$$

i.e.:   *either it is determinate that φ or it is determinate that ¬φ*
i.e.:   *it is determinate whether φ*

In sum: thanks to its intolerance, $\mathrm{PA}_{\mathrm{int}}$ articulates our *natural number* concept sufficiently precisely, that *every arithmetical claim is determinate*.

Allow me to summarise this section. The theory PA_{int} can be stated very briefly – it has just four conjuncts – so there is no difficulty in acquiring or manifesting either the theory itself or the concepts it articulates. Plenty of arithmetical claims are not decided by PA_{int}; it articulates the *number* concept incompletely. But PA_{int} articulates our *number* concept sufficiently precisely, that (provably) every arithmetical claim is determinate.

In short, PA_{int} gives us a way to respond to the Skolem-Gödel Antinomy of §IV, in the specific case of the *number* concept. That is the response I want to offer. And here is a more general statement of internalism (about arithmetic):

> I affirm PA_{int} unrestrictedly and unreservedly. With Dummett, I agree that the *number* concept is given to us primarily in terms of proof. Unlike Dummett, though, I rely upon an algorithmically-checkable proof-system. Then, with the modelist, I aim to prove the precision of my *number* concept, by proving the categoricity of my arithmetical theory. But, unlike the modelist, I am successful; and I succeed because my categoricity result is *internal*.

VI Intersubjectivity, Objectivity, and Objects

One moral of §V can be put as follows: *intolerance yields intersubjectivity*. More specifically: when a theory is intolerant, people using that theory are not just deploying *private* concepts, but are drawn into genuine (dis)agreement with each other. So, internalism provides an account of mathematical *intersubjectivity*. It is worth, though, briefly connecting this with issues about mathematical *objectivity* and mathematical *objects*.

As an internalist, I am committed to PA_{int}. I affirm it without reservation. And, in affirming it, I affirm that there *are* numbers: the axioms carry existential commitment. (I should be frank, and admit that I am not sure exactly how best to answer the question: *How do you know that there are numbers?* Still, as an internalist, I am committed to their existence.)

Moreover, this existential commitment is indispensable to the story I told in §V. To see why, suppose that there were no PA_{int}-ish number properties, i.e. that $\neg \exists N \exists s PA(N, s)$. Then we would vacuously have that both $\forall N \forall s (PA(N, s) \to \varphi)$ and $\forall N \forall s (PA(N, s) \to \neg \varphi)$, for each relevant φ. It would follow that that it is both determinate that φ and determinate that $\neg \varphi$. This would be catastrophic. So, contraposing, the satisfactoriness of my account of determinacy (and hence intersubjectivity) implicitly requires that $\exists N \exists s PA(N, s)$.

To repeat, then: internalists are committed to the *existence* of numbers. But I have said very little about their *nature*. I have said that (my) numbers behave

PA$_{int}$-ishly, but I have been silent about many things: about whether the numbers are mind-independent or theory-independent; about whether any number is a Gallic emperor, or a set (and, if so, which); and, returning to the trivial illustration in §V, even about whether the numbers are hungry.

I believe that I could say whatever I like about such matters. For this reason, I would really prefer to say nothing at all. It is fortunate, then, that there is a principled way for an internalist to insist that *all such matters are indeterminate.*[28]

In §V, I glossed $\forall N \forall s(PA(N, s) \rightarrow \varphi) \vee \forall N \forall s(PA(N, s) \rightarrow \neg\varphi)$ as "it is determinate whether φ." At the time, I restricted this gloss to sentences of a particular form (second-order formulas with only N and s free, and whose quantifiers are all restricted to N). But if I extend this gloss to cover sentences in richer languages, then I will get to say that it is indeterminate whether the number 2 is equal to Julius Caesar, or is hungry, or is (in)tangible. For if there are any PA$_{int}$-ish number properties, then there will be a number-property which takes 2 to be a hungry, tangible, Caesar, and another which takes it to be an abstract singleton set. More generally, on this approach, all questions about the "metaphysical nature" of numbers will have indeterminate answers. They can simply be ignored.

A "hardcore realist" might complain that this brisk response simply trivialises some *very important* questions in the metaphysics of mathematics.[29] Let them complain. My point is just that internalists get to say that all the facts about the numbers can be expressed in the language of arithmetic. And that strikes me as a nice "bonus point" in favour of internalism.[30]

VII Internalism about Set Theory

There is much more to say about internalism about arithmetic. I will say some of it in §X. First, I want to consider internalism about set theory. In brief, I want to lift the story of §§V–VI over from the *number* concept to the *set* concept.

As in §V, I will start by introducing an "internalised" theory of pure sets. Rather than using a Zermelo-Fraenkel-style theory, though, I prefer to use a set theory which captures the "minimal core" of the cumulative iterative notion of

---

28 This line is developed in Button and Walsh, *Philosophy and Model Theory*, §10.7.

29 The "hardcore realist" is a character from Putnam "Realism and Reason," 490. Thanks to Wesley Wrigley for suggesting I address this point.

30 Something similar also sounded good to Putnam; see his comments on "whether the number 2 is identical with a set, and if so, which set is identical with." ("Comments and Replies," in *Reading Putnam*, edited by Peter Clark and Bob Hale (Oxford: Blackwell, 1994), 248–251)

set. This *Level Theory* has its origins in work by Montague, Scott, Derrick, and Potter.[31]

I want to articulate a theory of pure sets. This is not to say that there is no set of the cows in the field; only that (for present purposes) I will ignore that set if it exists. To restrict attention to pure sets in this way, I need a predicate, "*P(x)*," to be read as "*x* is a pure set." Unsurprisingly, I will also need a membership predicate, "$\in$." Using these symbols and the abbreviations of §V, I can then write down some axioms:

(1) $\forall x \forall y (x \in y \rightarrow (P(x) \wedge P(y)))$
    i.e. we restrict our attention to membership facts between pure sets
(2) $(\forall x{:}\ P)(\forall y{:}\ P)[\forall z(z \in x \leftrightarrow z \in y) \rightarrow x = y]$
    i.e. pure sets are extensional entities
(3) $\forall F(\forall x{:}\ P)(\exists y{:}\ P)\forall z(z \in y \leftrightarrow (F(z) \wedge z \in x))$
    i.e. pure sets obey separation
(4) $(\forall x{:}\ P)(\exists v{:}\ Level)x \subseteq v$
    i.e. every set is found at some level

As written, principle (4) uses an undefined predicate, "*Level*". However – and this is the neat trick about the approach – we can explicitly define "*Level*" in terms of set-membership.[32] As such, the only primitives we need are "*P*" and "$\in$." Let LT$_{\text{int}}$ (for *Level-Theory, int*ernalised) be the conjunction of these four axioms.

---

31 I present a simple version of the theory in Tim Button, "Level Theory, Part 1: Axiomatizing the Bare Idea of a Cumulative Hierarchy of Sets," in *Bulletin of Symbolic Logic* 27, no. 4 (2021): 436–460. For the origins of Level Theory, see: Richard Montague, "Set Theory and Higher-Order Logic," in *Formal Systems and Recursive Functions. Proceedings of the Eight Logic Colloquium, July 1963*, edited by John Crossley and Michael Dummett, 131–148 (Amsterdam: North-Holland, 1965); Richard Montague, Dana Scott, and Alfred Tarski, "An Axiomatic Approach to Set Theory" (BANC MSS 84/69c, carton 4, folder 29–30, Bancroft Library, University of California, Berkeley); Dana Scott, "The Notion of Rank in Set-Theory," in *Summaries of Talks Presented at the Summer Institute for Symbolic Logic, Cornell University, 1957*, 267–269 (Princeton: Institute for Defence Analysis, 1960); Dana Scott, "Axiomatizing Set Theory," in *Axiomatic Set Theory II. Proceedings of the Symposium in Pure Mathematics of the American Mathematical Society, July-August 1967*, 207–214 (Providence: American Mathematical Society, 1974) and Michael Potter, *Set Theory and Its Philosophy* (Oxford: Oxford University Press, 2004), especially Ch. 3. Thanks to Charles Parsons for making me aware of Montague's work. For a brief presentation of all that is required for the purposes of this paper, see Button and Walsh, *Philosophy and Model Theory*, §§8.B–C, 11.C–D.
32 For the definition, see Button, "Level Theory, Part 1," Definition 2.2. This simplifies a definition due to Potter, *Set Theory and Its Philosophy*, 24, 41, which is also used in Button and Walsh, *Philosophy and Model Theory*, §§8.5, 8.C.

Crucially, LT$_{int}$ proves that the levels are well-founded by membership. This is why LT$_{int}$ provides the "minimal core" of the cumulative iterative conception of sets. It is the "core," since it tells us that sets are stratified into well-ordered levels. It is "minimal," because it makes no comment at all about how far the sequence of levels runs. (There is no powerset axiom; no axiom of infinity; no axiom of replacement.) Indeed, thinking model-theoretically for a moment, (the pure parts of) the full second-order models of LT$_{int}$ are, up to isomorphism, exactly the arbitrary stages of the (pure) cumulative hierarchy of sets, as axiomatised by second-order ZF.[33] But I mention this fact, only to make LT$_{int}$ feel a bit more familiar. I will treat LT$_{int}$ deductively, just as I treated PA$_{int}$ in §V.

Working deductively, then, we can recover an "internal" counterpart of Zermelo's quasi-categoricity theorem. Roughly, this says: if both Solange's and Tristan's pure sets behave LT$_{int}$-ishly, then their sets are isomorphic, as far as they go, but Solange's might go further than Tristan's (or vice versa). However, to keep this paper short, I will leave the details of internal quasi-categoricity for elsewhere,[34] and skip straight to a theory which is internally (totally) categorical. I call this theory CLT$_{int}$, for *Categorical Level-Theory*. We obtain it by adding a fifth conjunct to LT$_{int}$ (where "*f*" is a second-order function-variable):

(5) $\exists f\,(\forall x P(f(x)) \wedge \forall y(P(y) \rightarrow \exists! x\, f(x) = y))$
   i.e. *there are exactly as many pure sets as there are objects simpliciter*
   (i.e. objects which are either pure sets or not).

In the deductive system for impredicative second-order logic, we can then prove internal categoricity for CLT$_{int}$. Informally, this says that there is a membership-preserving bijection from Solange's pure sets to Tristan's. Formally:[35]

Internal Categoricity of CLT.
$\vdash \forall P_1 \forall \in_1 \forall P_2 \forall \in_2([CLT(P_1, \in_1) \wedge CLT(P_2, \in_2)] \rightarrow$
$\exists R\,[\forall v \forall y(R(v, y) \rightarrow [P_1(v) \wedge P_2(y)]) \wedge$
$(\forall v{:}P_1)\exists! y R(v, y) \wedge$
$(\forall y{:}P_2)\exists! v R(v, y) \wedge$
$\forall v \forall x \forall y \forall z([R(v, y) \wedge R(x, z)] \rightarrow [v \in_1 x \leftrightarrow y \in_2 z])])$

---

33 See Button and Walsh, *Philosophy and Model Theory*, §8.C.
34 Interested readers should look to Button and Walsh, *Philosophy and Model Theory*, §§11.2, 11.C and Button, "Level Theory, Part 1", §6.
35 See Button and Walsh, *Philosophy and Model Theory*, §§11.4, 11.D.

From internal categoricity, we can also obtain intolerance. Informally, this says that no two CLT_{int}-ish set concepts can diverge over any pure set-theoretic claim. Formally:[36]

Intolerance of CLT. For each second-order formula φ, whose only free variables are P and $\in$, and whose quantifiers are all restricted to P:

$$\vdash \forall P \forall \in (CLT(P, \in) \to \varphi) \vee \forall P \forall \in (CLT(P, \in) \to \neg\varphi)$$

The situation, then, is as with PA_{int}. The theory CLT_{int} gives *internalists about set theory* a concrete response to the Skolem-Gödel Antinomy of §IV, in the specific case of the *set* concept. It explains how, using an incomplete theory, we can acquire and manifest a *set* concept which is so precise, that any purely set-theoretic claim is determinate.[37]

VIII Internalism about Model Theory

I will say more about set theory in §X. First, I want to say a bit about model theory. I dismissed modelism in §II. But my complaint against modelism is not a complaint against model theory itself. Rather, it is a complaint against a philosophical misuse of model theory. Allow me to explain.

Modelists insist on using model theory to explicate mathematical concepts. This is a mistake, as the model-theoretic arguments show. From this, Putnam correctly concluded that we must (sometimes)[38] "foreswear reference to models in [our] account of understanding" mathematical theories and concepts. But the modelist's mistake is no part of the branch of pure mathematics known as *model theory*. So, as Putnam also emphasised, we do not "have to foreswear forever the notion of a model."[39] We just need to treat the pure-mathematical *model* concept in a suitably internalist fashion.

This is quite straightforward. In common with almost every branch of mathematics, model theory is largely carried out informally: the proofs are discursive,

---

36 See Button and Walsh, *Philosophy and Model Theory*, §11.5.

37 The approach, and invocation of a technical result, is greatly indebted to Vann McGee, "How We Learn Mathematical Language," *Philosophical Review* 106, no. 1 (1997): 35–68. For more on the similarities and differences, see Button and Walsh, *Philosophy and Model Theory*, §11.A.

38 Why only sometimes? See §IX.

39 Putnam "Models and Reality," 179. See also Dummett "The Philosophical Significance of Gödel's Theorem," 191, 193.

they omit tedious steps, and so forth. But we can easily grasp the idea that, "officially," model theory is implemented within set theory. After all, model-theorists freely use set-theoretic vocabulary and set-theoretic axioms to describe and construct models, and, in principle, all of the definitions of ordinary model theory could be rewritten in austerely set-theoretic terms.

So, in what follows, let MT_{int} (for *Model Theory, internalised*) be a suitable set theory to be used for model-theoretic purposes. There is no need to go into great detail about MT_{int}; I only need to explain how it relates to CLT_{int}. There are three crucial points:[40]

(1) MT_{int} deals with a pure set property, P, and a membership relation, $\in$.
   It might have other predicates too, but it has at least those.
(2) MT_{int} proves CLT_{int}.
   This means that MT_{int} is internally categorical with respect to pure sets.
(3) MT_{int} proves that there are infinitely many pure sets.
   This gives MT_{int} the resources to carry out basic reasoning concerning arithmetic and hence (arithmetised) syntax.

These points ensure that MT_{int} has all the basic vocabulary and conceptual resources for developing model theory as a branch of pure mathematics. Working model-theorists will certainly want to add more axioms to the underlying set theory – I will return to this in the next section – but we need nothing more at present.

Internalists about model theory affirm MT_{int}, and insist that model theory is "officially" carried out deductively within MT_{int}. The internal categoricity and intolerance of CLT_{int} then transfers across to MT_{int}, so that any purely model-theoretic claims are determinate. As per the earlier pattern, this provides an account of how we can acquire and manifest a perfectly precise *model* concept, via a deductively-understood theory.

(At some point, of course, we might want to consider impure model-theoretic claims. For example, we might want to consider a model whose domain encompasses the cows in the field. But the internalist about model theory can deal with this straightforwardly: the specifically model-theoretic features of an impure model will be determinate, provided that there is some isomorphic model with a pure domain.)

---

40 If we want to develop an account of truth for MT_{int} itself, then we should also insist that MT_{int} is a single formula, so that we can continue to use it in the course of internal categoricity results, in the form of conditionals like $\forall P \forall \in (MT(P, \in) \to \varphi)$. For details, see Button and Walsh, *Philosophy and Model Theory*, §§12.4, 12.A.

IX Revisiting Putnam's Mathematical Internal Realism

I have outlined internalist approaches to arithmetic, set theory, and model theory. I now want to consider the interactions between internalism about these three branches of mathematics, with an aim to illuminating Putnam's mathematical internal realism.

Suppose that Charlie has mastered arithmetic, in the form of PA_{int}, but that he knows no model theory. Nevertheless, we – who know some model theory – can pose a question: *Are any particular models of arithmetic "intended," from Charlie's perspective?*

The short answer is: *Yes: Charlie's use of PA_{int} makes certain models "intended."* But, to unpack this short answer, I will work within MT_{int}, and I will also augment the assumptions of §VIII, by assuming that MT_{int} proves second-order ZF.[41]

For any number-property, N, and any successor-function, s, let $\|N, s\|$ be the model (as the notion is defined in MT_{int}, of course) whose domain is the set whose members are exactly the instances of N, i.e. $\{n: N(n)\}$, and whose interpretation of the successor-symbol is the set whose members are similarly determined by s, i.e. $\{(m, n) : s(m) = n\}$. Now, the internal categoricity of PA_{int} almost immediately yields the following:

$$MT_{int} \vdash \forall N_1 \forall s_1 \forall N_2 \forall s_2 \left([PA(N_1, s_1) \wedge PA(N_2, s_2)] \rightarrow \right.$$
$$\left. \|N_1, s_1\| \text{ is isomorphic to } \|N_2, s_2\|\right)$$

And we can gloss this formal result as follows:

> *MT_{int} proves that all PA_{int}-ish number concepts determine isomorphic models.*

Since internalists about model theory affirm MT_{int}, they can affirm that PA_{int} pins down a unique model (up to isomorphism). Admittedly, if our *model* concept were somehow imprecise – that is, if the *model* concept could be sharpened in different ways – then although the previous result would show that each sharpening would yield only one "model of arithmetic," different possible sharpenings

---

41 I could get away with much less than second-order ZF, but I certainly need more than just (1)–(3) of §VIII. Without some extra assumptions, I cannot prove that $\{n: N(n)\}$ exists for each property N with countably many instances, nor that $\{(m, n): s(m) = n\}$ exists for each successor-ish function s on N. So, without some augmentation, I would only be able to prove a result which we might gloss as follows: all PA_{int}-ish *number* concepts which determine a model at all determine the same model (up to isomorphism).

might allow for different "models of arithmetic." Fortunately, MT_{int}'s intolerance precludes this situation from arising: given rival sharpenings of the *model* concept, only one of them can be right.

The situation, then, is simple. Working within MT_{int}, internalists get to say that Charlie's deductive "use [of PA_{int}] already fixes the [model-theoretic] 'interpretation'."[42]

All of this has a potentially surprising consequence: internalists can (and should) agree with modelists, that the *natural number* concept is *precise up to isomorphism*. In a sense, then, one might say that internalism employs "a similar picture" to modelism, only "within a theory."[43] *But this does not vindicate modelism itself.* For, to show that the *number* concept is precise up to isomorphism, internalists work within some model theory. And they claim to understand that model theory *deductively*, rather than *semantically*.

This observation is the key which unlocks the cryptic but beautiful closing line of Putnam's "Models and Reality." Since modelists always insist on working semantically, they embark on a futile regress, and end up treating models as "lost noumenal waifs looking for someone to name them"; this is just a poetic restatement of the lessons we learned in §II. However, by working deductively, internalists treat models as "constructions within our theory itself, [with] names from birth."[44] Saying this does not, though, involve any constructivist metaphysics; it is simply a way to summarise the central observations of this section.[45] In detail, the point is as follows: we understand our model theory deductively;[46] we define the expression "model" within that deductively-understood theory; we "construct models" by working deductively within that model theory; and we work within MT_{int} when we prove that all models of PA_{int} are isomorphic, to draw the conclusion that Charlie's deductive use of PA_{int} picks out a unique isomorphism type.

I expect the modelist to raise one last complaint against the internalist's insistence that we should understand MT_{int} deductively:

---

42 Putnam, "Models and Reality," 482.

43 Putnam, "Realism and Reason," 484, commenting on how to regard the relationship between internal realism (in general) and metaphysical realism (in general).

44 Putnam, "Models and Reality," 482. Cf. also Dummett, "The Philosophical Significance of Gödel's Theorem," 191.

45 Cf. Button, *The Limits of Realism*, 217.

46 Following Putnam, "Models and Reality," 482, I might say that "the metalanguage [i.e. the model theory itself] is completely understood." But there is a slight risk that the word "completely" might be misunderstood; treated deductively, the model theory is of course *incomplete* (on Gödelian grounds).

Working semantically, I can show that MT_{int} itself has many models if it has any. And if you insist on only ever working deductively, then you will be unable to rule out the worry that we are "trapped" in some non-standard model of MT_{in} itself. But, if you want to say that Charlie pins down the standard model by using PA_{int}, then you must rule out this worry. After all: if we are all trapped in a non-standard model of MT_{int}, then we will be right (speaking from within our non-standard model of MT_{int}) to say "all PA_{int}-ish number properties determine the same model (if they determine one at all)," but what we happen to call "the intended model of arithmetic" will be grotesque (as viewed from the outside).[47]

I can dismiss this complaint quite briskly. Suppose, for reductio, that we are "trapped" in some non-standard model, **M**, of MT_{int}. Working in MT_{int}, I can trivially prove: *every model's domain omits some element*. So now – if I can understand the modelist's worry that I am "trapped" in **M** *at all* – then I know, specifically, that **M**'s domain omits some elements.[48] And if I can grasp *that* point, then I know that I am not "trapped" in **M**, since I just managed to quantify over the supposedly omitted elements. So: we are not "trapped" in a non-standard model of MT_{int}.

We should not infer from this, though, that we "inhabit the standard model" of MT_{int}. The same line of thought which shows that we are not "trapped" in **M** generalises to show that we do not "inhabit" any particular model of MT_{int}. Or, to drop the homely metaphors, it shows that no model of MT_{int} is "intended."[49] And if that initially sounds shocking, it really should not. Once we have abandoned modelism, there is no reason to think that a theory *needs* an "intended" model.

The overarching moral is encapsulated in a single quote from Putnam: for any theory, "either the use already fixes the 'interpretation', or nothing can."[50] But I read this as a genuine disjunction, rather than a rhetorical flourish.

In the case of PA_{int}, the use *already fixes* the interpretation. That is what we saw when we considered Charlie.

In the case of MT_{int}, by contrast, *nothing can* fix the interpretation, for there *is* no intended interpretation (in the model-theoretic sense of "intended

47 Cf. Toby Meadows, "What Can a Categoricity Theorem Tell Us?" *The Review of Symbolic Logic* 6, no. 3 (2013): 539–540.

48 The modelist might object: *maybe we don't even understand (at all) the worry that we are "trapped" in **M**!* At that point, their sceptical challenge has become ineffable, and I feel we have earned the right to walk away from it. But for more on this, see Button and Walsh, *Philosophy and Model Theory*, Ch. 9, §11.6.

49 Cf. Button and Walsh, *Philosophy and Model Theory*, §11.6 on "indefinite extensibility" in this context.

50 Putnam, "Models and Reality," 482.

interpretation"). Nevertheless, our model theory is not "uninterpreted syntax." We know how to use it – deductively – and our usage manifests perfectly precise concepts. What more understanding could we want or need?[51]

X Coda: On Intolerance and Conceptual Relativity

In this paper, I have explained how internalism develops Putnam's internal realism, to provide an account of mathematical concepts which faces up to the Skolem-Gödel Antinomy. In this coda, I want to draw some speculative connections between internalism and conceptual relativism; but I relegate these remarks to a coda, precisely because they are so speculative.

In §V, I glossed the significance of PA_{int}'s intolerance result as follows: *If* Solange and Tristan share a logical language, *then* they just have to say "one of us is wrong," when one affirms Goldbach's Conjecture and the other affirms its negation. Thereafter, though, I basically acted as if the antecedent is guaranteed to hold, without further comment. So I should come clean: I cannot prove that Solange and Tristan share a logical language. Moreover, if Solange and Tristan do not share a logical language, then in principle Solange might affirm φ, and Tristan might affirm $\neg\varphi$, and each could be right in their own languages.[52]

Having raised this abstract possibility, though, I should immediately point out that it is hard to see how it could actually come about. Indeed, it is not obvious that this abstract possibility is even intelligible to internalists. After all, the logical language in question is to be understood deductively rather than semantically, and we can take it for granted that Solange and Tristan accept exactly the same rules of inference. But, given this, it is hard to see what it could even *mean*, to say that they do not share a logical language.

Still, I might *just* be able to illustrate the possibility, by drawing an analogy with Putnam's discussions of mereology.[53] (To repeat: this is extremely speculative, and I am genuinely unsure what to make of it.)

Imagine two characters, Stan and Rudy. Stan is a mereological universalist, and thinks that *any things compose a fusion*. Rudy is a nihilist, and thinks that

---

51 Cf. Putnam's "*Internal realism is all the realism we want or need.*" Putnam, "Realism and Reason," 489.

52 Thanks to Sharon Berry, Cian Dorr, Hartry Field, and Luca Incurvati for discussion here.

53 See in particular Hilary Putnam, "Truth and Convention," *Dialectica* 40, no. 1–2 (1987): 69–77; for commentary, see Button, *The Limits of Realism*, Chs. 18–19.

there are no fusions. Stan and Rudy might argue vociferously about which of them is right. But at least one reasonable response to their dispute is to see them not as disagreeing, but as operating with different conceptual schemes (or frameworks, or languages, or whatever). This response is reinforced by the idea – which Putnam affirmed – that we can translate back and forth between Stan and Rudy's ways of talking. Roughly: Stan is to interpret all of Rudy's quantifiers as restricted to what Stan calls "simples"; Rudy is to interpret Stan's talk of "fusions, composed of simples" as talk of "plurals, among which there are simples." The devil, here, will be in the details. But the specific details about mereology are not relevant here. At a high level of description, the thought is just this: Rudy and Stan can offer deviant interpretations of each other's "logical concepts," and thereby dissolve their apparent disagreement.

Returning from mereology to arithmetic: *in principle*, a similar thing might happen with Solange and Tristan. If they apparently disagree, then we might (for all I know) be able to give them a suitable translation manual which smooths over the difference. And, in principle, perhaps, that might be the right thing to do.

But I emphasise: *in principle*. Rudy and Stan are equally successful in navigating their way around the world. Confronted with the same situation, they systematically give different – but wholly predictable – answers to the question "how many things are there?" So it is deeply reasonable to think that they are simply speaking different languages; that they are just using different words in the same situations. It is vastly harder to see what would prompt a similar thought in the arithmetical case. (I cannot think of anything, but maybe this is just lack of imagination on my part.)

It is also worth emphasising that the in-principle-possibility of reinterpreting logical vocabulary is compatible with everything I said in §VI about objects and objectivity. Tolerance concerning reinterpretation "is not a facile relativism that says 'Anything goes'."[54] It simply makes room for the in-principle-possibility that we might be free to choose between different languages, such that φ is the right thing to say in one language and $\neg\varphi$ is the right thing to say in the other. Still, if Solange has fixed a language and affirms φ, and if Tristan now affirms $\neg\varphi$, then Solange must regard Tristan either as speaking falsely or as speaking a different language. Embracing this disjunction yields no sacrifice of objectivity, for it is entirely commonplace. If Tristan says "I have a pet dragon," I have the same two options – regard him either as speaking falsely or as speaking a different language – but this does not make it "up to me" whether dragons exist.

---

54 Cf. Putnam, *Reason, Truth and History*, 54.

To summarise, then, here is the more cautious statement of the significance of an intolerance theorem. For now, I am (just about, in principle) open to tolerance, when it comes to choosing a logical language. But, within a logical language, and in the presence of an intolerance theorem, divergence cannot be tolerated. Moreover, given what I just said about pet dragons, this latter kind of intolerance suffices to secure all of the objectivity – and hence all the realism – that we could ever want or need.[55]

I now want to turn from arithmetic to set theory. Internalism about arithmetic delivers the verdict that every arithmetical claim is determinate. That is one of its main virtues. However, internalism about set theory also delivers the verdict that every pure-set-theoretical claim is determinate. It is less clear that this is a virtue. After all, can it really be that easy to arrive at the conclusion that the continuum hypothesis (for example) is determinate?

I fully feel the force of this concern. But I will close by saying a few things, to try to diminish its force a little.

First: I am only claiming that the continuum hypothesis is determinate. I am not suggesting that we will ever be able to know whether it holds. (The existence of unknowable mathematical truths is perfectly compatible with internalism.)

Second: to prove the intolerance of CLT, we need to use an impredicative principle of second-order comprehension.[56] So: maybe those who think that the continuum hypothesis is indeterminate should reject impredicativity.

Third: a few paragraphs ago, considerations about conceptual relativity led me to offer a slightly more cautious statement of the significance of an intolerance theorem. In the case of the intolerance of CLT, the more cautious statement would be as follows: once you have fixed a logical language, the claim "there is no cardinal between the cardinality of the naturals and the cardinality of the reals" becomes *determinate* (if not *decided* by the theory); but, *in principle*, different logical languages may settle it differently. So, perhaps the in-principle-possibility of tolerance in *choosing a logical language* is all that is needed, for those who want to explore set-theoretic indeterminacy.

---

55 To echo Putnam, "Realism and Reason," 489 again.
56 For a proof that impredicativity is necessary, see Button and Walsh, *Philosophy and Model Theory*, §11.C.

Tim Maudlin
The Labyrinth of Quantum Logic

Abstract: Quantum mechanics predicts many surprising phenomena, including the two-slit interference of electrons. It has often been claimed that these phenomena cannot be understood in classical terms. But the meaning of "classical" is often not precisely specified. One might, for example, interpret it as "classical physics" or "classical logic" or "classical probability theory." Quantum mechanics also suffers from a conceptual difficulty known as the measurement problem. Early in his career, Hilary Putnam believed that modifications of classical logic could both solve the measurement problem and account for the two-slit phenomena. Over 40 years later he had abandoned quantum logic in favor of the investigation of various theories – using classical logic and probability theory – that can accomplish these tasks. The trajectory from Putnam's earlier views to his later views illustrates the difficulty trying to solve physical problems with alterations of logic or mathematics.

I Introduction: The Siren Song of Quantum Theory

It has often been said that quantum mechanics is mysterious to us because it requires concepts that we cannot readily comprehend and displays behavior that cannot be understood in any classical way. And the term "classical" in this dictum has been taken in many senses. At the more trivial end of the spectrum, quantum theory is incompatible with classical Newtonian mechanics, which is not very surprising. But some claim that it is incompatible with a "classical" physical picture in a broader sense, for example demanding the amalgamation of the seemingly incompatible concepts of a particle and a wave. Classical probability theory has been fingered as the culprit, with quantum mechanics demanding negative probabilities. The "classical" idea that there must exist a complete description of the physical world has been questioned. And in the most extreme variation, "classical" logic has been called into question.

There has, from the beginning, been a penchant for *wanting* quantum theory to shock our whole conceptual system. Niels Bohr was fond of making gnostic pronouncements about the theory, and then touting their very incomprehensibility as an indicator of their profundity. He is quoted by his son as saying that there are "two sorts of truth: profound truths recognized by the fact that the

https://doi.org/10.1515/9783110769210-008

opposite is also a profound truth, in contrast to trivialities where opposites are obviously absurd."[1] The Theory of Relativity certainly required a substantial conceptual retooling, but it never provoked this sort of oracular commentary.

Are the phenomena associated with quantum theory intrinsically more difficult to account for than those associated with Relativity? It is said that the deepest mysteries of quantum theory are illustrated by the 2-slit interference of electrons. If an electron beam is sent through a single slit towards a fluorescent screen, there will be a somewhat fuzzy patch that lights up on the screen. Close that one and open a slit a bit to the right and the patch reappears on the right. But with both slits open alternating light and dark bands appear, the signature of the interference of waves. Turn the source down until only one spot at a time appears on the screen and the accumulated data still shows the interference bands. Individual electrons seem to somehow interfere with themselves.

These phenomena are referred to as particle/wave duality. Insofar as the interference bands emerge, the electron behaves like a wave. Insofar as individual local marks form on the screen, it behaves like a particle. What is it then? A wavicle? What does that mean?

Bohr's approach was to point to the experimental environment. In some circumstances the electron behaves like a particle, in others like a wave, and never like both. In itself it is both or neither. Classical concepts such as particle and wave, or position and momentum, only have content in particular experimental situations. Furthermore, those experimental situations may exclude each other, so at best only one of the two concepts can be deployed at a time. Which of the two is up to us. Thus the doctrine of complementarity was born. Our puzzlement about quantum theory arises from the habit of trying to use both concepts at the same time, as is done in classical physics.

This narrative, starting with experimental results and ending with conceptual revolution, appears to move smoothly from link to link. It certainly convinced several generations of physicists. So it can come as a shock to see how flimsy the whole construction is. Almost contemporaneously with the birth of quantum mechanics, Louis de Broglie suggested understanding the formalism in terms of particles guided by a "pilot wave," which was represented by the quantum wavefunction. De Broglie's theory was clear and comprehensible, and adequate to explain the phenomena. But it was roundly attacked and he abandoned it for many decades.

What was so objectionable about de Broglie's approach? Perhaps it was distasteful at the time due to its very comprehensibility. John Bell called such

---

1 Stefan Rozental (ed.), *Niels Bohr: His Life and Work as Seen by His Friends and Colleagues* (Amsterdam: North-Holland, 1967), 328.

accounts of quantum phenomena "unromantic," as contrasted with the bracing radicalism of Bohr. He writes:

> The last unromantic picture I will present is the "pilot wave" picture. It is due to de Bro-glie and Bohm. While the founding fathers agonized over the question
>
> "particle" *or* "wave"
>
> de Broglie in 1925 proposed the obvious answer
>
> "particle" *and* "wave."
>
> Is it not clear from the smallness of the scintillation on the screen that we have to do with a particle? And is it not clear from the diffraction and interference patterns that the mo-tion of the particle is directed by a wave? . . . This idea seems so natural and simple, to resolve the wave-particle dilemma in such a clear and ordinary way, that it is a great mys-tery to me that it was so generally ignored.[2]

What I hope this little historical prologue indicates is the seductiveness of the notion that quantum theory presents us with an even more radical break from "classical" patterns of thought and explanation than Relativity's break from the "classical" account of space and time. So seductive is the idea that rather plain and conceptually clear solutions to puzzles have been ignored while ever more outrageously baroque approaches are embraced. This pattern appeared – for a definite and delimited time – in Hillary Putnam's consideration of quantum theory. This is the story of that episode.

II Beginnings: 1965

In 1965, Putnam published two papers touching on quantum theory: "Philosophy of Physics"[3] and "A Philosopher Looks at Quantum Mechanics."[4] Both of these pieces are notable for their clarity concerning the main problems confronting the theory. Putnam focuses almost entirely on what is called the measurement prob-lem or the problem of Schrödinger's cat. The standard Copenhagen interpretation, associated with Bohr, is not a clear doctrine but it does have some constantly

---

2 J.S. Bell, *Speakable and Unspeakable in Quantum Mechanics*, 2nd edition (Cambridge: Cam-bridge University Press, 2004), 191.
3 Hilary Putnam, "Philosophy of Physics" (1965), reprinted in *Mathematics, Matter and Method: Philosophical Papers*, Vol. 1, 79–92 (Cambridge: Cambridge University Press, 1975).
4 Hilary Putnam, "A Philosopher Looks at Quantum Mechanics," reprinted in *Mathematics, Matter and Method: Philosophical Papers*, Vol. 1, 130–158.

repeated themes. One is that there is no "anschaulich" or "visualizable" picture of the microscopic realm that the theory addresses. "Classical" intuitions and expectations fail there. But in a curious twist, the macroscopic realm of everyday experience *must* be described in "classical" terms. Not via classical physics, of course: if classical physics could account for the behavior of macroscopic objects then it would be completely empirically adequate and there would be no call to adopt quantum theory. But the basic classical vocabulary of objects with both positions and velocities that move continuously through space must be used for describing both the configuration of experimental conditions and the outcomes of experiments. Those outcomes, in turn, must depend on the microscopic realm somehow. The main question was how to get a clear physical story about the relationship between these two domains.

John von Neumann had famously presented an axiomatized account of quantum theory, and in his account the interface between the microscopic realm of atoms and the macroscopic realm of everyday life took a particularly shocking form. Von Neumann postulated two completely different dynamical equations for the wavefunction that is used to represent the physical state of a quantum system. So long, von Neumann said, as the system was not *measured*, its evolution was the smooth, deterministic change given by Schrödinger's equation. But when the system is intervened upon by a *measurement*, it suddenly and unpredictably jumps into one of the *eigenstates* associated with the operator that represents the measured quantity. The chances for the different possible outcomes are given by Born's rule.

Here are von Neumann's own words:

> We therefore have two fundamentally different types of interventions that can occur in a system **S** or in an ensemble [$\mathbf{S}_1$, ..., $\mathbf{S}_N$]. First, the arbitrary changes by measurements which are given by the formula (**1.**) [Here von Neumann writes the transition from a single initial state to a statistical mixture of final eigenstates, each with a probability.] . . . Second, the automatic changes that occur with the passage of time. These are given by the formula (**2.**) [Here von Neumann gives the Schrödinger evolution.].[5]

For all of its seeming mathematical rigor, von Neumann's scheme is, as Bell would say, unprofessionally vague. Surely a measurement is just some sort of physical interaction between systems just as otherwise occurs with the passage of time. After all, what *physical* characteristic could distinguish measurements from other sorts of interactions, a characteristic so precise that its presence or absence makes the difference between smooth deterministic evolution and stochastic jumpy "collapses." This, in a nutshell is the measurement problem.

---

5 John von Neumann, *Mathematical Foundations of Quantum Mechanics* (Princeton: Princeton University Press, 1955), 351.

The Putnam of 1965 was rightfully scandalized by the state of the foundations of quantum theory. He finds the Copenhagen approach unsatisfactory as it seems to imply that particles only have positions and momenta when they are measured and not in between measurements.[6] Furthermore, and rather ironically, this interpretation is forced to say that the physical procedures we call "making a measurement" are really no such thing: they do not *reveal* some pre-existing property of the target system but rather serve to *create* a new property. Because of these strange features, Putnam discusses so-called "hidden variables" theories in which there is more to the physical state of a system than is reflected in the wavefunction. The de Broglie/Bohm " "pilot wave" theory was even then the most famous example, and Putnam discusses it in detail. He says that he doesn't like it because it is mathematically contrived, and also raises a problem that, oddly, requires applying classical physics to a quantum-mechanical situation.

Putnam also discusses Eugene Wigner's attempt to tie collapse of the wavefunction to human consciousness.[7] He finds all such approaches that take the collapse to be a physical event – rather than just an updating of subjective probabilities on receipt of new information – to be unacceptable, concluding that

> *no* satisfactory interpretation of quantum mechanics exists today. The questions posed by the confrontation between the Copenhagen interpretation and the hidden variable theorists go to the very foundations of microphysics, but the answers given by the hidden variable theorists and the Copenhagenists are alike unsatisfactory.[8]

What is notable about these two examinations of quantum theory from 1965 is that the question of logic is never raised. The next time Putnam weighs in, the situation is quite different.

III The Quantum Logic of David Finkelstein

Putnam returns to quantum theory with "The Logic of Quantum Mechanics"[9] As the title indicates, questioning – or at least discussing – logic itself is now on the main menu. Our quick review of the 1965 works has set the table: in those, Putnam rejects real physical collapses of the wavefunction, "hidden"

---

6 Putnam, "A Philosopher Looks at Quantum Mechanics," 141.

7 Putnam, "A Philosopher Looks at Quantum Mechanics," 147.

8 Putnam, "A Philosopher Looks at Quantum Mechanics," 157.

9 Hilary Putnam, "The Logic of Quantum Mechanics" (1968), Reprinted in *Mathematics, Matter and Method: Philosophical Papers*, Vol. 1, 174–197 (Cambridge: Cambridge University Press, 1975).

variables, and the Copenhagen interpretation because none of them could deliver what he regarded as a plausible account of measurement as a purely physical interaction between physical systems. The question that we must keep foremost in our minds is how the introduction of a new logic, or even more radically the replacement of classical logic with a new logic, could even in principle help to resolve this problem.

The main conceptual issue here concerns the question of what *empirical* import the logical connectives in a language can have. Let's take & as a clinical example. In propositional logic, & is a sentential connective: two well-formed formulas connected by & constitute another well-formed formula. The "meaning" of the connective can be given by a truth table or by a set of valid inferences. If every well-formed formula is either true or false, then the truth table is simple to specify: A & B is true if both A and B are true and is false otherwise. In terms of inferences, we give &-Introduction and &-Elimination rules. &-Introduction says that from A and B as premises one can derive A & B as a conclusion. &-Elimination says that from A & B one can derive A and one can derive B. It is easy to see that the validity (truth-preservingness) of &-Introduction requires that the truth of both A and B be sufficient for the truth of A & B, and &-Elimination requires that it be necessary.

Now if one were to reject bivalence, and allow well-formed formulas to be other than True or False, then the semantics of & would have to be revisited. If this new scheme retains the old inference rules, then again the truth of both A and B would still have to be necessary and sufficient for the truth of A & B. But if the truth values expand beyond "true" and "false" then the conjunctions that include the new values have to be addressed.

But what possible *empirical* consequences could such a change in logic have? How could anything like this solve the *physical* issues that must be confronted when trying to make clear sense of quantum theory? That is the main question we must bear in mind in the sequel.

The Putnam of 1965 thought something had to be done, but did not know what. By 1968, the idea that logic had to be amended came forward, but not because Putnam's own investigations had led him in that direction. Rather, as he makes clear, he was brought to the approach by David Finkelstein. Finkelstein, in turn, was working in a tradition that goes back to von Neumann and Garrett Birkhoff.[10] The mathematical core of this approach adverts to the structure of subspaces of Hilbert space.

---

10 Garrett Birkhoff and John von Neumann, "The Logic of Quantum Mechanics," *Annals of Mathematics* (2nd series) 37, no. 4 (1936): 823–843.

Hilbert space is the space of all quantum-mechanical wavefunctions. It is an infinite dimensional space, essentially just because wavefunctions are *functions*, and a function is specified at an infinitude of points. The other piece of mathematical machinery we need are *Hermitian operators*, also commonly called *observables*. These operators, as their name suggests, operate on wavefunctions: hand an operator a wavefunction and it hands another back to you. In special cases if you hand the operator a wavefunction it hands back the very same wavefunction multiplied by a number. Such a wavefunction is called an *eigenfunction* of the operator and the number is called its *eigenvalue*.

At this point, a key physical assumption is made. The "observable" operators are associated with *physical magnitudes* and the condition for a system to have a definite physical magnitude is that its wavefunction be an eigenfunction of the associated operator. The value of the physical magnitude is then its eigenvalue. Any wavefunction that is *not* an eigenfunction of the operator *fails to have any value for the magnitude at all*. Thus, a wavefunction that is not an eigenfunction of the position operator represents a system that fails to have any definite position, and a wavefunction that is not an eigenfunction of the momentum operator represents a system that fails to have any definite momentum. And since no position eigenfunction is a momentum eigenfunction, mathematics alone guarantees that no system can simultaneously have a definite position and a definite momentum. Indeed, the closer a system comes to having a definite momentum, the further it is from having a definite position and vice versa. This is an instance of the *uncertainty relation* or *complementarity*.

The final piece of the technical apparatus arises from the observation that the eigenfunctions of an observable that have the same eigenvalue form a *subspace* of the Hilbert space, called its *eigenspace*. So the condition for a system to have a particular value of an observable is that its wavefunction lies in that eigenspace. Therefore every proposition of the form "System S has value V for observable O" can be associated with a particular subspace of Hilbert space. The truth condition for the proposition is just the system wavefunction lying in the subspace. And the falsity condition is being perpendicular to the subspace. If S's wavefunction is neither in nor perpendicular to the eigenspace of the value V then the proposition is neither true nor false, and a measurement of the observable might or might not yield the value V.

Let's pause for a moment to think about this last case. There is some observable O and the wavefunction for the system S does not lie in any eigenspace of O, so the quantum predictive apparatus makes only a probabilistic prediction for what would happen were you to measure O. What options are there for assigning a truth value to the claim that S has a particular value of the quantity O?

One thing one might say is that if, in fact, S has the value V then, by the definition of what a "measurement" is, a measurement would have to return the outcome "V." And since there is no value that the measurement is certain to return if it should happen to be done, there is no value that S has.

But this chain of reasoning has several flaws. One is that what we usually call "measurements" just don't have the feature mentioned. If I put a thermometer into a liquid to "measure" its temperature, the reading is typically not the temperature that the liquid had before I "measured" it. If the thermometer was colder than the liquid then the equilibrium temperature of the liquid-thermometer system at the end is lower than the original temperature of the liquid, and if the thermometer was hotter then it is higher. Maybe one considers the discrepancy unimportant, or maybe it is important enough to try to compensate for. But to do that, one has to understand in complete physical detail how the "measurement device" physically interacts with the "system" to yield an outcome. And that, recall, just *is* the measurement problem! So on this approach one can't really know how to assign truth values to propositions without solving the measurement problem. To appeal to a new logic to solve the problem would be a viciously circular procedure.

The second problem is that the fact that quantum mechanics only generates probabilistic predictions about the outcomes of measurements does not, by itself, imply anything about the systems themselves. It might be that the dynamics of the system is fundamentally indeterministic, and the system is neither disposed to yield a particular value nor not to yield it. Or it could be that the probabilities, and consequent statistical predictions, only reflect an inadequacy in the quantum formalism, and that the wavefunction used to make the predictions is, in Einstein's terminology, incomplete. That is, the wavefunction fails to specify all of the physical features of a system, and the statistical predictions arise because different systems assigned the same wavefunction are physically different. Among these differences could be the value of the observable quantity O. In that case, the fact that quantum mechanics makes no definite prediction for the outcome of an O measurement would not imply that S fails to have any value for O. To understand whether it does or does not again requires solving the measurement problem.

So there are two essential questions that the standard presentation of quantum mechanics fails to answer: 1) Is the wavefunction a complete physical description of a system or not? And 2) How does the pre-interaction-with-a-"measuring"-device state of a system relate to its post-interaction state? What does the outcome of the measurement indicate about the system before it was measured? Without answers to these questions – physical answers – the truth value of many claims cannot even be addressed. The quantum logic of Finkelstein purported to address them.

The key to Finkelstein's approach lies in the observation that there are three purely mathematical operations on subspaces of a space that bear some formal resemblance to the operation of the classical truth-functional operators. Given two subspaces of a vector space one can form their *intersection*, which is just all the elements of the space that lie in both of the subspaces. The intersection is itself a subspace. And given two subspaces one can form their *span*, which is just the set of all vectors that can be formed by adding vectors from the two subspaces. The span, too, is a subspace of the vector space. Finally, given a subspace of a vector space one can form its *orthocomplement*, which is just all of the vectors orthogonal to the subspace. It is yet another subspace.

So if we have associated every subspace of a vector space with a proposition, the intersection and span operations are operations on a pair of propositions that yield a proposition, and the orthocomplementation operation is an operation on a single proposition that yields a proposition. How are these various propositions related to each other in terms of their truth values?

Clearly, if proposition A is true because the state of S lies in the A-subspace, and proposition B is true because the state of S lies in the B-subspace, then the proposition associated with the intersection of the two subspaces, call it "A⊓B," is true because the state of S lies in the intersection of the subspaces. (This notation is not standard, but it will help keep things straight.) And if either A or B is anything other than true, then A⊓B cannot be true, because if a state does not lie in a space it cannot lie in any subspace of that space. So ⊓ functions just like the classical & with respect to true and false sentences.

Let's indicate the proposition associated with the orthocomplement of the A-subspace "⊥A." Obviously, if A is true then ⊥A is not true, and if ⊥A is true then A is not true. Again, if the only truth values we had were true and false, ⊥ would operate just like the classical negation. But here the divergence from classical negation is more severe. Since there are vectors that lie neither in the A-subspace nor in the ⊥A-subspace (assuming neither is the whole space), there are propositions such that neither it nor its orthocomplement are true. So ⊥ does not work like classical ~ in the sense of mapping anything other than a true proposition to a true proposition.

Finally, what about the span? We will indicate the proposition associated with the span of the A-subspace and the B-subspace as "A⊔B." On the one hand, if the state of a system lies in the A-subspace or in the B-subspace then it lies in the span of the two. So if A is true or B is true then A⊔B is true. But there are many vectors that lie in the span of the A-subspace and the B-subspace but don't lie in either. If the state of a system is one of these vectors, then A⊔B is true even though neither A nor B is true. So although ⊓ functions just like &, ⊔ is quite unlike the classical ∨.

Interestingly, despite these differences, many tautologies of classical logic remain tautologies (i.e. propositions true for every state) when the corresponding operators are substituted for each other. Suppose, for example, we just *define* the falsehood of A in the new system as the truth of ⊥A. Then there are some propositions in the new language that are neither true nor false: we need a third truth value. And, mixing the different sets of operators, for any such proposition A, A ∨⊥A is not true. But still, A ⊔⊥A is true for all A since A ⊔⊥A is associated with the entire space.

Not all of the inferences that are valid in classical logic remain valid when the new operators are substituted. For example, in classical logic A & (B ∨ C) implies (A & B) ∨ (A & C) and vice versa. But in the new system A ⊓ (B ⊔ C) can be true while (A ⊓ B) ⊔ (A ⊓ C) is false. The analog of the distributive law fails. (To see an example, let C be ⊥B, and let the system state lie in the A-subspace, but neither in the B-subspace nor the ⊥B-subspace. Then A ⊓ (B ⊔⊥B) is true, but (A ⊓ B) ⊔ (A ⊓⊥B) is false.)

The structure of subspaces of Hilbert space under the operations of intersection, span, and orthocomplementation in this way becomes isomorphic to the structure of the lattice of associated propositions under the operations of meet, join, and orthocomplement. That, in technical terms, is what Finkelstein's "quantum logic" is.

It is here that we reach a critical point in the discussion. There are two crucial questions. First, are there any grounds for thinking of the operators ⊓ and ⊔ and ⊥ on these propositions as *alternatives* rather than *supplements* to the classical truth-functional operators &, ∨, and ~? And second, how could the induction of these new operators, whether as alternatives or as supplements, help us solve any interpretational problem of quantum theory?

IV Finkelstein's Logic and Understanding Quantum Theory

The most immediate question to ask when presented with something called "quantum logic" is whether it is being offered as a *supplement to* or a *replacement for* classical logic. If we don't know this, then we have no idea how to proceed.

If the new logic merely supplements the old, then adding the new logical connectives creates a more effective and extensive logical language, but does not revise any results of the old logic. All the old tautologies are still tautological, all the old valid inferences still valid. In this spirit, we could add ⊓ and ⊔ and ⊥ to a formal language alongside & and ∨ and ~. If the vector representing a system falls in the span of the subspaces A and B, but not in the A-subspace and not in the B-subspace, then we could truly write: (A ⊔ B) & ~(A∨B). In such a way, we could convey more using the new language than we could have in the old.

Such a change might be a *useful innovation* in logic, but certainly not a *conceptual revolution*. There would have been nothing strictly *wrong* in the old language, which remains as a fragment nestled inside the new. At worst, we might have been tempted to incorrectly use ∨ instead of the more appropriate ⊔, or ~ rather than ⊥.

Putnam's thought about quantum logic, though, is much more radical. The radical idea is that the new logic is to *replace* the old one rather than supplement it, and the formal similarity between ⊔ and ∨; ⊓ and &; and ⊥ and ~ makes clear how the substitution goes. In some sense disjunction *really is* ⊔ rather than ∨, and so on.

The key analogy here is supposed to be that of Euclidean and non-Euclidean geometry. For millennia, humans believed that they lived in a three-dimensional Euclidean space. Furthermore, they believed that they had some sort of *a priori* access to the structure of that space, codified in the theorems of Euclidean geometry. But eventually, empirical and explanatory pressures made it rational to supplant the Euclidean hypothesis with a non-Euclidean one. This was obviously a replacement rather than an enhancement: the old system is abandoned in favor of the new. One understands why the old worked as well as it did, but in the end it simply is regarded as a false approximation to the truth.

The analogy between geometry and logic is made explicitly in "How to Think Quantum-Logically,"[11] and is very telling. In the case of geometry, we definitely have a replacement rather than an expansion. The Euclidean geometry must die so that the non-Euclidean can live. And in the process, some empirical phenomena – such as the anomalous advance of the perihelion of Mercury – get explained.[12] Our main questions, then, are what could it even mean to *replace* classical logic with some other logic? And if we can get clear on that, how could any such replacement help solve any empirical problems?

It is useful to have an example here. What empirical problems did the switch from Special Relativity (flat space-time geometry) to General Relativity (curved space-time geometry) help account for? The anomalous advance of the

---

11 Hilary Putnam, "How to Think Quantum-Logically," *Synthese* 29, no. 1/4 (1974): 55–61.
12 Properly speaking, General Relativity does not so much demand replacing Euclidean with non-Euclidian geometry, as replacing flat Minkowski space-time with a variably curved space-time. But the analogy is very tight.

perihelion of Mercury, the bending of light passing near the Sun, the gravitational Red shift . . . these are the standard answers. None of these phenomena are logically incompatible with Special Relativity. Adjustments to overall physics elsewhere, that kept the flat space-time, are possible. But General Relativity accounts for them in a simple and satisfying way.

So what is the parallel example of a switch to quantum logic making the explanation of a physical phenomenon simpler and more elegant?

Interestingly, there isn't one. Instead, Putnam tries to argue that *classical* logic yields bad predictions, but not at all that *quantum* logic corrects these predictions. And the example he discusses is the famous two-slit interference effect. Let's quickly recap that.

If we fire elections or photons at a barrier with a thin slit, an image appears behind the barrier that is roughly the shape of the slit, but spread out in the direction that the slit is thin. It is brightest in the middle and shades off to either side. Let's call this the image formed when only slit A is open. If we close slit A and make a nearby parallel slit B, the image just moves to behind slit B. No surprise.

But what if both slits are opened? Then instead of just getting the sum of the two images, one gets a highly striped set of interference bands, rapidly alternating between bright and dark. The pattern is reminiscent of the interference patterns in water waves in similar circumstances. But curiously, the pattern persists even when the electrons are sent one at a time, and the images form one discrete spot at a time.

Now this behavior may be surprising, but Putnam makes a much, much stronger claim: it is not the behavior that *classical logic* leads us to expect! How does that argument go?

Putnam makes the following "classical" argument. If you want to know how likely it is for an electron to land in a particular region R on the screen (call the proposition that it lands there "R"), first close slit B and measure the number with only A open. Call the proposition that the particle passes through slit A "A." So we get a number: prob(R/A). Do the same by closing slit A and opening B to record prob(R/B), the chance of hitting R if the particle goes through B. Now what about with *both* slits open? In that case, says Putnam, the particle must either go through slit A or through slit B, so for every electron that makes it to the screen we have the truth of A ∨ B. What we want is prob(R/A ∨ B). Now by some fancy manipulations, Putnam "derives" that classical logic requires that prob(R/A ∨ B) = ½ prob(R/A) + ½ prob(R/B). The appearance of the ½ comes as a bit of a shock: offhand, one would suppose that the chance of getting to R by going either through A or B is just the *sum* of the chance going through A with the chance going through B. But let's leave that curiosity aside. What a moment's thought reveals is that, whatever Putnam has calculated, it can't *possibly* be a consequence of "classical logic" or any other kind of logic!

Consider the situation. We do one experiment with one slit open. We record a number. We do another experiment with the other slit open. We record another number. Now we wonder what will happen with *both* slits open. Well, as far as logic of any kind goes, *anything* could happen! The apparatus could blow up. All of the electrons could be reflected back to the source. The electrons could all turn into rabbits. *Logic* won't prevent it!

The fallacy, once you point it out, is glaringly obvious. The first experiment shows how many electrons get through slit A and land in R *when only slit A is open*. And the second how many get through slit B and land in R *when only slit B is open*. From the point of view of logic, this tells us exactly nothing about what will happen *when both slits are open*. Formally, let's let O(A) stand for only A is open, O(B) stand for only B is open, and O(A,B) stand for both A and B, and only A and B are open. Then the first experiment measures prob(R/A & O(A)), and the second measures prob(R/B & O(B)). And what the two-slit experiment measures, assuming the electron goes through one slit or the other, is prob(R/(A ∨ B) & O(A,B)). But since the first experiments carry no information at all about the condition O(A,B), no logic in the world, of any kind, will allow you to derive the third probability from the first two.

Further, all Putnam attempts to show is that classical logic yields a bad prediction, not that quantum logic yields a good one. When we replace the spacetime of Special Relativity with that of General Relativity, we not only abandon the Special Relativistic predictions, we acquire the new General Relativistic ones. If Putnam had tried to make a parallel argument, it would have become obvious that the first, classical, argument was invalid.

How could Putnam have been led so far astray? In "The Logic of Quantum Mechanics" he repeatedly emphasizes that the account of quantum logic is not his own: it is Finkelstein's. His account lies somewhere between reporting and endorsing. He is perhaps trying to set the large-scale stage for the very idea of logic being empirical rather than pushing a particular account of the right logic. Of course, since the example fails so spectacularly, we are left with no clue about how logic really could be empirical. But Putnam was not done with the topic yet.

V Gestures towards Yet Another Quantum Logic

In 1974 Putnam returns to the question of quantum logic with the very short paper entitled "How to Think Quantum-Logically." As already mentioned, this paper starts with the proportionality [Euclidean] Geometry:General Relativity:: [Classical] Logic:Quantum Mechanics. I have supplied the bracketed clarifications, which are clearly intended. Once again the overarching theme is that just as General Relativity demands the rejection of Euclidean geometry as the price for a tremendous simplification of physics, so Quantum Mechanics offers us an elegant account of physical phenomena at the price of replacing classical logic. The paper is written in a slightly coy way. Putnam begins by expositing what "the advocate of the quantum-logical interpretation of quantum mechanics claims,"[13] as if this were a dispassionate presentation of one approach to understanding quantum theory. But he soon enough slips into the revelatory locution "we advocates of this interpretation"[14] indicating that a defense of quantum logic rather than merely an exposition is in store.

We have already seen that Putnam's attempt to tie the two-slit experiment to some logical principle failed. In this paper, no such empirical phenomenon as the two-slit experiment is even mentioned. And in a further surprise, there is no trace of Finkelstein's quantum logic. Putnam is now setting out to create his own new logic, based on new arguments.

Finkelstein's logic, founded on the structure of subspaces of Hilbert space under the operations of intersection and span, made no change to the conjunction-like operation. The classical conjunction of two propositions is true iff the system's state lies in the intersection of the two propositions' subspaces. The novelty in Finkelstein's logic was all in the analogs of disjunction and negation. But Putnam's new logic is just the opposite. The novelty lies in the analog of conjunction! How is that supposed to work?

There are really two tricks that Putnam pulls here, one with disjunction and the other with conjunction. These tricks are both in service of one main contention: that the interactions called "measurements" really deserve the name. That is, a "measurement" merely reveals a pre-existing fact about a system, rather than playing a role in *creating* some new fact. The very first characteristic of what Putnam calls the "quantum logical view of the world" is:

---

13 Putnam, "How to Think Quantum-Logically," 55.
14 Putnam, "How to Think Quantum-Logically," 55.

(1) *Measurement only determines what is already the case: it does not bring into existence the observable measured, or cause it to "take on a sharp value" that it did not already possess.*[15]

There are two ways to understand this fundamental principle. One is merely as a stipulation, as a *definition* of what it takes to count as a "measurement" in the sense Putnam wishes to use that term. As such, it would have nothing to do with logic at all, because "measurement" is not a logical particle. And if this is just a stipulation, it is an open question whether, according to some theory, there are any "measurements." Since typical measurements are interactions, it is a question of theoretical analysis whether the "outcome" of the supposed "measurement" accurately indicates some pre-existing state of affairs.

Putnam evidently wants to take the term "measurement" a different way. He wants to regard certain experimental conditions as constituting paradigm "measurements," especially "measurements" of position and momentum. Having fixed that, principle (1) becomes a *constraint on the physical analysis of these paradigmatic "measurements."* The Putnam-style quantum logician is simply not open to a physics that analyzes these paradigm situations so that the outcome of the physical interaction between the system and the apparatus does not reveal a pre-existing physical magnitude. It is an odd thing to adopt such an *a priori* demand on these particular experimental arrangements. Surely *logic* cannot demand it! And even more than that, proofs due to Kochen and Specker,[16] Bell,[17] and Greenberger, Horne and Zeilinger[18] show that *no* physics can possibly meet the requirements of principle (1). The principle defies not classical logic but mathematics itself if we want to recover the quantum-mechanical predictions. It is simply off the table.

If one demands that an acceptable physics meet a condition that is mathematically impossible to meet there is bound to be trouble. And basically Putnam's new logic tries to defuse that trouble by abandoning classical logic. Let's trace the steps.

First, Putnam takes a page out of Finkelstein. There are *eigenstates* of the position operator, and according to the interpretation Putnam is using the only situation in which a particle has a particular position is when it is in an eigenstate

---

15 Putnam, "How to Think Quantum-Logically," 57.

16 Simon Kochen and Ernst Specker, "The Problem of Hidden Variables in Quantum Mechanics," *Journal of Mathematics and Mechanics* 17 (1967): 59–87.

17 J.S. Bell, "On the Einstein-Podolsky-Rosen Paradox," *Physics* 1, no. 3 (1964): 195–200.

18 Daniel M. Greenberger, Michael A. Horne and Anton Zeilinger, "Going beyond Bell's Theorem," in *Bell's Theorem, Quantum Theory and Conceptions of the Universe*, edited by Menas Kafatos, 69–72 (Dordrecht, Boston, and London: Kluwer, 1989).

with that eigenvalue. And there are many, many states that are not eigenstates of the position operator. Indeed, all but a set of measure zero are not position eigenstates but rather superpositions of position eigenstates. So if we are using classical logic it is correct to say than in most states the particle has no particular position.

But the *span* of all the position eigenstates is the whole Hilbert space, which includes every possible wavefunction. Similarly, the set of momentum eigenstates is a set of measure zero in the Hilbert space, but the span of that set is the whole Hilbert space. Putnam now considers a single particle, which, he says, has a position and has a momentum:

In symbols, taking "Oscar" to be the name of one of these particles:

(*Er*) the position of Oscar is *r*. (*Er'*) the momentum of Oscar is *r'*.

But it must not be concluded that each of these particles has a position *and* a momentum! For the following is *rejected*:

(*Er*)(*Er'*)(the position of Oscar is *r*. the momentum of Oscar is *r'*).[19]

Since these two sentences are logically equivalent in classical logic, quantum logic must depart from classical logic. But how?

Finkelstein's logic has the logical inequivalence of the two sentences because a "disjunction" (i.e. span) of two propositions can be true without any of the "disjuncts" being true. The existential claim is just an infinitary disjunction, so for Finkelstein it can be true without any instance being true. So each conjunct in the first conjunction is true – even necessarily true – making the conjunction necessarily true as well. But the second sentence, instead of being a conjunction of (infinite) disjunctions, is an (infinite) disjunction of conjunctions. In Finkelstein's logic, each of the conjunctions is false, since the intersection of a position eigenstate and a momentum eigenstate is zero. Since every conjunction is false, so is their infinite disjunction. It is true on Finkelstein's logic that every particle has a position and every particle has a momentum, but no particle has both a position and a momentum. At least if we translate the span into English as if it were a disjunction.

Putnam's quantum logic cannot achieve the inequivalence of the two sentences in the same way that Finkelstein's does. Putnam's requirement that "measurements" merely reveal pre-existing physical facts demands that such physical facts *always* exist. Individual particles do not merely have position-in-general without any specific position, as Finkelstein would have it, but they always have some particular position just as the classical disjunction would

---

19 Putnam, "How to Think Quantum-Logically," 57.

demand. And similarly for Putnam's particle's momentum: unlike Finkelstein's, it has not merely momentum-in-general but always a particular (albeit unknown) momentum. For Putnam, unlike for Finkelstein, the existential sentences are true because some specific instance is true. The semantics of disjunction is just classical semantics. And the conjunction of the existentials is true because each conjunct is true.

The pressing question, then, is how Putnam intends to achieve the semantic difference between the conjunction of the existentials and the double existential over the conjunction. If Oscar really has some specific position and some specific momentum, how can Oscar fail to have both a specific position and momentum?

Putnam bites the only bullet he has left: the problem with classical logic is not disjunction, but conjunction! In classical logic, the truth of the conjuncts separately implies the truth of the conjunction. But for Putnam, each of the conjuncts can be true without the conjunction being true. This is not a possibility that Finkelstein ever suggested.

But how can that be? How can A be true and B be true but A & B fail to be true? What does that even mean? Are there any vaguely analogous examples of the failure of conjunction in an everyday context?

Unfortunately, Putnam never directly confronts this issue. He simply says that the conjunction of a particular position and a particular momentum cannot be true, since otherwise we would not have the principle of complementarity! Here is the relevant passage:

> Complementarity is fully retained. For any particular r and any particular r' the statement "Oscar has position r and Oscar has momentum r'" is a logical contradiction. It is, of course, just the sacrifice of the distributive law that we mentioned a few moments ago that enables us to simultaneously retain the objective conception of measurement as finding out something which exists independently and the objective conception of complementarity as a prohibition on the simultaneous existence of certain states of affairs, not just as a prohibition on simultaneous knowledge.[20]

But the distributive law has really nothing to do with the case. If position measurements always reveal pre-existent positions and momentum measurements always reveal pre-existent momenta, then the particles always have pre-existent positions and pre-existent momenta. One need not appeal to any distributive law to conclude that Oscar always has both.

What Putnam has in mind is only revealed on the last page of the article. There he asserts – contrary to both Finkelstein and to quantum theory – that a

20 Putnam, "How to Think Quantum-Logically," 58.

system does not have one wavefunction ("state vector") but *many*. Since no single wavefunction can ascribe both a position and a momentum to Oscar, and Putnam wants to maintain that Oscar always has both a position and a momentum, he is forced into this position. But somehow, although Oscar is described by both of these state vectors simultaneously, one is not allowed to *say* so! For that, according to Putnam, would be a quantum-logical contradiction.

If this situation sounds incoherent, that's because it is. Here is part of the next to last paragraph of the paper:

> Thus we get: a system *has* more than one state vector, on the quantum-logic interpretation, but one can never *assign* more than one state vector! Or, to drop talk of "state vectors" altogether . . . we may say: A system has a position *and* it has a momentum. But if you *know* the position (say *r*), you cannot *know* the momentum. For if you did, say, know that the momentum was *r'*, you would know "Oscar has the position *r*. Oscar has the momentum *r'*," which is a logical contradiction.[21]

It is really impossible to make sense of this paragraph.

First, the mention of *knowledge* comes out of nowhere: up until now, no epistemic issues have even been raised. But further, if all propositions of the form "Oscar has the position *r*. Oscar has the momentum *r'*" are logical contradictions, then if I know Oscar has position *r*, it is not just that I can't *know* Oscar's momentum, but Oscar can't *have* a momentum. Whether I know it or not is neither here nor there. So Putnam's desire for Oscar to have both a definite position and a definite momentum collapses.

Clearly, Putnam's new original quantum logic was a work in progress at this point. In his last paper on this topic, he tries to clarify the situation.

VI Quantum Logic as the Logic of Prediction

Putnam's attack on the "logic" of conjunction finally gets a coherent explication in the 1981 paper "Quantum Mechanics and the Observer."[22] Once again, all of our foundational questions arise. Is "quantum conjunction" supposed to *replace* classical conjunction or *supplement* it? And what could possibly go *empirically* wrong with the classical truth-functional operator? If one just stipulates that A & B is true iff A is true and B is true, how could such a stipulation

---

21 Putnam, "How to Think Quantum-Logically," 61.
22 Hilary Putnam, "Quantum Mechanics and the Observer," *Erkenntnis* 16, no. 2 (1981): 193–219.

lead to any new empirical consequences at all? There certainly seems to be no bearing of conjunction on the two-slit experiment, where at least the issue of disjunction ("the particle goes through slit A or the particle goes through slit B") appears to be relevant to any proposed explanation. What issue is there with conjunction?

We last left Putnam in a bind. On the one hand, he wants the experiments we call "measurements" to just reveal some pre-existing physical property of a system rather than play a causal role in creating the property. And since position measurements and momentum measurements always have outcomes, it follows that particles always have both positions and momenta. But according to the Finkelstein quantum logic, the conjunction of a proposition assigning a particle a position and a proposition assigning the particle a momentum is *logically false*. No state vector assigned to the system can make both true. What to do?

In "Quantum Mechanics and the Observer," Putnam doubles down on the assertion that particles always have both position and momentum. This is true even though position (at a time) and momentum (at that time) are quantum-mechanically incompatible observables. Even more than that, he asserts that sometimes we can *know* both of these two incompatible observables to arbitrary accuracy, so long as the knowledge is about some time in the past. Suppose, for example, there is a source with a shutter in it surrounded by a spherical screen. If the shutter is opened briefly at t_0, resulting in a spherical wavefunction propagating outwards, and a flash is observed in some small region R of the screen at t_1, then the experiment tells us both that a particle escaped at t_0 and that it was in R at t_1. But, as Putnam points out, the quantum-mechanical states associated with these properties are incompatible: one cannot prepare any state that is certain to both pass through the open shutter and arrive the appropriate time later at R. Each of these properties has an associated quantum state, $|\psi_0\rangle$ and $|\psi_1\rangle$, but these states are incompatible. Their quantum-logical conjunction is necessarily false. Nonetheless, says Putnam, we can know that both are true of the system!

His conclusion is twofold. First, that a system may be described by not just one quantum state but two (or more). In some sense, each of these quantum states provides a true description of the system. Second, that these two quantum states need not be quantum-logically compatible.

Both of these claims are anathema to standard accounts of quantum theory. But quite apart from that, the results appear to run contrary to the whole quantum-logical approach. If $|\psi_0\rangle$ truly describes S, and $|\psi_1\rangle$ is logically incompatible with $|\psi_0\rangle$, then one would think that $|\psi_1\rangle$ cannot truly describe S. But in an unpredictable twist, Putnam tries to bring quantum logic to the rescue here. Since $|\psi_0\rangle$ and $|\psi_1\rangle$ are incompatible, their quantum logical conjunction is logically false. Nonetheless, each of the conjuncts is true! The solution, Putnam opines, is that *each of a pair of propositions may be true but their conjunction false*. That is what quantum logic, together with Putnam's decision to let more than one wavefunction describe a system, inexorably entail. But how to make sense of a false conjunction with two true conjuncts?

After all, it still seems perfectly acceptable to have a connective – call it # – defined so that A#B is true just in case each of A and B are true. From the truth of each of the pair one can validly infer the truth of A#B, and from the truth of A#B one can infer A and one can infer B. In all other cases, A#B is not true. What is gained by denying the very possibility of such a connective, and insisting on the quantum-logical one instead?

Here is his explication of the significance of quantum conjunction:

> In effect, not allowing ourselves to conjoin all the statements we know to be true means that we have what amount to two different kinds of conjunction: One amounts to asserting statements in two different "frames" as I shall call them (different Boolean sublogics); and the other, for which we reserve the *and*-sign, is conjunction of statements which lie in a common frame.[23]

Note that Putnam reserves the *and*-sign exactly for the "conjunction" that does not respect classical logic and designates no symbol at all for classical conjunction. That is, Putnam intends to *replace* the classical & with the quantum one. But why not at least leave the classical "&" alone and introduce a new symbol for the quantum operator? And what, after all, does the quantum conjunction *mean*?

With regard to the classical conjunction, Putnam thinks that certain aspects of quantum theory *refute* classical logic. But we know that that cannot be correct: given the usual truth-functional semantics of the classical connectives, we know that classical inferences are non-ampliative. If you require that A and B both be true in order that A & B be true, and that the truth A and B separately follow from the truth of A & B, then you have defined the classical conjunction willy-nilly. It is quite irrelevant what "frames" A and B come from. You can't derive any non-conjunctive claim after conjunction has been introduced in this way that you couldn't already derive without it.

It is precisely here that Putnam introduces a new and unheralded consideration: predictive value. So far, as is appropriate, we have been concerned with the truth of propositions and nothing else. We have seen that we can stipulate that A & B is true exactly when A is true and B is true without harm. But predictive value is clearly a different property than truth. Putnam's claim is then

---

23 Putnam, "Quantum Mechanics and the Observer," 212.

twofold: 1) When using quantum conjunction of propositions we are concerned not with their truth but their predictive value and 2) there are some pairs of propositions such that they cannot both simultaneously have predictive value.

To sum up the situation, and contrary to Putnam's convention about the use of the & sign, we will use & to mean classical conjunction and $\wedge$ to mean "quantum conjunction." Now suppose that A and B are propositions such that their quantum conjunction A $\wedge$ B is the zero proposition, a zero-dimensional subspace. The conventional quantum logic, such as Finkelstein's concludes that A and B cannot both be true, and *a fortiori* cannot both be known to be true. In other words, A & B cannot both be true and known. But according to Putnam, sometimes A and B can both be true and be known to be true. So A & B is true and knowable. Nonetheless, the unacceptability of A $\wedge$ B indicates that A and B cannot both have predictive value. If A makes good predictions, then B cannot, and vice versa.

In essence, Putnam proposes using the vocabulary of classical logic for the connectives of a different logic, the "logic of predictive value." So what does it mean that one true proposition about a system has predictive value and another does not?

Perhaps a slight variation of Putnam's example will help. Once again, a shutter briefly opens, which may or may not release a photon. The shutter hole is covered by a polarizing filter that allows only horizontally polarized light through. Some distance away is a second polarizer oriented at 45° from the first, and then finally a screen.

The shutter is opened and a flash occurs on the screen. What can we infer about the photon from this result?

First, as Putnam notes, we can infer that a photon was indeed released while the shutter was opened at t_0. But more than that, we can infer that the photon passed the first polarizer, and was therefore horizontally polarized after that time. Because the photon made it all the way to the screen, we can infer that it passed the second polarizer at t_1, and thereafter was polarized at 45°. These conclusions are unassailable from any interpretive point of view. Passing each polarizer counts as a "measurement" of the photon's polarization in the corresponding direction.

But Putnam's personal, and rather idiosyncratic insistence that the interactions we call "measurements" simply reveal some pre-interaction property of the measured system yields another, unexpected conclusion. It means that at the times between t_0 and t_1, when it is between the two polarizers, the photon was *both* polarized in the horizontal direction (as confirmed by having passed the first polarizer) *and* polarized in the 45° direction (as confirmed by later passing the second). But these two states are quantum-mechanically incompatible! Both are true, but the quantum conjunction of them is necessarily false.

Putnam's idea that measurements simply reveal pre-existing values without disturbing the system, though, cannot survive more experimentation. Adding yet another polarizer oriented in the 45° direction would not change the output data at all: the same number of photons reach the screen. In other words, every photon that passes the second polarizer will, in this case, pass the third, which is oriented in the same direction. However, if the third polarizer is oriented in the horizontal direction, the number of photons will be reduced by half. Apparently, even though every photon that reaches the second polarizer is horizontally polarized, not every photon that passes the second polarizer is. The second polarizer can at least disturb the *horizontal* polarization, even if, as Putnam insists, it leaves the 45° polarization intact.

This effect of the second polarizer even appears somewhat startling if we change the third polarizer from horizontal to vertical. Now, with the second polarizer *removed*, no photons at all get through: every photon that passes the first polarizer is horizontally polarized and therefore is absorbed by the vertical polarizer. But re-inserting the 45° polarizer between these two – adding yet another filter between the two that are already blocking all the light – suddenly allows some light to get through! The beam is only 1/8 the brightness of the beam with no polarizers at all, but more light gets through three than just two in the same sequence. Obviously, the middle polarizer alters the photons that pass it.

The idea that "measurements" simply *reveal* pre-interaction values rather than *create* post-interaction values is, indeed, the hallmark of Putnam's take on quantum theory:

> Although the interpretation I have suggested is not realistic in the sense of assuming a copy theory of truth (metaphysical realism), or even in the sense of assuming that all observables have determinate values, it is *internally realistic* in the sense that *within the interpretation* no distinction appears between "measured values" and "unmeasured values."[24]

But how can this picture be even internally *coherent*? Suppose that a system *has* no determinate value for an observable, but is subject to a "measurement interaction" for that observable. Putnam's dictum seems to imply that *there can be no outcome at all*. For an outcome would assign a "measured value," which would clearly be distinct from the pre-interaction *lack* of any value.

The only way that "quantum logic" could come to the rescue here is to insist that although the pre-measurement system *had* no determinate value, and

---

24 Putnam, "Quantum Mechanics and the Observer," 217–218.

the post-measurement system *does have* a determinate value, you are not *allowed* to say both of these truths together, and draw the obvious conclusions from them, because they don't belong to "the same frame." And this is, indeed, the sort of thing that some quantum logicians do say. But such a position is, to put it bluntly, madness. If you can't always talk about the pre- and post-measurement situations in the same breath, then you can't always assert that there is no distinction between the values in the two cases, which is exactly what Putnam wants to say!

And anyway, what would this prohibition on drawing conclusions from pairs of true sentences even have to do with conjunction? No need to conjoin A and B to infer from the premise set {"The pre-measurement system had no value for O.", "The post-measurement system had a value for O."} the conclusion "The pre-measurement state differs from the post-measurement state with respect to the value of O."

In short, Putnam's foray into his own version of quantum logic ended in self-contradiction and failure.

Putnam did come to recognize this. By the time of his reply to Michael Redhead in *Reading Putnam*,[25] he had abandoned quantum logic, never to take it up again. He came to see that one can't just stipulate how so-called "measurement interactions" work and then trim logic itself to fit. The issue facing quantum theory is bringing "measurement interactions" and "measurements" under the same physical laws and principles of physical analysis as everything else. What is left, then, is the legacy of a research program that did not pan out. There are always things to learn from such projects, insights about the conditions for success and failure of a strategy. The main moral here is that the analogy to the fate of Euclidean geometry was flawed from the beginning. Abstract geometry has a clear physical counterpart that it can be used to describe: space or space-time. But there is no corresponding physical counterpart of the logical connectives.

Kant went wrong when he took something extra-mental – space and time – and tried to make them merely the forms of our intuition. Since space and time are not just in our minds, our theories of space-time structure can get negative feedback from experience. But logical structure is not like space-time structure: there is no physical counterpart. As a result, physics cannot be simplified or improved by changing logic. Putnam wandered for three decades in the labyrinth of quantum logic, but he finally found his way out again.

---

25 Bob Hale and Peter Clark (eds.), *Reading Putnam* (Oxford: Blackwell, 1994).

Roy T. Cook
Fulfillability, Instability, and Incompleteness

Abstract: The purpose of this essay is to publicize, and to a more limited extent, further develop, an alternate proof of Gödel's incompleteness theorem due to Saul Kripke, based on a notion called *fulfillability*. Kripke's work has been publicized in talks, but at the time of writing this essay the only published discussion of the material appears in Putnam (2000). Here, a more detailed and more accessible overview of the approach is given, centered on a novel generalization – the Instability Theorem. After setting up the technical machinery and demonstrating the Instability Theorem, we prove both the first incompleteness theorem and Lob's theorem. We conclude with some observations regarding potential directions for future research along these lines.

I Two Incompleteness Proofs

As is well known, Kurt Gödel provided the first proof of the incompleteness of Peano arithmetic (and consistent extensions of the same).[1] His tools were primarily syntactic/proof-theoretic. In the 1980s, Saul Kripke formulated an alternative proof of the (first) incompleteness theorem. His tools were primarily semantic/model-theoretic.

Kripke's proof is far less well known, however, and the reason is simple: Kripke has never published the proof.[2] Hilary Putnam, however, published a version of Kripke's proof in a paper titled "Non-standard models and Kripke's Proof of the Gödel theorem".[3] His reasons for publishing a paper devoted to *someone else's* result are not hard to decipher: He notes in a footnote that:

---

[1] Kurt Gödel, "Über Formal Unentscheidbare Sätze der *Principia Mathematica* und Verwandter Systeme: I." *Monatshefte für Mathematik und Physik*: 38 no. 1 (1931): 173–198.

[2] There is a very brief discussion of the methods in Simon Kochen and Saul Kripke, "Nonstandard models of Peano arithmetic." *L'enseignement Mathématique* 28 (1981): 211–231, however.

[3] Hilary Putnam, "Nonstandard models and Kripke's proof of the Gödel theorem." *Notre Dame Journal of Formal Logic* 41, no. 1 (2000): 53–58. There is also a brief discussion of the proof in Hilary Putnam, "After Gödel", *Logic Journal of the IGPL* 14, no. 5 (2006): 745–754.

https://doi.org/10.1515/9783110769210-009

This paper is developed from a lecture to the Department of Computer Science at Peking University, June 1984. I have decided to publish this lecture at this time because Kripke's proof is *still* unpublished.[4]

Sadly, despite Putnam's efforts, the proof is still not well known beyond the small group of specialists working on completeness proofs and/or non-standard models of arithmetic. In fact, I am aware of only three other logicians that have investigated the main tool used in the proof – the notion of *fulfillability* – in any depth: Joseph Quinsey, Alex Wilkie, and Stella Moon.[5] Of these, only the first directly investigates the use of fulfillability in proving incompleteness (although Moon's thesis does contain a brief overview of Putnam's paper), and only the second is "officially" published (the other two are final theses for graduate degrees). This is unfortunate, since the methods mobilized in the proof are not only beautiful and astonishingly simple in and of themselves, but they also promise to provide powerful new methods for proving all sorts of metatheoretic results regarding arithmetic and related systems.[6] With this in mind, I will here attempt to complete the task begun by Putnam: to draw more attention to Kripke's proof of Gödel's (first) incompleteness theorem and, perhaps more importantly, to the novel method he uses in the proof. I will not merely re-present the extremely simple and clear version of the incompleteness proof already given by Putnam, however. Instead, I will attempt a more general introduction to the methods by proving a very general theorem regarding fulfillability – what I will call the *Instability Theorem* – and then using this theorem to obtain a number of familiar-looking results (including a version of the Kripke/Putnam incompleteness proof) as simple corollaries.

---

4 Putnam, "Nonstandard models", 58, emphasis Putnam's.
5 See Joseph Quinsey, "Some problems in logic." PhD Dissertation, Oxford University, 1980; Alex Wilkie, "On schemes axiomatizing arithmetic." In *Proceedings of the International Congress of Mathematicians*, 331–337. Providence, RI: American Mathematical Society, 1986; and Stella Moon, "Isaacson's thesis and Wilkie's theorem", MSc Thesis, University of Amsterdam, 2017, respectively. There are many papers that discuss Wilkie's 1986 paper and the proof of Wilkie's theorem contained therein, but as far as I can tell none of these examine the notion of fulfillability beyond its use in this proof. In addition, Warren Goldfarb, "Herbrand's theorem and the incompleteness of arithmetic." *Iyyun: The Jerusalem Philosophical Quarterly* 39 (1990): 45–64 utilizes fulfillability in his examination of Herbrand's theorem.
6 There is another aspect of the methods used in the Kripke proof that is worth mentioning: Putnam's claim that Kripke's proof, which unlike Gödel's proof, requires neither diagonalization nor a formal provability predicate: ". . . is one that establishes independence by means that could, in principle, have been understood by nineteenth-century mathematicians." Putnam, "Nonstandard models", 54–55. I will not address this claim here, although it deserves additional discussion.

The remainder of the essay will proceed as follows. In §2 I will set out the technical machinery needed for the results to follow, and present some simple preliminary results. In §3 I will then prove the *Instability Theorem*. I will then present extremely simple proofs of analogues of the first and second incompleteness theorems, as well as some related results (e.g., a purely semantic version of Löb's theorem for fulfillability) in §4. Finally, in §5 I will tie up a few loose ends, and suggest some directions for further work.

A final note before moving on. The primary purpose of this chapter, as already stated above, is not to generate any new mathematics. The methods used here are due to Kripke, and I make no claim to priority. Most of the results proven in §4 are versions of results already extant in the work of others (Gödel, Kripke, Quinsey, and Putnam in particular) or are modifications of, or relatively straightforward extensions of, this work (with a few exceptions). Nor is the purpose to give the most powerful, most general, or most informative version of each of the theorems discussed below. Doing so would obviously interfere with the primary goal of this essay, which is to provide a new *introduction* to the topic – one that is more extensive than Putnam's essay and more accessible than Quinsey's dissertation (both in terms of actually getting one's hands on the essay in question, and in terms of the difficulty of the mathematics contained in the essay itself!) Hence, the real novelty of the present approach is the organization of these results around the *Instability Theorem* given in §3, and the use of this theorem to provide a new way of introducing fulfillability.[7]

II Fulfillability: The Basics

We work (here and below) in a first-order language for first-order Peano arithmetic $\mathcal{L}_{PA}$ containing non-logical symbols 0, 1, and $+$, $\times$. Given a formula $\Phi \in \mathcal{L}_{PA}$, $\ulcorner\Phi\urcorner$ is the Gödel code of Φ. If S is a sequence of natural numbers (S possibly infinite, and possibly including non-standard numbers – see below), then σ_S is the Gödel code of the sequence S (if such exists), $\lambda(\sigma_S)$ is the length of S, and $\sigma_S(n)$ is the nth element of S (when $1 \leq n \leq \lambda(\sigma_S)$). We assume we are using a coding such that, for any finite sequence S, $\sigma_S > \lambda(\sigma_S)$ (the code of the sequence is greater than the length of the sequence) and, for all $n \leq \lambda(\sigma_S)$, $\sigma_S > \sigma_S(n)$ (the code of the sequence is greater than any entry in the sequence). A sequence (finite or infinite) $S = \langle n_1, n_2 \ldots \rangle$ is *good* if and only if:

---

7 A slightly snarky way of describing the task undertaken here is that I am Leibnizing Kripke's Newton.

1. $\sigma_S(1) > \lambda(\sigma_S)$ (the first number in the sequence is greater than the length of the sequence).
2. For all $n < \lambda(S)$, $\sigma_S(n+1) > (\sigma_S(n))^2$ (for any element in the sequence, if there is a next element in the sequence, then it is greater than the square of its predecessor in the sequence).

We will abbreviate the recursive relation expressing that σ codes a good sequence as $\mathsf{Gd}(\sigma)$.

PA will be used in an ambiguous manner to denote both some standard set of axioms for first-order Peano arithmetic, and the classical theory (in $\mathcal{L}_{PA}$) entailed by those axioms. A PA-model is any model satisfying all of the axioms of PA. We will write $\vDash_{PA}\Phi$ to abbreviate:

For any PA-model $\mathcal{M}$:

$$\mathcal{M} \vDash \Phi$$

We assume the following familiar "facts" in what follows:
- *Fact 1*: The standard model of arithmetic exists, and all of the axioms of PA are true on this model. We will use $\mathbb{N}$ to represent both the standard model and the set of (standard) natural numbers that is its domain.
- *Fact 2*: Given any set Δ of $\mathcal{L}_{PA}$ formulas true on $\mathbb{N}$, there is a non-standard model $\mathcal{M}$ such that all formulas in Δ are true on $\mathcal{M}$. In particular, if Φ is any $\mathcal{L}_{PA}$ formula true on $\mathbb{N}$, then there is a non-standard PA-model that satisfies Φ.

In a full, text-book style treatment of fulfillability, we would of course want to either *prove* these claims (in the case of *Fact 2*), or (in the case of *Fact 1*), say more about their logical and epistemological status. Since our purpose here is to explore what further results we can obtain using purely model-theoretic constructions based on fulfillability, however – and, in particular, as already mentioned, no effort is being made to prove the *best* or *strongest* such results, but only to provide insightful examples that might inspire the reader to explore the topic further – we will make these assumptions and move on. It is worth noting, however, that our assumption of *Fact 1* is, in the present context, akin to assumptions of the consistency of PA on the Gödelian approach to proving the incompleteness of (and related results about) PA, and that *Fact 2* can be obtained via either an application of the compactness theorem or via familiar algebraic techniques (in other words, we need not obtain *Fact 2* as a corollary of Gödel's incompleteness theorems).

For any $\mathcal{L}_{PA}$ formula Φ, let $\Phi^\dagger$ be an (arithmetically) equivalent formula in prenex normal form:[8]

$$(\forall x_1)(\exists x_2)(\forall x_3)\ldots(\exists x_m)\Psi(x_1, x_2, \ldots x_m)$$

where $\Psi(x_1, x_2, \ldots x_m)$ (the matrix) is primitive recursive. Note that the function represented by $\dagger$ is recursive. A formula Φ of the form:

$$(\forall x_1)(\exists x_2)(\forall x_3)\ldots(\exists x_m)\Psi(x_1, x_2, \ldots x_m)$$

(where $\Psi(x_1, x_2, \ldots x_m)$ is primitive recursive) is *fulfilled* by a sequence S of length n coded by σ_S if and only if:

$$(\forall z_1 : 0 < z_1 \leq \lambda\,(\sigma_S))(\forall x_1 < \sigma_S(z_1))(\exists x_2 < \sigma_S(z_1 + 1))$$

$$(\forall z_3 : z_1 < z_3 \leq \lambda\,(\sigma_S))(\forall x_3 < \sigma_S(z_3))(\exists x_4 < \sigma_S(z_3 + 1))\ldots$$

$$(\forall z_{m-1} : z_{m-3} < z_{m-1} \leq \lambda\,(\sigma_S))(\forall x_{m-1} < \sigma_S(z_{m-1}))(\exists x_m < \sigma_S(z_{m-1} + 1))$$

$$\Psi(x_1, x_2, \ldots x_m)$$

The following inductive translation maps each pair $\langle \sigma, \ulcorner \Phi \urcorner \rangle$, where σ is the code of a sequence and Φ is a $\mathcal{L}_{PA}$ formula of the form:[9]

$$(\forall x_1)(\exists x_2)(\forall x_3)\ldots(\exists x_m)\Psi(x_1, x_2, \ldots x_m)$$

(where $\Psi(x_1, x_2, \ldots x_m)$ is primitive recursive) to the sentence expressing that the sequence coded by σ fulfills Φ:[10]

$$\tau((\forall x)\Psi, \sigma, 1) = (\forall z_1 : 0 < z_1 \leq \lambda(\sigma_S))(\forall x_1 < \sigma_S(z_1))\tau(\Psi, n + 1)$$

$$\tau((\forall x)\Psi, \sigma, n) = (\forall z_n : z_{n-1} < z_n \leq \lambda(\sigma_S))(\forall x_n < \sigma_S(z_n))\tau(\Psi, n + 1)$$

$$\text{if } n > 1$$

$$\tau((\exists x)\Psi, \sigma, n) = (\exists x_n < \sigma_S(z_n + 1))\tau(\Psi, n + 1)$$

$$\tau(\Psi, \sigma, n) = \Psi \text{ if } \Psi \text{ is quantifier-free}$$

Letting $\mathcal{F}_\tau(x, y)$ be the recursive function corresponding to this translation – that is, the function that maps $\langle \sigma, \ulcorner \Phi \urcorner \rangle$ where σ is the code of a sequence and Φ is of the form:

---

8 Note that either the initial universal quantifier or the final existential quantifier or both might be vacuous.

9 This translation function is adapted from Quinsey, "Some problems", 9–10.

10 I have left out the clauses requiring variable substitutions in Ψ, which are obvious but distracting.

$$(\forall x_1)(\exists x_2)(\forall x_3)\dots(\exists x_m)\Psi(x_1, x_2, \dots x_m)$$

(where $\Psi(x_1, x_2, \dots x_m)$ is primitive recursive) to the code of the sentence obtained by applying τ to σ and Φ – we can construct a recursive function $\mathcal{F}_{\mathsf{ful}}(x, y)$ that maps $\langle \sigma, \ulcorner\Phi\urcorner\rangle$, where σ is the code of a sequence and Φ is *any* sentence in the language of arithmetic whatsoever, to the code of the sentence expressing the fact that σ fulfills Φ as:

$$\mathcal{F}_{\mathsf{ful}}(x, y) = \mathcal{F}_{\tau}(x^\dagger, y)$$

Note that, given any formula Φ and sequence code σ, the claim that σ fulfills Φ is a Δ_0 sentence. Hence $\mathcal{F}_{\mathsf{ful}}(x, y)$ maps each pair $\langle \sigma, \ulcorner\Phi\urcorner\rangle$ to the code of a Δ_0 sentence. What we need, of course, is not a function symbol but a predicate. But PA contains a truth predicate $T_0(x)$ for Δ_0 sentences, which is itself Δ_0. Hence, we finally arrive at a recursive binary predicate expressing the claim that σ codes a sequence that fulfills Φ (taking σ and the code of Φ as arguments) via:

$$\mathsf{FUL}(x, y) = T_{\Delta_0}(\mathcal{F}_{\mathsf{ful}}(x, y))$$

The intuition underlying a sequence S coded by σ_S fulfilling a $\mathcal{L}_{\mathsf{PA}}$ formula Φ is given game-theoretically by Putnam as follows:

> [. . .] we can define "S fulfills Φ" to mean that there is a winning strategy for the defending player in a game [. . .] in which the attacking player gets to choose a new place in the sequence, each time it is his turn to play. The attacking player must also choose a number less than $\sigma_S(n)$ where n is the number of the position he chose in the sequence. [. . .] Each time he plays, the attacking player has to choose a place which is to the right of the place in the sequence he chose before (unless it is his first turn to play) and not the last place in the sequence (unless he has no legal alternative, in which case he loses), and the defending player must then pick a number less than $\sigma_S(n+1)$ (less than the number in the next place in the sequence). The game ends when as many numbers have been chosen as there are quantifiers in the prefix of the formula. (We assume that all quantifiers are prenex, and that quantifiers alternate universal, existential, universal, existential, . . .) The numbers chosen are then substituted for the variables in the matrix of the formula Φ in order [. . .] The resulting primitive recursive statement is evaluated and [. . .] the defending player wins if the statement is true and the first (attacking) player wins if the statement is false.[11]

Given this understanding, we will also generalize the treatment above in the obvious way, to talk (in the metatheory) about "external" (often infinite) sequences (not necessarily coded by a number in the domain) fulfilling an $\mathcal{L}_{\mathsf{PA}}$ formula $\Phi \in \mathcal{L}_{\mathsf{PA}}$. Care will be taken, however, to distinguish between the mere existence

---

11 Putnam, "Nonstandard models", 55–56, notation changed to match that here.

of a sequence S of objects from the domain of a model fulfilling a sentence Φ and the existence of a σ_S in the domain of the model that codes S, since, as we shall see, the existence of the former does not entail the existence of the latter.

An $\mathcal{L}_{PA}$ formula Φ is *n-fulfillable* if and only if there is a good (coded) sequence of length n that fulfills Φ – that is:

$$(\exists \sigma)(\mathsf{Gd}(\sigma) \wedge \lambda(\sigma) = n \wedge \mathsf{FUL}(\ulcorner\Phi\urcorner, \sigma))$$

Being n-fulfillable, for some particular n, expresses a kind of "weak kind of correctness": that there is at least one sequence that fulfills Φ – that is, there is at least one (coded) sequence such that the defending player in Putnam's game has a winning strategy with respect to that sequence.[12] Of course, the "weakness" of this notion is apparent from the fact that, for any $\Phi \in \mathcal{L}_{PA}$ and $n \in \mathbb{N}$, the claim that Φ is n-fulfillable is Σ_1.

We can easily construct stronger such "weak correctness conditions" in terms of fulfillability. For example, we can ask whether Φ is n-fulfillable for all n – that is, whether Φ is *universally fulfillable*:

$$(\forall y)(\exists \sigma)(\mathsf{Gd}(\sigma) \wedge \lambda(\sigma) = y \wedge \mathsf{FUL}(\ulcorner\Phi\urcorner, \sigma))$$

Universal fulfillability is obviously stronger than n-fulfillability for any particular n, but is nevertheless still very weak, being Π_2.

In what follows, we will be interested, not only in the fulfillability of particular sentences, but also in the fulfillability of PA itself, and in connections between the fulfillability of the axioms of PA and the fulfillability of other $\mathcal{L}_{PA}$ sentences. One particularly useful way to achieve this is as follows: Let:

$$P_1, P_2, P_3, \ldots$$

be some fixed recursive enumeration of our axioms for PA. Then we can introduce a new axiomatization of PA:

$$P_1^{\wedge}, P_2^{\wedge}, P_3^{\wedge}, \ldots$$

where the nth axiom in the new enumeration is the conjunction of the first n axioms in the original axiomatization. Letting $\mathcal{F}_{PA}^{\wedge}(x)$ be the recursive function that maps n to $\ulcorner P_n^{\wedge}\urcorner$, we can express the fact that, for any n, the first n axioms of PA (on our original axiomatization $P_1, P_2, P_3, \ldots$) and Φ are jointly n-fulfillable – that is, that Φ is *universally PA-fulfillable* – as follows:

---

11 Putnam, "Nonstandard models", 55–56, notation changed to match that here.
12 Putnam, "Nonstandard models", 56.

$$(\forall n)(\exists \sigma)(\mathrm{Gd}(\sigma) \wedge \lambda(\sigma) = n \wedge \mathrm{FUL}(\ulcorner \Phi \urcorner, \sigma) \wedge \mathrm{FUL}(\mathcal{F}_{\mathrm{PA}}^{\wedge}(n), \sigma))$$

Universal PA-fulfillability, like universal fulfillability, is Π_2. Universal PA-fulfillability will be the central topic of §3 and §4 below. First, however, it is helpful to prove some preliminary results regarding the simpler notion of universal fulfillability.

The first such result we will prove is that PA entails that every $\mathcal{L}_{\mathrm{PA}}$ sentence implies its own universal fulfillability:[13]

Lemma 2.1. *For all $\Phi \in \mathcal{L}_{\mathrm{PA}}$:*

$$\vDash_{\mathrm{PA}} \Phi \rightarrow (\forall x)(\exists \sigma)(\mathrm{Gd}(\sigma) \wedge \lambda(\sigma) = x \wedge \mathrm{FUL}(\sigma, \ulcorner \Phi \urcorner))$$

Proof. Assume we are given some arbitrary model $\mathcal{M}$ of PA. We prove the formula holds in that model by induction. Base case:

$$\mathcal{M} \vDash (\exists \sigma)(\mathrm{Gd}(\sigma) \wedge \lambda(\sigma) = 1 \wedge \mathrm{FUL}(\sigma, \ulcorner \Phi \urcorner))$$

Trivial. Induction step: Assume that there is a good sequence of length n coded by σ that fulfills Φ. Let m be the maximum of n^2 and the value obtained by applying the relevant Skolem function to the values in the sequence coded by σ. Let σ' be the code of the sequence obtained by appending m to the end of the sequence coded by σ. Then σ' is the code of a sequence of length $n+1$ that fulfills Φ. That is:

$$\mathcal{M} \vDash (\forall n)((\exists \sigma)(\mathrm{Gd}(\sigma) \wedge \lambda(\sigma) = n \wedge \mathrm{FUL}(\sigma, \ulcorner \Phi \urcorner))$$
$$\rightarrow (\exists \sigma)(\mathrm{Gd}(\sigma) \wedge \lambda(\sigma) = n+1 \wedge \mathrm{FUL}(\sigma, \ulcorner \Phi \urcorner)))$$

Since $\mathcal{M}$ is a model of PA and hence satisfies all instances of induction, we obtain:

$$\mathcal{M} \vDash (\forall n)(\exists \sigma)(\mathrm{Gd}(\sigma) \wedge \lambda(\sigma) = n \wedge \mathrm{FUL}(\sigma, \ulcorner \Phi \urcorner))$$

□

Thus, in any model of PA, any true $\mathcal{L}_{\mathrm{PA}}$ sentence is n-fulfillable for all n. The following corollaries will be useful in what follows:

---

[13] Both Putnam and Quinsey give this result as a fact about provability (i.e., in terms of $\vdash$). Given the completeness theorem for first-order logic, these claims are equivalent, but expressing it in terms of the double turnstile ($\vDash$) further emphasizes the purely model-theoretic nature of this result and the related incompleteness theorems to come.

Corollary 2.2. *For all* $n \in \mathbb{N}$:

$$\vDash_{PA}(\forall x)(\exists \sigma)(\mathsf{Gd}(\sigma) \wedge \lambda(\sigma) = x \wedge \mathsf{FUL}(\sigma, \ulcorner P_n \urcorner))$$
$$\vDash_{PA}(\forall x)(\exists \sigma)(\mathsf{Gd}(\sigma) \wedge \lambda(\sigma) = x \wedge \mathsf{FUL}(\sigma, \ulcorner P_n^{\wedge} \urcorner))$$

Proof. Immediate from **Lemma 2.1.** □

Thus, any axiom of PA is n-fulfillable for all n in any model of PA, as is the conjunction of the first m axioms, for any finite m. In addition, we have:

Corollary 2.3. *For all* $n \in \mathbb{N}$:

$$\vDash_{PA}\Phi \rightarrow (\forall x)(\exists \sigma)(\mathsf{Gd}(\sigma) \wedge \lambda(\sigma) = x \wedge \mathsf{FUL}(\sigma, \ulcorner \Phi \urcorner) \wedge \mathsf{FUL}(\sigma, \ulcorner P_n \urcorner))$$
$$\vDash_{PA}\Phi \rightarrow (\forall x)(\exists \sigma)(\mathsf{Gd}(\sigma) \wedge \lambda(\sigma) = x \wedge \mathsf{FUL}(\sigma, \ulcorner \Phi \urcorner) \wedge \mathsf{FUL}(\sigma, \ulcorner P_n^{\wedge} \urcorner))$$

Proof. Immediate from **Lemma 2.1** and the fact that:[14]

$$\vDash_{PA}(\forall x)(\exists \sigma)(\mathsf{Gd}(\sigma) \wedge \lambda(\sigma) = x \wedge \mathsf{FUL}(\sigma, \ulcorner \Phi \urcorner) \wedge \mathsf{FUL}(\sigma, \ulcorner \Psi \urcorner))$$
$$\leftrightarrow (\forall x)(\exists \sigma)(\mathsf{Gd}(\sigma) \wedge \lambda(\sigma) = x \wedge \mathsf{FUL}(\sigma, \ulcorner \Phi \dot{\wedge} \Psi \urcorner))$$

□

Although, as we shall see, the truth of a sentence Φ on an arbitrary PA-model $\mathcal{M}$ does not entail that Φ is universally PA-fulfillable on $\mathcal{M}$, this does hold in the special case where the model in question is the standard one:

Corollary 2.4. *For all* $\Phi \in \mathcal{L}_{PA}$:

$$\mathbb{N} \vDash \Phi \rightarrow (\forall x)(\exists \sigma)(\mathsf{Gd}(\sigma) \wedge \lambda(\sigma) = x \wedge \mathsf{FUL}(\sigma, \ulcorner \Phi \urcorner) \wedge \mathsf{FUL}(\sigma, \ulcorner P_x^{\wedge} \urcorner))$$

Proof. Immediate consequence of **Corollary 2.3** and the fact that:

$$\mathbb{N} \vDash (\forall x) \Psi(x) \text{ if and only if, for all } n \in \mathbb{N}, \mathbb{N} \vDash \Phi(n)$$

□

We conclude this section with the following lemma, which will allow us to construct purpose-built (often non-standard) models of PA:

Lemma 2.5. *If* Φ *is a formula in* $\mathcal{L}_{PA}$, $\mathcal{M} = \langle \Delta, I \rangle$ *is any model, and S is an ω-sequence of objects from* Δ *(S need not be coded by an $x \in \Delta$) such that:*

---

14 In other words, a conjunction is universally fulfillable if and only if each of the conjuncts is. We leave the tedious but straightforward verification of this fact to the ambitious reader (or see Quinsey, "Some problems", Chapter 2).

1. S is cofinal in Δ (on the standard ordering $<$)
2. S fulfills Φ.

then $\mathcal{M} \models \Phi$

Proof. If S is cofinal in Δ, then for any x serving as the 'choice' for a universal quantifier in the prefix of $\Phi^\dagger$, x is less than the mth member of S, for some $m \in \Delta$. Since S fulfills Φ, we can find a corresponding y less than the $m+1^{th}$ member of S to serve as the 'choice' for the subsequent existential quantifier. $\qquad\square$

This completes the preliminaries, and we are now in a position to prove our main result.

III The Instability Theorem

The following result – the *Instability Theorem* – shows, in effect, that universal PA-fulfillability cannot hold of any sentence in *all* PA-models:[15]

Theorem 3.1. *For any $\Phi \in \mathcal{L}_{PA}$, if there is a PA-model $\mathcal{M}$ such that:*

$$\mathcal{M} \models (\forall x)(\exists \sigma)(\mathsf{Gd}(\sigma) \wedge \lambda(\sigma) = x \wedge \mathsf{FUL}(\sigma, \ulcorner \Phi \urcorner) \wedge \mathsf{FUL}(\sigma, \mathsf{P}_x^\wedge))$$

then there is a PA-model $\mathcal{M}'$ such that:

$$\mathcal{M}' \models \neg(\forall x)(\exists \sigma)(\mathsf{Gd}(\sigma) \wedge \lambda(\sigma) = x \wedge \mathsf{FUL}(\sigma, \ulcorner \Phi \urcorner) \wedge \mathsf{FUL}(\sigma, \mathsf{P}_x^\wedge))$$

and:
$$\mathcal{M}' \models \Phi.$$

Proof. Let Φ be an arbitrary $\mathcal{L}_{PA}$ formula, and $\mathcal{M} = \langle \Delta, I \rangle$ be any PA-model such that:

$$\mathcal{M} \models (\forall x)(\exists \sigma)(\mathsf{Gd}(\sigma) \wedge \lambda(\sigma) = x \wedge \mathsf{FUL}(\sigma, \ulcorner \Phi \urcorner) \wedge \mathsf{FUL}(\sigma, \mathsf{P}_x^\wedge))$$

By *Fact 1*, we can assume that $\mathcal{M}$ is a non-standard model. Let v be any non-standard number in Δ. Then:

---

[15] The *Instability Theorem* is a generalization of the method used in Quinsey, "Some problems", 19–20 and Putnam, "Nonstandard models", 56–58 to prove the incompleteness theorem. We will see exactly how the proof discussed in the latter work (and due originally to Kripke) is a simple consequence of the *Instability Theorem* in §4.

$$\mathcal{M} \models (\exists \sigma)(\mathsf{Gd}(\sigma) \land \lambda(\sigma) = v \land \mathsf{FUL}(\sigma, \ulcorner\Phi\urcorner) \land \mathsf{FUL}(\sigma, \mathsf{P}_v^\land))$$

Let σ_S be the least (non-standard) number (coding a sequence S of non-standard numbers) such that:

$$\mathcal{M} \models (\mathsf{Gd}(\sigma_S) \land \lambda(\sigma_S) = v \land \mathsf{FUL}(\sigma_S, \ulcorner\Phi\urcorner) \land \mathsf{FUL}(\sigma_S, \mathsf{P}_v^\land))$$

Consider the model $\mathcal{M}' = \langle \Delta', I' \rangle$ where:[16]

$$\Delta' = \{\mu \in \Delta : \mu < \sigma_S(n) \text{ for some } n \in \mathbb{N}\}$$
$$I' = I \restriction \Delta'$$

The ω-sequence:

$$\sigma_S(1), \sigma_S(2), \sigma_S(3) \dots$$

fulfills each axiom of PA (since it fulfills the conjunction of the first v axioms), and is cofinal in Δ'. Hence (by **Lemma 2.5**) $\mathcal{M}'$ is a PA-model. In addition, $v \in \Delta'$ (since $\sigma_S(1) > v$).[17] But there is no $\sigma' \in \Delta'$ such that σ' is the code of a sequence of length v that fulfills the conjunction of the first v axioms of PA and fulfills Φ. Assume for *reductio* that there was such a $\sigma' \in \Delta'$. Then $\sigma' < \sigma_S$ (since $\sigma_S \notin \Delta'$) and:

$$\mathcal{M}' \models (\mathsf{Gd}(\sigma') \land \lambda(\sigma') = v \land \mathsf{FUL}(\sigma', \ulcorner\Phi\urcorner) \land \mathsf{FUL}(\sigma', \mathsf{P}_x^\land))$$

But since the formula above is recursive, and recursive relations are preserved upwards, we have:

$$\mathcal{M} \models (\mathsf{Gd}(\sigma') \land \lambda(\sigma') = v \land \mathsf{FUL}(\sigma', \ulcorner\Phi\urcorner) \land \mathsf{FUL}(\sigma', \mathsf{P}_x^\land))$$

contradicting the fact that σ_S is the *least* code of such sequence in Δ. Hence:

$$\mathcal{M}' \models \neg(\exists \sigma)(\mathsf{Gd}(\sigma) \land \lambda(\sigma) = v \land \mathsf{FUL}(\sigma, \ulcorner\Phi\urcorner) \land \mathsf{FUL}(\sigma, \mathsf{P}_\sigma^\land))$$

which entails:

$$\mathcal{M}' \models \neg(\forall x)(\exists \sigma)(\mathsf{Gd}(\sigma) \land \lambda(\sigma) = x \land \mathsf{FUL}(\sigma, \ulcorner\Phi\urcorner) \land \mathsf{FUL}(\sigma, \mathsf{P}_x^\land))$$

In addition, $\sigma_S(1), \sigma_S(2), \sigma_S(3) \dots$ fulfills Φ (and, again, is cofinal in Δ'). Hence (by **Lemma 2.5**):

---

16 This is where we need the second clause in the definition of a good sequence.
17 This is where we need the first clause in the definition of a good sequence.

$$\mathcal{M}' \vDash \Phi$$

□

Thus, for any $\mathcal{L}_{PA}$ formula Φ, if the claim that Φ is universally PA-fulfillable is satisfiable, then so is the conjunction of Φ and the claim that Φ is not universally PA-fulfillable.

The following is an immediate consequence of the *Instability Theorem*:

Corollary 3.2. *For all $\Phi \in \mathcal{L}_{PA}$:*

$$\nvDash_{PA} (\forall x)(\exists \sigma)(\mathsf{Gd}(\sigma) \wedge \lambda(\sigma) = x \wedge \mathsf{FUL}(\sigma, \ulcorner \Phi \urcorner) \wedge \mathsf{FUL}(\sigma, \mathsf{P}_x^\wedge))$$

Proof. Assume, for *reductio*, that there is a $\Phi \in \mathcal{L}_{PA}$ such that:

$$\vDash_{PA} (\forall x)(\exists \sigma)(\mathsf{Gd}(\sigma) \wedge \lambda(\sigma) = x \wedge \mathsf{FUL}(\sigma, \ulcorner \Phi \urcorner) \wedge \mathsf{FUL}(\sigma, \mathsf{P}_x^\wedge))$$

Then, given *Fact 1*, there is at least one PA-model $\mathcal{M}$ such that:

$$\mathcal{M} \vDash (\forall x)(\exists \sigma)(\mathsf{Gd}(\sigma) \wedge \lambda(\sigma) = x \wedge \mathsf{FUL}(\sigma, \ulcorner \Phi \urcorner) \wedge \mathsf{FUL}(\sigma, \mathsf{P}_x^\wedge))$$

But then, by the *Instability Theorem* there is a PA-model $\mathcal{M}'$ such that:

$$\mathcal{M}' \vDash \neg(\forall x)(\exists \sigma)(\mathsf{Gd}(\sigma) \wedge \lambda(\sigma) = x \wedge \mathsf{FUL}(\sigma, \ulcorner \Phi \urcorner) \wedge \mathsf{FUL}(\sigma, \mathsf{P}_x^\wedge))$$

Contradiction. □

Thus, for no $\Phi \in \mathcal{L}_{PA}$ is the claim that Φ is universally PA-fulfillable a theorem of PA. Given that we characterized universal PA-fulfillability as a weak notion of "correctness", this is surprising, but it is not yet an incompleteness theorem. To get that, we need to know that there is also at least one $\Phi \in \mathcal{L}_{PA}$ such that the claim that Φ is not universally PA-fulfillable is also not a theorem.

IV Incompleteness and Other Stuff

The (semantic) incompleteness of PA is an easy corollary of the *Instability Theorem* and an earlier lemma:

Theorem 4.1. *For any* $\Phi \in \mathcal{L}_{PA}$, *if*:

$$\mathbb{N} \models \Phi$$

then:[18]

$$\nvdash_{PA}(\forall x)(\exists \sigma)(Gd(\sigma) \wedge \lambda(\sigma) = x \wedge FUL(\sigma, \ulcorner\Phi\urcorner) \wedge FUL(\sigma, P_x^\wedge))$$
$$\nvdash_{PA} \neg(\forall x)(\exists \sigma)(Gd(\sigma) \wedge \lambda(\sigma) = x \wedge FUL(\sigma, \text{'}\Phi\text{'}) \wedge FUL(\sigma, P_x^\wedge))$$

Proof. The first claim is a consequence of **Corollary 3.2**, the second a consequence of **Corollary 2.4**. □

At this point, it is worth slowing down a bit and clarifying what, exactly, we
have shown. One way to do this is to look at a specific case – in particular, the
instance of **Theorem 4.1** used in the incompleteness proof given by Putnam.
Putnam (setting aside notational variation) considers the following sentence:[19]

$$(\forall x)(\exists \sigma)(Gd(\sigma) \wedge \lambda(\sigma) = x \wedge FUL(\sigma, P_x^\wedge))$$

Since any sequence fulfills a tautology, this is equivalent to the claim that T is
universally PA-fulfillable:

$$(\forall x)(\exists \sigma)(Gd(\sigma) \wedge \lambda(\sigma) = x \wedge FUL(\sigma, \ulcorner T \urcorner) \wedge FUL(\sigma, P_x^\wedge))$$

Since T is obviously satisfied on $\mathbb{N}$, **Theorem 4.1** entails that neither this sentence nor its negation is a theorem of arithmetic. In addition, this formula is
equivalent to:

$$(*) : (\forall y)(\forall x)(\exists \sigma)(Gd(\sigma) \wedge \lambda(\sigma) = x \wedge FUL(\sigma, \ulcorner T \urcorner) \wedge FUL(\sigma, P_y^\wedge))$$

Now, **Corollary 2.2** provides:

$$\models_{PA}(\forall x)(\exists \sigma)(Gd(\sigma) \wedge \lambda(\sigma) = x \wedge FUL(\sigma, P_1^\wedge))$$
$$\models_{PA}(\forall x)(\exists \sigma)(Gd(\sigma) \wedge \lambda(\sigma) = x \wedge FUL(\sigma, P_2^\wedge))$$
$$\models_{PA}(\forall x)(\exists \sigma)(Gd(\sigma) \wedge \lambda(\sigma) = x \wedge FUL(\sigma, P_3^\wedge))$$

etc.

---

18 Note that, as is made evident in the proof of **Lemma 4.1**, it is the first claim:

$$(\forall x)(\exists \sigma)(Gd(\sigma) \wedge \lambda(\sigma) = x \wedge FUL(\sigma, \ulcorner\Phi\urcorner) \wedge FUL(\sigma, P_x^\wedge))$$

that is satisfied on the standard model $\mathbb{N}$ – hence true but not a theorem of PA.
19 Putnam, "Nonstandard models", 56.

These are obviously equivalent to:

$$\vDash_{PA}(\forall x)(\exists\sigma)(Gd(\sigma) \wedge \lambda\,(\sigma) = x \wedge FUL(\sigma,\ulcorner T\urcorner) \wedge FUL(\sigma, P_1^{\wedge}))$$

$$\vDash_{PA}(\forall x)(\exists\sigma)(Gd(\sigma) \wedge \lambda\,(\sigma) = x \wedge FUL(\sigma,\ulcorner T\urcorner) \wedge FUL(\sigma, P_2^{\wedge}))$$

$$\vDash_{PA}(\forall x)(\exists\sigma)(Gd(\sigma) \wedge \lambda\,(\sigma) = x \wedge FUL(\sigma,\ulcorner T\urcorner) \wedge FUL(\sigma, P_3^{\wedge}))$$

etc.

But these are nothing more than the instances of the formula marked by ($*$) above (and, via the aforementioned equivalences, are in effect instances of Putnam's original sentence). Hence what we have is nothing more than a straightforward instance of the semantic analogue of ω-incompleteness.

Theorem 4.1 is akin to Gödel's first incompleteness theorem: we have shown, of a great many sentences, such that neither they nor their negations are theorems of PA – and we have done this without diagonalization! But what about the second incompleteness theorem?

At first glance, it would seem that the most natural way to formulate a fulfillability analogue of the second incompleteness theorem would be to show that, for some or all $\Phi \in \mathcal{L}_{PA}$, that:

$$\neg(\forall x)(\exists\sigma)(Gd(\sigma) \wedge \lambda\,(\sigma) = x \wedge FUL(\sigma,\ulcorner\neg\Phi\urcorner) \wedge FUL(\sigma, P_x^{\wedge}))$$

is not a theorem of PA. After all, if universal PA-fulfillability is a weak kind of *correctness*, then this suggests that universal PA-fulfillability is some sense a semantic analogue of the syntactic provability predicate $Bew(x)$. But then, the failure of the negation of Φ to be universally PA-fulfillable – the dual of this notion of correctness (a sort of weak *non-incorrectness*) – would correspond to a semantic analogue of the Gödelian consistency predicate $\neg Bew(\neg x)$. Put more simply, this suggests the following associations:[20]

$$Bew(\ulcorner\Phi\urcorner) \rightsquigarrow (\forall x)(\exists\sigma)(Gd(\sigma) \wedge \lambda\,(\sigma) = x \wedge FUL(\sigma,\ulcorner\Phi\urcorner) \wedge FUL(\sigma, P_x^{\wedge}))$$

$$\neg Bew(\ulcorner\neg\Phi\urcorner) \rightsquigarrow \neg(\forall x)(\exists\sigma)(Gd(\sigma) \wedge \lambda\,(\sigma) = x \wedge FUL(\sigma,\ulcorner\neg\Phi\urcorner) \wedge FUL(\sigma, P_x^{\wedge}))$$

Since the second incompleteness theorem amounts to the proof-theoretic independence of:

$$\neg Bew(\ulcorner\neg T\urcorner)$$

---

[20] The squiggly arrow $\rightsquigarrow$ is meant to suggest an intuitive association based on similarities in the formal behavior of provability and fulfillability – nothing more.

the parallel just drawn would seem to suggest that the fulfillability analogue of the second incompleteness theorem amounts to something like the semantic independence of:

$$\neg(\forall x)(\exists \sigma)(\mathsf{Gd}(\sigma) \wedge \lambda(\sigma) = x \wedge \mathsf{FUL}(\sigma, \ulcorner \neg \mathsf{T} \urcorner) \wedge \mathsf{FUL}(\sigma, \mathsf{P}_x^\wedge))$$

But no such result will be forthcoming, for the following simple reason: For each $\Phi \in \mathcal{L}_{\mathsf{PA}}$, Φ being a theorem (i.e. being satisfied on all PA-models) entails the failure of the negation of Φ to be universally PA-fulfillable on the standard model $\mathbb{N}$:[21]

Theorem 4.2. *For any* $\Phi \in \mathcal{L}_{\mathsf{PA}}$ *if*:

$$\vDash_{\mathsf{PA}} \Phi$$

then:

$$\vDash_{\mathsf{PA}} \neg(\forall x)(\exists \sigma)(\mathsf{Gd}(\sigma) \wedge \lambda(\sigma) = x \wedge \mathsf{FUL}(\sigma, \ulcorner \neg \Phi \urcorner) \wedge \mathsf{FUL}(\sigma, \mathsf{P}_x^\wedge))$$

Proof. Proof by contraposition. For any arbitrary $\Phi \in \mathcal{L}_{\mathsf{PA}}$ and PA-model $\mathcal{M}$, assume that:

$$\mathcal{M} \nvDash \neg(\forall x)(\exists \sigma)(\mathsf{Gd}(\sigma) \wedge \lambda(\sigma) = x \wedge \mathsf{FUL}(\sigma, \ulcorner \neg \Phi \urcorner) \wedge \mathsf{FUL}(\sigma, \mathsf{P}_x^\wedge))$$

Then:

$$\mathcal{M} \vDash (\forall x)(\exists \sigma)(\mathsf{Gd}(\sigma) \wedge \lambda(\sigma) = x \wedge \mathsf{FUL}(\sigma, \ulcorner \neg \Phi \urcorner) \wedge \mathsf{FUL}(\sigma, \mathsf{P}_x^\wedge))$$

But then the *Instability Theorem* provides a PA-model $\mathcal{M}'$ such that:

$$\mathcal{M}' \vDash \neg \Phi$$

Hence:

$$\nvDash_{\mathsf{PA}} \Phi$$

$\square$

So what has gone wrong? The answer is simple: the reasoning just rehearsed associating provability in PA with universal PA-fulfillability gets things exactly backwards. Universal PA-fulfillability does not correspond to Bew(x),

---

21 The biconditional strengthening of this theorem – that is, the claim that Φ being a theorem (i.e. being satisfied on all PA-models) *is equivalent to* the failure of the negation of Φ to be universally PA-fulfillable on the standard model $\mathbb{N}$ – seems to be true, although the simple methods mobilized in this paper seem insufficient to prove the right-to-left direction.

but instead corresponds to $\neg\mathsf{Bew}(\dot{\neg}x)$, or, put another way, the fulfillability analogue of $\mathsf{Bew}(x)$ holding of (the code of) a formula Φ is not the universal PA-fulfillability of Φ, but the failure of the negation of Φ to be universally PA fulfillable. Thus, we should reject the informal associations given above, and replace them with:

$$\mathsf{Bew}(\ulcorner\Phi\urcorner) \leftrightsquigarrow \neg(\forall x)(\exists\sigma)(\mathsf{Gd}(\sigma) \wedge \lambda(\sigma) = x \wedge \mathsf{FUL}(\sigma, \ulcorner\neg\Phi\urcorner) \wedge \mathsf{FUL}(\sigma, \mathsf{P}_x^\wedge))$$

$$\neg\mathsf{Bew}(\ulcorner\neg\Phi\urcorner) \leftrightsquigarrow (\forall x)(\exists\sigma)(\mathsf{Gd}(\sigma) \wedge \lambda(\sigma) = x \wedge \mathsf{FUL}(\sigma, \ulcorner\Phi\urcorner) \wedge \mathsf{FUL}(\sigma, \mathsf{P}_x^\wedge))$$

And, once we note that these are the correct correspondences between fulfillability and provability, it turns out that we have already proven a fulfillability version of the second incompleteness theorem since, on this understanding, the fulfillability analogue of the second incompleteness theorem just is **Corollary 3.2**.

Another way of putting all of this is to note that:

$$\neg(\forall x)(\exists\sigma)(\mathsf{Gd}(\sigma) \wedge \lambda(\sigma) = x \wedge \mathsf{FUL}(\sigma, \ulcorner\dot{\neg}y\urcorner) \wedge \mathsf{FUL}(\sigma, \mathsf{P}_x^\wedge))$$

is (or is something much like) a *theoremhood in* PA predicate, and hence universal PA-fulfillability is (or is something much like) the dual of this: a *satisfiable on some* PA *model* predicate. Thus, **Corollary 3.2** expresses (something like) the fact that there is no $\Phi \in \mathcal{L}_{\mathsf{PA}}$ such that it is a theorem of PA that Φ is true on some PA-model.

Now that we have gotten all of this straight, it is perhaps unsurprising that we can provide a very simple proof of a fulfillability analogue of Löb's theorem:[22]

Theorem 4.3. *For all* $\Phi \in \mathcal{L}_{\mathsf{PA}}$, *if:*

$$\vDash_{\mathsf{PA}} \neg(\forall x)(\exists\sigma)(\mathsf{Gd}(\sigma) \wedge \lambda(\sigma) = x \wedge \mathsf{FUL}(\sigma, \ulcorner\neg\Phi\urcorner) \wedge \mathsf{FUL}(\sigma, \mathsf{P}_x^\wedge)) \to \Phi$$

then:

$$\vDash_{\mathsf{PA}} \Phi$$

Proof. Assume, for arbitrary $\Phi \in \mathcal{L}_{\mathsf{PA}}$, that:

$$\vDash_{\mathsf{PA}} \neg(\forall x)(\exists\sigma)(\mathsf{Gd}(\sigma) \wedge \lambda(\sigma) = x \wedge \mathsf{FUL}(\sigma, \ulcorner\neg\Phi\urcorner) \wedge \mathsf{FUL}(\sigma, \mathsf{P}_x^\wedge)) \to \Phi$$

---

22 As far as I am aware, this is the first time fulfillability has been used *in print* to prove a version of Löb's Theorem. This result and the next could be given even briefer proofs by invoking **Corollary 3.2**, but, given that the purpose of this essay is to introduce Kripke's fulfillability method and demonstrate the power of this notion – and, in particular, the power of the *Instability Theorem* – the more explicit proof given here is more useful.

Assume, for *reductio*, that there is a PA-model $\mathcal{M}$ such that:

$$\mathcal{M} \models \neg\Phi$$

Then, by *modus tollens*:

$$\mathcal{M} \models (\forall x)(\exists \sigma)(\mathsf{Gd}(\sigma) \wedge \lambda(\sigma) = x \wedge \mathsf{FUL}(\sigma, \ulcorner\neg\Phi\urcorner) \wedge \mathsf{FUL}(\sigma, \mathsf{P}_x^\wedge))$$

But then, by the *Instability Theorem*, we obtain a PA-model $\mathcal{M}'$ such that:

$$\mathcal{M}' \models \neg(\forall x)(\exists \sigma)(\mathsf{Gd}(\sigma) \wedge \lambda(\sigma) = x \wedge \mathsf{FUL}(\sigma, \ulcorner\neg\Phi\urcorner) \wedge \mathsf{FUL}(\sigma, \mathsf{P}_x^\wedge))$$

and:

$$\mathcal{M}' \models \neg\Phi$$

This contradicts our initial assumption. Hence, there is no PA-model $\mathcal{M}$ such that:

$$\mathcal{M} \models \neg\Phi$$

Hence

$$\models_{\mathsf{PA}} \Phi$$

$\square$

Before moving on, it is worth making the following consequence of **Theorem 4.4** explicit, since it will be convenient in the next section:

Corollary 4.4. *For all* $\Phi \in \mathcal{L}_{\mathsf{PA}}$, *if:*

$$\models_{\mathsf{PA}} \Phi \rightarrow (\forall x)(\exists \sigma)(\mathsf{Gd}(\sigma) \wedge \lambda(\sigma) = x \wedge \mathsf{FUL}(\sigma, \ulcorner\Phi\urcorner) \wedge \mathsf{FUL}(\sigma, \mathsf{P}_x^\wedge))$$

then:

$$\models_{\mathsf{PA}} \neg\Phi$$

Proof. Substitute $\neg\Phi$ for Φ in **Theorem 4.3**, and contrapose. $\square$

These results are certainly enough to show that Kripke's notion of fulfillability is a fruitful technique for proving limitation results for **PA** (and related systems). But these results – especially the first two – also show something else. Although the discussion above about the parallels between fulfillability and Gödel's provability predicate was helpful in determining exactly how to prove something resembling the second incompleteness theorem within the fulfillability framework (or, more precisely, to identify something we had *already* proven as the desired analogue of the second incompleteness theorem), they should not be taken to suggest that the theorems and proofs given above are nothing more than a notational variation on Gödel's original proofs. Although fulfillability and provability might be closely related notions, the proofs above demonstrate that the manner in which they are manipulated in proofs of limitation results are quite different. In his discussion of these matters, Putnam claims that:

> I am going to show you a *different* proof of the Gödel theorem, not just a different *version* of Gödel's proof.[23]

The results above help to solidify exactly what makes these different proofs, rather than merely a different version of the same old proofs: the proof of incompleteness found in Putnam's paper (and due originally to Kripke), and the additional results given here, are not different merely because they avoid diagonalization or avoid proof-theoretic methods. In addition, they involve a genuinely *new* notion – fulfillability – one that is amenable to constructions and proofs (e.g., the *Instability Theorem*) that are different in kind from those used when mobilizing the Gödelian provability predicate.

V Further Directions

Obviously, the simple results given above barely scratch the surface of what might be done with fulfillability. Here I will mention just a few simple areas where much work is waiting to be done.

First, although much of the interest in fulfillability is to be found in the fact that these methods allow us to prove important metatheorems about **PA** (and related systems) without invoking Gödel's diagonalization lemma and without invoking proof-theoretic methods, it is nevertheless interesting to see what happens when we apply diagonalization to various predicates constructed in terms of fulfillability. In order to continue in the purely semantic vein we have been mining, we need to have at our disposal a semantic version of the Gödelian diagonalization lemma:

For any unary predicate $\Psi(y) \in \mathcal{L}_{PA}$, there is a sentence $\Phi \in \mathcal{L}_{PA}$ such that:

$$\vDash_{PA} \Phi \leftrightarrow \Psi(\ulcorner\Phi\urcorner)$$

We could obtain this result via Gödel's original proof, plus an application of the completeness theorem, although purely semantic proofs of the result are

---

23 Putnam, "Nonstandard models", 54.

possible as well. Diagonalizing on various fufillability predicates, we can obtain sentences like:[24]

$$\vDash_{PA} D_1 \leftrightarrow (\forall x)(\exists \sigma)(Gd(\sigma) \wedge \lambda(\sigma) = x \wedge FUL(\sigma, \ulcorner D_1 \urcorner) \wedge FUL(\sigma, P_x^{\wedge}))$$

$$\vDash_{PA} D_2 \leftrightarrow \neg(\forall x)(\exists \sigma)(Gd(\sigma) \wedge \lambda(\sigma) = x \wedge FUL(\sigma, \ulcorner D_2 \urcorner) \wedge FUL(\sigma, P_x^{\wedge}))$$

$$\vDash_{PA} D_3 \leftrightarrow (\forall x)(\exists \sigma)(Gd(\sigma) \wedge \lambda(\sigma) = x \wedge FUL(\sigma, \ulcorner \neg D_3 \urcorner) \wedge FUL(\sigma, P_x^{\wedge}))$$

$$\vDash_{PA} D_4 \leftrightarrow \neg(\forall x)(\exists \sigma)(Gd(\sigma) \wedge \lambda(\sigma) = x \wedge FUL(\sigma, \ulcorner \neg D_4 \urcorner) \wedge FUL(\sigma, P_x^{\wedge}))$$

These sentences (unsurprisingly, given the connections we drew in the previous section between the model-theoretic behavior of fulfillability and the proof-theoretic behavior of the provability predicate) provide additional examples of sentences with various sorts of model-theoretic properties relative to PA:

$$\vDash_{PA} \neg D_1$$

$$\nvDash_{PA} \neg D_2 \text{ and } \mathbb{N} \vDash \neg D_2$$

$$\nvDash_{PA} D_3 \text{ and } \mathbb{N} \vDash D_3$$

$$\vDash_{PA} D_4$$

In addition to constructing examples based on, and proving theorems inspired by, parallels between the Gödelian provability predicate $Bew(x)$ and fulfillability, there are other ways to connect fulfillability to extant proof-theoretic work. For example, we could investigate fulfillability conditions formulated in the style of J. Barkley Rosser's well-known construction, such as:[25]

$$(\forall x)[(\exists \sigma)(Gd(\sigma) \wedge \lambda(\sigma) = x \wedge FUL(\sigma, \ulcorner \neg z \urcorner) \wedge FUL(\sigma, P_x^{\wedge}))$$
$$\rightarrow (\exists y < x)(\exists \sigma')(Gd(\sigma') \wedge \lambda(\sigma') = y \wedge FUL(\sigma, \ulcorner z \urcorner) \wedge FUL(\sigma', P_x^{\wedge}))]$$

This predicate holds of (the code of) a sentence Φ if and only if, for any (coded) sequence of length n that fulfills $\neg \Phi$, there is a shorter sequence that fulfills Φ. Just as the Rosser provability predicate exhibits logical behavior different from that displayed by the Gödelian provability predicate,

---

24 If the Kripke proof is, as Putnam suggests, a genuinely *new* proof of incompleteness, since it uses new model-theoretic techniques, then there is some reason for thinking that sentences D_2 and D_3 provide a *third* proof of incompleteness, distinct from both the Gödel proof and the Kripke proof, since it combines methods from each.

25 J. Barkley Rosser, "Extensions of some theorems of Gödel and Church." *Journal of Symbolic Logic* 1 (1936): 87–91. This is far from the only way that one could adapt Rosser's "trick" to fulfillability.

this Rosser-style fulfillability predicate is no doubt worth comparing to the simpler conditions studied in the previous sections.

The sort of approach suggested by the examples above no doubt have much to teach us about incompleteness (and, in particular, the way that we might understand incompleteness as a purely model-theoretic phenomenon). But both the application of diagonalization and the exploration of Rosser-style fulfillability predicates are merely instances of mimicking techniques familiar from the older, Gödelian proof-theoretic approach to incompleteness and related results. Likely the most promising avenues of exploration with regard to fulfillability involve, not simplistic copying of proof-theoretic constructions and techniques, but the discovery of new methods that are purely model-theoretic in nature. The *Instability Theorem* is one such technique, providing us not only with the basic building blocks for an extremely simple proof of (both the first and second) incompleteness theorems, but also providing a simple method for obtaining, for each PA-model $\mathcal{M}$, a submodel $\mathcal{M}'$ whose domain is a proper initial segment of the domain of $\mathcal{M}$. This technique, although central to the proofs given in §4, is a purely model-theoretic technique, with (as far as I know) no existing proof-theoretic analogue. The hope, of course, is that the use of these purely model-theoretic techniques will lead – not only to new proofs of old theorems – but also to proofs of *new* theorems. This was, no doubt, part of the hope underlying Putnam's attempt to publicize Kripke's methods and proof (and, equally importantly, to provide a simple and accessible version of the proof). Hopefully this essay further contributes to a wider awareness of, and a wider use of, fulfillability within mathematical logic.[26]

---

26 Thanks are owed to Stella Moon for and Warren Goldfarb for helpful conversations on the material contained in this essay. All mistakes are, of course, solely the fault of the author.

Martha C. Nussbaum
Putnam's Aristotle

Abstract: Putnam felt a special affinity for Aristotle. He worked hard on Greek and regularly participated in an Aristotle reading group. This paper studies this deep affinity, as represented primarily in the papers "Changing Aristotle's Mind" (co-authored with Martha Nussbaum) and "Aristotle After Wittgenstein," considering not just affinities of argument, but also a more general affinity of philosophical method and approach.

I Putnam and Aristotle: Respect, Curiosity, Affinity

Putnam really liked Aristotle. He not only admired him, he also felt an affinity with him. In consequence, he thought he could learn something about his own philosophical problems by a close study of some of Aristotle's works. In *Realism With a Human Face* he mentions that he has been known to make the "rueful joke" that "As I get smarter, Aristotle gets smarter" (RHF 211)[1] – meaning, I suppose, that as his grasp of his own problems increases he is better able to appreciate Aristotle's own contributions. As a result of that developing engagement, Putnam discusses Aristotle more often and more substantively than any other pre-twentieth-century philosopher, usually with great sympathy. He relearned ancient Greek in order to read Aristotle seriously, and between around 1980 and around 1986 he attended regular Aristotle reading groups at my home in Cambridge with a group of graduate students and faculty from Harvard and Brown. We proceeded slowly and often stopped to translate difficult passages. Putnam's Greek was very good.[2] It was in consequence of this shared engagement with the

---

1 I shall use the abbreviation RHF to refer to Hilary Putnam, *Realism with a Human Face*, edited by James Conant (Cambridge, MA: Harvard University Press, 1990), and WL to refer to Putnam, *Words and Life*, edited by James Conant (Cambridge, MA: Harvard University Press, 1994). I shall mention the titles and dates of specific articles only where pertinent.

2 Putnam had a real flair for languages. He was always delighted when he could lecture in German or French; his Hebrew became very good; and he seemed to be able to relearn Greek without distraction from his other activities. Unlike Quine, who delighted in the structures of different languages and learning facts about them, Putnam mainly liked to *use* languages to communicate, and he prided himself on being able to connect with people and express himself well.

https://doi.org/10.1515/9783110769210-010

text that Putnam and I decided to co-author an article that appeared in 1983, which I shall discuss in section II.

So far as I know, Putnam never wrote about why he felt an affinity with Aristotle. Let me try to characterize some affinities that I see. Perhaps the most obvious one is that Aristotle is just about the only philosopher who, like Putnam, made contributions in every area of the subject: logic, philosophy of mathematics, philosophy of science, philosophy of mind, metaphysics, ethics, political philosophy, aesthetics. Aristotle talked about biology and cosmology, as Putnam did not; but Putnam talked about the philosophy of language, which did not really exist until after Aristotle, and the philosophy of religion, which engaged Aristotle little. (Thus Aristotle's accounts of virtues make no room for piety, a traditional Greek virtue; his god is relevant to cosmology, but not, it would seem, to poetics or ethics.) But the large areas are mostly the same. Like Aristotle, Putnam's work exudes a boundless curiosity about the world and all it contains, and there is no problem that does not excite him.

Both philosophers made bold claims, but both also showed an openness to new discovery and a willingness to change. In the case of Aristotle the presence of different and apparently shifting points of view on many topics gives rise to an endless industry of chronology-making – since Aristotle had a pretty long life (384–322 BCE) – but we have very little external evidence for the relative chronology of his works (apart from passages in which he discusses species of animal that he could not have seen before the period of his exile from Athens, after Plato's death in 347 BCE). Nor is the evidence of a changing prose style much help to us, as it occasionally seems to be in the case of Plato, since Aristotle's works are partially finished lectures, or lecture notes, not polished publications: there were in fact many such publications, famous in antiquity for their elegant style; but they don't survive except in fragments. With Putnam, we are lucky to have – in part thanks to the editorial work of Jim Conant – a complete set of his finished publications, with secure documentation of their dates of publication – which in Putnam's case is usually close to the date of composition. This is fortunate indeed, since we are able to chart shifts of position with precision. If we lost all evidence of the chronology of Putnam's writings, I wonder how well we would do! In any case, both were continually self-critical and open to argument, and they changed their views in the light of argument. *Pace* the scholastic appropriation of Aristotle as dogmatist, the "master of all those who know,"[3] the Aristotle who really comes across in

---

3 Dante, *Inferno*, canto IV.

his writings wants to learn from every source.[4] Neither Aristotle nor Putnam had any place for the anxious self-defensiveness that so often mars philosophy, or for authoritarianism in teaching. And this openness to criticism led, in both, to a serious interest in their predecessors, whom both expected to have gotten a lot of things right; they could therefore give us a lot of help in our search.

There is another more intangible affinity. Both were scientists without peer, but neither allowed science to become imperialistic, eclipsing human life. They were naturalists without being reductivists. Perhaps precisely because they knew so much real science and mathematics, they knew what those disciplines could do and what they could not. I recall a meeting at the World Institute for Development Economics Research in Helsinki at which numerous economists, as is their wont, were dismissing the insights of the humanistic disciplines of philosophy and history. Putnam, utterly lacking in true arrogance, knew how to parody the pretensions of scientism to make a humanistic point. Proclaiming that he was, after all, the Walter Beverly Pearson Professor of Modern Mathematics and Mathematical Logic, he then insisted (from that "lofty" vantage point!) that there was exactly as much objectivity in ethics as in science.[5] Aristotle would have put on just such a performance of knowingness, I think, had he had such arrogant economists to face![6] In all the areas in which he worked, Putnam shares with Aristotle a deep concern: that the messy matter of human life should not be squeezed to fit the demands of an excessively simple theory, that what Putnam calls "the whole hurly-burly of human actions" should be the context within which philosophical theory does its work. At the same time, and again like Aristotle, Putnam has never given way to irrationalism, has never taken up a skeptical and dismissive attitude to philosophical theorizing: for, as he stresses, the attempt to order our world by the work of reason is one of the most deep and pervasive aspects of the hurly burly of human life. Indeed, it's no exaggeration to say that for many, Putnam's work has reopened the possibility of philosophy in a post-Wittgensteinian era.

---

4 Far more accurate is Jonathan Swift's portrait of Aristotle in *Gulliver's Travels*, in the voyage to Laputa: Aristotle loves meeting Descartes and Gassendi, and quickly admits that many of his views were plain wrong!

5 See Hilary Putnam, "Objectivity and the Science-Ethics Distinction," in *The Quality of Life*, edited by Martha C. Nussbaum and Amartya Sen, 143–157 (Oxford: Clarendon Press, 1993).

6 Here's a difference, though: Putnam was a US citizen, and it was from that vantage point that he engaged in radical political activity. Aristotle was not a citizen at Athens, but what was then known as a "metic" or "resident alien." Metics had very few rights; they could not vote or sit on juries, and they had to make regular reports on their activities to a citizen "watcher." Because of his links with Macedonia, where he was born, Macedonia being an enemy of Athens, he was forced to leave Athens twice during his life; he died in exile.

In this paper I'll describe three examples of Putnam's humanistic anti-reductionism, all three being cases in which he turns to Aristotle for guidance. One example comes from the philosophy of mind; one from debates over intentionality; and one from ethics. In all three cases, Putnam's internal conversations with Aristotle help him to a powerful conclusion that is still of significance to our philosophical debates.

For reasons of space, I must unfortunately omit Putnam's exhilarating confrontation with reductive forms of economics, and his energetic defense of the Aristotle-inspired "Capabilities Approach" (CA), an approach to comparative quality of life measurement and to the foundation of normative political principles pioneered by me and Amartya Sen (with subtly different purposes and views). To talk about this debate would require describing the field of development economics and saying why the CA was needed; it would require both showing its Aristotelian roots and showing many ways in which it departs from Aristotle (not least in its insistence on the equal dignity of all human beings). And it would require distinguishing Sen's version of the CA from my own. Finally, it would require discussing the important critique of welfare and development economics made by Putnam's friend Vivian Walsh, which set the stage for Putnam's own intervention. Much of this has little direct connection to Aristotle. So I hope readers will follow this fascinating debate for themselves.[7]

II Text and Context

Before I launch in, it's useful to be aware that Putnam reflected explicitly about the job of interpreting a distant philosophical text. He believed that interpretation of a philosophical text was always in some sense interest-relative: our choices are rightly guided by our own language and our own questions. Interpretation, he thought (noting that he was following Quine), was a type of "correlation": correlation of the words and sentences of Aristotle with words and sentences in our own language. And this means, he added, that it is really a

---

7 For the essentials, see Vivian Walsh, "Sen after Putnam," *Review of Political Economy* 15, no. 3 (2003): 315–394; Hilary Putnam, "For Ethics and Economics without the Dichotomies," *Review of Political Economy* 15, no. 4 (2003): 395–412; Martha C. Nussbaum, "Tragedy and Human Capabilities: A Response to Vivian Walsh," *Review of Political Economy* 15, no. 3 (2003): 413–418; Amartya Sen, "Walsh on Sen after Putnam," *Review of Political Economy* 17, no. 1 (2005): 107–113; Putnam and Walsh, "Facts, Values, Theories and Destitution in the Work of Sir Partha Dasgupta," *Review of Political Economy* 19, no. 2 (2007): 181–202.

type of "human interaction." In RHF he illustrated this point using Aristotle as his key example.

> Aristotle's words depended for their life on particular "contexts" – which is to say, particular institutions, particular assumptions, particular positions that real people once occupied and no longer occupy. Any "translation manual" interprets Aristotle using words which depend for *their* life on different institutions, assumptions, and positions. It is not surprising, from such a perspective, that each century should require new interpretations.. . . (RHF 211)

If we think of interpretation as a type of human interaction, he continued, we will not "be dismayed (or driven to an insane relativism) by the open-ended character of the activity." (RHF 211)

In the case of Aristotle, however, he continued, interest-relativity has a further dimension. Because we read Aristotle looking for insight into our own philosophical questions, we can't stop with a translation of his words and sentences: we need to know what these imply for our questions. "Even if he had written 'Happiness is the activity of the psyche according to virtue in the complete life,' and not the Greek sentence he actually wrote," there would still be an interpretation problem, since we want to know not just the words but also their implications, "and in cases where what Aristotle wrote was vague or ambiguous, we are interested in knowing what (more precise) senses it could be given and what it implies about our problems when given these various possible more precise readings." (RHF 212)

What Putnam does here is to steer deftly between two bad views of interpretation that we scholars often encounter. One is the view that the aim of interpretation is to put aside the entirety of our own context and to see the text in its original context, as if through a perfectly clear pane of glass, bringing nothing of ourselves to the exercise. This is not even possible, of course, given the gappiness of our evidence, so there is a measure of self-delusion involved in all attempts of this type. Often the attempt to put ourselves to one side simply ends up revealing unconscious biases and prejudices rather than involving an intelligent effort to make those explicit. But also: this is hardly a way to conduct a *human interaction* with the past, from which we might learn something. We simply can't pretend we aren't ourselves, with our own context and our own questions. It would be like trying to understand your friend by pretending you aren't you but her. That would not only be remarkably pretentious and officious, presuming to understand the other as if you were that other, it would also be totally alien to the aims of friendship, which involve reciprocity, conversation, and learning.

The second bad view is to flip over into what I guess Putnam meant by an "insane relativism": we can't get access to Aristotle, so let's just use him for our own ends. We often see cheap and hasty attempts to recast the Greeks into the terms of some contemporary debate, as if it were clear that Plato is really Russell and Aristotle really Wittgenstein (to use an example from my own graduate education). This is no better than to say that Zeus is "really" the Christian God, as pious Victorian classicists so often did: it robs us of any chance to learn anything at all from the past. (Gay classicists of this era liked to point out that one reason to study Greek ethics was precisely to understand that another successful and admirable culture thought very differently from the Victorians about essential questions of sexual morality.[8]) Once again, to return to the friendship metaphor, it is a horrible way to converse with a friend: not listening, simply appropriating and using.

Putnam, I claim, avoids both of these errors. Unlike my first group of interpreters, he understands that we always bring ourselves to the encounter with the other, as in any human interaction. But just as the omnipresence of personal projects need not doom friendship and love, so too the omnipresence of one's own context need not doom the quest for learning from a text written in a different context. Just as love and friendship require active and unflagging curiosity and a constant awareness of one's own possible biases and prejudices, so too learning from Aristotle requires both curiosity and humility. (These are my metaphors, not Putnam's, but I think he would approve.[9])

III Philosophy of Mind: Aristotle Shows a Path

"Changing Aristotle's Mind"[10] was a joy to write. We were in great harmony about both the interpretation of Aristotle and the correct contemporary philosophical

---

8 A notable work in this effort to recover the difference of the past as a guide to the present was John Addington Symonds's *A Problem in Greek Ethics*, written in 1873 and privately published and circulated in 1883, the first work of European scholarship to see clearly what Greek homosexuality was and was not. The complete text can now be found at Project Gutenberg, https://www.gutenberg.org/ebooks/32022.

9 When I co-authored with Putnam I realized that he was surprisingly fond of military metaphors, including quotations from "The Charge of the Light Brigade" – so, just for fun, I used them too in my sections of "Changing Aristotle's Mind," thinking it an ironic commentary on Putnam's earlier antiwar stance. (I don't think he was ever a pacifist, though: he was just opposed to the lunacy of the Vietnam War.)

10 Martha C. Nussbaum and Hilary Putnam, "Changing Aristotle's Mind," in *Essays on Aristotle's De Anima*, edited by Martha C. Nussbaum and Amelie Rorty, 27–56 (Oxford: Clarendon Press, 1992), reprinted in WL 22–61.

position, so we just divided up the sections, Putnam being largely responsible for the first draft of those dealing with contemporary issues and I being first drafter of the parts dealing with the text – but we revised of everything jointly, and we knew going in that we would have fun. We had each defended a certain view about Aristotle in separate writings, and the article was motivated by an attack by Myles Burnyeat on what he called the "Nussbaum-Putnam interpretation."[11] Since Burnyeat called his interpretation "the Christian interpretation,"[12] we were amused to think that our approach, situating Aristotle squarely in this world, with a keen interest in material change, was supposed to be the Jewish interpretation.[13] (We loved joking about that.[14]) We rose to our mutual defense – which was also a defense of Aristotle, since Burnyeat maintained that Aristotle's philosophy of mind would have to be "junked," along with our interpretation. We decided that the article would have to be very textual and concerned with details of passages in several works. That part of it I won't try to summarize here; it's there to read. It's not hard to understand even if you don't know Greek. But from start to finish it had an unmistakable aim to vindicate Aristotle's insights as useful for present-day thought about mind and explanation.

Here is the essence of Burnyeat's challenge. Aristotle, being pre-Descartes and pre-Newton, had a view about matter that we can no longer take seriously. Pretty much all of what he says about perception and desire relies on this antiquated picture of matter, according to which the mental activities of animals (with the possible exception of desiring) take place with no describable or intelligible material change. Nussbaum and Putnam have not appreciated to what extent all of Aristotle's arguments about form and matter are hitched to the doomed picture of matter, and therefore their interpretation, and Aristotle with it, must be thrown out, now that we can no longer take this picture seriously.

Burnyeat, like many products of the British system of education, with its early specialization, didn't actually know any modern physics, and one point we make right away is that the picture Burnyeat is operating with is actually not the modern picture of matter, which is much more difficult and elusive that

---

11 I'll assume that those who want references can find them in the article.

12 In an earlier draft, not the ultimately published version, which was also billed as an unfinished draft, as had long been Burnyeat's custom, even before his problems with dementia made others seek to publish his drafts.

13 By this time, 1982–83, Putnam was very observant; I had converted in 1969 and continue to be seriously Jewish, though in a Reform style that was never Putnam's. (He once asked me whether he would be *permitted* to wear a kipoh to my temple!)

14 But we also included a section on Aquinas, showing that he, at least, did not hold the "Christian interpretation."

his simple Cartesianism. But that was a throwaway line. Our main concern was to defend ourselves and our Aristotle.

Burnyeat's error is a version of my first bad style of interpreting. Burnyeat is a great scholar, and he would not go wrong in any simple way, but he was at that stage enamored of the idea of Greek philosophy's utter strangeness and distance, which is as dogmatic as the idea that they are just like us, and just as wrong. We just have to look and see in each case – but not by pretending that we can study them through a clear pane of glass, without bringing ourselves. In this case, Burnyeat most definitely brings in himself, including his English schoolboy physics, but doesn't acknowledge his own situated position (except, perhaps, when he called his view "Christian"). We were hoping from the beginning to show that you can converse with Aristotle while explicitly having in mind some current concerns and questions, and tease out his thought in a way that makes it illuminating for us, without falling into the opposite error of cheaply using him instrumentally for our own ends, or ignoring serious scholarship. We tried to show that we were not doing that by the sheer textual detail of our article, but also by distancing ourselves from those who thought Aristotle was a contemporary functionalist. By this time Putnam had himself abandoned functionalism, and he showed how the insight that prompted that move brought him closer to Aristotle, and likely was a case of learning from Aristotle.

The first insight we found in Aristotle is one that I think philosophy of mind badly needs to relearn today. This is that many issues addressed in the philosophy of mind are not specific to "mind," but are actually more general issues about how we explain the life-activities of living things.[15] Aristotle's treatise *Peri psuchês*, usually translated *On the Soul*, is not about "souls" in the Christian sense, where "soul" connotes the presence of "higher" faculties such as reasoning.[16] Aristotle's word for "living thing" is *empsuchon*, meaning "that which has *psuchê* in it," and so, really, *psuchê* is just the livingness of the living, whatever that is. (He investigates a variety of views.) The work covers all the major classes of living thing: plants, non-human animals, humans. In some other works, Aristotle leaves plants to one side for a time, given that they do not move from place to place, and seeks what he calls a "common explanation

---

15 Also pertinent here is Putnam's "How Old Is the Mind," felicitously placed just before our "Changing" in WL 3–21. "Changing" was first presented at a conference in 1984, though not published until 1992, so it is actually very close to "How Old," published in 1986.

16 I put "higher" in quotes because I think each life-form is worthy of investigation and ethical concern for what it is, and the traditional medieval view of the "ladder of nature" confuses us. I don't suggest, however, that Aristotle is utterly free of that confusion.

of animal motion."[17] But always he organizes his inquiry around a group of life-activities that need principles of explanation, and he proposes broad such principles, treating what we now call the "mental" as a special case only when it does indeed require special principles of explanation. He argues that in all cases of explaining the behavior of living things, the level of "form," or functional organization, plays a privileged role, taking explanatory precedence over the changes of material constituents.

But his concern for explanation is more general yet, as it turns out. For the inquiry into living beings is a central part of a more general inquiry into "substance," that is to say relatively durable entities that we can trace through time, identify and reidentify. For Aristotle living beings are paradigmatic cases of "substance," since they have reasonably clear identity conditions, as artifacts do not: it is pretty clear when an animal is born and dies, much less clear when a statue, or a table, or a house, ceases to be the same statue, table, or house. However, to a certain extent the two classes can be treated together in a general inquiry into continuity. Putnam and I noted that this unifying concern for substance is not so common in contemporary philosophy, though we mentioned David Wiggins and Roderick Chisholm as exceptions. This lack of a general concern for continuity and explanation is a loss to the philosophy of mind, we argued.

Here's the basic point we made, drawing on Aristotle: To grant as we do, that every artifact and every living being is a material object, realized at every stage of its existence in some sort of suitable, and constantly changing, matter, does not license the inference that the best explanations of how artifacts and living beings function in the world – how they move, what changes they undergo – are given on the level of constituent matter. For good explanations include what is relevant and what is not relevant; they focus on what can be generalized and not on the sui generis; and they are not cluttered with a lot of stuff that does little or no explanatory work. And given that living and non-living substances are compositionally plastic, the material level would violate these criteria. Take a bronze sphere with radius r. That sphere will be able to pass through a wooden hoop with radius slightly greater than r, but not through a hoop with radius

---

17 This is especially the case in the little treatise *De Motu Animalium*, which I edited and translated and on which I wrote a commentary, all for my 1975 Harvard Ph.D. thesis, much of it published as *Aristotle's De Motu Animalium* (Princeton: Princeton University Press, 1978). A more technical article on text critical matters was published separately as "The Text of Aristotle's *De Motu Animalium*," *Harvard Studies in Classical Philology* 80 (1976): 111–159. I note that Oliver Primavesi of the University of Munich, who is preparing a new critical edition with newly discovered evidence, has found that the new evidence confirms a major conjecture of mine, that there is a third independent manuscript family.

slightly less than r. Why? Now we could start talking about bronze and wood. We could produce detailed atom charts tracing the movements of every atom at every stage of the transaction. But that's a particularist narrative, not an explanation. Armed with this chart we could not predict that a sphere made of marble (with radius r) could pass through a hoop of stainless steel with radius slightly greater than r. The material account would be completely different. And yet of course the same geometrical laws hold, and the prediction could be made if we focused on those, rather than on the superfluous information supplied by atom charts. The specific atoms are just not relevant to the story.

Now consider a cat. What do we need to know to explain its movements, predict what it can and cannot do, and what continuities must obtain as long as it is in existence? We need to know that at every stage of its existence it is instantiated in some type of suitable matter to be sure: it can't be like Alice's Cheshire cat, which faced to immateriality, leaving only its grin. But to talk about atom charts at every stage will, once again, obscure many relevant features and introduce many that are irrelevant. What we need to know about is the functional organization of that type of animal, what sorts of life-activities it is organized to be able to perform. That is where we should focus our gaze, if we want to be able to explain and predict.

Moving on to "mind," much the same thing holds true: perception, emotion, and desire are useful functional concepts, which should not be discarded simply because we understand that they are always realized in the particular movements of matter. We should, of course, be interested in learning as much as possible about the physiology underlying mental processes. (We praised David Huebel's work on the brain, and of course by now there is a lot more.) But unless it turns out that some functions are not, after all, compositionally plastic, then we still need to hold on to the psychological/functional concepts. (And it now turns out that the brain is more plastic than it was then thought to be.) Where we dug in our heels against Burnyeat was in our insistence that our interest in explanations at the functional level did not require us to adopt any untenable or mysterious picture of matter. Multiple realizability is all we need, and then we can happily say as much as seems interesting or true about changes on the material level.

Putnam once believed that the functional organization of a human being could be given as a Turing machine program. But, as we continue, he discarded that view when he realized that

mental states are not only compositionally plastic but also *computationally plastic*, that is, reasons to believe that physically possible creatures which believe that there are a lot of cats in the neighborhood, or whatever, may have an indefinite number of different "programs" . . . The "intentional level" is simply not reducible to the "computational level" any more than it is to the "physical level." (WL 47)

What we wanted to insist on, though, was that opposition to reductionism didn't entail Brentano's conclusion that intentionality is primitive and that nothing interesting could be said about material embodiment.

In short: we wanted science without reductionistic scientism. So, we insist, did Aristotle. In many ways his multifaceted inquiries into substance and life can still guide us.

I would like to point to a further advantage to Aristotle's way of organizing the inquiry into substance. We never forget that humans are but one type of living thing, enmattered forms. The term "philosophy of mind" splits humans off from other animals, suggesting that special principles of explanation are needed for the very special nature of our mental life, since the term usually connotes a focus on self-conscious awareness. (Some animals also have that, but many do not.) Aristotle says: let's see how far we can get with a "common explanation." In the case of life-activities such as perception and desire, we can get very far indeed. And not artificially separating our species off from the other animals makes it more likely, at least, that we will respect them and pursue ethical questions about our treatment of them. (I have to grant that Aristotle did not do well here, whereas the Platonist Porphyry wrote some of the best arguments against meat-eating ever produced.)

Did Putnam think about this advantage to the Aristotelian approach? He certainly did not write about animal rights. But I think a concern for the "common explanation" surfaces at one point in "Aristotle After Wittgenstein," when he notes, concerning his effort "to put myself in the frame of mind of a 'latter-day Aristotelian'": "I find that such thought experiments are best conducted while taking my dog, Shlomit, on a walk in the woods and marshes of Arlington and Lexington." (WL 71) A few paragraphs later, we find: "one idea that might occur to a latter-day Aristotelian (while walking his dog). . ." (WL 71) Now Putnam is not fond of gratuitous autobiographical insertions. One should proceed on the assumption that these two are purposive. I think their purpose is to point out that the Aristotelian approach, which focuses on the properties and capacities common to all animals, can best be understood when one is oneself in a close relationship with another animal species, preferably one whom one loves and respects.

IV Intentionality: Aristotle after Wittgenstein

Putnam returned to the question of intentionality in "Aristotle After Wittgenstein" (WL 62–81), focusing now not on substance generally but on the problem of how thoughts and language latch onto the world. And here, much to many readers' surprise – and informed by those long walks with Shlomit – Putnam comes emphatically to the conclusion that Aristotle does better than Wittgenstein (of the *Tractatus*) in helping us wrestle with this question. Aristotle is, then "after Wittgenstein" in two senses: he is alive for us in a way that the early Wittgenstein no longer is (Putnam claims); but also, Aristotle has to be made anew, to some extent, to make him speak to us after the linguistic turn and the shift to a metaphysics of events that characterize our post-Wittgensteinian world.

Putnam begins by noting a similarity between Aristotle's idea that the form of the object is isomorphic to the idea in the mind – an idea that sounds magical, but that actually resembles, to a surprising degree, the *Tractatus*'s picture theory of meaning. If we revise Aristotle by making him speak of the way language (rather than perception or thought) latches onto the world, the resemblance becomes yet stronger. And we must make one more revision to set him up to prevail in our current controversies: we must make him speak of a metaphysics of events, not just substances – as Putnam thinks, rightly, his texts are ready to do with only slight changes.

Both the Aristotelian and the Wittgensteinian pictures, however, appear to have been displaced by causal theories of reference. But claims of victory are premature. We must begin by recognizing, as Davidson has correctly argued, that events must have a structure of their own, in such a way that the same event can be described by different logically equivalent sentences. (Both Davidson and Putnam also hold that the same event can be described by different sentences that are not logically equivalent, but this plays no further role in the argument.) But if this is so, we can then show that causal connection cannot be a sufficient account of how language latches onto the world: what we are missing is the notion that events have a *form*. (The argument here is rather technical, and Putnam refers us to a yet more technical model-theoretic version that he has given elsewhere.) Both Aristotle and Wittgenstein now reenter the picture.

Aristotle and Wittgenstein mean something different by "form." Putnam now argues that the Aristotelian metaphysical notion of form, in which it means the structured capacities of everyday objects, is much more useful in arguing against the causal theorist than the abstract logical Wittgensteinian notion of form. Aristotle's metaphysics is rooted in the world. The idea that a thing's form is the "metaphysically best description of its nature" is far more useful in answering the causal theorist than the Tractarian vision of form as "the abstract characterization of the totality of its logical possibilities of combination with other objects." (WL 71) As the model-theoretic argument shows, that notion just doesn't do anything to distinguish one worldly object from another. "The idea that logic could do all the work of metaphysics was a *magnificent* fantasy, but fantasy it surely was." (WL 71) It's in this section of the paper that Putnam makes two references to walking his dog, in order to underline the everydayness of the Aristotelian notion. It would take a lot more work to unpack this argument in all its detail, but suffice it to say that Putnam here finds in Aristotle's metaphysics, suitably revised, a valuable philosophical picture of how language latches onto the world – a "metaphysics that does justice to the world as we know it." (WL 70)

Putnam now faces two objections to this use of the Aristotelian notion of form. First, we often have the structures of things completely wrong, and we had better not require the correct picture of the structure to be in the mind in order for reference to be secured. Putnam is very brief, perhaps too brief, with this objection. All he says is that we clearly can't require the representation to get the essential metaphysical properties right in order for reference to work: that requirement is much too strong. People successfully referred to water without knowing its atomic structure. This seems right, but I would have liked him to say more: how much do we need to get right in order to refer, and what sorts of properties are pivotal in accounting for our success?

The second problem is that Aristotle believes that species have timeless essences, and we do not. For the evolutionary biologist, species are really historical populations, and interbreeding, the handy heuristic, shifts over time. Nonetheless, Putnam rightly replies, evolutionary biology still finds the ordinary synchronic notion of species useful, in fact indispensable. (He then considers an alternative conception of species from molecular biology, with similar results.) Aristotle is still on his feet, despite all that he didn't know. I would like to add that recent work on Aristotle's biology by David Balme and others has shown us that his picture of species is far less rigid than the medieval "timeless essence" view that is sometimes ascribed to him. This reading makes Putnam's point even more powerful: Aristotle was already on the track of the truth about species.

I would like to end this section with a point about our profession. Philosophy has fads. Many young philosophers, especially in technical areas, read mainly the latest journal articles and converse mainly with the living. Often, too, they don't do a lot of looking at the world. Here we see a great philosopher out on those long walks with his dog, looking at the world of nature and conversing with Aristotle – both together informing his own ruminations. We can't force young hotshots to go out and look at nature (and after all Aristotle himself really was forced to look at nature, by being exiled from Athens for about twenty years, to the coast of Asia Minor, where he saw all those starfish and sea urchins). But we can require them to study the history of philosophy, reminding them continually that the ideas they encounter there can challenge contemporary fads and preconceptions, proving invaluable conversation-partners.

V Ethics: Rules and Perceptions

Putnam's interest in Aristotle's ethics, which was ongoing and serious, leaves fewer traces than his interest in Aristotle's philosophy of nature. And if with regard to philosophy of nature Putnam and I are in harmony, the main evidence for his view of the ethical thought comes from an article that is a somewhat stern criticism of me! I'll recapitulate the history, describe Putnam's approach to Aristotle, and try to argue that he (and, to some degree, Aristotle) are right against me in one important respect, but that I (and Aristotle) are right against Putnam in another. On a third issue, it's a draw: Putnam is right in some respects, but incomplete in another area, which my work emphasized. The article in question is "Taking Rules Seriously" (RHF 193–200), originally published in 1983[18] – thus a contemporary of "Changing Aristotle's Mind" and "Aristotle After Wittgenstein."

Here's the background. Invited to present an "Invited Paper" at the Pacific Division APA in (I believe) 1981, I decided to take a risk and present a paper that was not about ancient Greek philosophy, the first time I had done that publicly. I wanted to establish that I was not just a narrow specialist, though ultimately my long study of Aristotle very much shaped what I wrote. I thought, "now or never" if I was to get out of that box. I had been teaching a lecture course on "Literature and Moral Philosophy" at Harvard, in which the authors considered were Henry James, Marcel Proust, Virginia Woolf, and Samuel Beckett. I had some ideas about James's *The Golden Bowl*, long a favorite novel of mine, that I thought it worth developing into a paper about the relationship between literature and moral philosophy. (As I repeatedly taught the course over the years, I refined my ideas about all these authors, and the results appear in my book *Love's Knowledge: Essays on Philosophy and Literature*.[19] For the APA, I submitted the paper, "Flawed Crystals: James's *The Golden Bowl* and Literature

---

18 Hilary Putnam, "Taking Rules Seriously: A Reply to Martha Nussbaum," *New Literary History* 15, no. 1 (1983): 193–200.
19 Martha C. Nussbaum, *Love's Knowledge: Essays on Philosophy and Literature* (New York: Oxford University Press, 1990).

as Moral Philosophy,"[20] the first of two papers on that novel and of four on James that I ultimately published. The paper was rather radical and odd, in the context of the moral philosophy of the period, dominated as it was by rather abstract versions of Kantianism and Utilitarianism. It might have encountered a very hostile reception, or it might have been met by blank indifference – in which case I might have been discouraged about that part of my work and failed to develop it further. The Program Committee, however, made a decision so lucky for me, one that basically changed the course of my career: they invited Richard Wollheim to be the commentator. He understood right away what I was attempting to do, and while he totally disagreed with my reading of the novel, he put himself on the line, so to speak, as much as I had. The exchange was riveting for me, and to this day I cannot express enough gratitude to Wollheim, and to the APA, for this rare instance of genuine philosophical understanding and communication. When one adds the fact that this type of work could easily have been branded as "womanish" or even "girly," with its focus on love and the nuances of the moral emotions, it was also a rare instance of anti-sexism in our profession: a powerful man talking about emotional vulnerability, as Richard so often memorably did. I have more or less forgotten how the discussion went, apart from the fact that Ruth Marcus asked a good question. (I remember Richard whispering to me before we began, "This is California. Not one person out there will have read the novel.")

Wollheim and I decided that our exchange ought to be published, preferably with further commentaries. Ralph Cohen, editor of *New Literary History*, a great visionary editor in the literary world, knew me and what I was thinking about, and had long wanted a contribution; so we wrote to Ralph. He not only liked the idea, he decided right away to devote an entire issue to the topic. Since Patrick Gardiner had in the meantime commented on my paper at the Oxford Philosophical Society, we included him. Ralph then invited his friends Hilary Putnam and Cora Diamond. (Ralph and the journal had their home at the University of Virginia, Cora's home.) Those two accepted. Ralph then added several articles that were not about my paper. I must pause again to record my gratitude to Ralph – who died on his 99th birthday, February 23, 2016, thus just exactly a month before Hilary. He supported the work of a young and unknown scholar, and a woman, and made in so doing a huge difference to my career.

---

20 Martha C. Nussbaum, "Flawed Crystals: James' *The Golden Bowl* and Literature as Moral Philosophy," in *Love's Knowledge: Essays on Philosophy and Literature*, 125–148 (Oxford: Oxford University Press, 1990).

Putnam was, then, one of a group of commentators, and they ran the gamut from Diamond's radical assault on the whole project of having an account of the good life – she thought my own internal critique was far too timid – to Putnam's stern Kantian chastisement, with Wollheim somewhere to the Diamond side of me, insisting on the importance of the non-ethical material that psychoanalysis uncovers, and urging that this material not be domesticated by squeezing it into an Aristotelian search for the good life. I'm grateful to all of them to this day, and I draw attention to the fact that there were several men, along with one woman, who, instead of mocking a young woman in sexist terms, which many certainly did in those times, engaged with her work with the greatest seriousness, even to the point of putting their own most serious thoughts about life and love on the line.[21] May their memory be a blessing, *zichronom livracha*, as we say of the dead (omitting for these purposes, but still honoring, Diamond, who is very much alive).[22]

My paper argues that if one adopts a very inclusive account of the task of moral philosophy, according to which it is an Aristotelian search for the best account of a flourishing human life, then one has reason to include novels like *The Golden Bowl* alongside recognized works of moral philosophy. This is so, I argued, because anyone who accepts that framing account ought to agree that all the major competing accounts of this subject matter should be duly considered – the Kantian, the Utilitarian, the Aristotelian, and any others there might be – and that the Aristotelian account could not be fairly considered without texts like this novel, which make clear what it really means to accept two claims made by Aristotle. The first of these is that rules are limited in their usefulness, and that ultimately "the discernment rests with perception." The second is that ethical values are plural and non-commensurable and that profound conflicts between them are a ubiquitous part of the ethical life. I offered a reading of the novel focused on these two features: first on Maggie Verver's progress from a fearful rule-bound person to one who bravely confronts the whole complexity of ethical situations; second, on the novel's idea that the ethical life is inherently flawed, since fidelity to all commitments is made basically impossible by the structure of the family, of marriage, and of human love itself. That is why it is strewn with images of Eden and the fall from Eden. I must at this point refer you to the article for elaboration of these claims. But note that I never

---

21 Two more were, of course, Stanley Cavell and Bernard Williams, who for whatever reason were not included in the journal exchange.

22 Thanks to Saul Levmore for giving me the right plural form of this familiar phrase, typically used in the singular. I'm afraid that I have not yet learned as much Hebrew as Hilary, though I am working on it.

took it upon myself in this article to defend the Aristotelian picture of the moral life against its rivals. I was trying to be very inclusive, as I said in my reply to my critics in the journal. A Utilitarian like Sidgwick, or a Kantian like Rawls, should agree with me, since both adopt an Aristotelian framing account of the domain of the ethical and thereby commit themselves to taking seriously all the major accounts of the ethical life, Aristotle's among them. The specific literary qualities of the novel are an intrinsic part of its contribution: its long circumlocutions, straining to get it right; its agonized sense of tragedy, as characters defect from a commitment under pressure of another.

Putnam misunderstands the inclusive nature of my enterprise: he takes my phrase "the Kantian account" to express hostility to Kantian ethics. In the context it expresses nothing at all about the content of Kantian ethics. I only stated that Kant's own account of what the domain of the moral includes would exclude much that the Aristotelian framing account would include, such as the salience of contingent particulars; so it would be biased against the content of Aristotle's ethics from the start. (Rawls and Sidgwick understand the need to be more inclusive if we are to judge the major competitors fairly.)

But Putnam is not wrong to think that I also sympathized with the *content* of the Jamesian/Aristotelian picture. Although I didn't say this in the article, it was probably evident from the passionate conviction with which I described the view. And Putnam had by then had many occasions to talk philosophy with me, so he knew what I thought pretty well. Against that shadowy me, lurking behind the images of Maggie Verver and her choices, he makes two claims: first, that I wrongly slight the role of rules in the moral life, and, second, that I wrongly consider all choices between competing values to be mere trade-offs, with no sense of the binding importance of rules and commitments. He thinks that Aristotle is better than Martha on rules, and he does not make clear where he thinks Aristotle stands on conflict.

Putnam was not altogether right about me. In my slightly later article on James, "'Finely Aware and Richly Responsible',"[23] I make it clear that James and I both think that a focus on fine-tuned perceptions can easily go astray and become self-serving. I argue that James recommends a dialogue between rules and perceptions. But in the paper at issue that was by no means clear, and I did tilt too much toward the perception side. He is also not quite right about Aristotle: Aristotle compares the ethical life to both medical practice and navigation,

---

23 Martha C. Nussbaum, "'Finely Aware and Richly Responsible': Literature and the Moral Imagination," in *Love's Knowledge: Essays on Philosophy and Literature*, 148–167 (Oxford: Oxford University Press, 1990).

and says of all these that rules can take you only so far: you have to be alive to the new situation, which may be unlike anything for which you were prepared. I still think this sensible and powerful, both about ethics and about the law. Indeed the common law, with its incrementalism and its determination to take no universal rule as absolutely fixed, is very much in the spirit of my Aristotle. (And that's how I came to be lodged in a law school, since debates between the common law and Utilitarianism were raging, and I was seen as someone who could give the common law a principled defense.)

Still, in an important sense he was right: I had indeed underestimated the importance of rules in the moral life, failing to take account of a point made forcefully by Kant in the *Groundwork*: that a major source of moral error is a propensity to self-privileging, which he calls "quibbling." People who feel rules inconvenient because they forbid something they would like to do have ingenious ways of quibbling with the rule, exempting their case from its claims. Thus only a very robust commitment to the universalizability of moral rules can prevent selfishness from holding sway. Universals need not be highly general. Aristotle could and I think does accept the idea that moral norms should be universalizable, albeit highly refined and thus not highly general. But probably it's right to see a taste for a high degree of refinement as dangerous in its own way, since people can all too easily insulate themselves from moral demands by casting their situation in sui generis terms. Jeremy Bentham argues that many repellent pieces of Victorian morality are hypocritical in this way, insulating the behavior of a dominant group from scrutiny while using the rule to beat up on an unpopular minority. (Thus, one of his lead examples, the sexual pleasures of the majority are deemed fine, while same-sex acts are deemed hideous and baneful – even though there is no morally significant difference at all between them.)

Sidgwick, appreciating this point, goes to a repellant extreme by insisting that thoughtful people sometimes have reason to adopt a highly refined rule that deviates from the generally accepted rule, and that a highly refined rule of this type should be kept secret from common folks, who might take it as an invitation to lawlessness. In the context, he is talking about sexual morality, and it is now known that Sidgwick was a closeted gay man. So what he seems to be saying is, Keep the rules of Victorian society in place for most people, but let a few elites adopt in secret a more refined rule that exempts their own conduct from moral scrutiny. (Sidgwick had friends who did express their homosexuality, though he himself apparently did not.)

Obviously this is a bad way of being Aristotelian. The right way would be to provide arguments against the Victorian rule and to recommend a different rule. Bentham boldly did so, but most of his writing on this topic was not published in his lifetime. Sidgwick was less courageous. Putnam offers no guidance about how we ought to distinguish good rules from bad, or how we should proceed when greeted with a bad rule. But the general direction of his argument is correct, as I have long since recognized.

When we turn to law and politics, the need for rules takes on a further dimension. We simply cannot be fine-grained Aristotelians when recommending political and legal principles for all. Considerations of practicability and transparency weigh heavily in favor of a rule-governed politics. Rules may be highly complex: thus the Clean Air Act is approximately 2000 pages long. But you are supposed to obey it, and anyone can find out what is in it. When we turn to the judiciary, a more Aristotelian common-law method prevails for the most part, and there are still things to be said in its favor.[24] But by now we can see how easily it can be hijacked by special pleading of a type that both Kant and the British Utilitarians rightly opposed. I think we still need to listen to the common law and its defenders. But my sympathies have shifted. To some extent they have moved further even than the pro-rule aspect of Aristotle, which Putnam supports.

There is another issue, however, on which I continue to think Putnam wrong and both Aristotle's and my own account right. This is the issue of tragic conflicts of values. My reply to Putnam in the journal still seems right to me, but since that reply was not reprinted in RHF, I must recapitulate. (By now I've written a lot more on the topic as well, so please forgive the repetition.[25]) Putnam interprets me as saying that all conflicts between two values involve trade-offs, and he objects to seeing them this way: the violation of a rule has real costs. But this is precisely what I too affirm. In fact, the central argument in my attack on Maggie Verver's notion of ethical consistency was that it did not take rules *seriously enough*. It should be quite plain from my interpretation of the novel that I do not think the "adult" attitude toward morality involves the idea that everything is a matter of "trade-offs." It involves, instead, the idea that to take a commitment seriously is to regard oneself as bound by it *even when* it

---

24 See my "Janus-Faced Law: A Philosophical Debate," in *The Timing of Lawmaking*, edited by Saul Levmore and Frank Fagan, 249–229 (Cheltenham and Northampton: Edward Elgar, 2017). The best defense of the common law is given by David A. Strauss, "Common Law Constitutional Interpretation," *University of Chicago Law Review* 63, no. 3 (1996): 877–935.

25 I discuss the issue in *The Fragility of Goodness: Luck and Ethics in Greek Tragedy and Philosophy* (Cambridge and New York: Cambridge University Press, 1986), in several of the essays in *Love's Knowledge*, and most recently in "The Costs of Tragedy: Some Moral Limits of Cost-Benefit Analysis," *Journal of Legal Studies* 29, no. 2 (2000): 1005–1036, reprinted in *Cost-Benefit Analysis: Legal, Economic and Philosophical Perspectives*, edited by Matthew D. Adler and Eric A. Posner, 169–200 (Chicago: University of Chicago Press, 2000).

clashes, contingently, with another commitment. Maggie's attachment to consistency is childish because it leads her to deny or "round" away the conflicting claim. I say that this is morally reprehensible.

Let me in fact speak of Kant here. Kant, like Maggie Verver, is deeply attached to the idea of ethical consistency. He is also, like Maggie, deeply attached to the idea that nothing the world does ought to be able to cause a person to violate a genuine obligation. The requirement that objective practical rules be in every situation consistent overrides, for Kant, our intuitive feeling – which he acknowledges – that there is a genuine conflict of duties. It appears that our duties may conflict. But this cannot be so. Consistency requires us to see that at most one can be a genuine obligation; the other is only an apparent obligation, which has turned out, in this case, to be actually contrary to duty.[26]

What I want to say about this is that, paradoxically, it does not take duty and obligation seriously enough. For it says that a contingent feature of the world can cause something that would otherwise be a duty not to be a duty. This is an odd result for Kant. For it is a deep part of Kantian ethics to insist that obligations are obligations in all circumstances. I want to say that Kant is un-Kantian, just as innocent Maggie is guilty, when he lets his attachment to consistency lead him to deny the conflicting claim as merely apparent. I claim that James's novel shows us how a rigid attachment to the idea of consistency in conflict situations produces moral evasiveness and, in fact, moral inconsistency of a deeper sort. Maggie ends up being unfaithful to some commitments that ought to have been especially deep and binding. What would we actually think of an agent who, confronted with two conflicting claims, went cheerfully toward one with no compunction, saying that the other one had just turned out to be contrary to duty? (Think of Orestes in Sartre's *The Flies*.) James suggests, I believe correctly, that we would think this person irresponsible, childish, and even quite immoral. The kind of commitment we want from a moral agent is, instead, the sort that involves sticking by a commitment when it leads into difficulty, even moral difficulty, attending to and caring about it even when the world makes it impossible to do full justice to it.

Aristotle got this right, although he does not devote a lot of space to the topic.[27] A lot of good work has been done on the topic recently, in the spirit of both Greek tragedy and Aristotle.[28] Sidgwick, like Kant, goes disastrously wrong, by making normative consistency in the sense of freedom from conflict a methodological

---

26 See the Preface to the *Metaphysics of Morals*, AA VI, 223.
27 See Michael Stocker, *Plural and Conflicting Values* (Oxford: Oxford University Press, 1990).
28 See particularly Bernard Williams, "Ethical Consistency," in *Problems of the Self*, 166–186 (Cambridge: Cambridge University Press, 1973); Michael Walzer, "Political Action: The Problem

requirement of ethical correctness. If you do that, you do end up reducing all values to one, as his Utilitarianism recommends.

But what good is it to recognize that you are in a tragic situation. You can't honor both commitments, and you have to do something. Isn't the recognition of the losing commitment a bit of self-indulgent hand-wringing? Does it offer any guidance at all for the future? Yes! First of all, recognizing the force of the pro tempore losing commitment you can redouble your efforts to honor it in other situations. Second, where possible you can make reparations to the losing "side." But the most important point is made by Hegel: you can try to figure out how you got into that pickle and try to produce a world that does not keep thrusting agents into similar pickles. A good political order does not continually force people to choose between two values recognized as central (such as, in his *Antigone* example, religious commitment and good citizenship). It structures things so that tragic choice is rare and not daily. Civil war may still pose tragic dilemmas, but that can reasonably be expected to be rare. When women are forced on a daily basis to choose between good parenting and the requirements of their profession, because society inadequately supports child care and the professions embody structures hostile to parenting, that is the mark of a primitive and irrational society!

So Putnam was wrong about tragic conflict, I believe, and Aristotle and I (with Hegel, Bernard Williams, and others) are correct.

On one meta-issue, there's a standoff. Putnam denies my claim that a work of literature cannot be a work of moral philosophy. It is my philosophical commentary on James, not James's novel, that counts as moral philosophy. I was quick to grant his point that the commentary is important (although I noted that commentary is also important for Aristotle's works, and yet these are undoubted works of moral philosophy). I think I pushed a tiny bit too far here: the novel stands less on its own than do Aristotle's works, and it does take a philosophical commentary to make its relevance clear. (With Proust's novel, which incorporates large stretches of overt philosophizing, this is less clear.) However, I think that Putnam should not have said that it is my commentary *and not the novel* that contributes to philosophy. For my argument was that we cannot take the measure of several key parts of the Aristotelian view without novels like this. So I think the right conclusion is that the novel contributes to philosophy *when accompanied by a philosophical commentary*. They contribute together.

---

of Dirty Hands," *Philosophy and Public Affairs* 2, no. 2 (1973): 160–180; and Henry Richardson, *Practical Reasoning about Final Ends* (New York: Cambridge University Press, 1984).

The conversation continued. For a volume in Putnam's honor, I wrote about what an Aristotelian attitude to both perception and moral conflict could bring to the political life – selecting *The Princess Casamassima*, James's only novel of class conflict to frame my argument.[29] Reflecting about Putnam's own political commitments – the Marxism he espoused in 1970, when I first met him, and the left-liberalism he later preferred – I noted that the thread of continuity, as for James's hero, was in a keen perception of the sufferings of individual human beings, which are ultimately not honored (James suggest and I agree) by the abstractions of Marxian class politics but are better honored, I believe (and Putnam did too) by the social-democratic approach expressed in the "Capabilities Approach." I probably imputed too much of the position Putnam and I share to Henry James, but readers must judge for themselves. This engagement led directly to Putnam's writings on the Capabilities Approach, one of which was delivered as a plenary address at the Human Development and Capability Association.

In short, Putnam was engaged with Aristotelian ideas throughout his life. He did what he talked about: he filled in gaps in a way that enabled Aristotle to be a live voice in contemporary debates. More generally, his engagement with Aristotle was an example of his philosophical personality. He never stopped being respectful, responsive, generous, curious, zestful, and great.

---

29 Martha C. Nussbaum, "Perception and Revolution: *The Princess Casamassima* and the Political Imagination," in *Meaning and Method: Essays in Honor of Hilary Putnam*, edited by George Boolos, 327–354 (Cambridge: Cambridge University Press), reprinted in Nussbaum, *Love's Knowledge*, 195–219.

Mario De Caro
Davidson and Putnam on the Antinomy of Free Will

Abstract: This article discusses and compares Donald Davidson's and Hilary Putnam's views on free will. Those views have a two-fold motive of interest: first, they are the coherent expressions of the very influential conceptions that these authors held regarding the mind-body relation, causation, the nature of the laws of nature, and the meaning of our explanatory practices; second, both Davidson and Putnam tried to articulate liberal forms of naturalism according to which normative notions are not incompatible with scientifically explainable phenomena but not reducible to them either. In conclusion I will argue that Putnam's view is the more promising for approaching the free will issue since it is not committed to problematic form of ontological monism still accepted by Davidson.

I Introduction

Since Kant presented it in the *Critique of Pure Reason*, the antinomy of freedom has remained with us. The question raised by the antinomy was: how can we reconcile *the scientific view* of the world, which has no place for the galaxy of normative notions connected to free will, and *the agential view*, which makes these notions absolutely central?

The two most obvious solutions to this antinomy are (i) a radical form of dualism or idealism (e.g., a Cartesian or neo-Cartesian view), which makes the mind ontologically independent from the natural world and, consequently, impermeable to scientific investigation, and (ii) a reductionist view that has no place for our "cherished" notions of freedom and autonomy (e.g., the standard eliminationist/ reductionist views held by many contemporary physicalists). Many philosophers, however, follow Kant in searching for an alternative solution, which is able to reconcile the naturalistic view of the world with the idea that humans enjoy free will and, consequently, are morally responsible for (some of) their actions.

Among contemporary philosophers who have dealt with this classic problem are two of the main thinkers of the last half a century: Donald Davidson and Hilary Putnam. The views of freedom held by these philosophers can be usefully compared for two reasons. First, they are the coherent expressions of the very influential conceptions that these authors held regarding the mind-body relation, causation, the nature of the laws of nature, and the meaning of

https://doi.org/10.1515/9783110769210-011

our explanatory practices; second, both Davidson and Putnam tried to articulate liberal forms of naturalism according to which normative notions are not incompatible with scientifically explainable phenomena but not reducible to them either.

II Davidson's (Not Enough) *Anomalous* Monism

Even if it is not well known, Davidson believed that "anomalous monism" – his influential response to the mind-body problem – could satisfyingly do justice to Kant's insight about freedom.[1] In "Mental Events," he approvingly quotes a passage by Kant:

> We think of a man in a different sense and relation when we call him free, and when we regard him as subject to the laws of nature . . . [And] not only can both of these very well co-exist, but [. . .] both must be thought *as necessarily united* in the same subject.[2]

In this passage Kant argues that, in order to solve the problem of freedom, one has to reconcile the two perspectives we use to look at human beings: as *objects of nature* and as *free agents*. This is a task for which, according to Davidson, anomalous monism is perfectly adequate, thanks to its two-level structure.[3] Davidson's idea was that the monistic constraint of anomalous monism makes it possible to look at human beings as objects of nature, while its anomalous constraint makes it possible to look at them as agents who act freely:

> We explain a man's free actions [. . .] by appeal to his desires, habits, knowledge and perceptions. Such accounts of intentional behaviour operate in a conceptual framework removed from direct reach of physical law by describing both cause and effect, reason

---

1 A useful discussion of the literature on anomalous monism is in Steven Yalowitz, "Anomalous Monism," *The Stanford Encyclopedia of Philosophy*, edited by Edward N. Zalta, 2019, https://plato.stanford.edu/entries/anomalous-monism/ (last accessed October 15, 2021).

2 Quoted (from Kant's *The Fundamental Principles of the Metaphysics of Morals*) in Donald Davidson, "Mental Events" (1970), reprinted in *Essays on Actions and Events* (Oxford: Clarendon Press, 1980), 225.

3 I assume here the standards definitions of these two views in the contemporary debate on free will. Compatibilism is the view that free will is compatible with causal determinism (and indeed, according to some of the advocates of this view, free will actually *requires* causal determinism). Libertarianism states, on the contrary, that free will is incompatible with causal determinism and we enjoy it.

and action, as aspects of a portrait of a human agent. The anomalism of the mental is [. . .] a necessary condition for viewing action as autonomous.[4]

It should be remembered that Davidson conceived of freedom – notwithstanding the elusive phenomenon of the "deviant causal chains"[5] – as "a causal power of the agent," i.e., a power that is exercised when our intentional actions are caused by some appropriate mental events (which, according to the claims of anomalous monism, are *also* physical events).[6] To be more exact, for Davidson, the free actions of an agent are the intentional actions that are non-deviantly caused by the agent's mental events.

Davidson did not hold an idiosyncratic view of freedom. In fact, his anomalous monism was closely associated to the traditional compatibilist views defended by Locke and Hume (a circumstance that Davidson simply ignored when he compared his view to Kant's libertarian conception), but for the fact that Davidson attributed to some apt mental events the causal power that the old empiricists attributed to the mysterious faculty of "the will."

The vast majority of compatibilists share the idea that a necessary condition for an action to be free is that an adequate mental state of the agent is part of its sufficient cause. Accordingly, Davidson explicitly stated that an agent's free actions are (non-deviantly) caused by the agent's desires and beliefs; consequently, in order to account for free will, anomalous monism has to explain how (deviant causal chains aside) agents control their own free action through the causal power of their relevant conscious mental states.

On this issue, Quine – "without whom not," as in the dedication of Davidson's *Inquiries into Truth and Interpretation*[7] – held a very similar view:

> Like Spinoza, Hume, and so many others, I count an act as free insofar as the agent's motives or drives are a link in its causal chain. Those motives or drives may themselves

---

4 Davidson, "Mental Events," 225. Kant defended a strong form of libertarian incompatibilism, since he conceived freedom, at the transcendental level, as an *unconditioned* causal power. On Kant's theory of freedom, see Henry Allison, *Kant's Theory of Freedom* (Cambridge: Cambridge University Press, 1990).

5 On the impossibility of giving a complete causal account of intentional action because of deviant causal chains, cf. Donald Davidson, "Freedom to Act" (1973), reprinted in *Essays on Actions and Events* (Oxford: Clarendon Press, 1980), 63–81.

6 Davidson ("Freedom to Act," 81) admitted that there is no satisfying way for distinguishing the cases in which the agent's beliefs and desires cause a genuine intentional action from the cases in which (because of a deviant causal chain) such beliefs and desires cause actions that are not intentional. But this admission did not shake his trust in the idea that freedom is a causal power.

7 Donald Davidson, *Inquiries into Truth and Interpretation* (Oxford: Clarendon Press, 1984).

be as rigidly determined as you please . . . It is for me an ideal of pure reason to subscribe to determinism as fully as the quantum physicists will let me.[8]

As its name suggests, anomalous monism has two main tenets:
a) Ontological physicalism;
b) The thesis that the mental is anomalous, i.e., the mental is (epistemologically) irreducible to the physical.

The first tenet is composed of two claims. First, all causal relata are events, and all causal relations instantiate physical laws, *i.e.*, laws that are "as deterministic as nature can be found to be."[9] Second, all entities, events and processes are physical (with the possible exception of the abstract entities of mathematics).[10]

Some relevant consequences follow from these claims. First, all mental events are *also* physical events, i.e., events that can *also* be described in a physicalist vocabulary. Second, all causes and effects are physical events. Finally, no causal relation can escape the nomological network of the physical laws – not even the causal relations that involve human agents (and the mental events occurring in them), since, according to Davidson, by definition, a relation between two events has to instantiate a physical law in order to be causal.

---

8 W.V.O. Quine, "Things and Their Place in Theories," *Theories and Things* (Cambridge, MA: Harvard University Press, 1981), 11.

9 Donald Davidson, "Thinking Causes," in *Mental Causation*, edited by John Heil and Alfred Mele (Oxford: Oxford University Press, 1993), 8. It is worth noticing that Davidson changed his mind regarding the question of how deterministic the laws of nature are. While in "Mental Events," he had written, "Where there is causality, there must be a law: events related as cause and effect fall under strict *deterministic* laws" (my emphasis), in "Laws and Cause," *Dialectica* 49, no. 2–4 (1995), he instead wrote: "If physics cannot be made deterministic, if the ultimate laws of the universe, so far as we will ever know, are *probabilistic*, then we must think of causality as probabilistic. Singular causal statements will still entail the existence of strict laws, even at the quantum level, but the laws will not meet Hume's or Kant's or Einstein's standards" (278–279, my emphasis). However, even if he granted that such laws might be indeterministic, Davidson was never a libertarian, since he always believed in the compatibility of free and causal determinism – and this is a conceptual thesis that does not require causal determinism to be actually true. To my knowledge, however, Davidson never thought that determinism is a *necessary* condition of freedom, as many philosophers, including Ayer and Mill, have (on this Davidson was in agreement with influential contemporary philosophers such as Daniel Dennett and David Lewis).

10 I do not know any place in which Davidson discusses in some depth the ontological status of abstract entities; however, in conversation he told me that in this regard he shared Quine's view – that is, a form of Platonism based on the idea that mathematics is indispensable for physics.

The second tenet of anomalous monism, the "anomalism of the mental," states that mental properties are *irreducible* to physical properties because of their normative and holistic character. Therefore, in principle, mental properties cannot be subsumed under physical laws.

According to Davidson, the apparent contradiction between the two tenets of anomalous monism (ontological physicalism and the anomalism of the mental) can be dispelled by accepting the "token identity thesis." According to this thesis, between mental and physical *types* of events there is neither identity nor possible reduction, but each mental event, taken as a token, is still identical to a physical *event*, taken as a token.[11] In this light, mental properties *supervene* on physical properties – that is, there could not be a difference between the mental properties of two events without a difference in their corresponding physical properties.[12]

As said, according to the physicalist tenet of anomalous monism, all causal relations instantiate physical laws, which are "as deterministic as nature can be found to be."[13] Now, obviously such laws, being *physical* laws, can be stated (at least in principle) only by referring to the physical properties of the events that are involved in the causal relations. But this implies, as Kim has noticed, that events have the causal powers they have *only in virtue* of their physical properties. And this means that, no causal relation can exist in virtue of the mental properties of the events involved. As Kim puts it, anomalous monism "assigns no causal role to mental properties, [so it] can [. . .] reasonably be said to be epiphenomenalistic with regard to mental properties."[14]

It is true that, as Kim himself admits, anomalous monism makes the mental properties of an event causally *relevant*, because, according to the supervenience thesis defended by Davidson, the mental properties of an event make a difference for the physical properties it has (in virtue of the fact that different mental properties imply different physical properties); but this view also makes the mental properties of an event causally *inefficacious*. As Kim writes:

---

11 In his works, Davidson oscillated between two different uses of the word "event" (both common in contemporary literature): he sometimes distinguished between states and events, and sometimes lumped them together under the general category of "events." Here I follow the second usage.

12 The question of what kind of supervenience anomalous monism has to appeal to, and how satisfyingly it can do so, is a complex one: cf., for example, Jaegwon Kim, *Supervenience and Mind* (Cambridge: Cambridge University Press, 1993); Brian McLaughlin and Karen Bennett, "Supervenience," in *Stanford Encyclopedia of Philosophy*, edited by Edward N. Zalta, 2018, https://plato.stanford.edu/entries/supervenience/ (last accessed October 15, 2021).

13 Davidson, "Thinking Causes," 8.

14 Kim, *Supervenience and Mind*, 20–21.

> [The] causal relations [of an event] are fixed, wholly and exclusively, by the totality of its physical properties, and there is in this picture no causal work that mental properties can, or need to, contribute.[15]

Davidson tried to avoid the charge of epiphenomenalism by referring to his own extensional view of causation. According to this view, mental powers belong to events, not to their properties; and this, according to Davidson,[16] is no surprise since an event's being mental or physical depends only on the vocabulary with which *we* describe it ("an event, mental or physical, by any other name smells just as strong"). So, when an event causes (or does not cause) another event, it does so independently of the way in which *we* describe it:

> [I]f events described in physical terms are effective, and they are identical with those same events described in psychological terms, then the latter must also be causally effective.[17]

This strategy appeals to Davidson's peculiar, extensional view of causation and events. According to this view, events, which are the only possible causal relata, are ontological primitives – bare singulars that we "color" with properties when we describe them. Very few interpreters, however, have found this proposal very convincing or even perspicuous, and I suspect that Davidson himself was not entirely sure about it. Once, for example, he puzzlingly wrote:

> People have mental properties, which is to say that certain psychological predicates are true of them. These properties are constantly changing, and such changes are mental events.[18]

This definition raises two problems, at least, for Davidson's official view about causation and events. First, what is that makes the psychological predicates true, if not how things are, *i.e.*, the properties they have? And, if "people *have* mental properties," how can it be that properties depend on how *we* describe events? (Paraphrasing Davidson's above-mentioned phrase, we could say that from this passage it seems that properties *are* relevant for how strong events "smell"). Second, in this passage, events are said to depend on the changing of

---

15 Jaegwon Kim, *Mind in a Physical World: An Essay on the Mind-Body Problem and Mental Causation* (Cambridge, MA.: MIT Press, 1998), 34.

16 Davidson, "Thinking Causes," 12.

17 Donald Davidson, "Anomalous Monism," in *MIT Encyclopedia of Cognitive Sciences*, edited by Frank C. Keil and Robert A. Wilson (Cambridge, MA: MIT Press, 1999), 30.

18 Donald Davidson, "Self-Portrait," in *A Companion to the Philosophy of Mind*, edited by Samuel Guttenplan (Oxford: Blackwell, 1994), 231.

the properties, and this seems to suggest that events are *not* ontologically primitive (as Davidson's official doctrine should, on the contrary, normally imply).

So we have some clue, I think, that Davidson himself had a problem with his official view about events and causality. Be that as it may, Kim convincingly summarizes his case against anomalous monism:

> It makes sense to ask questions of the form "What is about events *c* and *e* that makes it the case that *c* is a cause of *e*?" and be able to answer them, intelligibly and informatively, by saying something like "Because *c* is an event of kind *F* and *e* is one of kind *G* [. . .]. This is only to acknowledge that the causal relation obtains between a pair of events because they are events of certain kinds, or have certain properties.[19]

This objection is, in my view, convincing. If so, from the tenets of anomalous monism it follows that events are causally related *because* of their physical properties (which are the ones in virtue of which the causal relations instantiate the physical laws that back them). Thus, the mental properties of events are causally inert, and this means that anomalous monism is just epiphenomenalism in disguise. And so, anomalous monism cannot be a satisfying proposal for the mind-body problem.

Now we can go back to the free will problem, and ask ourselves whether anomalous monism can at least represent a plausible solution to *that* problem. Unfortunately, it cannot.

The spirit of Davidson's proposal is Kantian: human beings can be viewed both as agents who act freely and as subjects that obey the laws of nature. As said, following the compatibilist tradition, Davidson thought that actions are free as long as they are (non-deviantly) caused by some of the agent's relevant conscious mental states. However, anomalous monism deprives mental events of *all* causal power. Therefore, if anomalous monism is the right conception of the mental, no mental state or event would have any causal powers, and never be a link in the causal chain that ends in an action. No motive, impulse, desire, belief or intention could ever contribute to cause any action whatsoever.

Davidson himself maintained that, in order to be free, actions have to be caused by desires and beliefs: this is how, in his opinion, in which agents exercise the necessary control over their own actions.[20] But then, since anomalous monism implies the impossibility of mental causation, it implies the impossibility of free will as well.

---

19 Kim, *Supervenience and Mind*, 22.

20 On this issue, the classic reference is Donald Davidson, "Actions, Reasons, and Causes" (1963), reprinted in *Essays on Actions and Events*, 3–19 (Oxford: Clarendon Press, 1980).

Davidson's view of free will was a brilliant attempt; but, as long as it made all forms of causation dependent on physical laws, it leaned too heavily towards the scientific view of the world. Therefore, if one had to summarize what the problem was with anomalous monism, one could say that it was not anomalous enough. Solving the antinomy of freedom requires one to look elsewhere.

III Putnam's Pluralism

Among contemporary philosophers, Putnam was one of the most influential advocates of the need to reconcile, in the Kantian spirit, the two images of the world – that expressed by science and that expressed by common sense. He shared this goal with Davidson. But whereas, as we have seen, Davidson still attributed a primacy to the scientific image, Putnam's view was equidistant between the two images, which he tried to harmonize in a liberal naturalist view.[21] And this, in my opinion, is a more promising starting point.

In order to understand Putnam's view on freedom, it is useful to first look at the ontological and epistemological background of the view. Putnam was always a stern realist about science – i.e., he believed that the scientific theories can be (and often are) true or approximately true and that scientific terms refer to real entities even when those are unobservable. It is from this perspective that Putnam developed the famous "no-miracles argument," which defends scientific realism by appealing to an inference to the best explanation.[22] The core of the argument is that realism recommends itself insofar as it offers a much more convincing account of the great success of modern science in predicting and explaining than antirealism does – since, for the latter view, the success of science is nothing less than an unexplainable miracle. So we have to take for true (or reasonably close to truth) our best scientific theories and, consequently, accept in our ontologies all the unobservable entities whose existence is implied by the truth of those theories.

---

21 For a general discussion of Putnam's liberal naturalism, cf. Mario De Caro, "Putnam's Liberal Naturalism," in *Mind and Meaning: Themes from Putnam*, edited by Michael Frauchiger (Berlin: De Gruyter, forthcoming), which expands what is said in this paragraph.
22 Hilary Putnam, "What Is Mathematical Truth," in *Mathematics, Matter and Method: Philosophical Papers*, Vol. 1, 60–78 (Cambridge: Cambridge University Press, 1975) and Hilary Putnam, "On Not Writing Off Scientific Realism," in Hilary Putnam, *Philosophy in an Age of Science*, edited by Mario De Caro and David Macarthur, 91–108 (Cambridge, MA.: Harvard University Press, 2012).

But, even if he was a scientific realist, Putnam (differently from Davidson) refused ontological physicalism for two main reasons. First, because some theories can be cognitively equivalent even if *prima facie* they appear incompatible – a phenomenon Putnam called "conceptual relativity," but could less equivocally be called "descriptive equivalence," since the other term may suggest a connection with relativism and antirealism, which would be wholly inappropriate.) As Putnam argued, in some scientific fields, such as mathematical physics, this phenomenon is ubiquitous.

> To take an example from a paper with the title "Bosonization as Duality" that appeared in Nuclear Physics B some years ago, there are quantum mechanical schemes some of whose representations depict the particles in a system as bosons while others depict them as fermions. As their use of the term "representations" indicates, real live physicists – not philosophers with any particular philosophical axe to grind – do not regard this as a case of ignorance. In their view, the "bosons" and "fermions" are simply artifacts of the representation used. But the system is mind-independently real, for all that, and each of its states is a mind independently real condition, that can be represented in each of these different ways. And that is exactly the conclusion I advocate . . . [These] descriptions are both answerable to the very same aspect of reality . . . they are "equivalent descriptions.[23]

The second reason Putnam refused the old physicalist view about ontology is more interesting for our purposes. It is that, on his view, the ontology of the world cannot be limited to the entities and properties described by natural science.

> I do indeed deny that the world can be completely described in the language game of theoretical physics; not because there are regions in which physics is false, but because, to use Aristotelian language, the world has many levels of form, and there is no realistic possibility of reducing them all to the level of fundamental physics.[24]

One of Putnam's favorite examples was that, depending on our interests, we can correctly and usefully describe a chair in the alternative languages of carpentry, furniture design, geometry, or etiquette. Each of these descriptions is useful, in its own way, without being reducible to any of the others. There is no fundamental theory of what being a chair is, so to speak. And this is valid with regard to a vast amount of entities (possibly all of them, with the exception of the entities of microphysics), since they can be described in different ways not just because of conceptual relativity, but also because things have different properties that belong to different ontological regions, to use Husserl's term.

---

23 Putnam, "On Not Writing Off Scientific Realism," 63–64.
24 Putnam, "On Not Writing Off Scientific Realism," 65.

In this pluralistic light, the old ontological project of providing a general inventory of the universe, which would supposedly encompass the referents of all possible objective statements – a project for which strict naturalism is the latest expression – has made us wander in Cloud Cuckoo Land for too long.[25] And this means that Ontology with a capital "o" is a dead project. But another form of ontology (one with a lower-case initial) is still possible, i.e., the search for the entities our best theories and practices commit us to. But this cannot be carried out if one is driven by the ideological bias that there is one, and only one, true theory of the world. Nor can it be carried out without noticing that reality has different levels. And it is a pragmatic question which level is relevant to a particular discursive practice.

However, the fact that reality is articulated in different levels raises a question about the relationship running between them. About this relationship, Putnam was straightforward: different levels of reality are linked by a relationship of supervenience (sometimes local, sometimes global) from the most basic to the less basic. In this context, it is useful to mention a discussion between Putnam and Stephen White. White defended the idea that the "agential perspective" and the "objective perspective" are categorically different and incommensurable, so that between them there is a relation of "asupervenience" (neither supervenience nor non-supervenience).[26] To this Putnam replied,

> I do think that all of our capacities, including "agential" ones (a category which, as Stephen White correctly argues, includes our perceptual capacities), supervene on the states of the physical universe, including, in a great many cases, past as well as present ones . . . I am a naturalist – a non-reductive naturalist – and I don't see how any naturalist can deny global supervenience of human psychological states and capacities. (And appealing to the murky doctrine of "incommensurability" is no help.) But there is no one simple answer to the question of whether our agential capacities are locally supervenient (supervenient on just the relevant brain-states) or globally supervenient on factors external to the brain, and even to the organism, because it depends on which agential capacities one is talking about, even if we restrict the issue to perceptual capacities.[27]

These ontological claims have, of course, important epistemological implications. In this respect Putnam held what can be called a "liberalized epistemological" view, claiming that many cognitively non-equivalent and mutually irreducible conceptual schemes have to be used to account for the different

---

25 Hilary Putnam, *Ethics without Ontology* (Cambridge, MA: Harvard University Press, 2004), 85.
26 Stephen White, "On the Absence of an Interface: Putnam, Direct Perception, and Frege's Constraint," *European Journal of Analytic Philosophy* 4, no. 2 (2008): 11–28.
27 Hilary Putnam, "Reply to Stephen White," *European Journal of Analytic Philosophy* 4, no. 2 (2008): 30.

levels of reality. And this means that, *contra* Quine, there is no such a thing as a "first-grade conceptual system" (i.e., the natural sciences, if not physics alone), which is in charge of describing reality, while all the other conceptual system are either reducible in principle to it or completely flawed. According to Putnam, we legitimately "employ many different kinds of discourses, discourses subject to different standards and possessing different sorts of applications."[28]

This view has an important implication regarding Putnam's view of causation. He strictly linked causation to explanation, in the sense that he thinks that causal notions are grounded on "why questions" that structure our explanatory practices. This view obviously implies that the notion of explanation cannot be reduced to the notion of causation. However, against the Humean and neo-Humean view, Putnam also denied that causation can be reduced to non-causal notions, such as that of explanation. As he wrote, "Our interests fix the criteria for saying that the relation holds, but it holds gives those criteria is a fact independent of us."[29] In his view, therefore, causation and explanation are interdependent and mutually irreducible notions.

An important consequence of this point, which is particularly interesting for the topic discussed here, is causal pluralism. Putnam approvingly quoted John Haldane, when he claims, "there are as many kinds of causes as there are senses of 'because.'"[30] In this context by the term "senses of because," Putnam meant "our ever-expanding repertoire of explanatory practices." Therefore, pluralism about explanation, on the one hand, and the conceptual link between explanation and causation, on the other hand, generate pluralism about causation.

As a consequence, Putnam refused the so-called "principle of the physical causal closure of the world,"[31] at least if one takes it in one of its classic

---

28 Putnam, *Ethics without Ontology*, 22. Putnam also endorsed a radical semantic view. Not only does he say that there are true judgments that do not concern scientifically accepted entities or properties, but he also says that some of these judgments are objective without describing anything; that is, there can be "objectivity without objects" (*Ethics without Ontology*, 77–78), as in the case of ethical and mathematical judgments. For example, no *special* moral entities (such as free-floating values) exist that make our moral judgments true or false, which is not to say that there are no *non-special* moral entities, since these certainly exist: they are the rational agents. But when we say that someone is good, there is no ontologically autonomous "goodness" to which we refer.

29 Hilary Putnam, *The Threefold Cord. Mind, Body, and World* (New York: Columbia University Press, 1999), 143.

30 Quoted in Putnam, *The Threefold Cord*, 77, 137, and 149–150.

31 Putnam, *The Threefold Cord*, 215.

formulations: "If x is a physical event and y is a cause or effect of x, then y, too, must be a physical event."[32] Given Putnam's pluralist and non-reductionist ontology, physical event *can* indeed be caused by non-physical events, which are irreducible to physical events. (But it should be noted that this does not mean that events cannot have physical causes as well). The point, for Putnam, was that different causal explanations generalize to different classes of cases. And whether we are interested in an event as a member of one or another classis a completely context-relative question. For example, we can be interested in the physiological chain of events that ended in the movement of my hand, but we can also be interested in the reasons why I intentionally moved it. Neither of these causal chains have priority on the other since their respective interest is context-relative.

A fundamental question about free will is still open, though: whether this ontological and epistemological framework is better complemented with a libertarian or a compatibilist account of free will. Inspired by Anscombe, at first Putnam argued for the former option.[33] Later he explained that that stance was backed by the idea that

> Mechanics indeterminacy does not arise only from localized 'chance events' [since] there is, a kind of holistic indeterminacy in quantum mechanics which arises simply from the Uncertainty Principle.[34]

That holistic indeterminacy, in Putnam's opinion, is the adequate foundation of agent causation. The reason is that it represents the kind of indeterminacy that one has to find at the macrolevel in order to justify the intuition that free agents are able to determine their own actions without being determined to do so. Later, however, Putnam changed his mind on this topic, because he came to realize that none of the major indeterministic interpretations of quantum mechanics support his way of appealing to the Uncertainty principle. In fact,

> either the indeterminacy does turn to be ontological, but then it can be traced to highly localized events ("quantum jumps," as it were), or else it turns out to be merely epistemological (the original Bohm theory, or Many-Worlds).[35]

---

32 Jaegwon Kim, *Philosophy of Mind* (Boulder: Westview, 1996), 147.

33 Hilary Putnam, "The Place of Facts in a World of Values" (1979), reprinted in Hilary Putnam, *Realism with a Human Face*, edited by James Conant, 142–162 (Cambridge, MA: Harvard University Press, 1990).

34 Mario De Caro and Hilary Putnam, "Free Will and Quantum Mechanics," in *The Monist* 103, no. 4 (2020): 415–426.

35 De Caro and Putnam, "Free Will and Quantum Mechanics," 423.

In this light, Putnam came to realize that his idea of backing libertarianism with the indeterminism of quantum mechanics does not work. For this reason, at the end of his life, he accepted compatibilism – interpreted in the context of his pluralistic epistemology and ontology – as the correct account of free will.[36]

Summarizing, like Davidson, Putnam thought that freedom is to be found in the intentional explanations of actions: an action is free as long as it is adequately caused by some relevant intentional state. However, differently from Davidson, Putnam did not think that all causal relations instantiate a universal (physical) law. And this implies that, according to Putnam, it is not the case that causal powers only belong to physical events, which is what made the mental epiphenomenal in the Davidsonian framework. Pluralism in ontology and in epistemology cannot solve all the problems regarding the free will issue, of course. However, it certainly represents a promising starting point.

---

36 The details of this line of reasoning, and an account of the development of Putnam's ideas about agent causation, are offered in De Caro and Putnam, "Free Will and Quantum Mechanics," a paper Hilary and I submitted to a journal just before he got sick. Two reviewers of that journal asked for some revisions on which we worked almost completely. However, Putnam's death stopped me from publishing that article for some years, until Juliet Floyd and I edited a special issue of *The Monist* ("Liberal Naturalism: The Legacy of Hilary Putnam," 103, no. 4, 2020) in which I thought it would fit well.

Duncan Pritchard

Putnam on Radical Scepticism: Wittgenstein, Cavell, and Occasion-Sensitive Semantics

Abstract: While there has been a lot of attention devoted to how Putnam applies content externalism to the problem of radical scepticism, there has been considerably less attention paid to his other writings on this subject. This paper examines Putnam's wider treatment of radical scepticism. It looks at his critiques of such figures as P.F. Strawson, Barry Stroud, and Michael Williams, and considers how, under the influence of Wittgenstein, Austin, Stanley Cavell, and (more recently) Charles Travis, Putnam has developed an anti-sceptical line that is built around an occasion-sensitive semantics. While taking a generally sympathetic line to Putnam's anti-scepticism, it is also argued on broadly Wittgensteinian grounds (albeit the Wittgenstein of *On Certainty*, rather than that of the *Philosophical Investigations*, which is the primary concern of Putnam and his key influences) that the need to adopt such a semantics in order to respond to radical scepticism is significantly overstated.

I Introductory Remarks

Hilary Putnam made numerous important contributions to core philosophical topics, but when it comes to the problem of radical scepticism his wide-ranging work in this area has been overshadowed by one aspect of his writing that has been particularly influential. I have in mind, of course, his famous writings on content externalism, and how this has the upshot that there is an important sense in which one cannot state that one is a brain-in-a-vat (BIV) and thereby speak truly.[1] It would be ironic if we let ourselves be side-tracked by outlining the details of this argument, and so I won't. Suffice it to say that there is a wealth of material exploring this ingenious piece of reasoning and trying to determine what, exactly, it demonstrates.[2] My concern is rather with Putnam's

---

1 The *locus classicus* in this regard is, of course, Putnam, *Reason, Truth and History* (Cambridge: Cambridge University Press, 1981), Ch. 1.
2 For some key texts in this regard, see, for example, Anthony Brueckner, "Brains in a Vat," *The Journal of Philosophy* 83, no. 3 (1986): 148–167; Gary Ebbs, "Skepticism, Objectivity and

https://doi.org/10.1515/9783110769210-012

other work on radical scepticism, which often runs completely orthogonal to his semantic externalism. Although there are various aspects to Putnam's writings on radical scepticism – as he engages with such figures as P.F. Strawson, Stanley Cavell, Barry Stroud, Michael Williams, and Charles Travis – we can discern a running Wittgensteinian (and Austinian) thread in these writings in terms of a distinctive form of contextualism about meaning.

These other writings on radical scepticism are particularly important because Putnam's content externalist response to radical scepticism, philosophically significant though it is, is not really a response to radical scepticism *simpliciter*, as even Putnam would admit. This is because such an argument, even if successful, at best only demonstrates that certain kinds of sceptical scenarios are incoherent.[3] In particular, it is only a BIV scenario where the subject is completely cut-off, including socially cut-off, from the target referents that ensures that Putnam is even in the market to generate his intended conclusion (this is why he appeals to super-computers to manage the BIVs, rather than, for example, other human beings, who may have had the relevant causal contact with the target referents). As such Putnam's content externalist argument is probably best understood as not being a general response to the problem of radical scepticism, but rather as demonstrating how content externalism imposes important limitations on the contents of one's thoughts, where this idea is being played out within the provocative context of a BIV scenario. With this point in mind, if we really want to get a handle on what Putnam thinks about radical scepticism, then we would be wise to look at his wider writings on the subject, and that is just what I propose to do.

Brains in Vats," *Pacific Philosophical Quarterly* 73, no. 3 (1992): 239–266 and "Is Skepticism about Self-Knowledge Coherent?" *Philosophical Studies* 105, no. 1 (2001): 43–58; André Gallois, "Putnam, Brains in Vats, and Arguments for Scepticism," *Mind* 101, no. 402 (1992): 273–286; and Crispin Wright, "On Putnam's Proof that We Are Not Brains-in-a-Vat," *Proceedings of the Aristotlian Society* 92, no. 1 (1992): 67–94. For a helpful survey of some of the issues in this regard, see Anthony Brueckner, "Skepticism and Content Externalism," *Stanford Encyclopedia of Philosophy*, edited by Edward Zalta, 2012, http://plato.stanford.edu/entries/skepticism-content-externalism/. (Last accessed December 19, 2021).

3 I say "at best," because many have argued that Putnam's BIV argument, even if successful, in fact demonstrates a much weaker conclusion. See, for example, Crispin Wright, "On Putnam's Proof that We Are Not Brains-in-a-Vat," *Proceedings of the Aristotelian Society* 92, no. 1 (1992): 67–94.

II Putnam *Contra* Strawson

We begin with Putnam's insightful response[4] to Strawson's naturalistic, neo-Humean line on radical scepticism.[5] Strawson's response to the problem of radical scepticism broadly mirrors the naturalistic line he had previously taken on the problem of induction.[6] The basic idea in that regard was that in showing that induction could not be given a non-circular justification, Hume had in effect demonstrated that it didn't need one. The point was that the lack of a non-circular justification didn't entail that induction was a mere convention, but rather demonstrated that it was a natural inclination that, as such, did not stand in need of a justification. Conventions, after all, are a matter of choice, whereas natural inclinations are not.

Strawson attempts a similar line as regards radical scepticism about the external world. The fact that we are unable to answer sceptical doubts does not put our overall epistemic standing in jeopardy, but rather demonstrates that attempts to answer such doubts are pointless. As he puts it:

> They [*i.e., sceptical doubts*] are to be neglected because they are idle; powerless against the force of nature, of our naturally implanted disposition to belief.[7]

Rather like our natural conviction in the uniformity of nature that underpins our use of induction, we have similar natural inclinations to believe such things as that there is an external world, and there is nothing that argumentation, sceptical or otherwise, can do to shake such natural convictions. As before, we are not to think of these natural inclinations as mere conventions, since they are not optional on our part.

This is certainly an unusual philosophical line to take on the problem of radical scepticism.[8] Indeed, if anything, wouldn't the discovery that one has no rational response to the sceptical problem, and that we ultimately believe as do merely as natural unavoidable inclination, *accentuate* the paradoxical nature of radical scepticism, rather than alleviate it? In this regard, Strawson's only

---

4 Hilary Putnam, "Strawson and Skepticism," in *The Philosophy of P.F. Strawson*, edited by Lewis Edwin Hahn, 273–287 (Chicago, IL: Open Court, 1998).
5 P.F. Strawson, *Skepticism and Naturalism: Some Varieties* (New York: Columbia University Press, 1985).
6 See, in particular P.F. Strawson, *Introduction to Logical Theory* (London: Meuthen, 1952).
7 Strawson, *Skepticism and Naturalism*, 13.
8 As Alex Byrne quips, the idea that radical sceptical doubts are idle in this sense, and hence can be ignored, "is a curious view for an erstwhile Waynflete Professor of Metaphysics, to say the least." ("How Hard are the Sceptical Paradoxes?" *Noûs* 38, no. 3 (2004): 302).

response seems to be to reiterate that the question of whether or not there is an external world has no practical bearing (which ensures that it is "idle" in the relevant sense), the point being, presumably, that there cannot be anything paradoxical about a natural commitment to something that has no practical bearing either way.

In support of his naturalistic line, Strawson takes inspiration from Wittgenstein's final notebooks, published as *On Certainty* (=OC).[9] In particular, he draws on the fact that in this work Wittgenstein argues that our most basic commitments – the so-called "hinge" commitments of which we are most certain (OC, §§341–343) – are completely immune to rational evaluations. Moreover, these arational commitments are held in a visceral, "animal" fashion. (OC, §359) Strawson takes from this idea that our most basic commitments, including our anti-sceptical commitment to there being an external world, is not to be evaluated along rational lines at all, much less treated as a convention, but rather understood as a being the product of nature. As Wittgenstein puts the point at one juncture:

> It is always by favour of Nature that one knows something. (OC, §505)

Interestingly, in his critique of Strawson Putnam also draws on OC. But rather than seeing in OC support for the idea that we are naturally compelled to be committed to holding that there is an external world, Putnam argues that the Wittgenstein of OC shows us that such a claim is simply incoherent. OC is an impressionistic work, comprised of unedited notebooks, so one would not expect to find a canonical interpretation. And yet Putnam is surely right that the idea that "There is an external world" is contentless is one of the few things that Wittgenstein is emphatic about in OC, especially in the first notebook that comprises this work (i.e., §§1–65). As Wittgenstein puts it, in the context of a discussion of G.E. Moore's proof of an external world,[10] "'There are physical objects' is nonsense." (OC, §35) He goes on:

> "A is a physical object" is a piece of instruction which we give only to someone who doesn't yet understand either what "A" means, or what "physical object" means. Thus it is instruction about the use of words, and "physical object" is a logical concept. (Like colour, quantity, . . .) And that is why no such proposition as: "There are physical objects" can be formulated. Yet we encounter such unsuccessful shots at every turn.

---

9 Ludwig Wittgenstein, *On Certainty*, edited by G.E.M. Anscombe and Georg Henrik von Wright, translated by Denis Paul and G.E.M. Anscombe (Oxford: Blackwell, 1969).
10 G.E Moore, "Proof of an External World," *Proceedings of the British Academy* 25 (1939): 273–300.

> But is it adequate to answer to the scepticism of the idealist, or the assurances of the real-
> ist, to say that "There are physical objects" is nonsense? For them after all it is not non-
> sense. It would, however, be an answer to say: this assertion, or its opposite is a misfiring
> attempt to express what can't be expressed like that. (OC, §§36–37)

And it is clear from the context that what goes here for "There are physical objects" would also apply, if anything *a fortiori*, to "There is an external world."

Strawson is thus committed to arguing that the sceptical possibility that there
is no external world is a genuine one, that we have no rational basis for our commitment to it, but that we have it nonetheless because it is our unavoidable natural
inclination. In contrast, Putnam's line enables us to argue, in a Wittgensteinian
spirit, that what has the first appearance of a genuine possibility turns out to be a
mere trick of language, as when we confuse the meaningful use of "This is a physical object," used to explain to someone what the words "physical object" mean,
and those same words, used in the context of Moore's proof, which attempt to
meaningfully say something against idealism but which is completely meaningless. Putnam's anti-sceptical line in this regard, unlike Strawson's, does not commit us to absurdity.

This brings us to another important feature of Putnam's anti-scepticism that
is noticeably lacking in Strawson's. Strawson seems to think that the problem of
external world scepticism – i.e., the difficulty of demonstrating, *contra* the ideal-
ist, the legitimacy of our belief that an external world exists – just *is* the problem
of radical scepticism. In doing so, he fails to recognise that one can generate
such a difficulty without making any kind of metaphysical claim about an "external" world, whatever that is supposed to mean. Indeed, radical sceptical arguments that proceed in this way – i.e., by merely appealing to radical sceptical
hypotheses, like the BIV hypothesis – are arguably far more persuasive ways of
making the sceptical case, in that they do not carry the same metaphysical bag-
gage, and hence are harder to undermine.

Wittgenstein was certainly aware of this point. This is why although he dismisses idealism, and thus defences of an "external" world, as meaningless in
the first notebook that makes up OC, he clearly doesn't think his task is over.
Rather, the next three notebooks continue to be devoted to the problem, albeit
now in terms of radical sceptical hypotheses that expose important features
about the nature of the structure of rational evaluation.[11] Putnam is similarly

11 See Michael Williams, "Wittgenstein's Refutation of Idealism," in *Wittgenstein and Scepticism*, edited by Denis McManus, 76–96 (London: Routledge, 2004) for an early defence of the
idea that the first notebook of OC should be kept apart from the other three for this very reason. See also Duncan Pritchard, *Epistemic Angst: Radical Skepticism and the Groundlessness of
Our Believing* (Princeton: Princeton University Press, 2015), Part 2.

sensitive to this issue. For as we will see, he clearly doesn't suppose that treating such a metaphysical claim as there is an external world (or that there isn't, for that matter) as meaningless by itself suffices to resolve the problem of radical scepticism, as we will also need to engage with the difficulties posed by specific radical sceptical scenarios. That's not to say that he doesn't also find the latter meaningless too (the issue is complex, as we will see). The point is just that Putnam recognises that making a case for the meaninglessness of a metaphysical claim such as that there is an external world is very different from making such a case as regards a specific radical sceptical scenario.[12]

III Putnam on Cavell

This brings us to the source of Putnam's Wittgensteinian sympathies. By his own admission,[13] this is emphatically the work Cavell, and in particular his *magnum opus, The Claim of Reason: Wittgenstein, Skepticism, Morality, and Tragedy*.[14] There are many aspects to Cavell's thinking on scepticism, but let's explore some key interconnected themes that are particularly relevant for our purposes, as they will help us to understand the philosophical ground that Putnam also occupies in this regard.

Let's begin with the idea that Cavell is not in the business of simply refuting scepticism. He argues, instead, that there is something deep and important to be learnt from it; there is, as he puts it, a "truth in skepticism." It is worthwhile reminding ourselves of what Cavell has in mind here. Here is the full passage from where it appears:

> An admission of some question as to the mystery of existence, or the being, of the world is a serious bond between the teaching of Wittgenstein and that of Heidegger. The bond is one, in particular, which implies a shared view of what I have called the truth of skepticism, or what I might call the moral of skepticism, namely, that the human creature's

---

12 I offer a critical discussion of Strawson's anti-scepticism in the context of a Wittgensteinian epistemology in Pritchard, *Epistemic Angst*, Ch. 4. See also P.F. Strawson, "Reply to Hilary Putnam," in *The Philosophy of P.F. Strawson*, edited by Lewis Edwin Hahn, 288–292 (Chicago, IL: Open Court, 1998), where he responds to Putnam, "Strawson and Skepticism."
13 See for example Hilary Putnam, "Philosophy as the Education of Grownups: Stanley Cavell and Skepticism," in *Reading Cavell*, edited by Alice Crary and Sanford Shieh, 119–130 (London: Routledge, 2006).
14 Stanley Cavell, *The Claim of Reason: Wittgenstein, Skepticism, Morality, and Tragedy* (Cambridge, MA: Harvard University Press, 1979).

basis in the world as a whole, its relation to the world as such, is not that of knowing, anyway not what we think of as knowing.[15]

I'm not qualified to comment on Heidegger in this regard (though I strongly suspect that Cavell was entirely right on this score), but he is spot-on with regard to Wittgenstein. The Cavell of *The Claim of Reason* has Wittgenstein's *Philosophical Investigations* (=PI)[16] in mind, but the point he makes here about how our fundamental relationship to the world is not one of knowing comes through even more clearly in OC. As already noted above, in this work Wittgenstein reminds us time and again that our most everyday certainties, far from being that which is most epistemically secure, are in fact completely arationally held, though no less appropriately held nonetheless. At the root of our practices of rational evaluation are thus not rational evaluations of a special sort, but rather a primitive kind of hinge certainty that must be in place in order for rational evaluations to be even possible.

In saying that there is a truth in scepticism, Cavell is clearly ruling out an approach to the sceptical problem that completely dismisses it. Since Cavell's focus, following Wittgenstein, is on the oddity of sceptical (and, for that matter, anti-sceptical) uses of language, this means that his approach is not simply to claim that the sceptic's utterances are completely meaningless. Putnam here makes an interesting contrast between Cavell and Austin:[17]

> To read either *Philosophical Investigations* or The *Claim of Reason* as if it were a longer and more careful attempt to say what John Austin said in "Other Minds" is to look at Wittgenstein's and Cavell's work in the wrong way.[18]

Austin famously argued that once we focus on how the sceptic is using our everyday folk epistemic concepts in such different ways to our ordinary usage, then that in itself licences us to disregard sceptical doubts. Here is a famous passage, remarking on what is required to be able to know that the creature before one is a goldfinch:

> Enough is enough: it doesn't mean everything. Enough means enough to show that (within reason, and for present intents and purposes) it "can't" be anything else, there is

---

15 Cavell, *The Claim of Reason*, 241.

16 Ludwig Wittgenstein, *Philosophical Investigations*, edited by G.E.M. Anscombe and Rush Rhees, translated by G.E.M. Anscombe (Oxford: Blackwell, 1953).

17 J.L. Austin. "Other Minds," in J.L. Austin, *Philosophical Papers*, edited by J.O. Urmson and G.J. Warnock, 76–116 (Oxford: Clarendon Press, 1961).

18 Putnam, "Philosophy as the Education of Grownups," 120.

no room for an alternative, competing description of it. It does not mean, for example, enough to show it isn't a stuffed goldfinch.[19]

Austin is surely right that the epistemic practices of the radical sceptic are far removed from our own, and hence that they are using epistemic language in a very different way to how we use it. Cavell would surely grant that point, as would Putnam; indeed, they would similarly grant, following Wittgenstein, that the sceptic's assertions don't clearly make sense. But they would resist the Austinian conclusion – at least in "Other Minds," anyway (the point of this *caveat* will become apparent in due course) – that it follows that they are therefore clearly senseless.[20]

For Cavell, the reason for this is that he believes that we can get ourselves into a sceptical frame of mind. Consider his treatment of other minds scepticism, whereby one can see clearly that someone is in pain and yet one can be of a frame of mind that one still feels the pull of the sceptical concern that perhaps there is no pain behind the pain behaviour on display. As Cavell would put it, this would manifest a failure on one's part to *acknowledge* the other person. In particular, it is not due to a lack of evidence, as one has all the evidence that one could want on this score. The failure is thus more ethical than epistemic.[21]

More generally, I take it that it is Cavell's commitment to there being a truth in scepticism, such that our fundamental relationship to the world is not one of knowing, that enables the possibility of adopting this sceptical condition. For what an engagement with sceptical arguments does is expose the way in which our fundamental, often everyday, commitments which manifest our most fundamental relationship to the world – i.e., our hinge commitments – are not epistemically rooted at all, and hence not in the market for knowledge. This is something that is ordinarily hidden in our everyday practices, since these most fundamental commitments, as Wittgenstein memorably put it, "lie apart from the route travelled

---

19 Austin, "Other Minds," 84.

20 Interestingly, there is another reason to be suspicious of the Austinian line, which relates to a challenge posed for ordinary language responses to radical scepticism posed by Barry Stroud, *The Significance of Philosophical Scepticism* (Oxford: Clarendon Press, 1984) – see note 42.

21 This way of understanding scepticism about other minds is brought out vividly by Cavell, *The Claim of Reason*, Part 4, in his fascinating interpretation of Othello, whereby the hero effectively becomes a sceptic with regard to the specific other mind of Desdemona) – in particular, in terms of her faithfulness, whereby no evidence that could possibly be offered in this regard could ever suffice. See also Stanley Cavell, *Disowning Knowledge in Seven Plays of Shakespeare* (Cambridge: Cambridge University Press, 2003) which offers a range of similarly "sceptical" readings of Shakespeare plays. Indeed, Cavell makes a persuasive case for the thesis that these plays are responses to the crisis of knowledge of the late sixteenth and early seventeenth centuries, and the associated emergence of radical scepticism.

by inquiry." (OC, §88) They form, rather, the backdrop against which inquiry (ordinarily) takes place. When faced with them head-on, and with their groundless nature exposed, we are bound to feel a certain epistemic giddiness. We are thus led to a kind of *epistemic vertigo*, whereby abstracting away from our everyday perspectives ("ascending," if you will) offers an unsettling new perspective that in turn provokes a phobic response.[22]

So for Putnam, as for Cavell, the sceptical claims are not clearly meaningful, but also not clearly meaningless either. The former thesis is meant to be underwritten by the later Wittgenstein, while the latter thesis is meant to set their anti-sceptical stance apart from those, like Austin in "Other Minds," who do claim that sceptical doubts are simply meaningless. The importance of allowing that sceptical doubts are not completely meaningless is to enable us to make sense of the very human phenomenon (and, note, not merely *philosophical* phenomenon) of having a certain pathology that leads to a sceptical frame of mind. The thought seems to be that if sceptical doubts were simply meaningless, then we would not be able to account for the "naturalness" of this occurrence, much less the fact that it arises in non-philosophical contexts (and hence cannot be attributed to the kind of philosophical misunderstandings, such as a reification of language, that Wittgenstein famously railed against). Finally, notice that in taking this line Putnam, following Cavell, is clearly not focussing on metaphysical anti-sceptical claims like "there is an external world," but rather on the kinds of sceptical scenarios that might arise outside of such explicitly philosophical contexts. There is thus no tension between Putnam's response to Strawson's external world scepticism that we just looked at, whereby the thesis that Strawson wants to claim we are naturally inclined to accept is in fact simply contentless, and the line now being taken such that sceptical doubts are neither clearly meaningful nor clearly meaningless.

IV Problems for Putnam and Cavell

Ultimately, however, Putnam *does* think that Cavell provides us with the resources to refute a universalised scepticism, at least insofar as this is understood as a lived condition. The key is Cavell's notion of acknowledgement noted above. Putnam writes:

---

22 Indeed, this phrase is used by Cavell, and cited by Putnam, "Philosophy as the Education of Grownups," 121. I have argued elsewhere for a specifically Wittgensteinian treatment of this notion, albeit one that overlaps considerably with what Cavell (and, via Cavell, Putnam) has in mind. See Pritchard, *Epistemic Angst*, Part 4.

[. . .] skepticism universalized, skepticism that refused to acknowledge any human community, is, to the extent that it is possible, a posture that negates not only its own intelligibility, but also the very existence of a speaking and thinking subject, negates the subject's own existence and the world's.[23]

Putnam is surely right about this point about a universalised scepticism negating its own intelligibility, but what is puzzling is why Putnam thinks that this has any particular bearing on the sceptical problematic that he and Cavell are engaging with. After all, whoever thought that it was essential to the radical sceptical puzzle that it should be possible to coherently live one's radical scepticism?

We can bring this point out into sharper relief by distinguishing between radical scepticism as a *position* and scepticism as a putative *paradox*. Under the guide of the latter, radical scepticism purports to be exposing a deep tension in our fundamental epistemic concepts. Scepticism as a position, in contrast, involves embracing one of the horns of the paradox. But of course one can pose a paradox without endorsing *any* of its horns. Indeed, isn't that scepticism in its strongest form, as exposing a deep tension in our fundamental epistemic concepts and then simply stepping back to let us reflect on our predicament? After all, posing radical scepticism *qua* paradox involves no material commitments at all, since one is simply (one claims) employing the materials found in our folk epistemic concepts. In contrast, adopting a sceptical position does involve material commitments; for example, this needs to be a stance that can consistently be adopted. Putnam thus seems to be supposing that the import of radical *scepticism* depends on the plausibility of there being a coherent radical *sceptic*. But that's an odd line for someone who follows Cavell in taking the sceptical problem seriously, particularly when we reflect that radical scepticism in its strongest guise is in the form of a putative paradox.

A further worry about Putnam (and Cavell's) anti-sceptical line is the way in which it treats the issue of the meaningfulness of sceptical claims as so central to our understanding of radical scepticism. This reveals, I think, the influence of PI in this regard, as there the overwhelming focus is indeed on claims about meaning. But once we bring OC into the picture, and in particular the radical new conception of the structure of rational evaluation that it offers, then it ceases to be so clear that the problem in hand is to be wholly understood in terms of meaning. After all, if Wittgenstein is right that it is in the nature of rational evaluation that it should presuppose these arational hinge certainties – he tells us, for example, that this is a matter of "logic," rather than being, say, a lack

---

23 Putnam, "Philosophy as the Education of Grownups," 128.

of imagination, consistency, etc., on our parts (e.g., OC, §342) – then surely it follows that radical scepticism is simply incoherent. This is because – just like traditional forms of *anti*-scepticism, for that matter – it is essential to this enterprise that it undertakes universal rational evaluations (negative in the case of radical scepticism, positive in the case of traditional anti-scepticism), and yet the very idea of such a thing has been shown to be unintelligible. We thus have an undercutting response to the problem of radical scepticism, in that we have shown that what has the surface appearance of a paradox is in fact nothing of the sort. Rather than arising out of our own folk epistemic concepts, the radical sceptic is in fact smuggling in contentious theoretical claims that should be rejected. The putative paradox thus dissolves.[24] And yet at no point in these proceedings has any claim been made about the meaningfulness, or otherwise, of sceptical doubts.[25]

This is not to say, I should emphasise, that the Wittgenstein of OC is conceding that the sceptic's claims are clearly meaningful. Indeed, like the Wittgenstein of PI, he also makes the point in this work that it is hard to make sense of the sceptic's utterances (and the traditional anti-sceptic's utterances too, I should add, such as G.E. Moore's). As he nicely puts it at one juncture, they rather sound like someone saying "good morning" in the middle of a conversation. (OC, §464) Moreover, if radical scepticism is trading on an incoherent

---

24 Undercutting responses to putative paradoxes are thus to be contrasted with *overriding*, or revisionary, responses. While the former demonstrates that what looks like a paradox is in fact nothing of the sort, since it imports dubious theoretical commitments that we should jettison, the latter grants that the paradox is genuine, but argues nonetheless that there are compelling grounds for embracing one of the horns of the paradox so posed. One finds a distinction of this kind in a number of works (though often with different nomenclature in play). See, for example, Michael Williams, *Unnatural Doubts: Epistemological Realism and the Basis of Scepticism* (Oxford: Blackwell, 1991), Ch. 1 and Quassim Cassam, *The Possibility of Knowledge* (Oxford: Oxford University Press, 2007), Ch. 1. I discuss this contrast, and its dialectical import for the problem of radical scepticism, in Pritchard, *Epistemic Angst*, Part 1.
25 This is broadly the interpretation of OC that I offer in Pritchard, *Epistemic Angst*, Part 2. For some alternative proposals, see Marie McGinn, *Sense and Certainty: A Dissolution of Scepticism* (Oxford: Blackwell, 1989); Williams, *Unnatural Doubts*; Danièle Moyal-Sharrock, *Understanding Wittgenstein's On Certainty* (London: Palgrave Macmillan, 2004); Crispin Wright, "Warrant for Nothing (and Foundations for Free)?" *Proceedings of the Aristotelian Society* 78 (2004): 167–212; Annalisa Coliva, *Moore and Wittgenstein: Scepticism, Certainty, and Common Sense* (London: Palgrave Macmillan, 2010) and *Extended Rationality: A Hinge Epistemology* (London: Palgrave Macmillan, 2015) and Genia Schönbaumsfeld, *The Illusion of Doubt* (Oxford: Oxford University Press, 2016). For a recent survey of Wittgenstein's treatment of radical scepticism in OC, see Duncan Pritchard, "Wittgenstein on Hinge Commitments and Radical Scepticism in *On Certainty*," in *Blackwell Companion to Wittgenstein*, edited by Hans-Johann Glock and John Hyman, 563–575 (Oxford: Blackwell, 2017).

picture of the structure of rational evaluation, then that is at least *prima facie* grounds for treating sceptical claims as meaningless anyway. The issue is just that one can settle the radical sceptical problem without having to make appeals to the clear meaningfulness, or otherwise, of sceptical claims, and this is something that both Putnam and Cavell seem to miss.

With the foregoing in mind, what would be amiss with arguing that radical scepticism is *both* incoherent *and* that the claims it issues are meaningless? That is, it is far from clear to me why it is so important to Putnam and Cavell to maintain that the sceptical claims, while not clearly meaningful, are not clearly meaningless either. The idea, recall, was that this was needed to capture the natural pathology of getting oneself into a sceptical frame of mind. But it seems to me that there are ways of doing this while treating radical scepticism as incoherent and radical sceptical claims as meaningless.

I think that what is key to understanding this possibility is to take seriously what Wittgenstein says about the visceral, animal nature of our hinge commitments. As we saw, Strawson took this point very seriously indeed, perhaps too seriously, as he ended up missing the important thesis about the structure of rational evaluation and taking on board instead only the non-optional nature of our hinge commitments. Crucially, however, it is the former that does the heavy-lifting in Wittgenstein's response to radical scepticism in OC, not the latter, even though the latter thesis is also present. The import of the latter thesis rather reminds us that there are limits to the extent to which it is even possible to get into the sceptical frame of mind.

We can see this point in action by considering what it is like to discover that one's rational evaluations are essentially local in the manner that Wittgenstein outlines. Remember that this is a fact that is ordinarily obscured in our ordinary practices, as we are never usually brought to attend to our hinge commitments *qua* hinge commitments; they are, instead, hidden from view. For example, one is taught to do things with one's hands, but not that one has hands. (OC, §153) The hinges are rather "swallowed down" with everything else that one is taught. (OC, §143) But there is nothing to prevent our becoming aware of them and the role that they play. Indeed, that is precisely our predicament as epistemologists who have engaged with the ideas in play in OC.

Becoming aware of our hinge commitments *qua* hinge commitments, however, is by its nature an unsettling experience. As Cavell would put it, one is hereby encountering the "uncanniness of the ordinary," in the sense that that which is most ordinary is also that which is most hidden from view in normal circumstances (even though it is in plain sight), and hence can now seem extraordinary once it is the subject of one's focus. Indeed, even if one has engaged with the putative sceptical paradox and then become convinced by the Wittgensteinian thesis that undercuts the "paradox" altogether, this is not going to return one to state of epistemic innocence. Although our everyday epistemic practices do not involve universal rational evaluations (but only localised ones), it's not as if there is anything in those practices that makes manifest that such rational evaluations would be impossible. And yet that's precisely what we discover once we appreciate the role that hinge commitments play in our epistemic practices. This realisation, even when coupled with the philosophical explanation that Wittgenstein offers, is bound to generate the kind of epistemic vertigo that we described earlier. We are now looking at our epistemic position from a detached perspective, and in doing so are quite naturally feeling giddy about out epistemic position.

This last point is crucial. If epistemic vertigo is compatible with one being in possession of an undercutting response to the sceptical problem, then it clearly isn't necessary to concede that there is a sense in which the sceptic's claims are not clearly meaningless in order to account for this phenomenon. That is, we have seen that one can consistently be aware that radical scepticism essentially trades on an incoherent thesis that should be rejected and yet still be subject to epistemic vertigo. If that's right, then surely we can similarly account for the phenomenon of epistemic vertigo even if the sceptic's claims are shown to be meaningless.

Note too that the reason why this is possible is precisely because epistemic vertigo does not involve actual doubt of the hinge commitments. Indeed, once we take seriously the visceral, animal nature of hinge commitments, then there simply is no sense to the idea that one can doubt them. This is why epistemic vertigo is a *phobic* reaction to one's epistemic position. Just as one can experience vertigo while high up – more accurately, *acrophobia* – even while being aware that one is not in fact in any danger at all, so one can experience epistemic vertigo even while being aware that there is no significant epistemic risk of error in play. Of course, for those who are not availed of the Wittgensteinian account of why radical scepticism should be rejected, the awareness of the uncanny nature of our hinge commitments is not coupled with an opposing awareness of why this is nothing to be concerned about. This is why epistemic vertigo is a more troubling condition for them than it is for us. Even so, the point remains that this realisation cannot in fact shake their hinge commitments; it rather just results in a more unsettling phobic response.

The crux of the matter is that, *contra* Putnam and Cavell, we can accommodate the phenomenon of epistemic vertigo, and thereby the idea that one can get oneself into a sceptical frame of mind, while nonetheless treating the sceptical problem as trading on incoherence, and even while treating sceptical claims as clearly meaningless. It follows that epistemic vertigo does not in itself provide any rationale for supposing that we must treat sceptical claims as not clearly meaningless.[26]

V Putnam on Contextualism and Occasion-Sensitivity: *Contra* Stroud

We noted earlier that Putnam dismisses treatments of Cavell's anti-scepticism that equate it with Austin's. The reader might therefore be puzzled to learn that in Putnam's other writings on radical scepticism he adopts a distinctive line on meaning that he attributes, in part, to Austin (and also to Wittgenstein, via Cavell). The puzzle is resolved once we realise that Putnam is distinguishing between the Austin (1961) of "Other Minds" and the Austin of *Sense and Sensibilia* (1964).[27] While Putnam clearly views the former work as being committed to demonstrating the meaninglessness of radical sceptical doubts, he sees in the latter work an approach to meaning more amenable to his purposes.[28] In particular, he finds in the latter work a way of thinking about the sceptical puzzle such that sceptical claims are neither clearly meaningful nor meaningless, in just the manner described above in our discussion of Cavell.

---

26 Another issue that might be lurking in the background here is the nature of Wittgensteinian quietism. It is clear that the Wittgenstein of PI endorsed a thesis of this kind, but its exact nature is controversial. On a radical reading, Wittgenstein is advocating a kind of quietism that aims to get us to abandon philosophy altogether. But there is a more constructive reading according to which philosophy can be the solution to philosophical problems even if (bad) philosophy is usually the cause of those problems in the first place. For further discussion of such a constructive Wittgensteinian quietism, see John McDowell, "Wittgensteinian 'Quietism'," *Common Knowledge* 15, no. 3 (2009): 365–372 and Duncan Pritchard, "Wittgensteinian Epistemology, Epistemic Vertigo, and Pyrrhonian Scepticism," in *Epistemology After Sextus Empiricus*, edited by Justin Vlasits and Katja Maria Vogt, 172–192 (Oxford: Oxford University Press, 2019).

27 J.L. Austin, *Sense and Sensibilia*, edited by G.J. Warnock (Oxford: Oxford University Press, 1964).

28 Note that this is a charitable interpretation on my part, as Putnam himself is never explicit about this contrast between his readings of the two Austin texts. And yet I think this must be the explanation, for otherwise there is a direct contradiction between remarks Putnam makes in "Philosophy as the Education of Grownups," 120, and "Skepticism and Occasion-Sensitive Semantics," in Hilary Putnam, *Philosophy in an Age of Science: Physics, Mathematics and Skepticism*, edited by Mario de Caro and David Macarthur (Cambridge, MA: Harvard University Press), 515ff.

The approach to meaning in question is *occasion-sensitive semantics*, which as Putnam notes constitutes a particular kind of contextualism about language. While it has its roots in the work of Austin and (via Cavell) Wittgenstein, Putnam clearly holds that it gains its fullest expression in the more recent work of Charles Travis.[29] Roughly, the driving thought behind occasion-sensitive semantics is that, independently of a concrete context of use (or an occasion of use, as Travis puts it), a statement need have no truth-evaluable content at all. In particular, from the meaning of a particular sentence we cannot simply deduce what, in a particular context of use, truth-evaluable content, if any, is generated by an assertion of that sentence.[30] To illustrate this proposal, Putnam offers an example that he attributes to Travis. Suppose one has a tree in one's garden with bronze coloured leaves, but which has been painted green by a prankster. Putnam points out that depending on "who says it, and to whom, and why" the sentence "The tree has green leaves" (said about the tree in question) could count as true or false, or even as lacking a determinate truth-value at all.[31]

Putnam employs this account of meaning to critique, on the one hand, Barry Stroud's sympathetic treatment of radical scepticism,[32] and, on the other hand, Michael Williams' own brand of contextualist response to radical scepticism.[33] Let's take these critiques in turn.

---

29 See Charles Travis, *The True and the False: The Domain of Pragmatics* (Amsterdam: John Benjamins, 1981); *The Uses of Sense: Wittgenstein's Philosophy of Language* (Oxford: Clarendon Press, 1989); "Pragmatics," in *A Companion to the Philosophy of Language*, edited by Bob Hale and Crispin Wright, 87–107 (Oxford: Blackwell, 1997); *Unshadowed Thought: Representation in Thought and Language* (Cambridge, MA: Harvard University Press, 2000); "The Silence of the Senses," *Mind* 113, no. 449 (2004): 57–94; "A Sense of Occasion," *Philosophical Quarterly* 55, no. 219 (2005): 286–314; *Thought's Footing: A Theme in Wittgenstein's Philosophical Investigations* (Oxford: Oxford University Press, 2006); *Occasion-Sensitivity: Selected Essays* (Oxford: Oxford University Press, 2008). See also James Conant, "Wittgenstein on Meaning and Use," *Philosophical Investigations* 21, no. 3 (1998): 222–250 for the presentation of a similar idea in the context specifically of the work of the later Wittgenstein.
30 Here is Putnam: "[*What occasion-sensitive semantics denies*] is that the 'meaning' of a sentence [. . .] determines the *truth-evaluable content* of that sentence. The thesis of [*occasion-sensitivity*] is that in general the *truth-evaluable content of sentences depends both on what they mean (what a competent speaker knows before encountering a particular context) and on the particular context, and not on meaning alone.*" Hilary Putnam, "Skepticism, Stroud, and the Contextuality of Knowledge," *Philosophical Explorations* 4, no. 2 (2001): 3, italics in the original.
31 Putnam, "Skepticism and Occasion-Sensitive Semantics," 516.
32 Stroud, *Significance of Philosophical Scepticism*. See also Barry Stroud, "Scepticism, 'Externalism,' and the Goal of Epistemology," *Proceedings of the Aristotelian Society* (suppl. vol.) 68 (1994): 290–307.
33 Williams, *Unnatural Doubts*.

Let's begin by examining how Stroud sets-up the sceptical argument. A key move in this regard is his claim[34] that the following condition on knowledge is highly plausible, and also rooted in our everyday epistemic practices:

Descartes' Principle

In order to have knowledge that p, one must be able to know any condition which one knows is necessary for knowledge that p.[35]

So, for example, if I know that if I am presently dreaming, then I am not in a position to know my present surroundings (that I am driving to work, say), and I am aware of this fact. It follows via this principle that I need to know that I am not dreaming if I am to have knowledge of my present surroundings. Stroud's next move is to give examples of someone raising far-fetched error-possibilities in everyday contexts, error-possibilities that the subjects concerned cannot rule out. For example, one takes oneself to know, on excellent grounds, that John will be at the party, but the possibility is then raised (by a "boorish host") that perhaps he might get struck down by a meteorite on the way. Since one cannot exclude such a possibility, which would be incompatible with one knowing that John will be at the party, hence Stroud concludes that there is an open question over whether one counts as knowing what one took oneself to know, given that one cannot rule out the error-possibility that was raised.

Putnam's main complaint to reasoning of this kind is to appeal to occasion-sensitive semantics. Here is Putnam (where note that by "contextualism" in this regard he has in mind occasion-sensitive semantics):

[. . .] what contextualists maintain – or at least, what Wittgenstein teaches us – is that neither "Stroud knows that John will be struck by a meteorite on his way to the party" nor "Stroud does not know that John will be struck by a meteorite on the way to the party" has a unique truth-evaluable content that automatically accompanies it (like a shadow) every time it is uttered. Here and now, if you ask "Hilary, do you know or not know that Jim will not be struck down by a meteorite tomorrow," I would not say either "I know" or "I do not know"; I would say "What do you mean?" If it is "not true" that "I know that John will not be struck down by a meteorite tomorrow," that is because, uttered here and now, with no specified context other than the empty context of "it's a logical possibility," "I know that John will not be struck down by a meteorite tomorrow" isn't

---

34 Stroud, *Significance of Philosophical Scepticism*, 29.
35 Note that Stroud himself never makes this principle as explicit as we do here, though it is clear that it is implicit in his discussion of the sceptical argument. In describing this principle in the manner set out I am following Wright's discussion of Stroud, *Significance of Philosophical Scepticism*, at Crispin Wright, "Scepticism and Dreaming: Imploding the Demon," *Mind* 100, no. 1 (1991): 91.

merely something that is "not true," it is something that hasn't been given a determinate content (or a determinate context, for that matter). By assuming that the negation of the knowledge claim "Stroud knows that John will not be struck down by a meteorite on his way to the party" is true, Stroud has assumed that that knowledge claim has a truth-evaluable content, and this is precisely the move in the conjuring trick that gives the game away to the skeptic.[36]

Putnam is here using occasion-sensitive semantics to argue that we simply do not understand what the boorish host means when he raises, out of the blue, the mere logical possibility that John might have been hit by a meteorite. Until we do gain an understanding of what is meant by raising this claim, then the statement that "I know that John will not be struck down by a meteorite tomorrow" has no determinate truth-evaluable content, and hence cannot be assessed as either true or false. It rather falls through the cracks of meaning.

I'm broadly sympathetic to such an approach to semantics, though I would want to press the idea that what this line shows is that the sceptical claims are not clearly meaningful or meaningless. After all, if we can identify no determinate truth-evaluable content for the sceptical claims, then why not simply dismiss them as clearly meaningless? Isn't the onus on them to demonstrate that their claims have content? Even setting this point aside, however, I am also somewhat unconvinced that appealing to occasion-sensitive semantics is necessary to meet Stroud's challenge as Putnam clearly supposes, much less the challenge posed by radical scepticism more generally.

Indeed, although Putnam's main focus when responding to Stroud is to appeal to occasion-sensitive semantics, it is telling that he elsewhere offers a completely independent response to Stroud, albeit without it seems realising that it is independent. Putnam notes that Stroud effectively glosses over the crucial distinction between an error-possibility that is raised because it has a serious chance of obtaining, and an error-possibility that has no serious possibility of obtaining, and is merely a logical possibility.[37] And yet this distinction makes all the difference in the context of radical scepticism. If there is a serious chance that John might get hit by a meteorite – or even if our boorish host has reasonable grounds for thinking that there is such a serious chance – then it

---

36 Putnam, "Skepticism, Stroud, and the Contextuality of Knowledge," 8–9. Note that after the remark about Wittgenstein at the start of this quotation, Putnam cites Cavell's interpretation of PI in *The Claim of Reason*, Part 2.

37 See especially Putnam's discussion ("Skepticism, Stroud, and the Contextuality of Knowledge," 12) of Stroud's (*Significance of Philosophical Scepticism*, 67–68) commentary on Clarke's "plane-spotter" case in Thompson Clarke, "The Legacy of Skepticism," *Journal of Philosophy* 69, no. 20 (1972): 754–769.

would be entirely legitimate both to raise this error-possibility and to expect that one can exclude it if one is to count as knowing that John will be at the party. But if it is a mere logical possibility of error, then why would anyone think that one must be able to exclude this error-possibility if one is to count as having knowledge?

There is a deeper issue here, which is the kind of epistemic principles that the sceptic is appealing to. We noted earlier that Stroud is appealing to a principle – Descartes' Principle, as we called it – according to which in order to have knowledge one has to be able to know that all the known necessary conditions for that knowledge are met. That principle would suffice to make the mere (known) logical possibility of an error-possibility sufficient to ensure that one must exclude it before one can have knowledge. But that is an absurdly demanding principle, and it is hard to see why anyone would ever accept it, much less grant that it is rooted in our everyday epistemic practices as Stroud claims.

For example, this principle entails the iterativity of knowledge – i.e., that when one knows, one also knows that one knows. After all, knowing that p is trivially a (known) necessary condition for knowing that p, and hence in knowing that p one must know that one knows that p. (Indeed, one can continue this line of reasoning to third-order knowledge and beyond, but we won't press that particular point). But is it really part of our everyday epistemic practices to demand that first-order knowledge is always accompanied by the corresponding second-order knowledge? That seems at least *prima facie* unlikely.

One card that Stroud can play here is to point out that a principle can be genuinely rooted in our everyday epistemic practices even if our actual practices don't on the face of it manifest this fact. As Stroud points out, what we are interested in as epistemologists is, as it were, what a "purified" version of our everyday practices would look like, once we strip away everything that is extraneous to those practices. For example, while it is undoubtedly true that we don't insist that every known necessary condition is known to have obtained before attributing knowledge, isn't this just because of the practical limitations that we ordinarily operate under, such as limitations of time, imagination, and so forth? Once these practical limitations are set to one side and we consistently follow-through on our everyday epistemic principles, can we be so sure that they would not lead to epistemic practices that licence scepticism-friendly constraints on knowledge such as Descartes' Principle?

This is an important point, one that we will return to presently. For now, however, it suffices to note that there is a principle in the vicinity of Descartes' Principle that can do the job that Stroud wants and which is far less contentious. Accordingly, rather than getting bogged down in a debate about the plausibility of Descartes' Principle, we would be wiser to re-run Stroud's scepticism-friendly line with the alternative principle in play. Consider the following claim:

Competent Deduction Closure

If S knows that p, and S competently deduces from p that q, thereby forming a belief that q on this basis while retaining her knowledge that p, then S knows that q.[38]

Although much less demanding than the principle that Stroud was employing, and hence far more plausible as a result – it doesn't entail the iterativity of knowledge, for one thing – this principle seems sufficient for the sceptic's purposes. After all, if one knows full well that what one takes oneself to know is incompatible with the target error-possibility, and one knows that one cannot rule out (i.e., know to be false) that error-possibility, then it follows via this principle that one cannot have the knowledge that one takes oneself to have after all (since otherwise, via competent deduction closure, one could know the denial of the error-possibility, something we have granted is impossible). So mere logical possibility of error that one cannot rule out, plus competent deduction closure, seems sufficient to motivate the sceptical paradox after all. Accordingly, so long as radical sceptical error-possibilities are in play, and we grant that we cannot rule them out, then in conjunction with competent deduction closure they can deliver radical sceptical conclusions.[39]

Interestingly, however, the Wittgensteinian line on the structure of rational evaluation that we described earlier gives us the resources to meet closure-based radical scepticism head-on, and without making any essential appeal to claims about meaning. Recall that we noted above the importance of taking Wittgenstein's remarks about the visceral, animal nature of our hinge commitments seriously. Crucially, however, once we do so, then it becomes hard to see how they could possibly be in conflict with the competent deduction principle in the way that they would need to be for the set-up of the putative sceptical paradox. After all, what makes the competent deduction principle so compelling is that it involves the acquisition of a belief via a paradigmatic case of a rational process: competent deduction from known premises. How could what results from such a process be any less than knowledge? But notice that for

---

38 This is essentially the formulation of the closure principle put forward by Timothy William-son in *Knowledge and Its Limits* (Oxford: Oxford University Press, 2000), 117, and John Hawthorne in "The Case for Closure," in *Contemporary Debates in Epistemology*, edited by Ernest Sosa and Mathias Steup (Oxford: Blackwell, 2005), 29.

39 For further discussion of the logical structure of the sceptical argument, Pritchard, *Epistemic Angst*, Part 1.

such a principle to have application to the sceptical puzzle it would need to be possible to acquire beliefs in our hinge commitments (e.g., that we are not BIVs, for example) via this paradigmatically rational process. This is precisely the juncture where the radical sceptic becomes unstuck on the Wittgensteinian conception, for our hinge commitments are not beliefs in the relevant sense, nor are they the kinds of propositional attitude that could ever be acquired via rational processes.

We have already encountered the point that our hinge commitments are not acquired via rational means (but rather "swallowed down" with everything else we are taught). But what of the claim that they are not beliefs? Belief, of course, is a notion that is used in lots of different ways by different philosophers (and still more ways once we move beyond philosophy and move into other areas, such as cognitive science, say).[40] But what epistemologists mean by belief is clearly that propositional attitude that is a constituent part of propositional knowledge. Belief in this sense, however, has certain properties in virtue of being directed at the truth, one of which is that it is not the kind of propositional attitude that would survive the realisation that one had no rational basis whatsoever for the truth of the target proposition. And yet that is precisely the nature of our hinge commitments. Even when we recognise, outside the context of normal inquiry, that they are arational, we continue to hold them with no less conviction. This is what I mean by my remark that hinge commitments are not beliefs.

Wittgenstein's description of our hinge commitments as arational, animal, visceral etc., is thus vital to understanding his proposal. It offers us a way of dealing with the sceptical problem that is independent of the claim that the sceptic (and anti-sceptic) are trading in contentless claims. As I say, I find the latter thesis plausible as well; my point is just that we don't need this thesis to undermine the putative radical sceptical paradox and thereby show that it is illusory (in that it trades on an implausible philosophical assumption regarding the viability of fully general rational evaluations).[41]

Note too that responding to the sceptical puzzle in this fashion, as opposed to letting one's anti-scepticism rest exclusively on a claim about meaning, also helps us evade a worry that was raised above concerning Stroud's use of Descartes' Principle. Recall that the thought was that the fact that we don't employ

---

40 See Leslie Stevenson, "Six Levels of Mentality," *Philosophical Explorations* 5, no. 2 (2002): 105–124 for a useful taxonomy of some of the different ways that the notion of "belief" is employed.
41 I develop this interpretation of Wittgenstein's anti-scepticism in a number of places, but see especially Pritchard, *Epistemic Angst*, Part 2.

such a principle in our everyday epistemic practices does not by itself demonstrate that this principle is not rooted in our everyday epistemic practices. After all, what we are interested in as epistemologists is surely a purified version of our everyday epistemic practices, one that is stripped of all extraneous features. And such a purified version of our everyday practices may well manifest a commitment to Descartes' Principle.

More generally, the nub of the worry is that the existence of important differences between our everyday epistemic practices and sceptical epistemic practices is entirely consistent with the latter being a "purified" version of the former (i.e., once we consistently apply our epistemic standards, aren't side-tracked by practical limitations, and so on). For if the latter were a purified version of the former, then one could argue that the sceptical practices are grounded in our everyday practices after all, and so can derive their content from them. If that's right, however, then we should be very wary of making claims about the lack of clear meaning of the sceptical epistemic practices based on how they diverge from our everyday epistemic practices.

Significantly, however, Wittgenstein is not susceptible to this charge at all. For it is precisely part of his case against universal rational evaluations that they do not differ merely as a matter of degree from ordinary localised rational evaluations, but rather are different in kind. In particular, while the transition from localised doubt to universal doubt might initially look like a mere difference in scope, Wittgenstein is emphatic that we have instead shifted from a viable rational evaluation to attempting an impossible rational evaluation. For example, here he is comparing doubt that a planet exists and doubt (in ordinary circumstances) that one's hand exists:

> For it is not true that a mistake merely gets more and more improbable as we pass from the planet to my own hand. No: at some point it has ceased to be conceivable. (OC, §54)

This is why Stroud's worry doesn't get a grip on Wittgenstein's anti-sceptical line in OC, in that Wittgenstein doesn't merely show that the sceptic's epistemic practices are very different to ours, but he further emphasises that they are also in an important sense *discontinuous* with our practices.[42]

---

42 A good point of contrast here is, arguably anyway, Austin in "Other Minds." While Austin makes an excellent case for the claim that sceptical epistemic practices come apart from our everyday epistemic practices, he doesn't speak to the idea that the former is discontinuous with the latter at all, and hence he seems to be susceptible to Stroud's point about how sceptical epistemic practices could consistently be purified versions of our everyday epistemic practices. For further discussion of this point, see Duncan Pritchard, "Sceptical Intuitions," in

VI Putnam on Contextualism and Occasion-Sensitivity: *Contra* Williams

Putnam often refers to his brand of occasion-sensitivity as a form of "contextualism," which indeed it is, as it emphasises the important of context for determining truth-evaluable content. Putnam's proposal isn't specific to knowledge ascriptions, of course, as it is a general claim about meaning, but there are "contextualist" theses in epistemology that are specific in this way. One of these theses is due to Williams' *Unnatural Doubts*, and superficially at least it shares some key features with Putnam's account, not least in terms of how Williams' contextualism is brought to bear on the problem of radical scepticism. As we will see, however, there are also some important differences between these two forms of contextualism.

Before getting to the details of Williams' view, it may be helpful to first set-out a variety of contextualism that is very familiar within epistemology. According to a standard *attributer contextualism* – of a kind found in the work of such figures as Stewart Cohen,[43] Keith DeRose,[44] and David Lewis[45] – we are to understand "knows" as a context-sensitive term. In particular, when the epistemic standards are high, assertions of the form "S knows that p" will tend to express falsehoods, whereas when the epistemic standards are low, those very same assertions will tend to express truths. More specifically, it can *both* be true that in an everyday low-standards context that an assertion of "John knows that he has hands" expresses a truth while in a sceptical high-standards context that very same assertion will express a falsehood. In this way, so the thought goes, we can explain the "pull" of radical scepticism, since when the sceptic asserts, relative to their high-standards context, an assertion to the effect that we lack knowledge, she speaks truly, since "knows" in this context picks out that high epistemic standard that we cannot satisfy. Nonetheless, when we attribute knowledge to each other in everyday epistemic contexts we also tend to speak truly, since "knows" in these contexts picks out the low epistemic standards

Intuitions, edited by Darrell P. Rowbottom and Anthony Robert Booth, 213–231 (Oxford: Oxford University Press, 2014).

43 Stewart Cohen, "How to Be a Fallibilist," *Philosophical Perspectives* 2 (1988): 91–123; "Contextualism, Skepticism, and the Structure of Reasons," *Philosophical Perspectives* 13 (1999): 57–89; "Contextualism and Skepticism," *Philosophical Issues* 10 (2000): 94–107.

44 Keith DeRose, "Solving the Skeptical Problem," *Philosophical Review* 104, no. 1 (1995): 1–52.

45 David Lewis, "Elusive Knowledge," *Australasian Journal of Philosophy* 74, no. 4 (1996): 549–567.

that we can satisfy. In effect, then, the sceptical problem on this view trades on a simple failure to recognise the context-sensitivity of "knows."[46]

There are lots of problems that face contextualist responses to radical scepticism of this kind, though this is not the place to review them here.[47] The important point is that attributer contextualism differs in fundamental ways to the kind of contextualism put forward by Putnam. For one thing, attributer contextualism is applied only to a particular term, "knows," and not to expressions as a whole as occasion-sensitive contextualism is. For another, notice that there is a hierarchy of contexts in play in attributer contextualism, individuated by the demandingness of the epistemic standards in operation. There is nothing like this inherent to occasion-sensitivity. In particular, the idea is not that changes in the epistemic standards can strip an assertion of its truth-evaluable content; the issue is rather just that we need a concrete occasion of use in order to determine such a content. This means that Putnam is not claiming that sceptical assertions are meaningful in sceptical contexts but meaningless otherwise, but rather that they simply fail to ever pick out a determinate meaning.

Attributer contextualism also differs in fundamental ways to the variety of contextualism proposed by Williams. While Williams' would grant that "knows" is a context-sensitive term, he doesn't think that it is only the context of the attributer that has a bearing on this context-sensitivity. Moreover, as we just saw with Putnam's contextualism, Williams' contextualism does not involve a hierarchy of contexts individuated by the stringency of the epistemic standards in play. So what is Williams' brand of contextualism?

For Williams, "contextualism" is the rejection of *epistemological realism*, which is the thesis that a proposition can have an inherent epistemic status simply in virtue of its content. In particular, Williams is concerned to reject what he calls *epistemic priority*, which he takes to be a consequence of epistemological realism, at least when it comes to traditional post-Cartesian epistemology. This is the idea that propositions concerning the "inner" realm of one's mental states have an inherent epistemic priority over propositions concerning the "outer" realm of the empirical world around us, such that the epistemic standing of our beliefs in the latter can only ever be inferred from our beliefs in

---

46 Oddly, Putnam in "Skepticism, Stroud, and the Contextuality of Knowledge," "Philosophy as the Education of Grownups," and "Skepticism and Occasion-Sensitive Semantics," seems completely oblivious to attributer contextualism of this kind, even though it was part of the epistemological mainstream by the time he was writing, and hence would surely have been in the mind of readers when they consider Putnam's variety of "contextualism."

47 I offer a detailed account of the limitations of contextualist responses to radical scepticism in Pritchard, *Epistemic Angst*, passim.

the former (which have a privileged non-inferential epistemic standing). Of course, once epistemic priority is in place, then it is much easier to pose a sceptical question about the epistemic status of our empirical beliefs, as their epistemic standing is now in a sense derivative on the epistemic standing of our beliefs about our mental states. But Williams wants to resist this line of argument, and that means blocking it at its source: epistemological realism.

For Williams, epistemological realism is false because one always needs a context in order to determine epistemic standing. In particular, Williams takes a broadly Wittgensteinian line and argues that all contexts incorporate certain foundational and ungrounded commitments – which he terms *methodological necessities* – that determine the inferential structure of that context (i.e., what can count as reasons for what, and so forth). Accordingly, whether, for example, a belief about one's mental states can count as a reason for one's belief about the empirical world around one, rather than *vice versa*, will depend on one's context of inquiry, and hence on the methodological necessities in play. In the context of traditional post-Cartesian epistemology – and thus in the sceptical context which has the same fundamental methodological necessities – epistemic priority *will* hold. Crucially, however, it will not hold universally (i.e., across all contexts) as it is supposed to, for there are other contexts of inquiry, such as psychological investigation, which have different methodological necessities and where, accordingly, it can be epistemically legitimate to infer beliefs about someone's mental states from beliefs about the empirical world (e.g., their observed behaviour).

This last point highlights something that Williams shares with attributer contextualism, which is the idea that there is an epistemic legitimacy to sceptical doubts, it is just that it is entirely context-bound. The sceptic believes that they have demonstrated that there is an inherent problem with the epistemological standing of our beliefs, particularly regarding the empirical realm, but in fact all that they have demonstrated is that there is an inherent problem with the epistemological standing of our empirical beliefs *relative to the ungrounded methodological necessities of their context of inquiry*. Here is Williams:

> The sceptic takes himself to have discovered, under the conditions of philosophical reflection, that knowledge of the world is impossible. But in fact, the most he has discovered is that knowledge of the world is *impossible under the conditions of philosophical reflection.*[48]

Note that this is a very different line to that taken by Putnam, and hence unsurprisingly he takes issue with this aspect of Williams's view. In particular, he claims that once we attend to the actual context-sensitivity of "knows," via

---

48 Williams, *Unnatural Doubts*, 130. Emphasis in original.

occasion-sensitivity, we see that there is no sense to the idea that context can influence whether or not one counts as having "knowledge" as Williams (and the attributer contextualist) maintain. As he puts it, statements of the form "I would have known that p if you had not mentioned q," or "I know that p in that context, but I do not know that p in this context" are simply incoherent.[49]

Although I think that Putnam is right to criticise Williams on this score, I don't think the particular way that he pushes his critical line works. For one thing, there are perfectly legitimate situations in which it would make perfect sense to say that one would have known something had not a certain error-possibility been raised, which is when the error-possibility turns out to be a misleading defeater. Misleading defeaters which are not in turn defeated are sufficient to undermine knowledge, after all, but once one discovers that they were misleading, one realises that, prior to them being raised, one did know what one took oneself to know. Of course, the kinds of cases that Williams has in mind don't involve misleading defeaters, but that's not the point, which is that Putnam cannot charge Williams with misunderstanding the nature of our epistemic language via the particular claim that he makes.

Moreover, Williams has a response to statements that make context-change explicit, which is that by doing so they effectively force one into the epistemically more demanding context, whichever one that is. So, for example, Williams can grant that a statement like "I know that p relative to everyday contexts, but not relative to sceptical contexts" is awkward, but that's because on his view it is simply false. Once the sceptical context is explicitly in play, as it is in this statement, then it is sceptical contextual standards that are relevant, and that means that the first part of this conjunction is false, and hence the statement as a whole is false too.

So if Putnam's objection fails to hit its target, what would be a better way to object to Williams' view? Well, we have already seen that if we take Wittgenstein's line on hinge commitments and the essential structure of rational evaluation seriously, then there is no need to concede anything of this contextual kind to the radical sceptic. Rather, radical scepticism trades on dubious theoretical claims that we should dispense with, *period*. Williams fails to see this since he opts of a construal of our hinge commitments such that rather than being basic arational commitments that are held in a visceral, non-optional fashion, they are instead methodological posits, akin more to assumptions or hypotheses, and hence the kinds of commitments that one can alter at will, simply by changing one's inquiry. And yet Wittgenstein is adamant that we are not to

---

49 Putnam, "Skepticism and Occasion-Sensitive Semantics," 530–531.

think of hinge commitments along these "optional" lines, still less as assumptions/hypotheses.[50]

The upshot is that once the Wittgensteinian line is on the table, then there is no longer any impetus to go contextual in the sense offered by either Williams or the attributer contextualist. But, similarly, this also reminds us of the point made above, which is that even if the kind of contextualism represented by occasion-sensitivity is correct (as I'm inclined to think that it is), it is even so a *secondary* anti-sceptical resource, as the Wittgensteinian line all by itself undercuts the sceptical problematic without need of any essential appeals to meaning.[51]

VII Concluding Remarks

As I hope the foregoing has demonstrated, Putnam's treatment of radical scepticism extends well beyond his remarks on the import of content externalism to the coherence of certain radical sceptical hypotheses. Moreover, what Putnam has to say is both enlightening and distinctive. Nonetheless, his reliance on occasion-sensitive semantics blinds him to the fact that there is another Wittgensteinian response to radical scepticism available which, while closely related to the Cavellian line that Putnam takes, is also more radical. In particular, it offers is a way of undercutting the radical sceptical problematic without having to depend on claims about the meaningfulness, or otherwise, of sceptical moves. This is not to deny the correctness of occasion-sensitive semantics, much less that such an idea has relevance to the problem of radical scepticism, but only that its real import to radical scepticism comes after we have already diagnosed the putative sceptical threat as illicitly trading on dubious theoretical claims masquerading as common sense.

---

50 Recall this passage, which we quoted earlier (OC, §343): "But it isn't that the situation is like this: We just can't investigate everything, and for that reason we are forced to rest content with assumption. If I want the door to turn, the hinges must stay put."
51 I offer a sustained critique of Williams' anti-scepticism (which I call *inferential contextualism*) in Pritchard, *Epistemic Angst*, passim.

Yemima Ben-Menahem
Natural Laws and Human Language

Abstract: The paper addresses an apparent tension in Putnam's philosophy between, on the one hand, his realism, which suggests an objective understanding of natural laws, and, on the other hand, his acknowledgment of the role of human language – in particular its sensitivity to context and personal experience – in shaping our beliefs and methods of justification. Understanding Putnam's position on the relation between human language and objective reality also involves examining his views on reduction and non-scientific truth – issues that he was deeply concerned with in his later philosophy.

I Introduction

Putnam's long-standing avowal of realism in general, and in the philosophy of science, in particular, is indisputable. And yet, it is clear from his numerous writings on the subject – his critique of certain versions of realism, and the new versions he proposed in response to this critique – that Putnam's engagement with realism involved a struggle between conflicting inclinations. To make sense of this struggle, we must identify not only the core tenets of realism that Putnam upheld, but also arguments and considerations that seemed to him to lead in the opposite direction, that is, away from realism, or at least, away from overly naïve versions of realism. The attraction of such non-realist routes, I would like to suggest, stemmed from Putnam's conception of meaning and the role language plays in our grasp of reality. Although externalism – the backbone of Putnam's conception of meaning – was conceived as a realist theory of meaning, there are aspects of meaning and representation that Putnam took to speak against the naïve belief in the feasibility of a single, uniquely correct, description of reality. In short, the challenge was to embrace objectivity and mind-independence while taking into account the limitations that language imposes on the satisfaction of these desiderata.

Putnam sets the stage very clearly in *The Threefold Cord*, henceforth TTC.[1] He first reiterates his commitment to realism: "I agree . . . that the world is as it is independently of the interests of describers. [The] suggestion that the world

---

1 Hilary Putnam, *The Threefold Cord: Mind, Body, and World* (New York: Columbia University Press, 1999).

https://doi.org/10.1515/9783110769210-013

we know is to an indeterminate extent the product of our own minds is one I deplore." He immediately adds, however, that "the traditional realist way of putting what is wrong with [this] position involves a metaphysical phantasy." (TTC 6)[2] The tension verged on paradox. Indeed, when reviewing the evolution of his thought on the problem of realism, Putnam tells us that at one point "The whole realism problem came to look to me like one giant antinomy of reason." (TTC 13) Putnam points to two interrelated flaws in the traditional realist position: a naive conception of meaning and a naïve conception of objects and their properties. These flaws underlie the "metaphysical phantasy . . . that there is a totality of Forms, or Universals, or 'properties,' fixed once and for all, and that every possible meaning of a word corresponds to one of these Forms or Universals or properties. The structure of all possible thoughts is fixed in advance – fixed by the Forms." (TTC 6)

Although this phantasy was formulated by Putnam (deliberately, I suppose) in the somewhat archaic language of forms and universals, one can see how the same view could be formulated in terms of fundamental physics with its fundamental "beables" and their properties.[3] And one can see, further, how one could be led from a commitment to such a view – the commitment Putnam wanted to distance himself from – to *reductionism*. For if one believes that there is a complete and uniquely correct description of the world in terms of its fundamental beables and their properties, then it would also seem plausible to expect that objects, properties, and theoretical claims that are not part of this fundamental description are nonetheless reducible to it. One could even acknowledge that at this point in time we have not yet discovered the ultimate fundamental theory, nor (*a fortiori*) do we have any idea as to how to reduce every non-fundamental description to the fundamental one, but the belief that such a fundamental theory and such reduction schemes must, in principle, exist, could still seem plausible. It is only natural therefore, that Putnam devoted the second part of TTC to the critique of reduction and reductionism.[4]

Reductionism is also the focus of the present paper. In what follows, I review some of Putnam's arguments against reductionism and augment them

---

2 Putnam uses William James as backdrop for this discussion of realism. Instead of the square brackets above, he refers to James, i.e., "James's suggestion" and "James's position."

3 The term "beable" was coined by John Bell in the context of his celebrated work on quantum mechanics, as, for example, in "Beables for Quantum Field Theory" (1984), reprinted in *Speakable and Unspeakable in Quantum Mechanics* (Cambridge: Cambridge University Press, 1987), 173.

4 One can endorse a particular reduction, say the reduction of thermodynamics to statistical mechanics (which Putnam cites as an example of a successful reduction, but is considered by many scholars to face serious problems), without committing oneself to reductio*nism* – the position that *every* higher-level theory is reducible to fundamental physics.

with my own. Before doing so, it would be helpful to remind ourselves (briefly, of course) of those aspects of Putnam's conception of meaning that are pertinent to understanding his anti-reductionist position. Similarly, it is useful to bear in mind the close connection between Putnam's conception of meaning and his philosophy of mind, an area in which the viability of reductionism is pivotal, though deeply controversial.

II Putnam on Meaning and the Philosophy of Mind

Putnam's externalist theory of meaning was set forth in "Explanation and Reference,"[5] and "The Meaning of 'Meaning'."[6] The crucial idea was that "'meanings' just ain't in the *head*,"[7] that is, they reach out to reality. "Explanation and Reference" defends the realist intuition that Kuhn's *Structure of Scientific Revolutions* had denied, namely, that different theories (paradigms) can refer to the same world, thus obliterating the threat of truth relativized to theory and the notorious "incommensurability" of different theories (paradigms). Speakers espousing different definitions of a term, holding different beliefs about the entity the term refers to, and having different mental images of this entity, can still refer to the very same entity. In other words, the different mental states of such speakers do not prevent them from sharing the same world. "The Meaning of 'Meaning'" focuses on the complementary situation: Speakers can be in the very same mental state, share the same beliefs and images, and still diverge in the meaning and reference (extension) of their terms. The famous Twin Earth thought experiment (discussed in "The Meaning of 'Meaning'") was designed to demonstrate this possibility: Despite the fact the speakers on the two planets associate the same images and beliefs with the word "water," the word "water" on Twin Earth does not refer to water – the substance referred to by the word "water" on Earth. Together, these two facets of externalism provide the realist with a theory of meaning that meets the realist desideratum of anchoring language in a mind-independent reality.

---

5 Hilary Putnam, "Explanation and Reference," in *Mind, Language and Reality*: *Philosophical Papers*, Vol. 2, 196–214 (Cambridge: Cambridge University Press, 1975).
6 Hilary Putnam, "The Meaning of 'Meaning'," in *Mind, Language and Reality*: *Philosophical Papers*, Vol. 2, 215–271 (Cambridge: Cambridge University Press, 1975).
7 Hilary Putnam, "The Meaning of 'Meaning'," 227.

Despite this achievement, problems soon piled up. First, Putnam realized that the *uniqueness* of the word-world relation is not guaranteed by externalism. Even though words are required by the externalist to be linked to reality, there might be different reference schemes that meet this requirement. This was the message of the model-theoretic argument of which Putnam presented slightly different versions in the late 1970s and early 1980s.[8] The argument (especially the "Models and Reality" version) was inspired by the Löwenheim-Skolem theorem, according to which mathematical theories rich enough to contain arithmetic must have non-isomorphic models, that is, they can be variously interpreted. Here externalism is of no avail; reality itself, so to speak, offers too many options. Only a magical conception of reference, Putnam thought, could single out a particular interpretation, the "intended" one, from its competitors. A related concern was that if realism mandates the uniqueness of truth and reference, then truth becomes radically non-epistemic. For, by the model-theoretic argument, a theory could meet every epistemic criterion – perfect empirical adequacy, coherence, simplicity, and so on, and still be false in the sense that it does not use the "intended" reference relation. But, Putnam contended, what could "false" mean here? Worse, this conception of truth and falsehood puts the realist in the same boat with the skeptic, who likewise doubts the truth of the ideal theory of the world, regardless of the amount of evidence in its favor. For all of these reasons – the problem of uniqueness, the radically non-epistemic conception of truth, and the analogy with skepticism – Putnam came to the conclusion that there are versions of realism (which he dubbed "metaphysical realism" or "naïve realism") that he could not accept.[9] Another characteristic of meaning that Putnam examined in detail in TTC was its sensitivity to context and occasion. He illustrated context sensitivity by means of the sentence "there is a lot of coffee on the table," which, depending on context, could refer to coffee cups, coffee beans, bags of coffee, spilt coffee and so on (TTC 87–88). The abundance of examples of

---

8 E.g., the last chapter of Hilary Putnam, *Meaning and the Moral Sciences* (London: Routledge and Kegan Paul, 1978), the first chapter of Putnam, *Reason Truth, and History* (Cambridge: Cambridge University Press, 1981) and "Models and Reality" (1980), reprinted in *Realism and Reason: Philosophical Papers*, Vol. 3, 1–26 (Cambridge: Cambridge University Press, 1983).
9 Note that although Putnam felt he was abandoning a position he had been wedded to, it is not clear that his earlier realism should in fact be deemed "metaphysical." After all, he never explicitly embraced the features he now identified as troublesome and which had not been clearly defined before the discovery of the model-theoretic problem. Be this as it may, Putnam presented the change in his position as a transition from metaphysical to *internal* realism. In the "internal" phase of his philosophy he endorsed a verificationist theory of truth, a move he later regarded as erroneous. Since internal realism was short lived, I do not discuss it further in this paper.

this kind shows that context sensitivity is a prevalent characteristic of human language.

The connection between realism and meaning-theoretical considerations was further complicated by its bearings on the philosophy of mind. When writing "The Meaning of 'Meaning'," Putnam was still wedded to functionalism, a position that gives priority to function over matter in understanding the mind, and which he had developed a decade earlier. "The question of the autonomy of our mental life does not hinge on and has nothing to do with that all too popular . . . question about matter or soul-stuff. We could be made of Swiss cheese and it wouldn't matter."[10] What matters, Putnam argued, is functional organization. Putnam's guiding analogy for such functional organization was the computer (or Turing machine). The computer analogy suggested that mental states are computational states, characterized syntactically, the projected research program being to provide the "software" for their interaction. Evidently, different machines need not share the same hardware to carry out the same computation. Similarly, Putnam claimed, pain-states or jealousy-states can be functionally alike though physically different – a characteristic that has come to be known as the multiple realizability of the mental.[11] This is the root of nonreductionism: Since the same type of mental state could be realized by different types of physical states, there is no reduction of a particular type of mental state to a specific type of physical state.

As functionalism became exceedingly popular among philosophers of mind, Putnam began to have his doubts about his former position. He continued to give priority to function over matter, but he no longer believed that the computational states that carry out mental functions are completely internal. Externalism played a crucial role in this argument. Thinking of something – the play one saw last week – seems like a simple enough example of a mental state, but if the externalist is right, there is more to meaning than internal computational states. The response of some theorists, notably Jerry Fodor and Ned Block, was to save the computational picture by using a distinction (introduced by Putnam in "The Meaning of 'Meaning'") between narrow and wide content. Though acknowledging the contribution of physical and cultural environments to meaning in the wide sense, they held on to computationalism with respect to meaning in the narrow sense. Putnam's concern over intentionality led him to reject this solution. As he argued in

---

10 Hilary Putnam, "Philosophy and Our Mental Life," in *Mind, Language and Reality*: *Philosophical Papers*, Vol. 2 (Cambridge: Cambridge University Press, 1975), 291.
11 The term was coined by Jerry Fodor in his "Special Sciences, or the Disunity of Science as a Working Hypothesis," *Synthese* 28, no. 2 (1974): 97–115.

Representation and Reality[12] narrow-content computationalism is still an attempt to reduce the intentional to the non-intentional. Against this attempt, he argued that even the ascription of meaning in the narrow sense involves interpretation, that is, it involves the attribution of reasonable beliefs, norms, and individual experiences to the speaker. It is obvious, Putnam argued, that such norms and context-dependent interpretations are irreducible to the language of physics. Functionalism had conceived the computational level as autonomous, that is, irreducible to the physico-chemical level. Putnam's critique of his earlier functionalism makes an analogous point with regard to the autonomy and irreducibility of the mental vis-à-vis the computational. This critique, in turn, buttressed non-reductionism.

III Putnam on Reduction

In the second part of TTC, Putnam further articulates his non-reductionist philosophy of mind. Revisiting Jaegwon Kim's critique of Donald Davidson, he defends Davidson's non-reductionist position in "Mental Events"[13] against the various charges made by Kim in numerous papers, many of which are collected in *Supervenience and Mind*.[14] To follow Putnam's arguments, we must therefore review Davidson's position and Kim's critique. Davidson characterized mental events in terms of their description, namely, they are physical events that have mental descriptions. He endorsed the identity thesis for individual mental events – every mental event is a physical event. Yet, while each event-*token* has a physico-chemical realization, mental events of a certain *type*, say, being surprised, do not constitute a corresponding physical type. Thus, no reduction of the type 'being surprised' to a physico-chemical type is certified or indeed, allowed.

Underlying the denial of type identity is the observation Davidson made in his seminal "Causal Relations"[15] regarding the description-sensitivity of nomological explanations. Laws involve types fundamentally, as they invariably connect types of events rather than individual events. Types, in turn, are referred to via descriptions. In order for individual events to be subsumed under and explained by laws, they must be described in terms of the predicates appearing in

---

12 Hilary Putnam, *Representation and Reality* (Cambridge, MA: MIT Press, 1988).
13 Donald Davidson, "Mental Events" (1970), reprinted in *Essays on Actions and Events*, 207–224 (Oxford: Clarendon Press, 1980).
14 Jaegwon Kim, *Supervenience and Mind* (Cambridge: Cambridge University Press, 1993).
15 Donald Davidson, "Causal Relations" (1967), reprinted in *Essays on Actions and Events*, 149–162 (Oxford: Clarendon Press, 1980).

those laws. (The types connected by the laws are the extensions of these predicates.) If we do not describe an event appropriately, that is, in the language of the laws, but rather use some alternative description, the derivation of the (description of the) event we seek to predict or explain by means of the laws may be blocked.[16]

Here again, as in Putnam's functionalism, we find multiple realizability – a mental type is realizable by physical events that fall under multiple physical types. Davidson refers to this relationship between the two kinds of events as the supervenience of the mental on the physical. Worlds that differ in the mental states of their inhabitants necessarily differ in their physical states, but the converse need not hold, for worlds differing in their physical states may still occupy the same mental states. The relation between physical and mental events is a many-one relation.

Combining these insights, Davidson managed to reconcile three assumptions that at first sight seem hopelessly at odds: the causal interaction of mental and physical events; the Humean understanding of causation in terms of law-like regularities; and the repudiation of laws couched in terms of mental predicates. The significance of description underpins this reconciliation. An individual event that is predictable and explicable by the laws of physics under one of its descriptions may elude prediction and explanation under numerous other descriptions, and in particular, under mental descriptions. Since mental types do not correspond to physical types, there may be no physical law (or set of physical laws) that invokes the mental type in question, either directly, or indirectly via its correspondence with a physical type that is subject to law. And although an individual mental event can be the cause or the effect of a physical event, and although there is a law – a nomological connection – underlying any such causal relation, the law will refer to the mental event in question only under its physical description, not its mental description. Mental events can therefore be covered by physical laws, though not by laws formulated in terms of mental types (or by mixed laws that connect mental types with physical types). The compatibility of the above assumptions is therefore saved. Davidson calls his position anomalous monism – it is monistic in the sense that the mental is physical, and anomalous in the sense that the mental does not fit into the web of physical laws. Another common name for this position is non-reductive physicalism.

---

16 E.g., when we describe a free-falling object in terms of its initial height above the ground and its initial velocity, we can predict the velocity with which it hits the ground, whereas if we describe it in terms of its color and chemical structure, we cannot.

Kim's critique of Davidson is that non-reductive physicalism is incoherent. In a nutshell, the idea is that irreducible causal relations between mental events (or between mental events and events on the fundamental level) threaten to disrupt the physical order at the fundamental level. Were such higher-level causal relations to exist, Kim argues, they would interfere with the causal autonomy – *the physical closure* – of the fundamental level. Irreducible causal relations of this kind are therefore impossible. If Kim is right, then, Davidson notwithstanding, all higher-levels events and properties, including, of course, mental events and properties, are either reducible to fundamental ones, or causally inert.

Putnam is in agreement with the general thrust of Davidson's approach, namely, that mental types are multiply realizable by various physical events (states) and are therefore irreducible to physical types. Nonetheless, there are significant differences between their positions such as the ontology of events and the Humean analysis of causation in terms of laws, assumptions that are fundamental for Davidson, but which Putnam eschews. Moreover, Davidson embraces the identity thesis for individual events (token identity), whereas Putnam, as we will see shortly, questions the very intelligibility of this application of the notion of identity. Given these differences, the version of non-reductive physicalism that Putnam defends is more radical than Davidson's; it is equally non-reductive but, arguably, less physicalistic.

Putnam opens his discussion of Kim with William James's example of "an automatic sweetheart" – "a soulless body . . . absolutely indistinguishable from a spiritually animated maiden." To the question of whether we should regard this automatic sweetheart as a human being, James replies (and Putnam concurs) "Certainly not." (TTC 73) And we can speculate that even if creatures like the automatic sweetheart would be identical to human beings in their physical constitution (an assumption that James does not make explicitly), they would not count as human beings by James and Putnam or, for that matter, by common-sense intuitions. According to Putnam, Kim's critique of Davidson amounts to the claim that Davidson has no choice but to accept the highly counter-intuitive conclusion that these soulless creatures are after all human. The reason is that on Kim's reading, "under Davidson's anomalous monism, mentality does no causal work."[17] "You would not disturb a single causal relation if you randomly and arbitrarily reassigned mental properties to events, or even removed mentality entirely from the world."[18] Kim's reading implies that Davidson denies not only the causal role of the mental, but also its explanatory role. He should deny, for

---

[17] Kim, *Supervenience and Mind*, 269.
[18] Kim, *Supervenience and Mind*, 269.

instance, that Mary's belief that it might rain (together with other beliefs of hers) explains her taking her umbrella. The mental, in other words, is epistemologically useless; a mere epiphenomenon. But if so, isn't Davidson forced to consider James's imaginary automatic sweetheart as human? And worse, isn't he forced to consider *actual* humans to be no different from such automata?

Kim's way out is to urge the *type* identity of mental and physical states, thereby allowing the reduction of the mental to the physical that Davidson repudiates. Once type-type identity is upheld, redistributing the mental over the physical, or removing it altogether, is no longer possible. We can therefore use the postulated type-type identity to reduce mental states and properties, as well as causal and explanatory relations among them, to states, properties and causal relations on the fundamental physical level. But this way out is unavailable to Putnam, whose non-reductionism is as firm as Davidson's. Putnam is aware that Kim's reductionist way of handling the scenario of mindless automata is not the only one. The verificationist, for example, could claim that, since the allegedly mindless creatures are, by hypothesis, indistinguishable from humans, there is no empirical test that could tell them apart, or certify the absence of the mental. But again, for Putnam, verificationism is not an option.[19]

Putnam proposes a different way of avoiding the inertness of the mental that Kim takes to follow from nonreductive physicalism: He casts doubt on the *intelligibility* of both versions of the identity thesis – type identity as well as token identity. The very notion of identity, he contends, and thus also the notion of reduction, have not been given a determinate meaning in this context. The "thought experiment" that was supposed to enhance our understanding – the scenario of redistributing or removing mental properties – lacks the context that would enable us to envisage it, answer questions about it, and so on. Compare this scenario, Putnam suggests, with "Cinderella's coach turned into a pumpkin" and you will realize that the only reason for the intelligibility of the latter is that we have a background that makes it accessible – we know it is a fairy tale, we are familiar with this genre, and we can imagine what would happen (in the fairy tale) under the circumstances described by that sentence.

> But if we detach the statement "sometimes coaches turn into pumpkins" from a very particular sort of context and try to discuss the question "What would happen if a coach turned into a pumpkin?" as if this were, for example, a serious scientific question, we would be talking nonsense. (TTC 83)

---

19 Putnam was (for a number of years) attracted to verificationism as a solution to the model-theoretic problem of reference, but when writing TTC, he had long given it up.

Putnam notes the difference between the alleged reducibility of the mental and scientific examples of reduction, such as the reduction of thermodynamics to statistical mechanics. In the latter, there are two developed theories – thermodynamics and mechanics – such that their concepts are correlated by technical definitions, and the laws of the reduced theory are derived from the fundamental, reducing, theory.[20] Since no theories that even remotely resemble such developed scientific theories exist in either folk psychology (supposedly the reduced body of knowledge) or in the computational research program (that is expected to generate the reducing theory), Putnam concludes that the notions of identity and reduction have not been made fully intelligible.

To justify this claim, Putnam summarizes the major characteristics of his conception of meaning – externalism, the division of linguistic labor, context sensitivity, and the role of the environment – and shows that Kim's arguments are incompatible with this conception. For example, Kim thinks of mental states as internal, involving solely the speaker's brain, a view that is clearly at odds with externalism and the significance of the environment. In fact, Kim retains an early version of Putnam's functionalism, a version that, as we have seen, Putnam criticized on the basis of meaning-theoretic considerations. Since these considerations have been outlined above, we can conclude that it is Putnam sophisticated theory of meaning that is at the root of his rejection of both reductionism and physicalism.

IV More on Kim's Reductionism

In the reminder of this paper I would like to strengthen Putnam's critique of Kim by using a different line of reasoning. Unlike Putnam, I will not question the token identity of the mental with the physical, but like Putnam, I will defend Davidson's non-reductionism against Kim's arguments. Let me note, however, that whereas Davidson takes mental events, and only mental events, to be anomalous, my view is that the division between the lawful and the lawless does not coincide with the division between the physical and the mental. On the one hand, some mental events may well satisfy certain laws even under

---

20 The thermodynamic concepts of temperature, pressure, entropy, and so on, are defined in terms of mechanical properties of the fundamental particles that make up the substance in question and the laws of thermodynamics are derived from the laws of mechanics. For more on this example and the question of whether it exemplifies successful reduction, see the next section.

their mental description. On the other hand, there are concepts (and types of events) that, though not mental, cannot be captured by physical laws. Clearly, whether mental or not, concepts that lie outside the jurisdiction of physics pose a threat to the reductionist program. As we will see, we do not have to turn to folk psychology for examples of irreducible concepts; concepts and laws that are irreducible to the fundamental level of physics can be found *within* physics. Davidson's main point – the sensitivity of nomological explanations to the descriptions we use – remains valid regardless of this caveat, playing a crucial role in what follows.

To get started, recall the two basic approaches to reduction, one in terms of the logical relations between theories, the other in terms of causation. The former, proposed by Ernst Nagel,[21] requires that the concepts of the reduced, higher-level, theory be defined by means of fundamental-level concepts, and that the higher-level laws be derived from the laws of the fundamental level.[22] In view of the paucity of examples that satisfy these strong requirements, they are often weakened in the following way. The definitions in question need not establish the synonymy of the defined (reduced) terms with the defining terms, but rather, the definitions can be empirical laws (bridge laws) establishing co-extensionality rather than identity. And the laws derived from fundamental-level laws need not be identical to the laws of the reduced (higher-level) theory, but rather, it suffices that the latter constitute good-enough approximations of the fundamental laws. The fundamental laws can, for example, yield a probabilistic version of the laws of the reduced theory, as in the derivation of thermodynamics from statistical mechanics.

The second approach to reduction, focusing on causation, takes reduction to show that underlying the causal relations at higher levels are causal relations at the fundamental level. When reduction of this kind is achieved, genuine causation exists only at the fundamental level. Given the lack of consensus on the meaning of causation, the causal approach to reduction is more ambiguous than the Nagelian approach. For instance, depending on whether we understand causation in terms of lawful regularities, the two approaches to reduction can be seen as competing or complementary. In any event, on both approaches, successful reduction makes higher-level theories (in principle, even if not in practice) redundant. Reduction*ism*, in turn, (on either account) seeks to reduce *all* higher-level theories (and phenomena) to the most basic level of fundamental

---

21 Ernst Nagel, *The Structure of Science* (London: Routledge and Kegan Paul, 1961), Ch. 11.

22 This formulation may not be faithful to the letter of Nagel's account, but is consonant with its sprit. Note that I am only discussing what Nagel refers to as "heterogeneous reduction." (*The Structure of Science*, 342).

physics. Although the foregoing summary of reduction is highly schematic, it suffices to enable us to address the concerns that motivate Kim's critique of nonreductive physicalism.[23]

Let us distinguish between types of relations that may obtain between different levels, or between the laws operative at those levels. Consider a fundamental level F and a higher level H. At the outset, we should note that the laws of F and the laws of H can be consistent or inconsistent with each other. As already mentioned, there are actually very few cases where higher-level theories are rigorously consistent with lower-level ones; typically, the laws of the basic level contradict those of the higher level.[24] But let us agree to settle for a weaker condition than perfect consistency – one theory being consistent with a good-enough approximation of the other – and assume that this condition is satisfied in the case of F and H. There are still at least three possibilities:

1. Reduction: All H-laws can be reduced to F-laws, so that H-laws are eliminated in favor of F-laws. In this case H-laws are redundant, and phenomena on H are deemed epiphenomena.
2. Lacunae: There are H-laws that cover (predict and explain) phenomena that F-laws do not cover (lacunae).
3. Overdetermination: There are H-laws that are irreducible to F-laws, but provide alternative predictions and explanations of phenomena that F-laws suffice to explain. Being entailed by two distinct sets of laws, these phenomena are thus overdetermined.

---

23 As Thomas Nickles, "Two Concepts of Intertheoretic Reduction," *Journal of Philosophy* 70 (1973): 181–201, observed, on a different (and indeed, opposite) usage of the notion of reduction, common among physicists, it is the fundamental theory that is reduced to the higher-level theory, meaning that the former converges on the latter in the limit. Thus, whereas the philosopher would take Newtonian mechanics to be reducible to the special theory of relativity at velocities much lower than that of light ($v \ll c$), the physicist might say that special relativity reduces to Newtonian mechanics. I will use "reduction" in the philosophers' sense, which is more apt for discussing the problems that concern us here.

24 This is clearly the situation in statistical mechanics – the reductionists' favorite paradigm case – but it is also what happens in simpler cases that are usually thought of in terms of generalization rather than reduction. Strictly speaking, Newtonian mechanics contradicts Galileo's law of free fall, but the affinity between the two theories' respective predictions for small enough terrestrial distances induces us to think of Galileo's law as an instance of Newton's more general law.

And similar relations can be formulated in terms of causality:

1. Reduction: All H-causes are actually F-causes, hence H-causes are redundant.
2. Lacunae: Some H-causes bring about effects that have no F-cause.
3. Overdetermination: Some H-causes, though irreducible to F-causes (that is, though not identical to any F-cause), bring about effects that F-causes also suffice to bring about.

Denying the possibility of lacunae and overdetermination, reductionists see only the first option as viable. Their reasoning involves the deterministic assumption of the physical closure of the basic level: the assumption that every basic-level event is determined (predictable, explicable) by the laws and initial conditions (or boundary conditions) of the system at that level.[25] This deterministic assumption only holds for closed systems, and is valid only for classical theories, not quantum mechanics. Nevertheless, if, for argument's sake, the assumption of physical closure is accepted, lacunae and overdetermination are ruled out. Reductionism is vindicated, or so it seems.

Are there any examples of the failure of reduction in physics? We saw that in the context of the philosophy of mind, multiple realizability has been taken by both Putnam and Davidson to suggest such failure. Note that neither of them actually demonstrated the multiple realizability of the mental; its role in their arguments is that of an assumption, or a conclusion derived from some other philosophical thesis, such as functionalism. Multiple realizability, however, is well-established and quite common in physics.[26] For example, macrostates in statistical mechanics – states characterized by macroproperties such as temperature, pressure entropy and so on – are multiply-realized by microstates. In particular, the entropy of a macrostate corresponds neither to a specific micro-property, nor to an average over micro-properties, but rather to the *number* of microstates belonging to that macrostate (or the volume in phase space that those microstates occupy), and thus to the probability of the macrostate. The concept of entropy therefore involves the higher-level concept of macrostate essentially, that is, it cannot be defined solely in terms of micro-properties. Furthermore, by singling out the *size* of a macrostate as its most significant physical property, this understanding of entropy highlights the remarkable indifference of macro-phenomena to the physical properties of individual microstates. Consequently, statistical-mechanical explanations of macro-phenomena such as the stability of one

---

25 Determinism does not actually guarantee predictability, a point further addressed below.

26 Scientists do not often use this philosophical term, but are aware of the many-one relation to which it refers.

macrostate – equilibrium – relative to others, or the limit on the efficiency of heat engines, are not based solely on laws operative at the fundamental level, but require higher-level concepts and laws.

The multiple realizability of macrostates in statistical mechanics illustrates Davidson's observation that the various descriptions of an event determine the types it might belong to, and therefore also determine the laws under which it can be subsumed. It makes perfect sense for an event to instantiate the laws of physics under one of its descriptions, and fail to do so under others. And we may now add that it also makes sense for an event to instantiate one law under one of its descriptions, and a different law under an alternative description (provided these laws are consistent with each other), an option Davidson did not consider.[27] Consider a system that, at a certain moment, is in a microstate belonging to the equilibrium macrostate. If characterized as a type of microstate, i.e., (per impossibile) in terms of the precise positions and momenta of its trillions of particles, that microstate and the subsequent evolution of the system can be subsumed under the laws of mechanics. But on its own, this description will tell us nothing about, let alone explain, the system's macrostate, for instance, it won't tell us the system is in a state of equilibrium. To explain the stability of this particular macrostate and the ramifications of this stability for the system's subsequent development, we must adduce the system under its macro-description, and the laws operative at the macro-level. In other words, the behavior of macrostates *qua macrostates* cannot be explained by the fundamental laws of the micro-level. By the same token, causal constraints on macro-level processes, constraints that determine which macro-level changes are more probable than others, are *additional* to the causal constraints characteristic of the micro-level. That there are such additional constraints does not attest to overdetermination of micro-events or to any lacunae at the micro-level. Rather, the additional laws and constraints involve *new*, higher-level, types, about which the fundamental laws are silent. As long as the laws applicable to these new types are consistent with the fundamental laws, there is no violation of the physical closure of the fundamental level.[28] These considerations, I should stress, remain valid even if

---

27 The consistency of statistical mechanics with the fundamental laws of physics remains an open problem, but here we can assume that it can be solved. The problem pertains primarily to the directionality of the second law, an issue that is not crucial for the present argument.

28 A deck of cards illustrates the same point. Individual series are equi-probable, but under the higher-level concepts of ordered and disordered decks, we can explain why disordered decks are more probable. This explanation does not conflict with, or invalidate, or render superfluous, the detailed explanation of how, by means of a number of specific steps, we get from one particular series to another.

macrostates supervene on microstates, namely, even if no change in the system's macrostate can occur without change in its microstate as well. Supervenience ensures that any transition from one macrostate to another is, *ipso facto*, also a transition from one microstate to another. It also ensures that every microstate belongs to a single macrostate, so that if we could identify the two microstates in question, the identity of the corresponding macrostates would also be fixed. Yet without the additional information about the relative size of these macrostates – information that is foreign to the micro-level – no explanation of their behavior *qua macrostates* can be gleaned from the laws of the fundamental level.

It is often thought that the fact that each macrostate is realized by a microstate suffices to establish the reducibility of macrostates. But this is a category mistake. A system that is in a particular macrostate (at a particular moment) is also in a particular microstate, that is, it instantiates both a macrostate and a microstate, but this identity falls short of reduction in both the logical and the causal senses of the term. Insofar as reduction pertains to laws operative on macrostates, no reduction is achieved by pinpointing the microstates that realize them. Insofar as it pertains to causal relations at the macro-level, the instantiating microstate in itself is likewise uninformative. If, for example, the stability of a macrostate is considered causally relevant to the macrostate's response to small perturbations, this causal efficacy cannot be ascribed to the particular microstate that happens to instantiate the stable macrostate at a particular moment. The fact that a small perturbation would alter the microstate, while most probably leaving the system in the same macrostate, is essential to our understanding of macro-phenomena. Such ascription of causal efficacy to macrostates does not entail that there are lacunae at the micro-level, or deficits in its physical closure. Concern about overdetermination is likewise misplaced. Macrostates are indeed insensitive to the precise nature of their realizing microstates; numerous *other* microstates would have produced the very same macro-behavior. This overdetermination, however, is not present at the level of microsrates and micro-events: only macrostates are multiply realizable, and thus overdetermined, in this way. The apprehensiveness regarding an alleged incompatibility between macro-level causality and the physical closure of the fundamental level is, again, unwarranted.

With this example in mind, we can now turn to arguments that, seeking to establish full-blown reductionism, purport to demonstrate the inconsistency of higher-level causation. Kim, as we have seen, focuses on Davidson's argument against the reducibility of the mental, but if valid, his arguments should also apply, *mutatis mutandis*, to inter-level relations in physics. Kim sees non-reductivism as dualism, albeit a dualism of properties, not substances:

> Nonreductive physicalism . . . consists of two characteristic theses of non-reductionism: its ontology is physical monism, the thesis that physical entities and their mereological aggregates are all that there is; but its "ideology" is anti-reductionist and dualist, consisting in the claim that psychological properties are irreducibly distinct from the underlying physical and biological properties. Its dualism is reflected in the belief that, though physically irreducible, psychological properties are genuine properties nonetheless, as real as underlying physical-biological properties.

> I shall argue that non-reductive physicalism and its more generalized companion, emergentism, are vulnerable to similar difficulties [i.e., similar to those of traditional dualism, YBM]; in particular it will be seen that the physical causal closure remains very much a problem within the stratified ontology of non-reductivism. Non-reductive physicalism, like Cartesianism, founders on the rocks of mental causation.[29]

Furthermore, Kim construes his opponent as claiming that "mentality . . . takes on a causal life of its own and begins to *exercise causal influence "downward" to affect what goes on in the underlying physical-biological processes.*"[30] Kim is arguing, then, that the danger ensuing from non-reductive physicalism is downward (higher-level to lower-level) causation. Let us take a closer look at this argument. Suppose, with Kim, that a higher-level property M is causally efficacious with respect to another higher-level property M* and suppose further that these higher-level properties are instantiated by fundamental properties P and P*. According to Kim,

> We seem to have two distinct and independent answers to the question, "Why is this instance of M* present?" *Ex hypothesi*, it is there because an instance of M caused it; that's why it's there. But there is another answer: it's there because P* physically realizes M* and P* is instantiated on this occasion. I believe these two stories about the presence of M* on this occasion create a tension.[31]

He continues:

> Is it plausible to suppose that the joint presence of M and P* is responsible for the instantiation of M*? No; because this contradicts the claim that M* is physically realized by P*. . . . This claim implies that P* alone is sufficient to bring about M*.[32]

Here, Kim conflates the relation of instantiation, which, for any specific case, is an *identity*, with that of causation, which is a relation between two different events. P* is not, as Kim contends, the cause sufficient to bring about M*, but rather an instantiation of M*. The cause of P* (on Kim's own assumptions) is a *different* micro-event, P, and the relation between them may be lawful and

---

29 Kim, *Supervenience and Mind*, 339.
30 Kim, *Supervenience and Mind*, 349; emphasis in original.
31 Kim, *Supervenience and Mind*, 351.
32 Kim, *Supervenience and Mind*, 352.

deterministic. P (rather than P*) is therefore also the cause of *this* instance of M*. So there is no overdetermination. As we saw, it is possible, and consistent with fundamental physics, that the causal relation between P and P* will not provide a good account of the relation between M and M*. This does not attest to any explanatory lacunae at the basic level, but merely to a change in our explanandum. We have moved from explaining the relation between P and P* to explaining the relation between M and M*. The latter relation, involving different types of events than the former, might be governed by different laws.

Kim, perhaps misled by the upward/downward metaphor, has saddled his opponent with an image of the higher level/basic level structure as akin to a duplex whose upstairs occupants meddle in the affairs of their downstairs counterparts. (Note that here it is the reductionist who slips back into dualism!) This account is a misunderstanding of Davidson: there are no interacting neighbors. Higher levels, as levels of description, are linked to lower levels by various kinds of identities, not by causal connections that can intervene in the causal network at the lower levels.

Kim adduces another argument against the causal efficacy of higher-level properties. It is based on a principle he calls the "Causal Inheritance Principle":

> If mental property M is realized in a system at t in virtue of physical realization base P, the causal powers of *this instance of M* are identical with the causal powers of P.[33]

In one sense the principle is trivial. The causal powers of this instance of M are indeed the causal powers of the physical state that "realizes" it, but this is true simply because this instance of M *is* a P state, so that there is only one entity exerting whatever causal influence it has. The idiom of inheritance, though, is misleading, suggesting two distinct entities, one of which inherits something from the other. Might the inheritance principle have a less trivial formulation, for instance, the principle that the causal powers of M are "inherited by" every physical state that realizes it? But on this reading, the principle is wrong. In statistical mechanics, we saw, the causal efficacy of macrostates qua macrostates (and their explanatory import) is not inherited by every microstate that realizes them. My conclusion is that, Kim's arguments notwithstanding, nonreductive physicalism is perfectly consistent with the physical closure of the fundamental level.

Having outlined the limits of reduction even in physics, I would like to turn to a claim made by Gilbert Ryle in *The Concept of Mind* and with which Putnam would certainly agree.

---

33 Kim, *Supervenience and Mind*, 326; emphasis in original.

> The fear that theoretically minded persons have felt lest everything should turn out to be explicable by mechanical laws is a baseless fear. . . . Physicists may one day have found the answer to all physical questions, but not all questions are physical questions.[34]

A parallel claim, more germane to the subject of reduction, is that not all concepts are physical concepts. Many physicalists take the existence of non-physical concepts for granted, but since radical physicalists (reductionists) have challenged the existence of such concepts, insisting on their reducibility to physical concepts, the issue deserves our attention.[35]

As Davidson has argued, there is an essential correspondence between scientific laws and the concepts (predicates, types, descriptions) they invoke. Scientific explanation is sensitive to the descriptions we use and the categories these descriptions refer to. Description-sensitivity does not render science subjective or arbitrary. On the contrary, by identifying the categories linked by natural laws, we can distinguish scientific representations of reality from non-scientific representations. In *Fact, Fiction, and Forecast*, Goodman pointed to *projectability* as the salient feature of scientific laws, the feature that distinguishes them from accidental regularities. The projectability of laws, however, is inseparable from the entrenchment of the predicates they use. Through his celebrated grue paradox,[36] Goodman shows that "all emeralds are grue," though at first glance analogous to "all emeralds are green," fails the projectability test due to the poor entrenchment of "grue." For simplicity, we can also speak of the projectability of concepts, referring to their appearance in projectable laws.[37]

There is no need to go as far as Goodman's "grue"-some predicates, or to confine the discussion to the mental, as per Davidson's anomalous monism, to find examples of concepts (predicates) that defy lawlikeness and projectability. Consider a stop sign. It is certainly a physical object and belongs to the category of physical objects. It satisfies the laws of physics and does not threaten to violate any laws or confound causal relations at the fundamental level. Nevertheless, there is no physical category that corresponds to the higher-level category

---

34 Gilbert Ryle, *The Concept of Mind* (London: Hutchinson, 1949), 74.

35 See, for example, Meir Hemmo and Orly Shenker, "Flat Physicalism" *Theoria* (forthcoming 2021), and Meir Hemmo and Orly Shenker, "Why Functionalism Is a Form of 'Token-Dualism'," in: *Levels of Reality in Science and Philosophy: Re-Examining the Multi-Level Structure of Reality*, edited by Meir Hemmo, Ioannidis Stavros, Orly Shenker, and Gal Vishne. (Cham: Springer forthcoming 2022).

36 Nelson Goodman, *Fact, Fiction, and Forecast* (Cambridge MA: Harvard University Press, 1955), Chapter 3.

37 See Abe Stone's insightful "On Scientific Method as a Method for Testing the Legitimacy of Scientific Concepts," *Reviews of Contemporary Philosophy* 8 (2009): 13–48. It notes, e.g., that even the paradigmatic example of a black raven may not pass the test for scientific concepts.

of stop signs. This is not just because stop signs are multiply realizable (which, of course, they are), but because the concept of a stop sign is open-ended and non-projectable. Any number of objects could serve as stop signs, and no physical property, structure, or set of specific laws, distinguishes stop signs from other objects. Examples of this kind suggest a refinement of Davidson's point about the mental. It is not a dramatic refinement that is needed, since after all, stop signs are symbols, and require an interpreting mind to understand them. Their open-endedness thus derives from their symbolic significance, and is ultimately predicated on mental activity. Such examples do suggest, however, that the crucial feature differentiating the lawful from the lawless in this context is symbolic meaning rather than mentality *per se*. Even if mental states such as fear, surprise, and so on were found to correspond to neurological types (which is, perhaps, not unreasonable) or physical types (which is far less plausible), the property of being frighte*ning* or surpris*ing* would still be open-ended and lawless. The same open-endedness and lawlessness also applies to the events and objects falling under these descriptions, for instance, unexpected meetings or frightening movies.

Looking back at the examples discussed in this paper, we can distinguish two kinds of problems confronting the reductionist assumption of the overarching sovereignty of the fundamental physical level. First, there were examples from physics where higher-level phenomena are subsumed under higher-level concepts and laws foreign to the fundamental level. Here stratification, supervenience, multiple realization, and the insensitivity of higher-level patterns to lower-level detail, play an essential role. While these cases do not illustrate lawlessness *tout court*, they do highlight the limited explanatory import of fundamental laws (or fundamental causal relations) and the indispensability of higher-level laws (or higher-level causal relations). Secondly, there is a radical mode of lawlessness manifested by open-ended, unprojectable concepts. Both kinds were shown to be compatible with determinism and the physical closure assumption.

The alternative line of reasoning outlined in this section of the paper runs parallel to Putnam's arguments described in the previous section and reaches the same conclusion. Realism commits us neither to the naïve view that there is a single description of the world that is correct, nor to the idea that every correct descriptions must be given in the language of fundamental physics. Moreover, the legitimacy and usefulness of a variety of descriptions, not all of which refer to physical concepts and physical categories speak against reductionism.

Putnam's summarized this conclusion succinctly in the final lecture of his mythological course on non-scientific knowledge:

> This talk of "limning the true and ultimate structure of reality" I believe to be nonsense. We are committed to an open plurality of ways of describing, ways of conceiving, ways of talking, ways of thinking: that, if you like, is pluralism.[38]

---

[38] Hilary Putnam, "To Think with Integrity," *The Harvard Review of Philosophy* 8 (2000): 9.

Maximilian de Gaynesford
Balance in *The Golden Bowl:* Attuning Philosophy and Literary Criticism

Abstract: This chapter argues that Henry James' treatment of balancing in *The Golden Bowl*, to which Putnam draws attention, calls for the attunement of philosophy and literary criticism. The process may undermine Putnam's own reading of the novel, but it also finds new reasons to endorse what his reading was meant to deliver: the confidence that philosophy and thoughtful appreciation of literature have much to contribute to each other, and the conviction that morality can incorporate (Kantian) seriousness about rules alongside (Aristotelian) sensitivity to character and situation.

I

I.1

Philosophy and thoughtful appreciation of literature have much to contribute to each other.[1] Hilary Putnam held this view with considerable enthusiasm, though his advocacy is not much remarked in studies of his work.[2] A pity perhaps, but predictable when analytic philosophers still have to defend their engagement with literature as serious philosophy. Putnam does so with earnest intent on a variety of occasions[3] and particularly in three investigations: his

---

[1] This paper is about *The Golden Bowl* by Henry James. Since the two foremost versions of the novel differ, and in ways that are particularly relevant to what follows, in-text page references will be to both versions in their currently-available editions: (a) "1905" represents the first English version, available in the Oxford World Classics series, edited by Virginia Llewellyn Smith (Repr., Oxford: Oxford University Press, 1999) and (b) "1909" represents the New York version, available in the Penguin Classics series, edited by Ruth Bernard Yeazell (Repr., London: Penguin, 2009).

[2] A useful foundation is laid in James Conant's reflections on the significance of Stanley Cavell's work for Putnam; see his "Introduction" to *Realism with a Human Face*, edited by James Conant (London: Harvard University Press, 1990), lvii–lxxix.

[3] Beside papers cited in the course of this chapter, they include Hilary Putnam, "The Craving for Objectivity," in *Realism with a Human Face*, edited by James Conant (London: Harvard University Press, 1990): 120–31 and "An Interview with Putnam," *Cogito* 3, no. 2 (1989): 85–91.

https://doi.org/10.1515/9783110769210-014

account of Henry James' *The Golden Bowl*,[4] his study of Pope's *Essay on Man*,[5] and his examination of attitudes towards literature and science.[6]

Central to Putnam's advocacy is his belief that moral thinking requires "reasoning in the full sense of the word," something that "involves not just the logical faculties, in the narrow sense, but our full capacity to imagine and feel, in short, our full sensibility."[7] And he thinks reasoning "in the full sense" requires literature. For "the sorts of descriptions that we need" in "situations requiring ethical evaluation" are – adopting a phrase from Iris Murdoch – "descriptions in the language of a 'sensitive novelist.'"[8] Putnam gives individual character to this overall position in various ways. Particularly significant is his conviction about the two-way nature of the dependency here. We need to appreciate literature to engage in moral reasoning, but equally we need to engage in moral reasoning to appreciate just why it is that we need literature.[9] Putnam also takes a careful stance on knowledge, cautioning that it is "wrong either to say that novels give knowledge of man or to say categorically that they do not."[10] We should say instead that novels "give us what we need if we are to *gain* any moral knowledge." Moreover, he urges care in specifying the kind of knowledge gained. It is not empirical but conceptual knowledge, by which he means knowledge of possibilities. What we learn from novels, for example, is *what it would be like if* the world were as it looks to a particular person, *how someone could possibly think that* the world is like this, and so on.[11]

Putnam's position on literature guides us without being particularly limiting. Indeed, it offers considerable leeway, as we shall see. One can adopt it in examining the novel to which Putnam himself gives the closest attention –

---

4 See Hilary Putnam, "Taking Rules Seriously: A Reply to Martha Nussbaum," *New Literary History* 15, no. 1 (1983): 193–200, reprinted in *Realism with a Human Face*, edited by James Conant, 193–200 (London: Harvard University Press, 1990). References to 1990 version.

5 See Hilary Putnam, "Pope's *Essay on Man* and Those 'Happy Pieties'," in *Pursuits of Reason: Essays in Honor of Stanley Cavell*, edited by Ted Cohen, Paul Guyer and Hilary Putnam, 13–20 (Lubbock: Texas Tech University Press, 1993), reprinted in Hilary Putnam, *Words and Life*, edited by James Conant, 513–522 (Cambridge, MA: Harvard University Press, 1994). References to 1994 version.

6 See Hilary Putnam, "Literature, Science and Reflection," *New Literary History* 7, no. 1 (1976): 483–491, reprinted in Hilary Putnam, *Meaning and the Moral Sciences*, 81–94 (London: Routledge and Kegan Paul, 1978). References to 1978 version.

7 Putnam, "Literature, Science and Reflection," 86.

8 "Objectivity and the Science/Ethics Distinction," in Hilary Putnam, *Realism with a Human Face*, edited by James Conant (London: Harvard University Press, 1990), 166.

9 Putnam, "Literature, Science and Reflection," 94.

10 Putnam, "Literature, Science and Reflection," 89.

11 Putnam, "Literature, Science and Reflection," 89–90.

Henry James' *The Golden Bowl*[12] – and yet arrive at very different views of its "situations requiring ethical evaluation," of what it gives us to "imagine and feel," and hence of its contributions to "conceptual knowledge."

I.2

On Putnam's reading of *The Golden Bowl*, there is a "fundamental asymmetry" to the four people on which the story focuses.[13] On one side, there is the American millionaire art-collector Adam Verver and his daughter Maggie. On the other side, there is Maggie's friend, the cosmopolitan Charlotte Stant, and the noble Italian Prince Amerigo. It is not just that Adam and Maggie are both wealthy, naturally reserved and want association with a brilliant and active society, while Charlotte and Amerigo are both poor and need to marry well to sustain their social brilliance. We would be "missing everything" about the novel, Putnam

---

12 Putnam had practical reasons for writing on this novel – to reply to Martha Nussbaum – but they seem fortuitous (if also felicitous), given what is worthier of note: the particular sources of resonance which make the choice of *The Golden Bowl* seem acutely apt. Chief amongst these is the crux of the novel to which the shopkeeper gives voice, "But if it's something you can't find out, isn't it as good as if it were nothing?" (1905, 86; 1909, 108) and which might serve equally well as a crux uniting Putnam's philosophical concerns on a range of issues, which we can see at once if we let the "it" stand for: (i) a third truth-value ("Three-Valued Logic" (1957), reprinted in *Mathematics, Matter, and Method: Philosophical Papers*, Vol. 1, 166–173 (Cambridge: Cambridge University Press, 1975)); (ii) human subjective experience ("Minds and Machines" (1960), reprinted in *Mind, Language, and Reality: Philosophical Papers*, Vol. 2, 362–385 (Cambridge: Cambridge University Press, 1975)); (iii) analytic statements ("The Analytic and the Synthetic" (1962), reprinted in *Mind, Language, and Reality: Philosophical Papers*, Vol. 2, 33–69 (Cambridge: Cambridge University Press, 1975)); (iv) the mental ("Brains and Behavior" (1963), reprinted in *Mind, Language, and Reality*, 325–341); (v) consciousness ("Robots: Machines or Artificially Created Life?" (1964), reprinted in *Mind, Language and Reality*, 386–407); (vi) the foundations of mathematics ("Mathematics without Foundations" (1967), reprinted in *Mathematics, Matter, and Method*, 295–313); (vii) semantics ("Is Semantics Possible?" (1970), reprinted in *Mind, Language, and Reality*, 139–152); (viii) meaning ("Explanation and Reference" (1973), reprinted in *Mind, Language, and Reality*, 196–214); (ix) reference ("The Refutation of Conventionalism" (1974), reprinted in *Mind, Language, and Reality*, 153–191); (x) testimony ("Meaning and Knowledge," in *Meaning and the Moral Sciences*, 1–80 (London: Routledge and Kegan Paul, 1978); and so on. That "good" might equally be replaced by "bad" in the shopkeeper's remark goes unnoted but seems significant.

13 Putnam, "Taking Rules Seriously," 199.

thinks, unless we see that the Adam-Maggie pair are essentially virtuous characters, whereas the Amerigo-Charlotte pair are not.[14]

This is visible enough on the surface, Putnam thinks. While Maggie and Adam retire back into comfortable seclusion after their respective marriages, Charlotte and Amerigo rekindle an old affair. What the former do "is open and above board," "they make clear what their motives and intentions are," whereas what the latter do is "done in secret."[15]

But Putnam offers a deeper account of the asymmetry, to which the key is the notion of balancing. Charlotte and Amerigo treat moral thinking as "a balancing act," he says, whereas Adam and Maggie refuse to do this.[16] This is crucial to Putnam because he thinks that to conceive of moral thinking as a balancing act is "precisely not to think morally at all."[17] It is in this light that Putnam interprets and justifies what is notoriously the most difficult aspect of the novel to interpret and justify: Maggie's behaviour in the second half, where she manages to draw her husband Amerigo back into her marriage with him while removing Charlotte and her father from the scene, indeed from the continent.[18] Maggie has to deceive Charlotte to do this, causing her considerable anxiety by never quite confirming that she knows of the affair with her husband. Some find this behaviour hard to square with the requirements of virtue.[19] But Maggie does what she does to preserve two marriages. And, what is crucial, in Putnam's view: she resists the invitation to engage in a balancing act, matching loyalty to a friend against telling the truth "and regretfully having to violate one."[20]

---

14 Putnam, "Taking Rules Seriously," 199. Putnam treats this secrecy as of fundamental significance because "it depends on a fundamental violation of the idea of a community in which one does not treat people in ways to which they would not consent."

15 Putnam, "Taking Rules Seriously," 199.

16 Putnam, "Taking Rules Seriously," 198–200. Putnam says explicitly that he will offer a "reading" of the novel that "moves away from the conception of morality as a balancing act." (198) This is the overall theme of his paper: to show how a Kantian emphasis on "rules" and "exceptions" can resist the most harmful effect of focusing on "values" and "conflicts," namely that "the metaphor of balancing quickly gets the upper hand." (195).

17 Putnam, "Taking Rules Seriously," 195.

18 Robert Pippin calls this "the key issue." Robert Pippin, *Henry James and the Moral Imagination* (Cambridge: Cambridge University Press, 2000), 67.

19 For the closest and most determinedly scrupulous analysis of Maggie's actions, see Dorothea Krook, *The Ordeal of Consciousness in Henry James* (Cambridge: Cambridge University Press, 1962), 232–324.

20 Putnam, "Taking Rules Seriously," 200.

This is a sketch, but we can already appreciate how Putnam's reading of *The Golden Bowl* is meant to model his recommended approach to literature. He chooses Henry James as his Murdochian "sensitive novelist." What interests him in *The Golden Bowl* is the way James imaginatively re-creates moral perplexities by setting up particular situations that call for ethical evaluation. He shows how James' descriptions and reflections on these situations might enrich the sensibility of suitably receptive readers. Such readers should thereby acquire and exercise the ability to perceive and respond to nuances; for example, what it would be like if the world were as it looks to Maggie Verver and her father, how Charlotte and Amerigo could possibly think the world is as they take it to be, and so on. And this awareness of possibilities amounts to "conceptual knowledge," which in this case takes mutually supporting forms. On the one hand, readers are able to resist the temptation to conceive of moral thinking as a balancing act in appreciating that there is a fundamental asymmetry between these couples. On the other hand, readers are able to appreciate that (and how) there is this fundamental asymmetry in bringing themselves to resist the temptation to identify moral thinking as a balancing act.

To acquire such conceptual knowledge is to call on that "conscious criticism of ways of life" with which Putnam identifies moral reasoning. Specifically, it helps guard against what he regards as a comforting dogmatism in certain regions of moral philosophy: that we should renounce a characteristically "Kantian" appeal to universalist "rules" or "principles" and their "exceptions" in favour of a characteristically "Aristotelian" appeal to particularist "values" and "conflicts."[21] And the danger Putnam identifies here is precisely the tendency to treat moral thinking as a balancing act. If we allow a perfectly appropriate attentiveness to context to squash or sideline the appeal to rules and principles, it becomes overwhelmingly tempting, he thinks, to conceive of moral thinking in this way. And to do this is to give up on moral thinking.[22]

I.3

So far as I know, Putnam is unique in making balancing central to *The Golden Bowl*.[23] To do so effectively requires what criticism of James so often lacks: apt

---

[21] Fairly or not, Putnam explicitly associates Martha Nussbaum with this view; it was to her that he was replying with his reading of *The Golden Bowl* in "Taking Rules Seriously."

[22] Putnam, "Taking Rules Seriously," 195.

[23] The commentaries ignore the theme, beginning with the very first: James' own "Preface," written for the New York edition of 1909, four years after the book's first publication. But

quotation and close analysis of the writing itself.[24] Though I shall disagree with Putnam about secondary matters, this seems to me a deeply valuable insight. So my aim in what follows is to explore it, being guided by Martha Nussbaum's dictum: that if a philosophical study of a work of literature is to "make any contribution worth caring about," it must really do philosophy, it must really do literary criticism, and it must explain why philosophers – and literary critics, we ought to add – should care.[25] I use "literary critics," as Nussbaum does, with a certain generality, to include all who use critical attentiveness to appreciate a literary work.

More specifically, I shall try to show (i) that James' treatment of balancing in *The Golden Bowl* is something both philosophers and literary critics should care about, (ii) that what matters to philosophy here cannot properly be dealt with or appreciated without doing literary criticism of the novel, and (iii) that what matters to literary criticism here cannot properly be dealt with or appreciated without doing philosophy. To summarise these claims in a slogan, James's treatment of balancing in *The Golden Bowl* calls for the attunement of philosophy and literature.[26]

---

whether or not this particular absence is evidence – and of what exactly – must remain unclear, since the "Preface" begins with James' famous remark about "a certain indirect and oblique view of my presented action" (1909, xxxiv), and though this is ostensibly a description of his "mode of treatment" in the novel itself, it seems knowingly and self-consciously apt as a description of his mode in this very "Preface." Elsewhere, there is simply this passing comment in Leon Edel's biography of James: "In *The Golden Bowl* the energies of the characters, and of the work, have as their goal an extraordinary attempt to maintain balance – without rocking the boat." *Henry James: The Master 1901–1916* (New York: Avon Books, 1972), 212.

24 For two exemplary exceptions, see Christopher Ricks' observation on James' use of "innocence" and related words in his "Introduction" to *What Maisie Knew* (London: Penguin, 2010), xx–xxiv; and Ian Watts, "The First Paragraph of *The Ambassadors*: An Explication," *Essays in Criticism* 10, no. 3 (1960): 250–274, reprinted in *Henry James: Modern Judgements*, edited by Tony Tanner, 283–303 (London: Macmillan, 1969). References to reprinted version. One caveat: Watt, usually so finely discriminating, is content to join with others in offhand talk of "the abstractness and indirection of James's style" which he ascribes to "the multiplicity of his vision." (292) I think this is exactly wrong – and of Watt's own analysis of the first paragraph of *The Ambassadors* helps show why it is wrong: it is not James's style which is abstract, even in this late period, but that he often takes abstract objects as the subject of what he (quite concretely) writes; and it is not that his style is indirect, but that he often takes indirection (the indirections of his characters) as his subject, writing about it as directly as can be conceived.

25 See Martha C. Nussbaum, "Stages of Thought," *The New Republic*, May 2008. Nussbaum has studies of Shakespeare as her focus, but her point is evidently meant generally.

26 See my "What is Attunement?" in Maximilian de Gaynesford, *The Rift in The Lute: Attuning Poetry and Philosophy*, 1–33. (Oxford: Oxford University Press, 2017).

Attunement of this kind, I argue elsewhere, should draw particularly on analytic philosophy.[27] I hope this is no cause for alarm.[28] Indeed, I hope Putnam might have approved, since it attempts modestly to re-shape analytic philosophy from within.[29] More specifically, I argue that attunement requires a speech act approach.[30] Here it may be that James himself would have approved, since he recommends in his "Preface" to *The Golden Bowl* that we "recognise betimes that to 'put' things is very exactly and responsibly and interminably to do them," and that "Our expression of them, and the terms on which we understand that, belong as nearly to our conduct and our life as every other feature of our freedom."[31] But there is potential for confusion here. For anyone familiar with work in the speech act tradition is likely to assume that adopting such an approach to literature will – as J.L. Austin, John Searle, and others do[32] – contrast spoken with written uses of language and treat the former as the paradigm and focus of attention while relegating the latter to secondary significance, deferring analysis of features peculiar to it, like punctuation, until the "standard" or "ordinary" features of speech have been well understood. This is not the approach that novels like *The Golden Bowl* require. To understand what they do, we need to understand punctuation. Overlooking it would prevent us taking seriously the call to attune literature and philosophy. My reasons for this bear directly on claims (i)–(iii), and James' treatment of balancing provides evidence in support, so we shall be reviewing it.

Putnam's own reading of *The Golden Bowl* raises many deep questions. On the more literary side, are these couples really asymmetric in the way Putnam suggests? And is the difference really grounded in the way they conceive of moral thinking? On the more philosophical side, do we really renounce moral thinking when we conceive of it as a balancing act? And are we really drawn to

---

27 Because this is what is most satisfying, therapeutic and efficient; see de Gaynesford, *The Rift in The Lute*, 12–14.

28 Simon Blackburn offers an amusing and acute rebuttal of some versions of the analytic philosopher stereotype in "Can an Analytic Philosopher Read Poetry?" in *The Philosophy of Poetry*, edited by John Gibson, 111–126 (Oxford: Oxford University Press, 2015).

29 See De Gaynesford, *The Rift in The Lute*, 24–26.

30 See De Gaynesford, *The Rift in The Lute*, 97–115.

31 1909, 21.

32 See J.L. Austin *How to Do Things With Words*, edited by J.O. Urmson and Marina Sbisà (Oxford: Clarendon Press, 1962), 60–61, 74; John Searle, *Speech Acts* (Cambridge: Cambridge University Press, 1969), 3–21. These passages give a characteristically speech act inflection to a very widely-held attitude, which is so grounded in analytic philosophy that foremost representatives present it as obvious and uncontroversial in instructional books on style: see Michael Dummett, *Grammar and Style* (London: Duckworth, 1993), 81.

conceive of it in this way when we appeal to particularist "values" and "conflicts"? More deeply still, and calling equally on philosophy and literary criticism, does the novel really stand out against treating moral thinking as a balancing act? All of these issues press for attention, and though I cannot deal fully and satisfyingly with them all in the scope of a single chapter, I shall attempt to say something about each.

II

II.1

"Balance" occurs so often in *The Golden Bowl* that it seems a preoccupation of James to fret the word.

"He felt therefore, just at present, as if his papers were in order, as if his accounts so balanced as they had never done in his life before and he might close the portfolio with a snap."[33] Thus James introduces Amerigo's subjective situation and his tenuous moral position at the very start of the novel. As the story darkens, he is still to be found musing on "a balance in his favour that he could pretty well, as a rule, take for granted."[34] He is someone whose mental habit is continually to think of things which will "redress the balance of his being so differently considered."[35] It is what others, like Maggie, are primed to see as going on in him: "she felt herself present at a process taking place rather deeper within him than the occasion, on the whole, appeared to require – a process of weighing something in the balance."[36] What is significant to him about meeting with Charlotte before his marriage to Maggie is that "his security hung in the balance."[37]

Other characters are similarly vulnerable: "It was a touch at which she again lost her balance, at which, somehow, the bottom dropped out of her recovered comfort."[38] Maggie is deeply affected by a balancing habit of mind. She

---

33 1905, 15; 1909, 38. The later version reduces the slight pause by removing the first two commas.

34 1905, 257; 1909, 284. Again, the later version removes these two commas.

35 1905, 13; 1909, 37.

36 1905, 318; 1909, 345.

37 1905, 43; 1909, 66.

38 1905, 207; 1909, 23. The earlier version involves itself touchingly in this loss of balance; we notice this more acutely when we compare it with the later version, which removes two of the commas and alters the word-order so as to create a flatter surface for the narrative voice to

tries to place others by reference to it: "Bearing in mind dear Amerigo . . . whom the homeliness in question didn't, no doubt, quite equally provide for – that would be, to balance, just in a manner Charlotte's very most charming function . . . ."[39] She is, even on relatively light-hearted matters, "not indifferent to her own opportunity to redress this balance."[40] It is what she likes about the thought of having both Charlotte and Fanny Assingham to hand: "as if the two would balance, one against the other"; "It would be like putting this friend into her scale to make weight – into the scale with her father and herself."[41] It is what Maggie and Charlotte are described as sharing in their sense of a place as "being vivid in its stillness," that "all its great objects" are "ordered and balanced."[42]

Balance most concerns Maggie in her own situation, as she becomes steadily aware: "that it was practically precarious, a matter of a hair's breadth for the loss of the balance."[43] "The happy balance that demanded this amount of consideration was truly thus, as by its own confession, a delicate matter."[44] "The balance persisted and triumphed" despite "a fresh distribution of the different weights"; "if they balanced they balanced – she had to take that."[45] In intense conversation with her father, when "It shook between them, this transparency, with their very breath," Maggie is described as "perched up before him on her vertiginous point and in the very glare of his observation," and there "she balanced for thirty seconds, she almost rocked: she might have been for the time, in all her conscious person, the very form of the equilibrium they were, in their different ways, equally trying to save."[46] In similarly intense congress with Amerigo, at the close of the novel, she feels "That consciousness in fact had a pang, and she balanced, intensely, for the lingering moment, almost with a terror of her endless power of surrender."[47]

---

progress sure-footedly upon: "It was a touch at which she again lost her balance, at which the bottom somehow dropped out of her recovered comfort."
39 1905, 233; 1909, 260.
40 1905, 349; 1909, 375.
41 1905, 370; 1909, 395.
42 1905, 477; 1909, 505.
43 1905, 310; 1909, 337.
44 1905, 310; 1909, 337.
45 1905, 351; 1909, 378.
46 1905, 494; 1909, 520.
47 1905, 555; 1909, 583. The later version removes three commas and adds an "and" so that the lingering is lessened: ". . . she balanced intensely for the lingering moment and almost with a terror . . .".

II.2

James evidently moves through different senses of "balance" when he uses the word. But we can discern an underlying structure here. The form that functions at a deep level to characterise both Amerigo and Maggie is that of balancing some thing against another thing. For Amerigo, this is primarily a matter of self-opinion, balancing what can be said to his credit and what cannot, and making sure that "on balance" he can retain a good opinion of himself. For Maggie, this is primarily a matter of social coordination, balancing relations between her father, her husband and her close friend, making sure they retain their "equilibrium."

Balance can involve two or more things, but there is a simpler form, involving just one thing, balanced in itself rather than against anything else. This simpler form – keeping *oneself* in balance, for example – functions at a deep level to characterise both Adam and Charlotte. The difference between them is the appearance of striving, the struggle to effect such balance, absent from Adam and all too present in Charlotte. As the novel progresses, we sense that Amerigo and Maggie are equally invested in this simpler form of balancing, but that it is not part of the way they present themselves to themselves. What commits Amerigo to the more complex form is his growing awareness of being divided against himself, so that he must work to retain his own good opinion, balancing one part of himself against another. What commits Maggie to the same form is what matters most to her, maintaining equilibrium between several different people whose happiness comes to conflict, so that she must balance the interests of some against that of others.

Around these forms, James works other senses of "balance," principally by drawing on what is *involved* in balancing. In balancing things, for example, one so places them that they "hang in the balance" and are "in suspense," which relates to a variety of further possibilities: pausing them, or risking them, or making them a source of anxiety, for example. All these senses are at work in the quoted presentations of Maggie as "balanced" in her intense conversations with her father and then her husband. Two further extensions of the theme are in play throughout the novel and take on emblematic form in the scene where Fanny Assingham holds up the golden bowl,[48] balances for a drawn-out hieratic

---

48 Earlier in the scene, when first introduced to it, Mrs. Assingham calls it "the gilt cup" (1905, 415; 1909, 441). The unconscious slight aptly prefigures the object's destruction at her hands (though one may feel there is something a little too convenient about the fact that, all unknowing, Mrs. Assingham nevertheless hits on an exactly symmetrical phrase for "the golden bowl").

moment, and then brings it down, dashing it to the floor "where she had the thrill of seeing it, with the violence of the crash, lie shattered."[49] First, in balancing things, one becomes aware of the weightiness of them – not just of the fact that they have weight, but of what weight they have – which relates to recognising their significance or their value. Second, in balancing things, one carries their weight, which relates to bearing a certain responsibility, taking on a certain duty. Thus this scene of destruction is aptly preceded by a balancing act, one that not only summons up and recalls all the various valuations of the golden bowl that have structured the novel up to this point, but represents a moment of judgement and decision, an assumption of responsibility for the acts that will follow:

> She went over it, looked at it afresh and yielded now to her impulse to feel it in her hands. She laid them on it, lifting it up, and was surprised, thus, with the weight of it – she had seldom handled so much massive gold. That effect itself somehow prompted her to further freedom and presently to saying: "I don't believe in this, you know."[50]

II.3

Here James makes the description imitate the action. The demonstrative "thus," particularly when raised by its surrounding commas, draws the reader into the act of weighing, so that balancing is not simply described but engaged in by the use of language.

Such mimetic balancing occurs throughout *The Golden Bowl*, though the general power of James' writing prevents it from being obtrusive,[51]

> so that, not to seem to understand where she couldn't accept, and not to seem to accept where she didn't approve, and could still less, with precipitation, advise, she invoked the

---

49 1905, 430; 1909, 454. The later version removes the commas and evens out the word-order so that it seems merely to describe the act of seeing something ("where she had the thrill of seeing it lie shattered with the violence of the crash") while the earlier version comes close to enacting that act. The significance of seeing and vision is discussed later on.

50 1905, 428; 1909, 453. The later version removes the commas around "thus."

51 And James' changes for the New York edition – as I have been noting – make it even less so. Editors who concentrate on the relatively superficial effect of such changes – Virginia Llewellyn Smith notes only that James' removal of commas gives sentences "a smoother rhythm" and "the text appears less broken up" ("Note on the Text" to *The Golden Bowl* by Henry James (Oxford: Oxford University Press, 1999), xxxiii) – miss the overall effect, which is to weaken the mimetic effort of the earlier version, its attempts to thrust the narrating voice within the enacting of the events it describes.

mere appearance of casting no weight whatever into the scales of her young friend's consistency.[52]

How carefully James balances his prose, which is itself balanced against the careful balancing in the thoughts being depicted, where both are done sufficiently self-consciously for him to invoke explicitly the image of balancing.

In evoking the act of balancing, James' punctuation is particularly punctilious, a subtle indicator of the way considerations may balance finely against every other:

> It further passed across him, as his imagination was, for reasons, during the time, unprecedentedly active, that he had, after all, gained more from women than he had ever lost by them; there appeared so, more and more, on those mystic books that are kept, in connection with such commerce, even by men of the loosest business habits, a balance in his favour that he could pretty well, as a rule, take for granted.[53]

Again, notice the punctuation here:

> The question of the amount of correction to which Charlotte has laid herself open rose and hovered, for the instant, only to sink, conspicuously, by its own weight; so high a pitch she seemed to give to the unconsciousness of questions, so resplendent a show of serenity she succeeded in making.[54]

The commas around "conspicuous" make the sinking itself conspicuous, and the semi-colon after "by its own weight" gives a weighty suspension that imitates a suspension in thought.

In these examples – and the novel is strewn with them – James' prose consciously develops an appreciation of the weight of words, and of the way that weight is felt, how it is allowed to fall, enabling us to appreciate the way certain words and phrases balance against others, reflecting the way that certain moral considerations balance against others, thus answering at depth to psychological plausibility, since we so often balance complex considerations by balancing the way we express them in language.

---

52 1905, 192; 1909, 217.

53 1905, 257; 1909, 284. The later version replaces commas with a dash at ". . . – as his imagination was, for reasons, during the time, unprecedentedly active – . . ." and loses them around "after all" and "as a rule." The punctuation that is left still subtly supports the balancing act, but some of the finer hesitancies go un-portrayed.

54 1905, 558; 1909, 587. The effect is comparable to that in a passage by J.L. Austin: "But now how, as philosophers, are we to proceed? One thing we might go on to do, of course, is to take it all back: another would be to bog, by logical stages, down." *How to Do Things With Words*, 13. The changes made to the later version here – where all but the last of the commas disappear – do seem to me openly regrettable.

This passage needs to be quoted in full, as the epitome of the method:

> *That* was at the bottom of her mind, that their equilibrium was everything, and that it was practically precarious, a matter of a hair's breadth for the loss of the balance. It was the equilibrium, or at all events her conscious fear about it, that brought her heart into her mouth; and the same fear was, on either side, in the silent look she and Amerigo had exchanged. The happy balance that demanded this amount of consideration was truly thus, as by its own confession, a delicate matter; but that her husband had also *his* habit of anxiety and his general caution only brought them, after all, more closely together. It would have been most beautifully, therefore, in the name of the equilibrium, and in that of her joy at their feeling so exactly the same about it, that she might have spoken if she had permitted the truth on the subject of her behaviour to ring out – on the subject of that poor little behaviour which was for the moment so very limited a case of eccentricity.[55]

Balance terms are very heavily used here: in order of their flow, "equilibrium"; "precarious"; "balance"; "equilibrium"; "on either side"; "balance"; "equilibrium"; "exactly the same." And the punctuation is equally heavy: across only four sentences, fifteen commas, two semi-colons and one dash. But the deployment is precisely purposeful, discriminating Maggie's way of separating out the various components of her thought into their essential elements and then weighing them up in relation to all the other elements. And the point is not simply about mimesis and James' technical skill. The fact that James does not simply describe balancing, as Maggie's approach to moral thinking, but engages in balancing, as a writer's approach to evaluating that thinking, gives endorsement to the practice, creating an articulated unity that applauds as it imitates the balancing in Maggie's thinking, the articulated unity of her moral thought.[56]

II.4

So James' treatment of balancing in *The Golden Bowl* has considerable dramatic significance. This gives literary critics reason enough to care about it. Reasons for philosophers to care are various, but those relevant to Putnam's position are equally clear. What he recommends as philosophically significant about *The*

---

55 1905, 310; 1909, 337. The changes to the later version are slight: only the commas around "after all" and "therefore" go.

56 Dorothea Krook identifies in James' late style its "power to reproduce, or rather to re-enact, every minute change in tone, pace and emphasis of the mind engaged in self-reflective discourse." (*The Ordeal of Consciousness in Henry James*, 390) I would only quibble that "re-enact" is too bound by the mimetic model, failing to capture those other occasions, vital to this late style, where the doing in the text is not a re-producing or re-presenting of an action but its own action, a doing that is unique and non-mimetic.

Golden Bowl is its imaginative descriptions of morally perplexing situations and the conceptual knowledge to be gained by reflecting on them. And balancing is central to both, as we have seen. It is not just the characters but James himself whose engagement in moral thinking takes, as we have seen, the form of balancing.

Once we grant (i) that James' treatment of balancing in *The Golden Bowl* is something both philosophers and literary critics should care about, it is a small step to the next claim (ii) that what matters to philosophy here cannot properly be dealt with or appreciated without doing literary criticism of the novel. For it is by doing such criticism that we come to see what is philosophically significant about balancing. It may seem a much greater step to claim (iii) that what matters to literary criticism here cannot properly be dealt with or appreciated without doing philosophy. If we have been doing well enough so far, why suppose literary criticism is not already admirably equipped to appreciate the dramatic significance of balancing in *The Golden Bowl*?

This is a natural objection, but it misleads about what is at stake. For it makes it look as if claim (iii) were denying that literary criticism is already sufficiently equipped. That is not the case. All the claim implies is that *if* literary criticism is already sufficiently equipped, it must already be engaged in doing philosophy. And now the step to this claim seems much more reasonable. For literary criticism quite clearly *is* already doing philosophy when it appreciates what is dramatically significant about balancing in the novel: that it represents the form that moral thinking can and, arguably, ought to take in engaging with morally perplexing situations.

III

III.1

If James' treatment of balancing in *The Golden Bowl* calls for the attunement of philosophy and literary criticism – as claims (i)–(iii) imply – what can be *done* with such attunement? The remainder of this paper will pursue one possibility.

Putnam's reading of *The Golden Bowl* presents us with a puzzle, a tension between claims, which we can express – necessarily roughly – in the following way.

(a) Putnam recommends *The Golden Bowl* as the kind of literature required for moral thinking if it is to amount to "reasoning in the full sense of the word";

(b) what Putnam takes from this novel is that to conceive of moral thinking as a balancing act is to give up on it;

(c) this novel conceives of moral thinking as, in part at least, a balancing act.

Suppose that we feel strongly moved to endorse each of these points; that we regard Putnam's considerations as persuasive about (a)–(b), and that we regard the novel itself as compelling about (c). We might claim that James is *not* actually directing us to conceive of moral thinking in terms of balancing; he does use the metaphor, but only ever to characterise the *wrong* approach to moral thinking. But this flies in the face of what we have seen: that characters are presented as acting well when they adopt balancing, that James approves of this, that his authorial voice adopts a balancing approach, and that his style reflects and supports the balancing acts of his characters. Alternatively, we might claim that the kind of balancing Putnam rejects is not the kind that James advocates. But again, this is not consistent with the textual evidence. No doubt we ought to distinguish various kinds of balancing: most importantly, perhaps, between that which consists in *weighing something up* and that which consists in *weighing one thing against another*. But we have seen examples of both these kinds of balancing, and others besides, each of which merits James' approval as acting well, eliciting the support of his authorial voice and use of language.

If we disregard these ways of resolving the tension, there are still several live options – indeed three of them, depending on which of the three claims we take issue with. I shall briefly describe each, focusing particularly on the price they exact, since this helps us appreciate what is involved in attunement.

The first option is to take issue with Putnam over (a). Given (b) and (c), we ought not to count *The Golden Bowl* as the kind of literature required for moral thinking if it is to amount to "reasoning in the full sense of the word." But this option threatens to make literature too insignificant in our philosophising. If we are convinced by Putnam's position on the value of literature, we have to be willing to give literature a real, effective role – standing ready to have our philosophising changed by it. The attitude that this first option reflects is the failure to treat literature seriously. Content to use literature merely as an illustration of already-decided philosophical views, philosophy employs literature only if it accords with those views.

The second option is to take issue with (c). Given (a) and (b), we might question whether *The Golden Bowl* really does conceive of moral thinking as in any way a balancing act. But the evidence we have reviewed is too strong: it is in this way that the characters and authorial voice conceive of such thinking.[57]

This leaves one last option: to take issue with Putnam over (b). Given (a) and (c), we ought not to think that conceiving of moral thinking as a balancing act is to give up on it. This is the best of the options, but we adopt it with caution: not to give literature *too* decisive a role in our philosophising (i.e. the opposite of the first option). If we are convinced by Putnam's outlook on literature, we have to be willing to give appreciation of *The Golden Bowl* a role, but one amongst other factors, with a willingness to question or correct the views presented by it.

III.2

All this makes one question pressing. Why is it that so acute a reader as Putnam, who sees the centrality of balancing in *The Golden Bowl*, believes – in the face of this novel – that to conceive of moral thinking as a balancing act is to give up on it? If we can answer this, we might be able to appreciate why he need not, and perhaps should not, believe this.

Putnam was under the influence of two considerations, I think, when he wrote on *The Golden Bowl*. Both relate to Martha Nussbaum, to whose reading of the novel Putnam responds with his own. The first is about vision and seeing. Putnam disagrees with Nussbaum about many aspects of her interpretation, but he endorses her view that vision, seeing, is central to the presentation of moral thought in the novel.[58] This is not surprising, perhaps. The claim is almost irresistibly appealing if one wants to make literary appreciation necessary

---

57 Moreover, this option threatens to make the novel more deeply pessimistic than even the most extreme commentators have thought it – that *none* of the characters reason morally. Indeed, the vision might be consciously self-defeating and nihilistic – that not even the authorial voice reasons morally. This is to take the deep questioning in which the novel engages beyond the point in which such questioning would have a point. If *none* of the characters (or the author) *ever* think morally, why bother ourselves with what the novel so clearly wants to keep us interested in asking: whether particular characters are thinking morally or virtuously on particular occasions?.

58 See in particular her "Flawed Crystals: James' *The Golden Bowl* and Literature as Moral Philosophy," in *Love's Knowledge: Essays on Philosophy and Literature* (Oxford: Oxford University Press, 1990), 130–131, 134, 136–137, 145 and "'Finely Aware and Richly Responsible': Literature and the Moral Imagination," in *Love's Knowledge*, 148, 150, 152, 157–158, 159–160, 163–164.

to morality and the life of virtue. For it enables one to move naturally and equably between reading a situation well and reading a novel well.[59]

What Putnam approves here he traces back to Iris Murdoch, and particularly to *The Sovereignty of Good*.[60] Here, Murdoch identifies seeing as "the characteristic and proper mark of the active moral agent."[61] She claims that "I can only choose within the world I can *see*, in the moral sense of 'see.'"[62] The claim remains vague, though Murdoch does expand somewhat, speaking of "the idea of *attention*, or looking"[63] and of "the idea of a just and loving gaze directed upon an individual reality."[64] But what is quite clear about Murdoch's position, and brought vividly to life in Putnam's paper, is her hostility and resistance to the balancing metaphor. Murdoch is explicit about this: if we identify seeing as the "proper mark" of moral agency, we must replace the metaphors that dominate "modern moral philosophy" – metaphors of "touching, handling and the manipulation of things"[65] which comprise the balancing approach. She contrasts these positions on moral thinking: on one it is a balancing act; on the other, it is a seeing act.

So this is one reason why Putnam feels the need to reject balancing. Agreeing with Nussbaum that James attributes great moral significance to seeing in *The Golden Bowl*, he agrees with Murdoch that James must be rejecting balancing. But this novel is itself an excellent corrective. James does indeed attribute great moral significance to seeing.[66] But this is perfectly compatible with conceiving

---

59 Philosophers naturally connect – though they do not always make this explicit – the seeing and reading metaphors; e.g. John McDowell: "We might gloss 'reading situations correctly' as: seeing them in the light of the correct conception of doing well"; in "Deliberation and Moral Development in Aristotle's Ethics," in *The Engaged Intellect* (Harvard: Harvard University Press, 2009), 49.

60 Putnam, "Taking Rules Seriously," 193. For her part, Nussbaum is explicit about her reliance on Murdoch; see *Love's Knowledge*, 53, 106, 148, 167.

61 Iris Murdoch, *The Sovereignty of Good* (London: Routledge and Kegan Paul, 1970), 34.

62 Murdoch, *The Sovereignty of Good*, 37.

63 Murdoch, *The Sovereignty of Good*, 36.

64 Murdoch, *The Sovereignty of Good*, 34.

65 Murdoch, *The Sovereignty of Good*, 5. Murdoch takes the phrase from Stuart Hampshire, whom she treats as "fairly central and typical" of "modern moral philosophy." (4).

66 Though exaggerating this leads Nussbaum to misunderstand the significance of the golden bowl to Maggie. Nussbaum is surely right that, when Maggie "dwelt musingly on this obscured figure" in conversation with Mrs. Assingham (1905, 456; 1909, 483), she is thinking of her own life ("Flawed Crystals," 125). But when Maggie thinks of the vulnerability of the bowl, of the harm it would suffer were it to have a flaw, she does not focus exclusively on the way it *looks* but attends at least equally to what it *does*. The bowl as *container* of things matters to her: "The bowl with all our happiness in it." So what really concerns her about the possibility of a flaw is not so much that this would spoil its "brilliant perfect surface" (as Mrs, Assingham

of moral thinking as a balancing act. Indeed, James presents seeing as sub-serving balancing. When he describes the Prince's attitude to "the romantic spirit," for example (a vital theme in the novel because it structures the Prince's relations to Maggie and her father, explaining why he can think of them as "poor dears"), he makes a point of treating vision first, but then immediately going beyond it: "having seen it, having tried it, having taken its measure."[67] The movement of the phrase, the pull, is from the act of seeing to the act of weighing up, balancing.[68] Something similar happens at the close of the novel; it is worth appreciating the final words, their effect on us, and how they achieve that effect:

> And the truth of it had, with this force, after a moment, so strangely lighted his eyes that, as for pity and dread of them, she buried her own in his breast.[69]

Finally Amerigo *does* see, and Maggie sees that he sees. But Maggie recognises that seeing is not enough, and so she allows her eyes to fall. To some extent in relief perhaps, that the Prince will never be up to recognising what she has done to rescue their marriage. But also in final disappointment; that the Prince will never be up to being an equal partner in their relationship.

The Golden Bowl assigns a high status to Murdoch's "clear vision." But it is the ability to balance considerations, itself dependent on a feeling for their sheer weight, that has the mark of what she regards as active moral agency, the deep "result of moral imagination and moral effort."[70] That is why, as Robert Pippin and others have noted, the most obvious and immediately notable feature of the

---

interprets her, which Maggie notably fails to endorse) nor so much that it would no longer be "a pure and perfect crystal, completely without crack or seam" (as Nussbaum interprets her; "Flawed Crystals," 125) – neither of which need threaten its function as a container – but that this might mean it has "a hole in it big enough for you to poke in your finger." What Maggie wants, explicitly, is a happiness without *that*. All of which makes her seem much less precious than on Nussbaum's reading, much more likely and equipped to commit herself to winning what she values in the way she chooses. Nussbaum herself appears to move from identifying Maggie's basic moral focus as a devotion to purity (in "Flawed Crystals") to identifying it with a devotion to consistency (in her "Reply," defending her paper against responses by Putnam and others in *New Literary History* 15, no. 1 (1983): 201–208).

67 1905, 14; 1909, 37.

68 Vision-seeing is not even treated as a unique foil to balancing-weighing. On occasion, it is further demoted by being replaced by sound-hearing – for example, in James' description of the effects of an utterance of Maggie's: "Her question had fairly resounded, but it had afterwards, like many of her questions, dropped still more effectively than it had risen." (1905, 148; 1909, 171).

69 1905, 567; 1909, 595. The later version removes all the commas from this sentence, and the rush this makes of it seems substantially to change the nature of the force being depicted.

70 Murdoch, *The Sovereignty of Good*, 37.

novel is its great "density."[71] By correcting our appreciation of *The Golden Bowl*, we remove an obstruction to philosophy. We need not regard seeing as replacing balancing as the proper mark of moral agency. Indeed, it gives us a start on a possibility: that we appreciate the moral significance of seeing when we appreciate the moral significance of balancing. The two are connected and even, perhaps, interdependent.

III.3

The second reason why Putnam feels the need to reject balancing has, I think, to do with his interpretation of Aristotle.

Putnam endorses Nussbaum's view that James' insights into morality are best conceived as essentially Aristotelian. And philosophical discussion of Aristotle on practical reasoning at the time they were discussing *The Golden Bowl* (in 1983) was heavily influenced by a series of papers by John McDowell (published between 1978 and 1980), whose core idea was that virtuous Aristotelian agents reject balancing, at least when moral reasons present a particular action as required by virtue.[72] Being virtuous, such agents simply do not recognise other considerations as having any weight.[73] They are "not seen as any reason."[74] They are "silenced altogether – not overridden."[75] And precisely because there is nothing to be weighed up on a notional "other side" of a notional scale, there is no room for balancing here either, no place for "outweighing or

---

71 Pippin, *Henry James and the Moral Imagination*, 72. His helpful observations on *The Golden Bowl* (at 66–82) focus on exploring this point, arguing persuasively that the complexity James tends to present here is less a matter of "introspective revelation" than of relations between minds (75).

72 McDowell developed the interpretation over three papers, published 1978–80: (a) "Are Moral Requirements Hypothetical Imperatives?" (1978), reprinted in *Mind, Value and Reality* (Cambridge, MA: Harvard University Press, 1998), 90–93; (b) "Virtue and Reason" (1979), reprinted in *Mind, Value and Reality*, 55–56; (c) "The Role of *Eudaimonia* in Aristotle's Ethics" (1980), reprinted in *Mind, Value and Reality*, 17–18. For a more recent treatment, see (d) "Some Issues in Aristotle's Moral Psychology" (1998), reprinted in *Mind, Value and Reality*, 46–49.

73 Jeffrey Seidman distinguishes two claims here: (1) A virtuous agent will not be tempted to act in a way which is incompatible with virtue; (2) A virtuous agent will not believe that he has any reason to act in a way which is incompatible with virtue. But he is right that, for McDowell, these two claims are aspects of the same single phenomenon. See "Two Sides of Silencing," *Philosophical Quarterly* 55 no. 218 (2005): 68–77.

74 McDowell, "Virtue and Reason," 56. See also "The Role of *Eudaimonia* in Aristotle's Ethics," 17: "in the circumstances, they are not reasons at all."

75 McDowell, "Are Moral Requirements Hypothetical Imperatives?" 90.

overriding."[76] "[T]he dictates of virtue, if properly appreciated, are not weighed with other reasons at all, not even on a scale that always tips on their side."[77] What distinguishes the moral agent, at least where "the dictates of virtue" are concerned, is thus a "lack of struggle," "a sort of serenity."[78]

Agreeing with Nussbaum that James' moral insights are essentially Aristotelian, Putnam also agrees with McDowell that James must be rejecting balancing. To confirm that James' insights into morality are Aristotelian is, it may have seemed to him, to acknowledge that he counts it as a mark of moral agency to reject balancing. But again, *The Golden Bowl* is itself an excellent corrective. James sets great store by an agent's ability to appreciate the sheer weight of relevant considerations for and against courses of action, to exert imagination and effort in the attempt to weight and balance them. And this is perfectly consistent with Aristotle. Indeed, if we look carefully enough, it is consistent with *McDowell's* Aristotle. For Putnam's position exaggerates what is already quite an extreme position, and in two ways.

First, McDowell's Aristotle thinks that to reject balancing is characteristic of the *virtuous* person, the *phronimos*. But if Putnam is right, to reject balancing is required of *anyone* who may be accounted a moral agent. If this were correct, then there would be no room for merely continent people, for whom McDowell's Aristotle leaves a significant place. These are people who are neither virtuous nor incontinent. They think and act morally, even though they engage in balancing. Failing to appreciate the dictates of virtue properly, moral thinking for them is often a balancing act, a struggle between considerations that tell for and against any particular action. But it is no less moral thinking for all that.

Second, McDowell's Aristotle thinks that to reject balancing is not required of the virtuous person in *all* circumstances. On many occasions, there is no single right action required by the dictates of virtue. Here, virtuous people are free to balance their inclinations, where it may well be practically sensible to recognise how one outweighs or even overrides another. But if Putnam is right, and moral thinking is never a balancing act, this is never even morally permitted, let alone the practically sensible thing to do. To think and act morally is to conceive of *every* situation as one in which there is a single right action, where there are no contrary considerations to be taken into account.

---

76 McDowell, "Virtue and Reason," 56.
77 McDowell, "Are Moral Requirements Hypothetical Imperatives?" 90.
78 McDowell, "Are Moral Requirements Hypothetical Imperatives?" 91.

Again, we remove an obstruction to philosophy by correcting our appreciation of *The Golden Bowl*. We are not to regard moral agency as rejecting balancing altogether, but as giving it a crucial role for all on some occasions, and for some on all occasions. Indeed, it gives us a start on a possibility: we appreciate the moral significance of the dictates of virtue when we appreciate the occasions where it is not just permissible but practically sensible to engage in balancing.

III.4

Dorothea Krook calls *The Golden Bowl* "James' most ambitiously conceived and most brilliantly executed long poem."[79] The observation is just. Not because it tempts us to stretch the notion of "poem" until it fits the novel, or to squeeze the novel until it takes on the dimensions of a "poem."[80] Indeed, Krook herself gives no particular reason for identifying the novel as a poem, beyond observing that it achieves a high degree of "generality and comprehensiveness" which she takes as "the measure of poetic excellence."[81] The real value of her remark lies in the way it rearranges the expectations we have of ourselves as readers. To approach the novel as we would a poem, with that characteristic willingness to look more attentively at passing elements of form and content, sharpens our sensitivity to features of philosophical interest that call on philosophy's peculiar attentiveness. Or so I have tried to show.

Guided by this approach, I have contested Putnam's reading of *The Golden Bowl*. But only to find new reasons to accept what his reading was meant to deliver: the conviction that philosophy can learn from works of literature. Philosophy and literary criticism both benefit from the attunement that James's

---

79 Krook, *The Ordeal of Consciousness in Henry James*, 233. She may be picking up James' own references to poetry and the poet in the "Preface" of 1909. But what is notable about these occasions is James' tendency to adopt the distancing-effects of quotation marks and broad connotation; e.g. "It is scarce necessary to note that the highest test of any literary form conceived in the light of 'poetry' – to apply that term in its largest literary sense . . ." (1909, 20).

80 Though it is certainly worth noting that, when James originally conceived the plot (in November 1892), he thought it best suited to the dimensions of a short story; see Edel, *Henry James*, 210.

81 Krook, *The Ordeal of Consciousness in Henry James*, 233. This tells us much about why Krook thinks it excellent, less about why she thinks it a poem. She may mean us to take the one for the other, of course, which would make for so liberal a definition that many (most? all?) works of philosophy, *inter alia*, would merit the title (which is bland enough to stomach, but hardly gives one an appetite).

treatment of balancing in *The Golden Bowl* calls for. By doing philosophy, we appreciate what matters to literary criticism: the dramatic significance of this theme. And by doing literary criticism, we appreciate what matters to philosophy: not only how seeing and balancing need not exclude each other, but how balancing may be consistent with an Aristotelian conception after all.

Bibliography

Abel, Guenter and Conant, James (eds.). *Rethinking Epistemology*. Vol. 2. De Gruyter, 2012.

Alleblas, Joost and Eisinger, Randy. "An Interview with Hilary Putnam." *Cimedart* (Magazine of the Faculty of Philosophy of the University of Amsterdam), 2001.

Allison, Henry. *Kant's Theory of Freedom*. Cambridge: Cambridge University Press, 1990.

Austin, J.L. *How to Do Things with Words*, edited by J.O. Urmson and Marina Sbisà. Oxford: Clarendon Press, 1962.

Austin, J.L. "Other Minds." In J.L. Austin, *Philosophical Papers*, edited by J.O. Urmson and G.J. Warnock, 76–116. Oxford: Clarendon Press, 1961.

Austin, J.L. *Sense and Sensibilia*, edited by G.J. Warnock. Oxford: Oxford University Press, 1964.

Auxier, Randall E., Anderson, Douglas R., and Hahn, Lewis Edwin (eds.). *The Philosophy of Hilary Putnam*. Chicago, IL: Open Court, 2015.

Bach, Kent. "A Rationale for Reliabilism." *The Monist* 68, no. 2 (1985): 246–263.

Baghramian, Maria (ed.). *Reading Putnam*. New York: Routledge, 2012.

Bell, J.S. "Beables for Quantum Field Theory" (1984). Reprinted in *Speakable and Unspeakable in Quantum Mechanics*, 173–180. Cambridge: Cambridge University Press, 1987.

Bell, J.S. "On the Einstein-Podolsky-Rosen Paradox." *Physics* 1, no. 3 (1964): 195–200.

Bell, J.S. *Speakable and Unspeakable in Quantum Mechanics*, 2nd edition. Cambridge: Cambridge University Press, 2004.

Bella, Michela, Boncompagni, Anna, and Putnam, Hilary. "Interview with Hilary Putnam." *European Journal of Pragmatism and American Philosophy* 7, no. 1 (2015). http://journals. openedition.org/ejpap/357 (last accessed January 15, 2022).

Benacerraf, Paul and Wright, Crispin. "Skolem and the Skeptic." *Proceedings of the Aristotelian Society* 59 (1985): 85–115, 117–137.

Ben-Menahem, Yemima (ed.). *Hilary Putnam*. Contemporary Philosophy in Focus. Cambridge: Cambridge University Press, 2005.

Bicchieri, Cristina. *The Grammar of Society: The Nature and Dynamics of Social Norms*. Cambridge: Cambridge University Press, 2006.

Birkhoff, Garrett and Neumann, John von. "The Logic of Quantum Mechanics." *Annals of Mathematics* (2nd series) 37, no. 4 (1936): 823–843.

Blackburn, Simon. "Can an Analytic Philosopher Read Poetry?" In *The Philosophy of Poetry*, edited by John Gibson, 111–126. Oxford: Oxford University Press, 2015.

Boghossian, Paul. "Content and Self-Knowledge." *Philosophical Topics* 17, no. 1 (1989): 5–26.

Boghossian, Paul. "Externalism and Inference." *Philosophical Issues* 2 (1992): 11–28.

Boghossian, Paul. "How Are Objective Reasons Possible?" *Philosophical Studies* 106, no. 1/2 (2001): 1–40.

Boghossian, Paul. "Knowledge of Logic." In *New Essays on the A Priori*, edited by Paul Boghossian and Christopher Peacocke, 229–255. Oxford: Oxford University Press, 2000.

Boghossian, Paul. "What the Externalist Can Know A Priori." *Proceedings of the Aristotelian Society* 97, no. 2 (1997): 161–175.

Bonjour, Laurence. *In Defense of Pure Reason*. Cambridge: Cambridge University Press, 1998.

Bonjour, Laurence. "Is Thought a Symbolic Process?" *Synthese* 89, no. 3 (1991): 331–352.

Brian McLaughlin and Bennett, Karen. "Supervenience." In *Stanford Encyclopedia of Philosophy*, edited by Edward N. Zalta, 2018. https://plato.stanford.edu/entries/superve nience/ (last accessed October 15, 2021).

https://doi.org/10.1515/9783110769210-015

Brown, Jessica. *Anti-Individualism and Knowledge*. Cambridge: MIT Press, 2004.

Brueckner, Anthony. "Brains in a Vat." *The Journal of Philosophy* 83, no. 3 (1986): 148–167.

Brueckner, Anthony. "Skepticism and Content Externalism." *Stanford Encyclopedia of Philosophy*, edited by Edward Zalta, 2012. http://plato.stanford.edu/entries/skepticism-content-externalism/ (last accessed October 25, 2021).

Brueckner, Anthony. "Transcendental Arguments from Content Externalism." In *Transcendental Arguments: Problems and Prospects*, edited by Robert Stern, 229–250. Oxford: Clarendon Press, 1999.

Burge, Tyler. "Individualism and Self-Knowledge." *Journal of Philosophy* 85, no.1 (1988): 649–663.

Button, Tim. "Level Theory, Part 1: Axiomatizing the Bare Idea of a Cumulative Hierarchy of Sets." *Bulletin of Symbolic Logic* 27, no. 4 (2021): 436–460.

Button, Tim. *The Limits of Realism*. Oxford: Oxford University Press, 2013.

Button, Tim and Walsh, Sean. *Philosophy and Model Theory*. Oxford: Oxford University Press, 2018.

Byrne, Alex. "How Hard Are the Sceptical Paradoxes?" *Noûs* 38, no. 3 (2004): 299–325.

Cantor, Georg. "Letter to Dedekind" (1899). Reprinted in *From Frege to Gödel: A Source Book in Mathematical Logic, 1897–1931*, edited by Jean van Heijenoort, 113–117. Cambridge, MA: Harvard University Press, 1967.

Carnap, Rudolf. *The Logical Syntax of Language*. New York: Humanities, 1937.

Carnap, Rudolf. *The Philosophical Foundation of Physics*, edited by Martin Gardner. New York: Basic Books, 1966.

Carnap, Rudolf. "The Task of the Logic of Science" (1934). Reprinted in *Unified Science: The Vienna Circle Monographs Series Originally Edited by Otto Neurath*, edited by Brian McGuinness, translated by Hans Kaal, 46–66. Dordrecht: D. Reidel, 1987.

Cassam, Quassim. *The Possibility of Knowledge*. Oxford: Oxford University Press, 2007.

Cavell, Stanley. *Disowning Knowledge in Seven Plays of Shakespeare*. Cambridge: Cambridge University Press, 2003.

Cavell, Stanley. *The Claim of Reason: Wittgenstein, Skepticism, Morality, and Tragedy*, Cambridge, MA: Harvard University Press, 1979.

Cervantes, Miguel de. *Don Quixote de la Mancha: The Putnam Translation*. New York: Viking, 1947.

Chakraborty, Sanjit. "Hilary Putnam: An Era of Philosophy Has Ended." *Philosophia* 45, no. 1 (2017): 1–6.

Chakraborty, Sanjit. "Pursuits of Belief: Reflecting on the Cessation of Belief," *Sophia*, 60, no. 3 (2021): 639–654.

Chakraborty, Sanjit. "Scientific Conjectures and the Growth of Knowledge." *Journal of Indian Council of Philosophical Research* 38, no. 1 (2021): 83–101.

Chakraborty, Sanjit. *The Labyrinth of Mind and World: Beyond Internalism-Externalism*. London and New York: Routledge, 2020.

Chakraborty, Sanjit. *Understanding Meaning and World: A Relook on Semantic Externalism*. New Castle and London: Cambridge Scholars Publishing, 2016.

Chalmers, David. "Epistemic Two-Dimensional Semantics." *Philosophical Studies* 118, no. 1 (2004): 153–226.

Chalmers, David. "The Foundations of Two-Dimensional Semantics." In *Two-Dimensional Semantics: Foundations and Applications*, edited by Manuel Garcia-Carpintero and Josep Macia, 55–140. Oxford: Oxford University Press, 2006.

Chalmers, David and Jackson, Frank. "Conceptual Analysis and Reductive Explanation." *The Philosophical Review* 110, no. 3 (2001): 315–360.

Chomsky, Noam. "Problems of Projection." *Lingua* 130 (2013): 33–49.

Chomsky, Noam. *The New Horizons in the Study of Language and Mind*. Cambridge: Cambridge University Press, 2000.

Christensen, David. "Skeptical Problems, Semantical Solutions." *Philosophy and Phenomenological Research* 53, no. 2 (1993): 301–321.

Clark, Peter and Hale, Bob (eds.). *Reading Putnam*. Cambridge and Oxford: Blackwell, 1995.

Clarke, Thompson. "The Legacy of Skepticism." *Journal of Philosophy* 69 (1972): 754–769.

Cohen, Stewart. "Basic Knowledge and the Problem of Easy Knowledge." *Philosophy and Phenomenological Research* 65, no. 2 (2002): 309–329.

Cohen, Stewart. "Contextualism and Skepticism." *Philosophical Issues* 10 (2000): 94–107.

Cohen, Stewart. "Contextualism, Skepticism, and the Structure of Reasons." *Philosophical Perspectives* 13 (1999): 57–89.

Cohen, Stewart. "How to Be a Fallibilist." *Philosophical Perspectives* 2 (1998): 91–123.

Coliva, Annalisa. *Extended Rationality: A Hinge Epistemology*. London: Palgrave Macmillan, 2015.

Coliva, Annalisa. *Moore and Wittgenstein: Scepticism, Certainty, and Common Sense*. London: Palgrave Macmillan, 2010.

Conant, James. "Introduction" to Hilary Putnam, *Realism with a Human Face*, edited by James Conant, xv–lxxiv. Cambridge, MA: Harvard University Press, 1990.

Conant, James. "Introduction" to Hilary Putnam, *Words and Life*, edited by James Conant, v–lxxvi. Cambridge, MA: Harvard University Press, 1994.

Conant, James. "Two Varieties of Skepticism." In *Rethinking Epistemology*, Vol. 2, edited by Guenter Abel and James Conant, 1–73. Berlin: De Gruyter, 2012.

Conant, James. "Wittgenstein on Meaning and Use." *Philosophical Investigations* 21, no. 3 (1998): 222–250.

Conant, James and Elliott, Jay (eds.). *The Norton Anthology of Western Philosophy*. Vol. 2: *After Kant: The Analytic Tradition*. New York: Norton, 2017.

Conant, James, Putnam, Hilary, and Rorty, Richard. "What Is Pragmatism?" *Think* 8 (Autumn) (2004): 71–78.

Conant, James and Zeglen, Urszula M. (eds.). *Hilary Putnam: Pragmatism and Realism*. London and New York: Routledge, 2002.

Cook, Roy T. and Hellman, Geoffrey. "Memories of Hilary Putnam." In *Hilary Putnam on Logic and Mathematics*, edited by Roy T. Cook and Geoffrey Hellman, 1–7. Cham, Switzerland: Springer, 2018.

Courant, Richard and Robbins, Herbert. *What Is Mathematics? An Elementary Approach to Ideas and Methods*. New York: Oxford University Press, 1958.

David, Marian. "Neither Mentioning 'Brains in a Vat' nor Mentioning Brains in a Vat Will Prove that We Are Not Brains in a Vat." *Philosophy and Phenomenological Research* 51, no. 4 (1991): 891–896.

Davidson, Donald. "A Coherence Theory of Truth and Knowledge." In *Truth and Interpretations*, edited by Ernest Lepore, 307–319. Oxford: Blackwell, 1986.

Davidson, Donald. "Actions, Reasons, and Causes" (1963). Reprinted in *Essays on Actions and Events*, 3–19. Oxford: Clarendon Press, 1980.

Davidson, Donald. "Anomalous Monism." In *MIT Encyclopedia of Cognitive Sciences*, edited by Frank C. Keil and Robert A. Wilson, 30–31. Cambridge, MA: MIT Press, 1999.

Davidson, Donald. "Causal Relations" (1967). Reprinted in *Essays on Actions and Events*, 149–162. Oxford: Clarendon Press, 1980.

Davidson, Donald. "Freedom to Act" (1973). Reprinted in *Essays on Actions and Events*, 63–81. Oxford: Clarendon Press, 1980.

Davidson, Donald. *Inquiries into Truth and Interpretation*. Oxford: Clarendon Press, 1984.

Davidson, Donald. "Laws and Cause." *Dialectica* 49, no. 2–4 (1995): 263–279.

Davidson, Donald. "Mental Events" (1970). Reprinted in *Essays on Actions and Events*, 207–227. Oxford: Clarendon Press, 1980.

Davidson, Donald. "Self-Portrait." In *A Companion to the Philosophy of Mind*, edited by S. Guttenplan, 221–236. Oxford: Blackwell, 1994.

Davidson, Donald. "Thinking Causes." In *Mental Causation*, edited by John Heil and Alfred Mele, 3–17. Oxford: Oxford University Press, 1993.

Davis, Martin. *Computability and Unsolvability*. New York: Dover, 1982.

Davis, Martin, Putnam, Hilary, and Robinson Julia. "The Decision Problem for Exponential Diophantine Equations." *Annals of Mathematics* 2, no. 74 (1961): 425–436.

De Caro, Mario. "Putnam's Liberal Naturalism." In *Mind and Meaning*: *Themes from Putnam*, edited by Michael Frauchiger. Berlin: De Gruyter, forthcoming.

De Caro, Mario and Putnam, Hilary. "Free Will and Quantum Mechanics." *The Monist* 103, no. 4 (2020): 415–426. Reprinted in Hilary Putnam, *In Dialogue*, edited by Mario De Caro and David Macarthur. Cambridge, MA: Harvard University Press, forthcoming.

De Gaynesford, Maximilian. *Hilary Putnam*. Montreal: McGill-Queens University Press/ Acumen, 2006.

De Gaynesford, Maximilian. *The Rift in The Lute: Attuning Poetry and Philosophy*. Oxford: Oxford University Press, 2017.

De Gaynesford, Maximilian. "What Is Atunement?" In Maximilian de Gaynesford, *The Rift in The Lute: Attuning Poetry and Philosophy*, 1–33. Oxford: Oxford University Press, 2017.

Dennett, Daniel (ed.). *The Philosophical Lexicon*. Newark, Delaware: American Philosophical Association, 1987.

DeRose, Keith. "Solving the Skeptical Problem." *Philosophical Review* 104, no. 1 (1995): 1–52.

Dickie, Imogen. "We Are Acquainted with Ordinary Things." In *New Essays on Singular Thought*, edited by Robin Jeshion, 213–245. Oxford: Oxford University Press, 2010.

Dummett, Michael. *Grammar and Style*. London: Duckworth, 1993.

Dummett, Michael. "The Philosophical Significance of Gödel's Theorem" (1963). Reprinted in Michael Dummett, *Truth and Other Enigmas*. London: Duckworth, 1978.

Ebbs, Gary. "Analyticity: The Carnap-Quine Debate and Its Aftermath." In *The Cambridge History of Philosophy: 1945–2015*, edited by Kelly Becker and Iain Thompson, 32–48. Cambridge: Cambridge University Press, 2019.

Ebbs, Gary. "Is Skepticism about Self-Knowledge Coherent?" *Philosophical Studies* 105, no. 1 (2001): 43–58.

Ebbs, Gary. "Putnam and the Contextually A Priori." In *The Philosophy of Hilary Putnam*, edited by Randall E. Auxier, Douglas R. Anderson, and Lewis Edwin Hahn, 389–411. Chicago, IL: Open Court, 2015.

Ebbs, Gary. "Putnam on Methods of Inquiry," *Harvard Review of Philosophy* 24 (2017): 121–125.

Ebbs, Gary. "Skepticism, Objectivity and Brains in Vats." *Pacific Philosophical Quarterly* 73, no. 3 (1992): 239–266.

Edel, Leon. *Henry James: The Master 1901–1916*. New York: Avon Books, 1972.

Eisenberg, Daniel. "*Don Quixote* as Seen through the Eyes of Its Modern English Translators." *Cervantes: The Bulletin of the Cervantes Society of America*, Spring-Fall (2006): 103–126.

Evans, Gareth. *The Varieties of Reference*. Oxford: Oxford University Press, 1982.

Falvey, Kevin and Owens, Joseph. "Externalism, Self Knowledge, and Scepticism." *The Philosophical Review* 103, no. 1 (1994): 107–137.

Farkas, Katalin. "Constructing a World for the Sense." In *Phenomenal Intentionality*, edited by Uriah Kriegel, 99–115. Oxford: Oxford University Press, 2013.

Farkas, Katalin. "Phenomenal Intentionality without Compromise." *The Monist* 91, no. 2 (2008): 273–293.

Farkas, Katalin. *The Subject's Point of View*. Oxford: Oxford University Press, 2008.

Florio, Salvatore and Linnebo, Øystein. "On the Innocence and Determinacy of Plural Quantification." *Noûs* 50, no. 3 (2016): 565–583.

Floyd, Juliet. "Wittgenstein, Mathematics, and Philosophy." In *The New Wittgenstein*, edited by Alice Crary and Rupert Read, 232–261. London: Routledge, 2000.

Fodor, Jerry. *Language of Thought*. Cambridge, MA: Harvard University Press, 1979.

Fodor, Jerry. "Special Sciences, or the Disunity of Science as a Working Hypothesis." *Synthese* 28, no. 2 (1974): 97–115.

Folina, Janet. "Realism, Scepticism, and the Brain in a Vat." In *The Brain in a Vat*, edited by Sanford Goldberg, 155–173. Cambridge: Cambridge University Press, 2016.

Forbes, Graeme. "Realism and Skepticism: Brains in a Vat Revisited." *The Journal of Philosophy* 92, no. 4 (1995): 205–222.

Frege, Gottlob. *Basic Laws of Arithmetic*, edited and translated by Philip A. Ebert and Marcus Rossberg. Oxford: Oxford University Press, 2013.

Gallois, André. "Putnam, Brains in Vats, and Arguments for Scepticism." *Mind* 101, no. 402 (1992): 273–286.

Gallois, André and O'Leary-Hawthorne, John. "Externalism and Scepticism." *Philosophical Studies* 81, no. 1 (1997): 1–26.

Gilson, Étienne. *The Unity of Philosophical Experience*. New York: Scribners, 1965.

Gödel, Kurt. "Some Basic Theorems on the Foundations of Mathematics and Their Implications" (1951). Reprinted in Kurt Gödel, *Collected Works*, Vol. 3, edited by Solomon Feferman, John W. Dawson Jr., Warren Goldfarb, Charles Parsons and Robert N. Soloway, 304–323. Oxford: Oxford University Press, 1995.

Gödel, Kurt. "Über Formal unentscheidbare Sätze der *Principia Mathematica* und Verwandter Systeme: I." *Monatshefte für Mathematik und Physik* 38, no. 1 (1931): 173–198.

Goldberg, Sanford. "Anti-Individualism, Comprehension, and Self-Knowledge." In *Externalism, Self-Knowledge, and Skepticism*, edited by Sanford Goldberg, 184–194. Cambridge: Cambridge University Press, 2015.

Goldberg, Sanford. "Anti-Individualism, Conceptual Omniscience, and Skepticism." *Philosophical Studies* 116, no. 1 (2003): 53–78.

Goldberg, Sanford. "Anti-Individualism, Content Preservation, and Discursive Justification." *Noûs* 41 (2007): 178–203.

Goldberg, Sanford. *Anti-Individualism: Mind and Language, Knowledge and Justification*. Cambridge: Cambridge University Press, 2007.

Goldberg, Sanford. "Do Anti-Individualistic Construals of the Attitudes Capture the Agent's Conceptions?" *Noûs* 36, no. 4 (2002): 597–621.

Goldberg, Sanford. "Experts, Semantic and Epistemic." *Noûs* 43, no. 4 (2009): 581–598.

Goldberg, Sanford. "The Dialectical Context of Boghossian's Memory Argument." *Canadian Journal of Philosophy* 35, no. 1 (2005): 135–148.

Goldberg, Sanford. "The Psychology and Epistemology of Self-Knowledge." *Synthese* 118, no. 2 (1999): 165–199.

Goldberg, Sanford. "What Do You Know When You Know Your Own Thoughts?" In *New Essays on Semantic Externalism and Self-Knowledge*, edited by Susana Nuccetelli, 241–256. Cambridge, MA: MIT Press, 2003.

Goldberg, Sanford (ed.). *The Brain in a Vat*. Cambridge: Cambridge University Press, 2016.

Goldfarb, W. "Herbrand's Theorem and the Incompleteness of Arithmetic." *Iyyun: The Jerusalem Philosophical Quarterly* 39 (1990): 45–64.

Goodman, Nelson. *Fact, Fiction, and Forecast*. Cambridge MA: Harvard University Press, 1955.

Greenberger, Daniel M., Horne, Michael A. and Zeilinger, Anton. "Going beyond Bell's Theorem." In *Bell's Theorem, Quantum Theory and Conceptions of the Universe*, edited by Menas Kafatos, 69–72. Dordrecht, Boston, and London: Kluwer, 1989.

Grice, Paul. "Reply to Richards." In *Philosophical Grounds of Rationality*, edited by Richard Grandy and Richard Warner, 45–106. Oxford: Clarendon Press, 1986.

Hale, Bob and Clark, Peter (eds.). *Reading Putnam*. Oxford: Blackwell, 1994.

Harlan, Josh. "Hilary Putnam: On Mind, Meaning, and Reality." Interview with Josh Harlan. *Harvard Review of Philosophy*, Spring (1992): 20–24.

Harris, Zellig S. *Methods in Structural Linguistics*. Chicago: University of Chicago Press, 1951.

Harris, Zellig S. et al. (eds.). *The Form of Information in Science*. Berlin: Springer, 1988.

Hawthorne, John. "The Case for Closure." In *Contemporary Debates in Epistemology*, edited by Ernest Sosa and Mathias Steup, 26–43. Oxford: Blackwell, 2005.

Hellman, Geoffrey and Cook, Roy T. (eds.). *Hilary Putnam on Logic and Mathematics*. Cham, Switzerland: Springer, 2018.

Hemingway, Earnest. *A Moveable Feast*. New York: Vintage, 1964.

Hemmo, Meir and Shenker, Orly. "Flat Physicalism." *Theoria*, forthcoming 2021.

Hemmo, Meir and Shenker, Orly. "Why Functionalism Is a Form of 'Token Dualism'." In *Levels of Reality in Science and Philosophy: Re-Examining the Multi-Level Structure of Reality*, edited by Meir Hemmo, Ioannidis Stavros, Orly Shenker, and Gal Vishne. Cham: Springer, forthcoming 2022.

Hickey, Lance. "Hilary Putnam." In *American Philosophers, 1950–2000*, edited by Philip B. Dematteis and Leemon B. McHenry, 226–236. Detroit: Gale Group, 2003.

Hill, Christopher. S. (ed.). *The Philosophy of Hilary Putnam*. Fayetteville, AR: The University of Arkansas Press, 1992.

Horgan, Terence. "Original Intentionality Is Phenomenal Intentionality." *The Monist* 96, no. 2 (2013): 232–251.

Horgan, Terence and Tienson, John. "The Intentionality of Phenomenology and the Phenomenology of Intentionality." In *Philosophy of Mind: Classical and Contemporary Readings*, edited by David Chalmers, 520–533. Oxford: Oxford University Press, 2002.

Horgan, Terence, Tienson, John and Graham, George. "Phenomenal Intentionality and the Brain in a Vat." In *The Externalist Challenge*, edited by Richard Schantz, 297–317. Berlin: De Gruyter, 2004.

Jackson, Frank. *From Metaphysics to Ethics: A Defence of Conceptual Analysis*. Oxford: Oxford University Press, 1998.

Jackson, Frank. "Narrow Content and Representation – or Twin Earth Revisited." *Proceedings of the American Philosophical Association* 77, no. 2 (2003): 55–71.

James, Henry. *The Golden Bowl* (1905). Edited by Virginia Llewellyn Smith. Reprint: Oxford: Oxford University Press, 1999.

James, Henry. *The Golden Bowl*. (1909). Edited by Ruth Bernard Yeazell. Reprint: London: Penguin, 2009.

Johnsen, Bredo C. "Of Brains in Vats, Whatever Brains in Vats May Be." *Philosophical Studies* 112, no. 3 (2003): 225–249.

Kallestrup, Jesper. "Brains in Vats, Causal Constraints on Reference and Semantic Externalism." In *The Brain in a Vat*, edited by Sanford Goldberg, 37–53. Cambridge: Cambridge University Press, 2016.

Kant, Immanuel. *Kant's gesammelte Schriften*, edited by the Royal Prussian, subsequently German, then Berlin-Brandenburg Academy of Sciences. Berlin: Reimer, subsequently De Gruyter, 1900–.

Katz, Jerrold. *Realistic Rationalism*. Cambridge, MA.: MIT Press, 1998.

Kim, Jaegwon. *Mind in a Physical World: An Essay on the Mind-Body Problem and Mental Causation*. Cambridge, MA: MIT Press, 1998.

Kim, Jaegwon. *Philosophy of Mind*. Boulder: Westview, 1996.

Kim, Jaegwon. *Supervenience and Mind*. Cambridge: Cambridge University Press, 1993.

Kleene, S.C. *Introduction to Meta-Mathematics*. Amsterdam: North-Holland, 1952.

Kochen, Simon and Kripke, Saul. "Non-Standard Models of Peano Arithmetic." *L'enseignement Mathematique* 28 (1981): 211–231.

Kochen, Simon and Specker, Ernst. "The Problem of Hidden Variables in Quantum Mechanics." *Journal of Mathematics and Mechanics* 17 (1967): 59–87.

Kotzen, Matthew. "Dragging and Confirming." *The Philosophical Review* 121, no. 1 (2012): 55–93.

Kriegel, Uriah. "Intentional Inexistence and Phenomenal Intentionality." *Philosophical Perspectives* 21, no. 1 (2007): 307–340.

Kriegel, Uriah. "Is Intentionality Dependent upon Consciousness?" *Philosophical Studies* 116 (2003): 271–230.

Kriegel, Uriah. "The Phenomenal Intentionality Research Program." In *Phenomenal Intentionality*, edited by Uriah Kriegel, 1–26. Oxford: Oxford University Press, 2013.

Kriegel, Uriah. *The Sources of Intentionality*. Oxford: Oxford University Press, 2014.

Kriegel, Uriah (ed.) *Phenomenal Intentionality*. Oxford: Oxford University Press, 2013.

Krook, Dorothea. *The Ordeal of Consciousness in Henry James*. Cambridge: Cambridge University Press, 1962.

Lewis, David. "Elusive Knowledge." *Australasian Journal of Philosophy* 74 (1996): 549–567.

Lewis, David. *Parts of Classes*. Oxford: Blackwell, 1991.

Loar, Brian. "Phenomenal Intentionality as the Basis of Mental Content." In *Reflections and Replies: Essays on the Philosophy of Tyler Burge*, edited by Martin Hahn and B. Ramberg, 229–258. Cambridge: MIT Press.

Macarthur, David. "Introduction." In Hilary Putnam and Ruth Anna Putnam, *Pragmatism as a Way of Life: The Lasting Legacy of William James and John Dewey*, 1–9. Cambridge, MA and London: Belknap Press of Harvard University Press, 2017.

MacIntyre, Jane. "Putnam's Brains." *Analysis* 44, no. 2 (1984): 56–61.

Malcolm, Norman. "Defending Common Sense." *Philosophical Review* 58 (1949): 201–220.

Matiyasevich, Yuri. "Martin Davis and Hilbert's Tenth Problem." In *Martin Davis on Computability, Computational Logic, and Mathematical Foundations*, edited by Eugenio G. Omodeo and Alberto Policriti, 35–54. Cham, Switzerland: Springer International, 2016.

McDowell, John. "Are Moral Requirements Hypothetical Imperatives?" (1978). Reprinted in *Mind, Value and Reality*, 77–94. Cambridge, MA: Harvard University Press, 1998.

McDowell, John. "Deliberation and Moral Development in Aristotle's Ethics." In *The Engaged Intellect*, 41–58. Harvard: Harvard University Press, 2009.

McDowell, John. *Mind and World*. Cambridge, MA: Harvard University Press, 1994.

McDowell, John. "Putnam on Natural Reason." In *The Philosophy of Hilary Putnam*, edited by Randall Auxier, Douglas Anderson, and Lewis Hahn, 3–110. Chicago, IL: Open Court, 2015.

McDowell, John. "Some Issues in Aristotle's Moral Psychology" (1998). Reprinted in *Mind, Value and Reality*, 23–49. Cambridge, MA: Harvard University Press, 1998.

McDowell, John. "The Role of *Eudaimonia* in Aristotle's Ethics" (1980). Reprinted in *Mind, Value and Reality*, 3–22. Cambridge, MA: Harvard University Press, 1998.

McDowell, John. "Virtue and Reason" (1979). Reprinted in *Mind, Value and Reality*, 50–70. Cambridge, MA: Harvard University Press, 1998.

McDowell, John. "Wittgensteinian 'Quietism'." *Common Knowledge* 15, no. 3 (2009): 365–372.

McGee, Vann. "How We Learn Mathematical Language." *Philosophical Review* 106, no. 1 (1997): 35–68.

McGinn, Marie. *Sense and Certainty: A Dissolution of Scepticism*. Oxford: Blackwell, 1989.

McKinsey, Michael. "Anti-Individualism and Privileged Access." *Analysis* 51, no. 1 (1991): 9–16.

McKinsey, Michael. "Externalism and Priviliged Access Are Inconsistent." In *Contemporary Debates in the Philosophy of Mind*, edited by Brian P. McLaughlin and Jonathan D. Cohen, 37–53. Oxford: Blackwell, 2007.

Meadows, Toby. "What Can a Categoricity Theorem Tell Us?" *The Review of Symbolic Logic* 6, no. 3 (2013): 524–544.

Miracchi, Lisa. "Perspectival Externalism Is the Antidote for Radical Skepticism." *Episteme* 14, no. 3 (2017): 363–379.

Montague, Richard. "Set Theory and Higher-Order Logic." In *Formal Systems and Recursive Functions. Proceedings of the Eight Logic Colloquium, July 1963*, edited by John Crossley and Michael Dummett, 131–148. Amsterdam: North-Holland, 1965.

Montague, Richard, Scott, Dana, and Tarski, Alfred. "An Axiomatic Approach to Set Theory." BANC MSS 84/69c, carton 4, folder 29–30. Bancroft Library, University of California, Berkeley.

Moon, S. "Isaacson's Thesis and Wilkie's Theorem." MSc Thesis, University of Amsterdam, 2017.

Moore, G.E. "Proof of an External World." *Proceedings of the British Academy* 25 (1939): 273–300.

Moyal-Sharrock, Danièle. *Understanding Wittgenstein's On Certainty*. London: Palgrave Macmillan, 2004.

Murdoch, Iris. *The Sovereignty of Good*. London: Routledge and Kegan Paul, 1970.

Nagel, Ernst. *The Structure of Science*. London: Routledge and Kegan Paul, 1961.

Nagel, Thomas. *The View from Nowhere*. Oxford: Oxford University Press, 1986.

Nickles, Thomas. "Two Concepts of Intertheoretic Reduction." *Journal of Philosophy* 70 (1973): 181–201.

Nussbaum, Martha C. *Aristotle's De Motu Animalium*. Princeton: Princeton University Press, 1978.

Nussbaum, Martha C. "'Finely Aware and Richly Responsible': Literature and the Moral Imagination." In *Love's Knowledge: Essays on Philosophy and Literature*, 148–167. Oxford: Oxford University Press, 1990.

Nussbaum, Martha C. "Flawed Crystals: James' *The Golden Bowl* and Literature as Moral Philosophy." In *Love's Knowledge: Essays on Philosophy and Literature*, 125–148. Oxford: Oxford University Press, 1990.

Nussbaum, Martha C. "Hilary Putnam (1926–2016)." Obituary published in *The Huffington Post*, March 14, 2016. https://www.huffpost.com/entry/hilary-putnam-1926-2016_b_9457774 (last accessed March 13, 2021).

Nussbaum, Martha C. "Janus-Faced Law: A Philosophical Debate." In *The Timing of Lawmaking*, edited by Saul Levmore and Frank Fagan, 249–229. Cheltenham and Northampton: Edward Elgar, 2017.

Nussbaum, Martha C. *Love's Knowledge: Essays on Philosophy and Literature*. New York: Oxford University Press, 1990.

Nussbaum, Martha C. "Perception and Revolution: *The Princess Casamassima* and the Political Imagination." In *Meaning and Method: Essays in Honor of Hilary Putnam*, edited by George Boolos, 327–354. Cambridge: Cambridge University Press.

Nussbaum, Martha C. "Reply." *New Literary History* 15, no. 1 (1983): 201–208.

Nussbaum, Martha C. "Stages of Thought." *The New Republic*, (2008): 37–41.

Nussbaum, Martha C. "The Costs of Tragedy: Some Moral Limits of Cost-Benefit Analysis." *Journal of Legal Studies* 29, no. 2 (2000): 1005–1036. Reprinted in *Cost-Benefit Analysis: Legal, Economic and Philosophical Perspectives*, edited by Matthew D. Adler and Eric A. Posner, 169–200. Chicago: University of Chicago Press, 2000.

Nussbaum, Martha C. *The Fragility of Goodness: Luck and Ethics in Greek Tragedy and Philosophy*. Cambridge and New York: Cambridge University Press, 1986.

Nussbaum, Martha C. "The Text of Aristotle's *De Motu Animalium*." *Harvard Studies in Classical Philology* 80 (1976): 111–159.

Nussbaum, Martha C. "Tragedy and Human Capabilities: A Response to Vivian Walsh." *Review of Political Economy* 15, no. 3 (2003): 413–418.

Nussbaum, Martha C. and Putnam, Hilary. "Changing Aristotle's Mind." In *Essays on Aristotle's De Anima*, edited by Martha C. Nussbaum and Amelie Rorty, 27–56. Oxford: Clarendon Press, 1992. Reprinted in Hilary Putnam, *Words and Life*, edited by James Conant, 22–61. Cambridge, MA: Harvard University Press, 1994.

Paris, J. and Harrington, L. "A Mathematical Incompleteness in Peano Arithmetic." In *Handbook of Mathematical Logic*, edited by J. Barwise, 1133–1142. North-Holland, 1977.

Parsons, Charles. "The Uniqueness of the Natural Numbers." *Iyyun* 39, no. 1 (1990): 13–44.

Parsons, Charles. *Mathematical Thought and Its Objects*. Cambridge: Harvard University Press, 2008.

Passmore, John. *A Hundred Years of Philosophy*. London: Duckworth, 1957.

Passmore, John. *Recent Philosophers*. London: Duckworth, 1988.

Peacocke, Christopher. "Explaining the A Priori: The Programme of Moderate Rationalism." In *New Essays on the A Priori*, edited by Paul Boghossian and Christopher Peacocke, 255–286. Oxford: Oxford University Press, 2000.

Pippin, Robert. *Henry James and the Moral Imagination*. Cambridge: Cambridge University Press, 2000.

Potter, Michael. *Set Theory and Its Philosophy*. Oxford: Oxford University Press, 2004.

Priest, Graham. "What Is So Bad about Contradictions?" *The Journal of Philosophy* 95, no. 8 (1998): 410–426.

Pritchard, Duncan. *Epistemic Angst: Radical Skepticism and the Groundlessness of Our Believing*. Princeton: Princeton University Press, 2015.

Pritchard, Duncan. "Sceptical Intuitions." In *Intuitions*, edited by Darrell P. Rowbottom and Anthony Robert Booth, 213–231. Oxford: Oxford University Press, 2014.

Pritchard, Duncan. "Wittgenstein on Hinge Commitments and Radical Scepticism in *On Certainty*." In *Blackwell Companion to Wittgenstein*, edited by Hans-Johann Glock and John Hyman, 563–575. Oxford: Blackwell, 2017.

Pritchard, Duncan. "Wittgensteinian Epistemology, Epistemic Vertigo, and Pyrrhonian Scepticism." In *Epistemology After Sextus Empiricus*, edited by Justin Vlasits and Katja Maria Vogt, 172–192. Oxford: Oxford University Press, 2019.

Pritchard, Duncan and Ranilli, Chris. "Putnam on BIVs and Radical Scepticism." In *The Brain in a Vat*, edited by Sanford Goldberg, 75–89. Cambridge: Cambridge University Press, 2016.

Pryor, James. "What's Wrong with McKinsey-Style Reasoning?" In *Internalism and Externalism in Semantics and Epistemolgy*, edited by Sanford Goldberg, 177–200. Oxford: Oxford University Press, 2007.

Pryor, James. "When Warrant Transmits." In *Mind, Meaning and Knowledge: Themes from the Philosophy of Crispin Wright*, edited by Annalisa Coliva, 269–303. Oxford: Oxford University Press, 2012.

Putnam, Hilary. "After Gödel." *Logic Journal of the IGPL* 14, no. 5 (2006): 745–754.

Putnam, Hilary. "A Half Century of Philosophy, Viewed from Within." *Daedalus: Journal of the American Academy of Arts and Sciences*, Winter (1997): 175–208.

Putnam, Hilary. "A Philosopher Looks at Quantum Mechanics (Again)." *British Journal for the Philosophy of Science* 56 (2005): 615–634.

Putnam, Hilary. "An Interview with Putnam." *Cogito* 3, no. 2 (1989): 85–91.

Putnam, Hilary. "Antwort auf Jürgen Habermas." In *Hilary Putnam und die Tradition des Pragmatismus*, edited by Marie-Luise Raters and Marcus Willaschek, 306–324. Frankfurt am Main: Suhrkamp, 2002.

Putnam, Hilary. "Aristotle after Wittgenstein." In *Modern Thinkers and Ancient Thinkers*, edited by Robert W. Sharples, 117–137, London: UCL Press, 1993.

Putnam, Hilary. "Aristotle's Mind and Contemporary Science." In Hilary Putnam, *Philosophy in an Age of Science*, edited by Mario De Caro and David Macarthur, 584–607. Cambridge, MA.: Harvard University Press, 2012.

Putnam, Hilary. "Brains and Behavior" (1963). Reprinted in *Mind, Language, and Reality: Philosophical Papers*, Vol. 2, 325–341. Cambridge: Cambridge University Press, 1975.

Putnam, Hilary. "Comments and Replies." In *Reading Putnam*, edited by Peter Clark and Bob Hale, 242–296. Cambridge, MA: Blackwell, 1994.

Putnam, Hilary. *Ethics without Ontology*. Cambridge, MA: Harvard University Press, 2004.

Putnam, Hilary. "Explanation and Reference" (1973). Reprinted in *Mind, Language, and Reality: Philosophical Papers*, Vol. 2, 196–214. Cambridge: Cambridge University Press, 1975.

Putnam, Hilary. "For Ethics and Economics without the Dichotomies." *Review of Political Economy* 15, no. 4 (2003): 395–412.

Putnam, Hilary. "How to Think Quantum-Logically." *Synthese* 29, no. 1/4 (1974): 55–61.

Putnam, Hilary. "Intellectual Autobiography." In *The Philosophy of Hilary Putnam*, edited by Randall Auxier, Douglas Anderson, and Lewis Hahn, 3–110. Chicago, IL: Open Court, 2015.

Putnam, Hilary. "Is Semantics Possible?" (1970). Reprinted in *Mind, Language, and Reality: Philosophical Papers*, Vol. 2, 139–152. Cambridge: Cambridge University Press, 1975.

Putnam, Hilary. "It Ain't Necessarily So" (1962). Reprinted in *Mathematics, Matter, and Method: Philosophical Papers*, Vol. 1, 237–249. Cambridge: Cambridge University Press, 1975.

Putnam, Hilary. *Jewish Philosophy as a Guide to Life*. Bloomington: Indiana University Press, 2002.

Putnam, Hilary. "Literature, Science and Reflection." *New Literary History* 7, no. 1 (1976): 483–491. Reprinted in *Meaning and the Moral Sciences*, 81–94. London: Routledge and Kegan Paul, 1978.

Putnam, Hilary. *Mathematics, Matter and Method: Philosophical Papers*, Vol. 1. Cambridge: Cambridge University Press, 1979.

Putnam, Hilary. "Mathematics without Foundations" (1967). Reprinted in *Mathematics, Matter, and Method: Philosophical Papers*, Vol. 1, 295–313. Cambridge: Cambridge University Press, 1975.

Putnam, Hilary. "McDowell's Mind and McDowell's World." In *Reading McDowell: On Mind and World*, edited by Nicholas H. Smith, 174–190. London: Routledge, 2002.

Putnam, Hilary. "Meaning and Knowledge." In *Meaning and the Moral Sciences*, 1–80. London: Routledge and Kegan Paul, 1978.

Putnam, Hilary. "Meaning and Reference." *The Journal of Philosophy* 70, no. 13 (1973): 699–711.

Putnam, Hilary. *Meaning and the Moral Sciences*. London: Routledge, 1976.

Putnam, Hilary. *Meaning and the Moral Sciences*. London: Routledge and Kegan Paul, 1978.

Putnam, Hilary. "Meaning Holism" (1986). Reprinted in Hilary Putnam, *Realism with a Human Face*, edited by James Conant, 278–302. Cambridge, MA: Harvard University Press, 1990.

Putnam, Hilary. "Minds and Machines" (1960). Reprinted in *Mind, Language, and Reality: Philosophical Papers*, Vol. 2, 362–385. Cambridge: Cambridge University Press, 1975.

Putnam, Hilary. *Mind, Language and Reality: Philosophical Papers*, Vol. 2. Cambridge: Cambridge University Press, 1975.

Putnam, Hilary. "Models and Reality." *The Journal of Philosophical Logic* 45, no. 3 (1980): 464–482. Reprinted in *Realism and Reason: Philosophical Papers*, Vol. 3, 1–26. Cambridge: Cambridge University Press, 1983.

Putnam, Hilary. *Naturalism, Realism, and Normativity*, edited by Mario De Caro. Cambridge, MA: Harvard University Press, 2016.

Putnam, Hilary. "Nonstandard Models and Kripke's Proof of the Gödel Theorem." *Notre Dame Journal of Formal Logic* 41, no. 1 (2000): 53–58.

Putnam, Hilary. "Objectivity and the Science/Ethics Distinction." In Hilary Putnam, *Realism with a Human Face*, edited by James Conant, 163–178. London: Harvard University Press, 1990.

Putnam, Hilary. "Objectivity and the Science-Ethics Distinction." In *The Quality of Life*, edited by Martha C. Nussbaum and Amartya Sen, 143–157. Oxford: Clarendon Press, 1993.

Putnam, Hilary. "On Not Writing Off Scientific Realism." In Hilary Putnam, *Philosophy in an Age of Science*, edited by Mario De Caro and David Macarthur, 91–108. Cambridge, MA.: Harvard University Press, 2012.

Putnam, Hilary. "Peirce: The Logician." In Hilary Putnam, *Realism with a Human Face*, edited by James Conant, 252–260. London: Harvard University Press, 1990.

Putnam, Hilary. "Philosophy and Our Mental Life." In *Mind, Language and Reality: Philosophical Papers*, Vol. 2, 291–303. Cambridge: Cambridge University Press, 1975.

Putnam, Hilary. "Philosophy as the Education of Grownups: Stanley Cavell and Skepticism." In *Reading Cavell*, edited by Alice Crary and Sanford Shieh, 119–130. London: Routledge, 2006. Reprinted in Hilary Putnam, *Philosophy in an Age of Science*, edited by Mario De Caro and David Macarthur, 552–557. Cambridge, MA: Harvard University Press, 2012.

Putnam, Hilary. *Philosophy in an Age of Science*, edited by Mario De Caro and David Macarthur. Cambridge, MA: Harvard University Press, 2012.

Putnam, Hilary. *Philosophy of Logic*. New York: Harper and Row, 1971.

Putnam, Hilary. "Philosophy of Physics" (1965). Reprinted in *Mathematics, Matter and Method: Philosophical Papers*, Vol. 1, 79–92 (Cambridge: Cambridge University Press, 1975).

Putnam, Hilary. "Pope's *Essay on Man* and Those 'Happy Pieties'." In *Pursuits of Reason: Essays in Honor of Stanley Cavell*, edited by Ted Cohen, Paul Guyer and Hilary Putnam, 13–20. Lubbock: Texas Tech University Press, 1993. Reprinted in Hilary Putnam, *Words and Life*, edited by James Conant, 513–522. Cambridge, MA: Harvard University Press, 1994.

Putnam, Hilary. *Pragmatism: An Open Question*. Oxford: Blackwell, 1995.

Putnam, Hilary. "Pragmatism and Moral Objectivity." Reprinted in Hilary Putnam, *Words and Life*, edited by James Conant, 151–181. Cambridge, MA: Harvard University Press, 1994.

Putnam, Hilary. "Pragmatism and Nonscientific Knowledge" (2002). Reprinted in Hilary Putnam and Ruth Anna Putnam, *Pragmatism as a Way of Life*, edited by David Macarthur, 55–70. Cambridge, MA: Harvard University Press, 2017.

Putnam, Hilary. "Pragmatism and Relativism." Reprinted in Hilary Putnam, *Words and Life*, edited by James Conant, 182–197. Cambridge, MA: Harvard University Press, 1994.

Putnam, Hilary. "Preface" to *The Form of Information in Science*, edited by Zellig S. Harris et al. Berlin: Springer, 1988.

Putnam, Hilary. "Quantum Mechanics and the Observer." *Erkenntnis* 16, no. 2 (1981): 193–219.

Putnam, Hilary. *Realism and Reason: Philosophical Papers*, Vol. 3. Cambridge: Cambridge University Press, 1983.

Putnam, Hilary. "Realism and Reason." *Proceedings of the American Philosophical Society* 50, no. 6 (1977): 483–498.

Putnam, Hilary. *Realism with a Human Face*, edited by James Conant. Cambridge, MA: Harvard University Press, 1990.

Putnam, Hilary. "Realism without Absolutes." Reprinted in Hilary Putnam, *Words and Life*, edited by James Conant, 279–294. Cambridge, MA: Harvard University Press, 1994.

Putnam, Hilary. *Reason, Truth and History*. Cambridge: Cambridge University Press, 1981.

Putnam, Hilary. "Reductionism and the Nature of Psychology" (1973). Reprinted in Hilary Putnam, *Words and Life*, edited by James Conant, 428–440. Cambridge, MA: Harvard University Press, 1994.

Putnam, Hilary. *Renewing Philosophy*. Cambridge, MA: Harvard University Press, 1992. Reprint: 1995.

Putnam, Hilary. "Reply to Gary Ebbs." In *The Philosophy of Hilary Putnam*, edited by Randall Auxier, Douglas Anderson, and Lewis Hahn, 412–417. Chicago, IL: Open Court, 2015.

Putnam, Hilary. "Reply to James Conant." In *The Philosophy of Hilary Putnam*, edited by Christopher. S. Hill, 374–777. Fayetteville: University of Arkansas Press, 1992.

Putnam, Hilary. "Reply to John McDowell." In *The Philosophy of Hilary Putnam*, edited by Randall Auxier, Douglas Anderson, and Lewis Hahn, 3–110. Chicago, IL: Open Court, 2015.

Putnam, Hilary. "Reply to Stephen White." *European Journal of Analytic Philosophy* 4, no. 2 (2008): 29–32.

Putnam, Hilary. *Representation and Reality*. Cambridge, MA: MIT Press, 1988.

Putnam, Hilary. "Rethinking Mathematical Necessity" (1990). Reprinted in Hilary Putnam, *Words and Life*, edited by James Conant, 245–263. Cambridge, MA: Harvard University Press, 1994.

Putnam, Hilary. "Richard Rorty on Reality and Justification." In *Rorty and His Critics*, edited by Robert Brandom, 81–86. Oxford: Blackwell, 2000.

Putnam, Hilary. "Robots: Machines or Artificially Created Life?" (1964). Reprinted in *Mind, Language and Reality: Philosophical Papers*, Vol. 2, 386–407. Cambridge: Cambridge University Press, 1975.

Putnam, Hilary. "Sixty-Five Years of Philosophy." In *Naturalism, Realism, and Normativity*, edited by Mario De Caro, 213–226. Cambridge, MA: Harvard University Press, 2016.

Putnam, Hilary. "Skepticism and Occasion-Sensitive Semantics." In Hilary Putnam, *Philosophy in an Age of Science: Physics, Mathematics and Skepticism*, edited by Mario De Caro and David Macarthur, 514–534. Cambridge, MA: Harvard University Press, 2012.

Putnam, Hilary. "Skepticism, Stroud, and the Contextuality of Knowledge." *Philosophical Explorations* 4, no. 2 (2001): 2–16. Reprinted in Hilary Putnam, *Philosophy in an Age of Science: Physics, Mathematics and Skepticism*, edited by Mario De Caro and David Macarthur, 495–513. Cambridge, MA: Harvard University Press, 2012.

Putnam, Hilary. "A Philosopher Looks at Quantum Mechanics." In *Beyond the Edge of Certainty: Essays in Contemporary Science and Philosophy*, ed. Robert G. Colodny, 75–101. Englewood Cliffs, N.J.: Prentice-Hall, 1965.

Putnam, Hilary. "A Philosopher Looks at Quantum Mechanics" (1965). Reprinted in *Mathematics, Matter and Method: Philosophical Papers*, Vol. 1, 130–158. Cambridge: Cambridge University Press, 1975, 2nd edition 1979.

Putnam, Hilary. "Strawson and Skepticism." In *The Philosophy of P.F. Strawson*, edited by Lewis Edwin Hahn, 273–287. Chicago, IL: Open Court, 1998.

Putnam, Hilary. "Taking Rules Seriously: A Reply to Martha Nussbaum." *New Literary History* 15, no. 1 (1983): 193–200. Reprinted in Hilary Putnam, *Realism with a Human Face*, edited by James Conant, 193–200. London: Harvard University Press, 1990.

Putnam, Hilary. "The Analytic and the Synthetic" (1962). Reprinted in *Mind, Language, and Reality: Philosophical Papers*, Vol. 2, 33–69. Cambridge: Cambridge University Press, 1975.

Putnam, Hilary. *The Collapse of the Fact/Value Dichotomy*. Cambridge, MA: Harvard University Press, 2002.

Putnam, Hilary. "The Craving for Objectivity." In Hilary Putnam, *Realism with a Human Face*, edited by James Conant, 120–131. London: Harvard University Press, 1990.

Putnam, Hilary. "The Diversity of the Sciences." Reprinted in Hilary Putnam, *Words and Life*, edited by James Conant, 463–480. Cambridge, MA: Harvard University Press, 1994.

Putnam, Hilary. "The Logic of Quantum Mechanics" (1968). Reprinted in *Mathematics, Matter and Method: Philosophical Papers*, Vol. 1, 174–197. Cambridge: Cambridge University Press, 1975.

Putnam, Hilary. *The Many Faces of Realism*. La Salle, IL: Open Court, 1987.

Putnam, Hilary. "The Meaning of 'Meaning'." In *Mind, Language and Reality: Philosophical Papers*, Vol. 2, 215–271. Cambridge: Cambridge University Press, 1975.

Putnam, Hilary. *The Meaning of the Concept of Probability in Application to Finite Sequences* (1951). Reprint: New York and London: Garland, 1990.

Putnam, Hilary. "The Nature of Mental States." In *Mind, Language and Reality: Philosophical Papers*, Vol. 2, 429–440. Cambridge: Cambridge University Press, 1975.

Putnam, Hilary. "The Place of Facts in a World of Values" (1979). Reprinted in Hilary Putnam, *Realism with a Human Face*, edited by James Conant, 142–162. Cambridge, MA: Harvard University Press, 1990.

Putnam, Hilary. "The Psychological Predicates." In *Art, Mind and Religion*, edited by W.H. Captain and D.D. Merrill, 37–48. Pittsburgh: University of Pittsburgh, 1967.

Putnam, Hilary. "The Refutation of Conventionalism" (1974). Reprinted in *Mind, Language, and Reality: Philosophical Papers*, Vol. 2, 153–191. Cambridge: Cambridge University Press, 1975.

Putnam, Hilary. *The Threefold Cord: Mind, Body, and World*. New York: Columbia University Press, 1999.

Putnam, Hilary. "There Is at Least One A Priori Truth" (1978). Reprinted in *Realism and Reason: Philosophical Papers*, Vol. 3. 98–114. Cambridge: Cambridge University Press, 1983.

Putnam, Hilary. "Three-Valued Logic." *Philosophical Studies* 8, no. 5 (1957): 73–80. Reprinted in *Mathematics, Matter, and Method: Philosophical Papers*, Vol. 1, 166–173. Cambridge: Cambridge University Press, 1975.

Putnam, Hilary. "To Think with Integrity." *The Harvard Review of Philosophy* 8 (2000): 4–13.

Putnam, Hilary. "Truth and Convention." *Dialectica* 40, no. 1–2 (1987): 69–77.

Putnam, Hilary. "'Two Dogmas' Revisited." In *Realism and Reason: Philosophical Papers*, Vol. 3, 87–97. Cambridge: Cambridge University Press, 1983.

Putnam, Hilary. "What Is Mathematical Truth." In *Mathematics, Matter and Method: Philosophical Papers*, Vol. 1, 60–78. Cambridge: Cambridge University Press, 1975.

Putnam, Hilary. "What Theories Are Not" (1960). Reprinted in *Mathematics, Matter and Method: Philosophical Papers*, Vol. 1, 215–227. Cambridge: Cambridge University Press, 1975.

Putnam, Hilary. "Wittgenstein: A Reappraisal" (2011). Reprinted in Hilary Putnam, *Philosophy in an Age of Science*, edited by Mario De Caro and David Macarthur, 482–494. Cambridge, MA: Harvard University Press, 2012.

Putnam, Hilary. *Words and Life*, edited by James Conant. Cambridge, MA: Harvard University Press, 1994.

Putnam, Hilary and Putnam, Ruth Anna. "Education for Democracy." In Hilary Putnam, *Words and Life*, edited by James Conant, 221–244. Cambridge, MA: Harvard University Press, 1994.

Putnam, Hilary and Putnam, Ruth Anna. *Pragmatism as a Way of Life*, edited by David Macarthur. Cambridge, MA: Harvard University Press, 2017.

Putnam, Hilary and Putnam, Ruth Anna. "William James's Ideas." In Hilary Putnam, *Realism with a Human Face*, edited by James Conant, 217–231. London: Harvard University Press, 1990.

Putnam, Hilary and Walsh, Vivian. "Facts, Values, Theories and Destitution in the Work of Sir Partha Dasgupta." *Review of Political Economy* 19, no. 2 (2007): 181–202.

Putnam, Hilary and Walsh, Vivian. *The End of Value-Free Economics*. New York: Routledge, 2012.

Putnam, Samuel. *Paris Was Our Mistress: Memoirs of a Lost and Found Generation*. New York: Viking, 1947. Reprint: Carbondale: Southern Illinois University Press, 1970.

Pynn, Geoff. "The Bayesian Explanation of Transmission Failure." *Synthese* 190, no. 9 (2013): 1519–1531.

Quine, W.V.O. *Pursuits of Truth*, Cambridge, MA and London: Harvard University Press, 1992.

Quine, W.V.O. *The Roots of Reference*. La Salle, IL: Open Court, 1974.

Quine, W.V.O. "Things and Their Place in Theories." In *Theories and Things*, 1–23. Cambridge, MA: Harvard University Press, 1981.

Quine, W.V.O. "Two Dogmas of Empiricism." *Philosophical Review* 60, no. 1 (1951): 20–43. Reprinted in *From a Logical Point of View*, 20–46. Cambridge, MA: Harvard University Press, 1953.

Quine, W.V.O. *Word and Object*. Cambridge, MA: MIT Press, 1960.

Quinsey, P. "Some Problems in Logic." PhD Dissertation, Oxford University, 1980.

Rathers, Marie-Luise and Willaschek, Marcus (eds.). *Hilary Putnam und die Tradition des Pragmatismus*. Frankfurt am Main: Suhrkamp, 2002.

Reichenbach, Hans. *The Philosophy of Space and Time*, translated by Maria Reichenbach and John Freund. New York: Dover, 1958.

Rey, Georges. "A Naturalistic A Priori." *Philosophical Studies* 92, no. 1/2 (1998): 25–43.

Richardson, Henry. *Practical Reasoning about Final Ends*. New York: Cambridge University Press, 1984.

Ricks, Christopher. "Introduction" to *What Maisie Knew* by Henry James, xiii–xxviii. London: Penguin, 2010.

Rips, Lance J., Bloomfield, Amber, and Asmuth, Jennifer. "From Numerical Concepts to the Concept of Number." *Behavioral and Brain Science* 31, no. 6 (2008): 623–687.

Rosser, J. "Extensions of Some Theorems of Gödel and Church." *Journal of Symbolic Logic* 1 (1936): 87–91.

Rozental, Stefan (ed.). *Niels Bohr: His Life and Work as Seen by His Friends and Colleagues*. Amsterdam: North-Holland, 1967.

Russell, Bertrand. "Letter to Frege" (1902). Reprinted in *From Frege to Gödel: A Source Book in Mathematical Logic, 1897–1931*, edited by Jean van Heijenoort, 124–125. Cambridge, MA: Harvard University Press, 1967.

Ryle, Gilbert. *The Concept of Mind*. London: Hutchinson, 1949.

Sawyer, Sarah. "In Defense of Burge's Thesis." *Philosophical Studies* 107, no. 2 (2002): 109–128.

Sawyer, Sarah. "Privileged Access to the World." *Australasian Journal of Philosophy* 76, no. 4 (1998): 523–533.

Sawyer, Sarah. "The Epistemic Divide." *Southern Journal of Philosophy* 39, no. 3 (2001): 385–401.

Schönbaumsfeld, Genia. *The Illusion of Doubt*. Oxford: Oxford University Press, 2016.

Scott, Dana. "Axiomatizing Set Theory." In *Axiomatic Set Theory II. Proceedings of the Symposium in Pure Mathematics of the American Mathematical Society*, July-August 1967. 207–214. Providence: American Mathematical Society, 1974.

Scott, Dana. "The Notion of Rank in Set-Theory" In *Summaries of Talks Presented at the Summer Institute for Symbolic Logic, Cornell University*, 1957. 267–269. Princeton: Institute for Defence Analysis, 1960.

Searle, John. *Speech Acts*. Cambridge: Cambridge University Press, 1969.

Seidman, Jeffrey. "Two Sides of Silencing." *Philosophical Quarterly* 55, no. 218 (2005): 68–77.

Sen, Amartya. "Walsh on Sen after Putnam." *Review of Political Economy* 17, no. 1 (2005): 107–113.

Smith, Martin. "Transmission Failure Explained." *Philosophy and Phenomenological Research* 79, no. 1 (2009): 164–189.

Smith, Virginia Llewellyn. "Note on the Text" to *The Golden Bowl* by Henry James, xxxii–xxxv. Oxford: Oxford University Press, 1999.

Stevenson, Leslie. "Six Levels of Mentality." *Philosophical Explorations* 5, no. 2 (2002): 105–124.

Stocker, Michael. *Plural and Conflicting Values*. Oxford: Oxford University Press, 1990.

Stone, Abraham D. "On Scientific Method as a Method for Testing the Legitimacy of Scientific Concepts." *Reviews of Contemporary Philosophy* 8 (2009): 13–48.

Strauss, David A. "Common Law Constitutional Interpretation." *University of Chicago Law Review* 63, no. 3 (1996): 877–935.

Strawson, P.F. *Introduction to Logical Theory*, London: Meuthen, 1952.

Strawson, P.F. "Reply to Hilary Putnam." In *The Philosophy of P.F. Strawson*, edited by Lewis Edwin Hahn, 288–292. Chicago, IL: Open Court, 1998.

Strawson, P.F. *Skepticism and Naturalism: Some Varieties*. New York: Columbia University Press, 1985.

Stroud, Barry. "Scepticism, 'Externalism,' and the Goal of Epistemology." *Proceedings of the Aristotelian Society* (suppl. vol.) 68 (1994): 290–307.

Stroud, Barry. *The Significance of Philosophical Scepticism*. Oxford: Clarendon Press, 1984.

Thorpe, Joshua Rowan. "Closure Scepticism and the Vat Argument." *Mind* 127, no. 507 (2018): 667–690.

Thorpe, Joshua Rowan. "Semantic Self-Knowledge and the Vat Argument." *Philosophical Studies*, forthcoming.

Travis, Charles. "A Sense of Occasion." *Philosophical Quarterly* 55, no. 219 (2005): 286–314.

Travis, Charles. "Engaging." In *The Philosophy of Hilary Putnam*, edited by Randall Auxier, Douglas Anderson, and Lewis Hahn, 283–310. Chicago, IL: Open Court, 2015.

Travis, Charles. "Meaning's Role in Truth" (1996). Reprinted in *Occasion-Sensitivity: Selected Essays*, 94–108. New York: Oxford University Press, 2008.

Travis, Charles. *Occasion-Sensitivity: Selected Essays*. Oxford: Oxford University Press, 2008.

Travis, Charles. "Pragmatics." In *A Companion to the Philosophy of Language*, edited by Bob Hale and Crispin Wright, 87–107. Oxford: Blackwell, 1997.

Travis, Charles. "The Silence of the Senses." *Mind* 113, no. 449 (2004): 57–94.

Travis, Charles. *The True and the False: The Domain of Pragmatics*. Amsterdam: John Benjamins, 1981.

Travis, Charles. *The Uses of Sense: Wittgenstein's Philosophy of Language*. Oxford: Clarendon Press, 1989.

Travis, Charles. *Thought's Footing: A Theme in Wittgenstein's Philosophical Investigations*. Oxford: Oxford University Press, 2006.

Travis, Charles. *Unshadowed Thought: Representation in Thought and Language*. Cambridge, MA: Harvard University Press, 2000.

Tymoczko, Thomas. "In Defense of Putnam's Brains." *Philosophical Studies* 57, no. 3 (1989): 281–297.

Väänänen, Jouko and Wang, Tong. "Internal Categoricity in Arithmetic and Set Theory." *Notre Dame Journal of Formal Logic* 56, no. 1 (2015): 121–134.

van Heijenoort, Jean (ed.). *From Frege to Gödel: A Source Book in Mathematical Logic, 1897–1931*. Cambridge, MA: Harvard University Press, 1967.

von Neumann, John. *Mathematical Foundations of Quantum Mechanics*. Princeton: Princeton University Press, 1955.

Walsh, Vivian. "Sen after Putnam." *Review of Political Economy* 15, no. 3 (2003): 315–394.

Walzer, Michael. "Political Action: The Problem of Dirty Hands." *Philosophy and Public Affairs* 2, no. 2 (1973): 160–180.

Watts, Ian. "The First Paragraph of *The Ambassadors*: An Explication." *Essays in Criticism* 10, no. 3 (1960): 250–274. Reprinted in *Henry James: Modern Judgements*, edited by Tony Tanner, 283–303. London: Macmillan, 1969.

West, Cornel. "The Third Enlightenment." In *The Philosophy of Hilary Putnam*, edited by Randall Auxier, Douglas Anderson, and Lewis Hahn, 757–767. Chicago, IL: Open Court, 2015.

White, Stephen. "On the Absence of an Interface: Putnam, Direct Perception, and Frege's Constraint." *European Journal of Analytic Philosophy* 4, no. 2 (2008): 11–28.

Wiggins, David. *Needs, Values, Truth*. Oxford: Blackwell, 1987.

Wikforss, Åsa. "Externalism and Incomplete Understanding." *The Philosophical Quarterly* 54, no. 215 (2004): 287–294.

Wikforss, Åsa. "Self-Knowledge and Knowledge of Content." *Canadian Journal of Philosophy* 38, no. 3 (2008): 399–424.

Wikforss, Åsa. "Semantic Externalism and Psychological Externalism." *Philosophy Compass* 3, no. 1 (2008): 158–181.

Wikforss, Åsa. "Social Externalism and Conceptual Errors." *The Philosophical Quarterly* 51, no. 203 (2001): 217–231.

Wilkie, A. "On Schemes Axiomatizing Arithmetic." In *Proceedings of the International Congress of Mathematicians*, 331–337. Providence, RI: American Mathematical Society, 1986.

Williams, Bernard. "Ethical Consistency." In *Problems of the Self*, 166–186. Cambridge: Cambridge University Press, 1973.

Williams, Michael. *Unnatural Doubts: Epistemological Realism and the Basis of Scepticism*. Oxford: Blackwell, 1991.

Williams, Michael. "Wittgenstein's Refutation of Idealism." In *Wittgenstein and Scepticism*, edited by Denis McManus, 76–96. London: Routledge, 2004.

Williamson, Timothy. *Knowledge and Its Limits*. Oxford: Oxford University Press, 2000.

Wittgenstein, Ludwig. *On Certainty*, edited by G.E.M. Anscombe and Georg Henrik von Wright, translated by Denis Paul and G.E.M. Anscombe. Oxford: Blackwell, 1969.

Wittgenstein, Ludwig. *Philosophical Investigations*, edited by G.E.M. Anscombe and Rush Rhees, translated by G.E.M. Anscombe. Oxford: Blackwell, 1953.

Wittgenstein, Ludwig. *Remarks on the Foundations of Mathematics*, translated by G.E.M. Anscombe. Oxford: Blackwell, 1956.

Wright, Crispin. "Cogency and Question-Begging: Some Reflections on McKinsey's Paradox and Putnam's Proof." *Philosophical Issues* 10, no. 1 (2000): 140–163.

Wright, Crispin. "Facts and Certainty." *Proceedings of the British Academy* 71 (1986): 429–472.

Wright, Crispin. "McKinsey One More Time." In *Self-Knowledge*, edited by Anthony Hatzimoysis, 80–104. Oxford: Oxford University Press, 2008.

Wright, Crispin. "On Putnam's Proof that We Are Not Brains-in-a-Vat." *Proceedings of the Aristotelian Society* 92, no. 1 (1992): 67–94. Reprinted in *Reading Putnam*, edited by Peter Clark and Bob Hale, 216–242. Cambridge, MA: Blackwell, 1994.

Wright, Crispin. "Replies Part IV." In *Mind, Meaning and Knowledge: Themes from the Philosophy of Crispin Wright*, edited by Annalisa Coliva, 451–472. Oxford: Oxford University Press, 2012.

Wright, Crispin. "Scepticism and Dreaming: Imploding the Demon." *Mind* 100 (1991): 87–116.

Wright, Crispin. "Some Reflections on the Acquisition of Warrant by Inference." In *New Essays On Semantic Externalism And Self-Knowledge*, edited by Susana Nuccetelli, 57–77. Cambridge, MA: MIT, 2003.

Wright, Crispin. "Warrant for Nothing (and Foundations for Free)?" *Proceedings of the Aristotelian Society* 78 (2004): 167–212.

Yalowitz, Steven. "Anomalous Monism," *The Stanford Encyclopedia of Philosophy*, edited by Edward N. Zalta, 2019. https://plato.stanford.edu/entries/anomalous-monism/ (last accessed October 15, 2021).

Contributors

James Conant is Humboldt Professor in Theoretical Philosophy at Leipzig, as well as Chester D. Tripp Professor of Humanities, Professor of Philosophy and Full Professor in the College at the University of Chicago. Conant works broadly in philosophy and has published articles on topics in Philosophical Logic, Epistemology, Philosophy of Language, Philosophy of Mind, Aesthetics, German Idealism, and the History of Analytic Philosophy, among other areas, as well as interpretative work on a wide range of philosophers, including Descartes, Kant, Emerson, Nietzsche, Kierkegaard, Josiah Royce, William James, Frege, Carnap, Wittgenstein, Putnam, Cavell, Rorty, Stroud, and McDowell, among others. His most recent book is *The Logical Alien – Conant and His Critics*, Sofia Miguens, ed. (Harvard University Press, 2020).

Sanjit Chakraborty is an Assistant Professor of the School of Social Sciences and Humanities at the Vellore Institute of Technology-AP University and Visiting faculty at the Indian Institute of Science Education and Research Kolkata, India. Before that, he has been a member of the teaching faculty at the Indian Institute of Management Indore and the Central University of Hyderabad. He has published many papers in renowned journals and edited volumes on the philosophy of language, philosophy of mind, ethics, epistemology, and Indian philosophy. His books include *Understanding Meaning and World: A Relook on Semantic Externalism* (CSP, 2016), *The Labyrinth of Mind and World: Beyond Internalism-Externalism* (Routledge, 2020), *Living without God: A Multicultural Spectrum of Atheism* (Special issue of *Sophia*, Springer, 2021), and *Human Minds and Cultures* (forthcoming). He is the co-editor of *Engaging Putnam* honorary volume.

Martha C. Nussbaum received her B.A. from NYU and her M.A. and Ph.D. from Harvard. She has taught at Harvard, Brown, and Oxford Universities. She is the Ernst Freund Distinguished Service Professor of Law and Ethics at the University of Chicago, appointed in the Philosophy Department and the Law School. She won the 2016 Kyoto Prize in Arts and Philosophy and was awarded the Berggruen Prize for Philosophy and Culture in 2018. In 2021, she won the prestigious Holberg Prize for her innovative contribution to research in philosophy, law and related fields. She has written more than twenty-two books, including *The Fragility of Goodness, Sex and Social Justice, Upheavals of Thought, Frontiers of Justice* and *From Disgust to Humanity*. Her most recent books are *The Cosmopolitan Tradition* (Harvard University Press 2019), *Citadels Of Pride: Sexual Abuse, Accountability, And Reconciliation* (W. W. Norton, 2021), and *Justice For Animals* (Simon And Schuster, 2022). She is internationally renowned for her work in Ancient Greek and Roman philosophy, feminist philosophy, political philosophy, and philosophy and the arts. She delivered the John Locke Lectures at Oxford in 2014 and the Jefferson Lecture for the National Endowment for the Humanities in 2016.

Crispin Wright, FBA, FRSE, FAAAS, MAE, is Global Professor of Philosophy at New York University, Professor of Philosophical Research at the University of Stirling and Regius Professor of Logic Emeritus at the University of Aberdeen. He has published extensively on topics in the philosophy of language, the philosophy of mathematics, and epistemology, and was the founder and first director of the *Arché* research center at St. Andrews.

https://doi.org/10.1515/9783110769210-016

Sanford Goldberg is Chester D. Tripp Professor in the Humanities and Professor of Philosophy at Northwestern University, and Professorial Fellow at the Arché Research Center at the University of St Andrews. He works in the areas of epistemology, philosophy of language, and philosophy of mind. He is the author of several books, including *Foundations and Applications of Social Epistemology* (Oxford University Press, 2021), *Conversational Pressure: Normativity in Speech Exchanges* (Oxford University Press: 2020), *To the Best of Our Knowledge: Social Expectations and Epistemic Normativity* (Oxford University Press, 2018), *Assertion: On the Philosophical Significance of Assertoric Speech* (Oxford University Press, 2015), *Relying on Others: An Essay in Epistemology* (Oxford University Press, 2010), and *Anti-Individualism: Mind and Language, Knowledge and Justification* (Cambridge University Press, 2007).

Duncan Pritchard is UC Distinguished Professor of Philosophy and Director of the Center for Knowledge, Technology and Society at the University of California, Irvine. His monographs include *Epistemic Luck* (Oxford University Press, 2005), *The Nature and Value of Knowledge* (co-authored, Oxford University Press, 2010), *Epistemological Disjunctivism* (Oxford University Press, 2012), and *Epistemic Angst: Radical Skepticism and the Groundlessness of Our Believing* (Princeton University Press, 2015). His most recent book is *Scepticism: A Very Short Introduction* (Oxford University Press, 2019).

Tim Maudlin (B.A. Yale, Physics and Philosophy; Ph.D. Pittsburgh, History and Philosophy of Science) has interests primarily focused in the foundations of physics, metaphysics, and logic. His books include *Quantum Non-Locality and Relativity* (Blackwell, 2011, 3rd edition), *Truth and Paradox* (Oxford University Press, 2004) and The *Metaphysics Within Physics* (Oxford University Press, 2007). *Philosophy of Physics*: *Space and Time* (Princeton University Press, 2012). The second volume for Princeton, on quantum theory is due out in 2019. He has a large project developing and applying alternative mathematical accounts of topological and geometrical structure, the first volume of which is *New Foundations for Physical Geometry: The Theory of Linear Structures* (OUP). He is a member of the American Academy of Arts and Sciences, the Academie Internationale de Philosophie des Sciences and the Foundational Questions Institute (FQXi). He has been a Guggenheim Fellow and a Fellow of the American Council of Learned Societies. He taught at Rutgers from 1986 to 2011, and has been a visiting professor at Harvard. He is the Founder and Director of the John Bell Institute for the Foundations of Physics.

Gary Ebbs is Professor of Philosophy at Indiana University, Bloomington. He is the author of *Rule-Following and Realism* (Harvard University Press, 1997), *Truth and Words* (Oxford University Press, 2009), and *Carnap, Quine, and Putnam on Methods of Inquiry* (Cambridge University Press, 2017), and co-author of *Debating Self-Knowledge* (Cambridge University Press, 2012). He has also published articles on a wide range of topics in the philosophy of language, logic, and mind, as well as epistemology and the history of analytic philosophy.

Roy T. Cook is CLA Scholar of the College and Professor of Philosophy at the University of Minnesota—Twin Cities. He is the author of *The Yablo Paradox: An Essay on Circularity* (Oxford University Press, 2014), *Key Concepts in Philosophy: Paradoxes* (Polity, 2013), and *The Dictionary of Philosophical Logic* (Edinburgh University Press, 2009). He is also the editor of *The Arché Papers on the Mathematics of Abstraction* (Springer, 2007), and co-editor of *LEGO and Philosophy* (Blackwell, forthcoming), *The Routledge Companion to Comics and Graphic*

Novels (Routledge 2016), and *The Art of Comics: A Philosophical Approach* (Blackwell, 2012). He has also written many articles.

Mario De Caro is Professor of Moral Philosophy at Università Roma Tre and regularly a Visiting Professor at Tufts University. He is Hilary Putnam's literary executor and with him he has written "Free Will and Quantum Mechanics" (*The Monist*, 2020). He has edited Putnam's collections of essays *Philosophy in an Age of Science: Physics, Mathematics and Skepticism* (with D. Macarthur, 2012), *Naturalism, Realism, and Normativity* (2016), and *Philosophy as Dialogue* (with D. Macarthur, 2022), all with Harvard University Press. He is interested in naturalism, virtue theory, free will, theory of action, and early modern philosophy.

Maximilian de Gaynesford, formerly Fellow of Lincoln College Oxford, is Professor of Philosophy at the University of Reading. He is the author of several books, including *The Rift in the Lute: Attuning Poetry and Philosophy* (OUP, 2017), *I: The Meaning of the First Person Term* (OUP, 2006) and *Hilary Putnam* (Queens-McGill University Press, 2006), as well as of numerous articles on the philosophy of logic, mind, language and aesthetics.

Yemima Ben-Menahem is professor of philosophy (Emerita) at the Hebrew University of Jerusalem. Ben-Menahem's work centers on the philosophy of science, the philosophy of modern physics in particular. She is author of *Conventionalism* (Cambridge University Press, 2006) and *Causation in Science* (Princeton University Press, 2018). Ben-Menahem is editor of *Hilary Putnam* (Cambridge University Press, 2005) and co-editor of *Probability in Physics* (Springer, 2011). Another volume she has recently edited, entitled *Rethinking the concept of Law of Nature*, is forthcoming with Springer.

Tim Button is an Associate Professor of Philosophy at University College London. His first book, *The Limits of Realism* (OUP, 2013), critically explores and develops several themes from Putnam's work: the model-theoretic arguments; the connection between truth and justification; the brain-in-vat argument; semantic externalism; and conceptual relativity. His second book, *Philosophy and Model Theory* (OUP, 2018), which is co-authored with Sean Walsh, explores both the philosophical uses of model theory and the philosophy of model theory itself.

Joshua Rowan Thorpe is a Teaching Fellow in Philosophy at the University of Edinburgh. Before that he worked as a Postdoctoral Fellow at the University of Campinas, and as a Visiting Postdoctoral Fellow at the *Knowledge Beyond Natural Science* project at the University of Stirling. He has published in epistemology, the philosophy of mind, and the philosophy of language.

Index

https://doi.org/10.1515/9783110769210-017